DATE DUE

THE REFORMATION OF
CATHEDRALS

Canterbury Cathedral, aerial photograph showing relationship of
cathedral and surrounding city.

The Reformation of Cathedrals

✣ ✣ ✣

CATHEDRALS IN ENGLISH
SOCIETY, 1485–1603

STANFORD E. LEHMBERG

PRINCETON UNIVERSITY PRESS
PRINCETON, NEW JERSEY

Copyright © 1988 by Princeton University Press
Published by Princeton University Press, 41 William Street,
Princeton, New Jersey 08540
In the United Kingdom: Princeton University Press,
Guildford, Surrey

LIBRARY OF CONGRESS CATALOGING-IN-PUBLICATION DATA

Lehmberg, Stanford E.
The reformation of cathedrals: cathedrals in English society,
1485–1603 / Stanford E. Lehmberg
p. cm.
Includes bibliographical references and index.
ISBN 0-691-05539-4 (alk. paper)
1. Cathedrals—England—History—16th century. 2. England—Church
history—16th century. 3. England
—Social conditions—16th century. I. Title.
BR757.L39 1988
262'.3'0942-dc19   88-9851

Publication of this book has been aided by a grant from
the Paul Mellon Fund of Princeton University Press

This book has been composed in Linotron Baskerville

Clothbound editions of Princeton University Press books are
printed on acid-free paper, and binding materials are chosen
for strength and durability. Paperbacks, although satisfactory
for personal collections, are not usually suitable
for library rebinding

Printed in the United States of America by
Princeton University Press,
Princeton, New Jersey

CONTENTS

ILLUSTRATIONS

TABLES

PREFACE

THIS IS a study of English cathedrals as social institutions during the sixteenth century. Although most people think of cathedrals as buildings, this is not a book about architecture: England's great cathedrals had been completed well before the beginning of the Tudor period, and only minor modifications and additions were made during the years between 1485 and 1603. Rather, this is an account of the cathedrals as living human organisms operating within the larger framework of Tudor society. It attempts to describe the cathedrals as they existed at the end of the Middle Ages, to trace the changes associated with the Reformation under Henry VIII and Edward VI and the Counter-Reformation of Mary Tudor, to examine the Elizabethan Settlement as it affected the cathedrals, and to study the lives of the men who served these institutions as clergy, singers, and in other capacities. The work is intended as a piece of social history, and my final goal is to analyze the role of cathedrals in English society during a time of intense political and theological change. The relationship between cathedral establishments and lay society is hinted at throughout and explored as fully as the limited sources permit in a concluding chapter.

My original plan was merely to discuss the cathedral musical establishments and to trace the changes dictated by the Reformation and the Prayer Book so far as cathedral musicians were concerned. Because of my own long interest in Anglican church music, this topic remains of special concern, and I shall deal with it in the following pages. But research in cathedral libraries convinced me that a wide variety of related matters needed attention as well, and the present work has been broadened to include virtually all aspects of cathedral organization and life.

It is surprising that such a study has not been attempted before. There are, of course, books about the Reformation, but they have little to say about cathedrals. There are books about individual cathedrals, too, but these are usually pieces of local history and make no attempt to describe the situation throughout the entire country. An amazingly large number of primary documents have been transcribed and printed, mainly in the publications of county record societies. These have made my task easier, but they are not in themselves works of general history. The present book is the first that attempts to trace the effect of the Reformation on cathedrals and to determine how it altered the lives of cathedral clergy as well as their role in English society.

THIS study has been in progress for a long time. In a sense it began more than thirty years ago, when I was a research student at Cambridge University and first began visiting the cathedrals in order to admire the buildings and enjoy the beauty of the sung services. The actual collection of materials has been underway for about a decade, mainly during research trips lasting a month or so each summer, fitted into a schedule of teaching and administration at the University of Minnesota.

During this long period I have accumulated a host of obligations, which it is a pleasure to acknowledge here. I am particularly grateful to the John Simon Guggenheim Memorial Foundation, which honored me with a second Fellowship for the academic year 1985–1986 so that I could devote my full energies to this project. The Graduate School and the College of Liberal Arts at the University of Minnesota provided additional support. Librarians, archivists, and friends in England have made research into cathedral muniments pleasant as well as productive. My special thanks go to Miss Anne M. Oakley, cathedral archivist at Canterbury, and Mrs. Margaret Sparks, coordinating editor of the cathedral history project there; Claire Cross and W. J. Sheils at York; the Reverend Chancellor and Mrs. John Nurser at Lincoln; Professor and Mrs. Derek Beales, Professor Sir Geoffrey Elton, Sir David Willcocks, and Mrs. Dorothy Owen at Cambridge; the Very Reverend Dean and Mrs. John Arnold at Rochester; the late Howard M. Nixon, Librarian, the late N. H. MacMichael, Keeper of the Muniments, and Michael Keall, former Headmaster of the Choir School at Westminster Abbey; the late Canon Frederick Bussby at Winchester; the late A.R.B. Fuller, Librarian of St. Paul's; the Reverend Canon J. R. Fenwick and Mrs. Winifred Young at Worcester; Pamela Tudor-Craig, Lady Wedgwood, who helped me with iconography at Worcester; the Reverend Canon David Welander at Gloucester; Patrick Mussett and Alan Piper of the Prior's Kitchen at Durham Cathedral; Professor G. Rex Smith of Durham University; the Governing Body of Christ Church, Oxford; L. S. Colchester, archivist, and Anthony Crossland, organist at Wells; Audrey M. Erskine, Nicholas Orme, and Joyce Youings at Exeter; Suzanne Eward at Salisbury; Penelope E. Morgan at Hereford; the Reverend Canon Anthony Barnard, Chancellor of Lichfield; the Reverend Canon K. M. Maltby, Subdean of Chester; the Reverend Canon R.J.W. Bevan, Librarian of Carlisle, and

Andrew Seivewright, organist there. Professional archivists in a number of county record offices have also been efficient and cooperative. Several research assistants at the University of Minnesota have sped and eased my work. The computer-assisted analysis of the careers of the cathedral clergy was undertaken by Alice Keeler, without whose knowledge and industry it would have been impossible. Robert Keeler, Minjae Kim, Ann Kavanaugh, Chris Duggan, Fred Suppe, and Tom Taylor also helped. James E. Mills drew the map. Professor J. J. Scarisbrick read the finished manuscript and offered valuable suggestions. To all I extend warm appreciation.

NOTE ON SOURCES AND
ABBREVIATIONS

THIS book is based in large part on archival materials surviving in cathedral libraries or, in a few cases, in other repositories to which they have been transferred. Full citations are given in the footnotes. In lieu of a bibliography, which would have been very long, complete citations to printed sources have also been given in the footnotes.

The only abbreviations used are these standard ones:

BL   British Library
HMC   Historical Manuscripts Commission
PRO   Public Record Office
VCH   Victoria County History

THE REFORMATION OF
CATHEDRALS

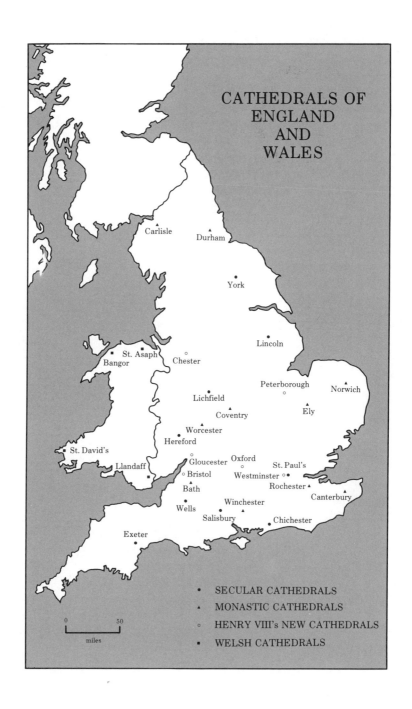

CATHEDRALS OF
ENGLAND
AND
WALES

Carlisle
Durham

York

Lincoln

St. Asaph
Bangor
Chester

Peterborough
Norwich

Lichfield
Coventry
Ely

Worcester
Hereford

St. David's

Gloucester
Oxford
St. Paul's

Llandaff

Bristol
Westminster
Bath
Rochester
Canterbury

Wells
Winchester

Salisbury
Chichester

Exeter

• SECULAR CATHEDRALS
▲ MONASTIC CATHEDRALS
○ HENRY VIII's NEW CATHEDRALS
▪ WELSH CATHEDRALS

0   50
miles

1

THE END OF THE OLD ORDER:
THE SECULAR CATHEDRALS

By basic definition a cathedral is a large church where a bishop has his seat (in Latin, *cathedra*). The notion of a cathedral as the mother church of a diocese was implicit from the beginning but not fully articulated until modern times. During the Middle Ages cathedrals became centers for the arts—architecture, sculpture, music—and for learning and education as well as liturgy, but there is little theoretical writing about the significance of these roles.

The oldest English cathedral, Canterbury, was founded as part of Augustine's mission in A.D. 597 and was dedicated in 602.[1] Its neighbor, Rochester, followed in 604. The first cathedral in London is also said to have been built in 604. A wooden minster is recorded at York in 627.

As dioceses were established, cathedrals were erected. By the end of the Anglo-Saxon period there were churches on the sites of all of the Tudor cathedrals, but virtually nothing is left from this era, since the Normans thought the earlier buildings too small and insignificant. Much remains from the great age of building following the Conquest in 1066—one thinks first of Durham, then of Ely, Norwich, Rochester, and Peterborough—and most of the cathedrals retain some Norman work.

The thirteenth century saw the beginning of a second great era of construction. This produced the masterpieces of the Early English Gothic style, or "first pointed architecture" so dearly loved by high-church Victorians—Salisbury, Wells, and Lincoln among others—and left its impress almost everywhere. Chapter houses, where the cathedral staff could hold meetings and conduct business, were built in many places during the thirteenth century. Beautiful examples, generally octagonal with a slender central column supporting a vaulted roof, may be seen at Lincoln, Salisbury, Wells, Lichfield, Worcester, Exeter, and York. The Decorated style transformed Gothic architec-

[1] See Nicholas Brooks, *The Early History of the Church of Canterbury* (Leicester: Leicester University Press, 1984); Jonathan Keates and Angelo Hornak, *Canterbury Cathedral* (London: Philip Wilson, 1980), p. 9.

ture during the years between 1250 and 1350, introducing a new sense of freedom and creativity and producing such marvelous works as the choir at Wells and the octagon at Ely. Finally, around 1330, the uniquely English Perpendicular style appeared; its fan vaults and enormous windows were to dominate church architecture until the Reformation brought building to a halt under Henry VIII.[2]

As the veneration of the Virgin Mary assumed greater importance during the later Middle Ages, Lady Chapels were added to the cathedrals. Some of these were not completed until the fourteenth or fifteenth century. At Wells an old Lady Chapel, built in the 1180s, was replaced by a new building between 1306 and 1319; this in turn was superseded by a large cruciform chapel off the cloisters, begun by Bishop Stillington in 1477. Remodeling of Norman buildings in the latest Perpendicular style was also characteristic of the fourteenth and fifteenth centuries, Winchester and Gloucester providing the most splendid instances of such work. Although additions and enrichments were still underway in many places (these will be described below), the cathedrals were essentially complete by 1485, and those familiar with the present structures would easily recognize the buildings as they stood when Henry VII came to the throne.[3]

In the early Tudor period there were nineteen cathedral churches in England. Nine of these—Salisbury, Lincoln, York, Exeter, Hereford, Lichfield, Chichester, Wells, and St. Paul's in London—were secular cathedrals, served by a dean, chapter, and inferior clergy who were in holy orders but not monks. The remaining ten cathedrals were monastic in organization. Canterbury, Winchester, Worcester, Rochester, Durham, Ely, Norwich, Coventry, and Bath were Benedictine priories, while the cathedral at Carlisle was staffed by Augustinian canons. In organization and finance the two types of cathedrals differed significantly. This chapter will describe the condition of the secular cathedrals during the decades immediately preceding the Reformation; the next will examine the cathedral priories in the half century before the dissolution of the monasteries.

THE clergy who staffed the secular cathedrals were called canons or prebendaries. The word *canon* originally meant "rule," and cathedral

---

[2] See Jean Bony, *The English Decorated Style* (Oxford: Phaidon, 1979); John Harvey, *The Perpendicular Style* (London: Batsford, 1978). Harvey prefers to think of the Perpendicular style as ending in 1485 and refers to later buildings simply as Tudor.

[3] St. Paul's is of course an exception, since the medieval cathedral was irreparably damaged in the Great Fire of 1666.

canons had at first lived under a rule, in a sort of communal life, even though they were not monks.[4] Their lives may have been regulated by rules drawn up by bishops; the most famous and most influential of these was the set of orders promulgated by Bishop Chrodegang of Metz about 755.

By the time of the Norman Conquest, canons had begun to acquire individual property. As this happened they abandoned their communal life and established homes in separate houses near the cathedral. For a time it was common for them to be married, but this arrangement ended by the thirteenth century.[5] They gained their financial support from individual endowments—lands and the right to collect rents, fees, and tithes from parish churches—which were called prebends. The canons thus became prebendaries, who could be referred to by naming their principal estate, such as the prebend of Masham at York. For my purposes the terms *canon* and *prebendary* are virtually synonymous, and they were used more or less interchangeably during the Tudor period. But they do have different origins and different technical meanings. For legal purposes they were often conjoined; the full title of a canon at Lincoln, for instance, was Canon of Lincoln and Prebendary of Buckden, or whatever other prebend he might hold.[6]

The number of canons in the secular cathedrals before the Reformation varied considerably, but it was always surprisingly large, at least in comparison to modern cathedral establishments. Lincoln—a vast and rich diocese before the 1540s—had fifty-eight prebendaries. Salisbury followed with fifty-two. York, though the seat of an archbishop, had only thirty-six. Lichfield, one of the poorest cathedrals, had more canons than St. Paul's in London; the numbers are thirty-two and thirty, respectively. There were twenty-seven canons at Hereford and Chichester, twenty-four at Exeter, and twenty-two at Wells.[7]

---

[4] Kathleen Edwards, *The English Secular Cathedrals in the Middle Ages* (Manchester: Manchester University Press, 1949), pp. 4–5.

[5] In the late eleventh and early twelfth century at least one-third of the canons of St. Paul's had wives, and some passed their positions on to their sons as if they were hereditary. See G. E. Aylmer and Reginald Cant, eds., *A History of York Minster* (Oxford: Clarendon Press, 1977), pp. 20–23.

[6] J. H. Srawley, *The Origin and Growth of Cathedral Foundations as Illustrated by the Cathedral Church of Lincoln* (Lincoln: Friends of Lincoln Cathedral, 1965), p. 6; Margaret Bowker, *The Secular Clergy in the Diocese of Lincoln, 1495–1502* (Cambridge: Cambridge University Press, 1968), p. 155. Exeter was unique in that its canons did not have separate prebendal estates, but controlled the cathedral's income in common. Each canon received £4 a year and weekly distributions of food and money when resident. See Nicholas Orme, *The Minor Clergy of Exeter Cathedral, 1300–1548* (Exeter: University of Exeter, 1980), p. xiii.

[7] Numbers from manuscript records; see also W. R. Matthews and W. M. Atkins, eds.,

The chief officer in every secular cathedral was the dean. The bishop was rarely present; he might celebrate mass or preach at Christmas and Easter, and he would normally be consecrated, enthroned, and eventually buried in the cathedral. But it was the dean who presided over meetings of the cathedral chapter, joined with the canons in holding title to cathedral property, and was generally responsible for all activities of the cathedral. He had the cure of souls for all the cathedral clergy. As will be seen shortly, his income was much larger than that of other canons, and he was expected to live grandly and entertain on a large scale. Many deans held other positions in the church concurrently, and a number were named bishops later in their careers. Although deans were supposed to be elected by members of the cathedral chapter, royal nomination became quite common in the later Middle Ages, with the actual election no more than a formal confirmation of the monarch's choice.[8] An extreme case is presented by the appointment of Henry VIII's great minister, Thomas Cromwell, as dean of Wells in 1537, for Cromwell was a layman as well as an obvious nonresident. But Cromwell was exceptional; most royal nominees were well qualified in addition to being well connected.[9]

Three other great officers were found in the secular cathedrals; they, together with the dean, formed the *quatuor personae* spoken of in medieval texts as forming the four cornerstones of the cathedral's spiritual and material fabric. Ranking next to the dean, though much inferior to him in wealth and prestige, was the precentor. He was in charge of the cathedral services, the music and liturgy, the choir and song school. The chancellor kept the seal of the chapter and acted as its secretary, but his most important functions related to education and scholarship. Most cathedrals had schools, which operated under the general supervision of the chancellor. He was usually the cathedral librarian and archivist, and he was often responsible for arranging the reading of lessons at services and for scheduling sermons. The treasurer was not, as one might expect, given control of cathedral finances. Instead he guarded the cathedral's treasures—plate, vestments,

---

A History of St. Paul's Cathedral (London: John Baker, 1957); L. S. Colchester, ed., *Wells Cathedral: A History* (Shepton Mallet: Open Books, 1982); Srawley, *Origin and Growth.*

[8] See K. Edwards, *Secular Cathedrals*, pp. 136–150; Aylmer and Cant, *York Minster*, pp. 62–67. The election of a new dean at Chichester in 1541 is described in W. D. Peckham, ed., *The Acts of the Dean and Chapter of Chichester, 1472–1544*, Sussex Record Society, no. 52 (Lewes, 1952), pp. 126–128. In 1529 it was quite clear that Henry VIII nominated Gamaliel Clifton as successor to Dean Edmund Froceter at Hereford; see Act Book 1, fols. 47, 60, Hereford Cathedral Library.

[9] These matters are considered more fully in Chapter 9 below.

relics—and provided the lights, candles, incense, bread and wine, and other things needed at the altars. He was also responsible for the regulation of the clock and bells.

Each of these great officers commonly had a deputy who assisted him and performed his duties in his absence. The subdean might be especially important in cases where the dean himself was nonresident or frequently absent from his cathedral church. At Lincoln the subdean was specifically charged with the duty of hearing confessions from members of the cathedral staff and assigning penances. As deputy to the precentor, the succentor was usually the real director of music in the choir and at the high altar during the later Middle Ages. At Exeter, for instance, we know that he lived with the choristers and taught in their song school.[10] The vice-chancellor's chief duty seems to have been arranging the lessons for the choir offices and assigning lectors. The sacrist—deputy to the treasurer—often assumed the routine duty of providing the material articles required by the liturgy (bread, wine, and lights). In some places archdeacons were also counted as officials of the cathedral. They were really assistants to the bishop and helped him oversee the parishes of the diocese, but they sometimes held prebends and were treated as guests of the cathedral, being allotted stalls in the choir next to those of the other great officers. In all, then, there could be nine principal officials in each secular cathedral, but they were rarely all present, and primary responsibility always remained in the hands of the dean and his three chief colleagues.[11]

One would hardly expect that such large numbers of canons would be resident at the cathedral continuously, especially when many of them held posts in parish churches, at court, or in the universities. In fact the problem of nonresidency presented great difficulties in the Middle Ages, and there were complaints of cathedrals being poorly served because few members of the senior staff were actually present. Eventually a satisfactory accommodation was reached, under which a small number of prebendaries would be designated residentiary canons. To them would be given the real responsibilities of running the cathedral, and they would receive additional compensation: as well as the revenue that came to individual canons from their prebends, the cathedral had common funds that were divided only among the resi-

---

[10] Sometimes, especially at Lincoln, the precentor was called the chanter and the succentor the subchanter. Cf. A. Hamilton Thompson, *Song-Schools in the Middle Ages* (London: SPCK, 1942), p. 13.

[11] On the history of these offices, see K. Edwards, *Secular Cathedrals*, pp. 150–255; Aylmer and Cant, *York Minster*, pp. 66–75; Srawley, *Origin and Growth*, pp. 8–12.

dentiaries. Besides these, the resident clergy received quite substantial sums for participation in obits (endowed masses and memorial observances).[12]

At York, where there were sometimes only two or three residentiaries in the fifteenth century, a clear distinction grew up between two types of canons. Those who did not actually reside were principally royal clerks and university scholars, while the four great officers and a few other active administrators formed the much smaller group of residentiaries. York appears to have been unique in that even the nonresidentiary canons had small houses in the immediate vicinity of the cathedral. As a result, the minster was "surrounded by a dense jungle of small and transient urban tenements."[13] At St. Paul's the residentiary canons were called stagiaries. There were ordinarily eight of them. Five canons generally resided at Lincoln, although there were occasionally only three and sometimes as many as seven.[14] Six or seven are common elsewhere; numbers fluctuate, and it is not unusual to find as few as four.

By the beginning of the period under discussion, the rewards of residence had grown so great that there were more canons wishing to reside than could easily be accommodated or paid without prejudice to those already residing. It was probably for this reason that the cost of assuming residence was set very high. A nonresidentiary who wished to come into full residence was required to declare his intention of doing so well in advance. If this was agreed to, the new residentiary would be required to attend every cathedral service for three-quarters of the first year. In addition, staggering responsibilities for hospitality were laid upon him. At St. Paul's new stagiaries had to keep open house daily at breakfast time; entertain the other stagiaries, one by one, at dinner each quarter; feast the choir twice a year; and provide semiannual banquets to which were invited the bishop and all the canons (including nonresidents) as well as the mayor and aldermen, judges, and other leading royal officials.

All of this could easily cost 1,000 marks (£667).[15] Indeed, new stat-

---

[12] An obit was an endowed mass for the dead, held annually on the anniversary of the testator's death. It was sometimes called a "year's mind," in contrast to the "month's mind" held a month following death.

[13] Barrie Dobson, "The Later Middle Ages, 1215–1500," in Aylmer and Cant, *York Minster*, p. 103.

[14] On St. Paul's, see Matthews and Atkins, *St. Paul's*, pp. 41, 87; on Lincoln, see Bowker, *Secular Clergy*, p. 161.

[15] Matthews and Atkins, *St. Paul's*, p. 87; cf. Aylmer and Cant, *York Minster*, p. 105. At Wells there was a tradition that each residentiary canon holding one of the great offices

utes enacted for York in 1541 complained that major residence (the term given to the first year, with its strict requirements) did cost 1,000 marks, so that only the richest clergy could contemplate it.[16] Even at a relatively remote and poor cathedral like Lichfield, no canon was allowed to take up residence unless he was able to spend at least £40 a year of his own money in the city, and he was required to pay the dean 100 marks, the money to be used partly for maintenance of the cathedral building and partly for church ornaments.[17] After the first year, or in some places a somewhat longer period of time, canons could enter into what was called the lesser residence, which required their presence for only half of the year.

At the beginning of the Tudor period, the residentiary canons were generally well established, well off, and prepared to live out their lives in the relative comfort of the cathedral close. Indeed all but one of the fifty residentiaries of York during the century and a half before 1500 died in office. (The single exception went on to become bishop of London.) They were educated men, almost all graduates of Oxford or Cambridge; occasionally, as at Hereford, they were given leaves of absence for a year or two so that they could undertake further study at the university.[18] A number of surviving wills of fifteenth-century canons testify to their wealth and the luxury of their homes. Their private libraries were often among the largest in the country.[19]

THE principal responsibility of the cathedral clergy was the maintenance of a daily round of services, the Opus Dei of praise and prayer. The mass was, of course, the central act of worship before the Reformation, and it was celebrated several times each day: there was the morrow mass at dawn and the mass of the Virgin Mary in the Lady Chapel as well as the solemn high mass. But the mass was not the only service sung in the cathedrals, for the Use of Salisbury or Sarum and

should provide refreshments, called "O.O.O.," for all the canons and vicars during Pentecost week (Liber Ruber, sec. II, Wells Cathedral Library; HMC, *Calendar of the Manuscripts of the Dean and Chapter of Wells*, 2 vols. [London, 1907, 1914], 2: 222).

[16] Aylmer and Cant, *York Minster*, p. 105. Precise requirements for the great residence varied from cathedral to cathedral; for details see K. Edwards, *Secular Cathedrals*, pp. 50–56.

[17] *VCH, Stafford*, 3: 152, 158.

[18] Act Book 1, fols. 28, 72, 73, Hereford Cathedral Library.

[19] Aylmer and Cant, *York Minster*, p. 106. See also Barrie Dobson, "The Residentiary Canons of York in the Fifteenth Century," *Journal of Ecclesiastical History* 30 (1979): 145–174.

its local variants, especially the Uses of Hereford, York, Lincoln, and Bangor, prescribed eight other daily observances. These were matins (sung during the night, before daylight), lauds (offered at daybreak), prime, terce, sext, none, vespers, and compline (celebrated just before retiring). By the fifteenth century some liberties had been taken with timing. At Lincoln, matins continued to be sung at midnight between Michaelmas and Easter until 1548, but between Easter and Michaelmas it was postponed until about 5 A.M.; elsewhere night matins was transferred to the early morning, just after the morrow mass, and was followed immediately by lauds. The Lady mass was usually celebrated at about 9 A.M. Terce was said while the celebrant was preparing for high mass, at 10 A.M. Sext and nones were sung after the mass, often together. Such a schedule occupied most of the morning but left the early afternoon free for other activities.[20]

All of these services included Psalms and prayers, and all were generally sung. Simple plainsong chant generally sufficed for the lesser offices of prime, terce, sext, and none. Although awkwardly timed, matins and lauds often contained some more elaborate polyphony, as did compline. Vespers, in which the liturgy included the Magnificat, had come by the late fifteenth century to be the most important of the offices musically. Antiphons and hymns were sung at matins, lauds, vespers, and compline; on Sundays and festivals the Te Deum concluded matins.

The principal mass of the day might be sung with relative simplicity on ordinary weekdays, but on Sundays and high holy days it was celebrated with great magnificence. Polyphonic music would then alternate with chant or replace it altogether in the Ordinary of the mass (the Gloria, Credo, Sanctus and Benedictus, and Agnus Dei), and antiphons and motets appropriate to the season could be included. The Marian masses sung in the Lady Chapels provided the greatest opportunity for the performance of elaborate polyphonic music sung by trained choirs of men and boys. Cathedrals that had shrines honoring

[20] On these services, see K. Edwards, *Secular Cathedrals*, pp. 56–57; J. D. Chambers, *Divine Worship in England* (London: Basil Montagu Pickering, 1877); G. J. Cuming, *A History of Anglican Liturgy* (London: Macmillan, 1969), pp. 15–31; F. E. Warren, ed., *The Sarum Missal*, Alcuin Club, no. 11 (London, 1913); J. W. Tyrer, *Historical Survey of Holy Week*, Alcuin Club, no. 29 (London, 1932); Hugh Benham, *Latin Church Music in England, c. 1460–1575* (London: Barrie and Jenkins, 1977); Frank L. Harrison, *Music in Medieval Britain* (London: Routledge and Kegan Paul, 1958); Peter Le Huray, *Music and the Reformation in England, 1549–1660* (London: Herbert Jenkins, 1967); and Denis Stevens, *Tudor Church Music*, 2d ed. (New York: Norton, 1966). Considerable material relating to pre-Reformation liturgy has been published in London by the Henry Bradshaw Society; e.g., *The Hereford Breviary*, 3 vols. (26, 1903; 40, 1910; 46, 1913), and *The Customary of Norwich* (82, 1945–1946).

the memory of saints and martyrs would provide regular services there as well.

In addition to these daily observances there were masses for the dead, celebrated at designated altars or in the chantry chapels that will be considered later. Distinctive liturgies were prescribed for Holy Week. Some other occasions demanded special observance: the installation of new bishops, deans, or mayors, for instance, or ceremonial visits by civic dignitaries or members of the royal family, or funerals of prominent persons. In addition, processions through the cathedral close and out into the streets of the city were common in the later Middle Ages; these might conclude with ceremonies just outside the west front of the cathedral, or they might culminate in high masses performed in the choir. Palm Sunday processions were especially elaborate and could include special liturgy, like that in which musicians at Wells sang through holes in the façade, concealed behind statues.[21]

It is impossible to say how frequently lay men and women attended cathedral services in the years preceding the Reformation.[22] Certainly some came to the masses on festival days, and many would have seen the processions of priests and singers. Civic ceremonies were probably well attended. Lady masses were also popular with lay people, perhaps because of the elegance of the music as well as on account of the growth of Marian devotion. The appeal of shrines may have been declining, but they remained a focus for worship and veneration of relics until they were dismantled under Henry VIII. The laity were unlikely to attend matins, lauds, and compline because of the inconvenience of the hours, and it is unlikely that many were attracted to the lesser offices. Evidence is lacking, but we may suppose that vespers appealed to some lay persons, just as its successor, evensong, does today. It is probably true, as John Stevens has suggested, that "good moral results and devotional stirrings were regarded as the natural by-product of good music."[23] Certainly John Wheathampstead, the abbot of St. Albans in the mid-fifteenth century, believed that "wherever the Divine Service is more honorably celebrated the glory of the church is increased and the people are aroused to much greater devotion."[24] But cathedral services were sung mainly for the glory of God, not the edi-

[21] There were also "holes" in the façade at Salisbury and probably elsewhere. The small spaces behind these acted as megaphones projecting sound into the churchyard. I am indebted to L. S. Colchester and Pamela Tudor-Craig, Lady Wedgwood, for sharing their research on this subject.

[22] The few bits of surviving evidence will be considered below in Chapter 10.

[23] John Stevens, *Music and Poetry in the Early Tudor Court* (London: Methuen, 1961), p. 64.

[24] Quoted in Benham, *Latin Church Music*, p. 4.

fication of man, and there was no provision for participation by a congregation of worshipers.

THESE elaborate services obviously could not be maintained by the small number of residentiary canons, who were not in any case chosen because of their skill in music. It was the vicars choral who actually sang the several daily masses and other canonical hours. These men are usually thought of as being deputies for the nonresident prebendaries—this is the origin of the term *vicar* and the accompanying notion that these men vicariously performed the duties of others who were absent. As early as the twelfth century, canons were required to appoint vicars, who initially lived in the homes of the canons and ate at their tables. However, residentiaries were often expected to have vicars just as were their nonresident colleagues, and it soon became clear that the vicars had duties that were quite different from those of the canons whom they represented.

Skill in singing was a requisite for vicars choral at least as early as the twelfth century. In a number of the cathedrals, medieval statutes provide that vicars serve a probationary year before achieving permanent tenure in their offices. During this time they were supposed to learn the Psalms, antiphons, and hymns by heart; if they had not mastered all this material they might (as at Wells in 1488) be granted permanent status on condition that they memorize the remaining Psalms and hymns by a certain date.[25]

The number of vicars choral varied from place to place. At the beginning there were theoretically as many vicars as there were canons in the cathedral chapter. Thus Lincoln, Wells, and Salisbury were supposed to have more than fifty vicars, York thirty-six. But these numbers were not in practice maintained during the early Tudor period. A visitation of 1437 had revealed that there were only thirty-four vicars at Wells, and only twenty-three were actually paid in 1500.[26] Salisbury had only thirty-one in 1468, fourteen in 1547.[27] At Lincoln there were twenty-five in 1501.[28] York could afford only twenty in 1509.[29] When John Colet became dean of St. Paul's in 1505, he was shocked

[25] Liber Ruber, fol. 21 (HMC, *Wells*, 2: 111).

[26] Fabric Accounts, 1390–1600, Wells Cathedral, ed. L. S. Colchester (typescript), Wells Cathedral Library.

[27] Act Book, MS. 80, p. 22, Salisbury Cathedral Library.

[28] A. R. Maddison, *A Short Account of the Vicars Choral, Poor Clerks, Organists, and Choristers of Lincoln Cathedral* (London, 1878), pp. 3–5.

[29] Aylmer and Cant, *York Minster*, p. 93.

to find that the thirty vicars had dwindled to six. But St. Paul's was unusual in having twelve minor canons who joined the vicars in singing its services.[30] Exeter had twenty-four vicars choral, Hereford twenty-seven.[31] At Chichester there were seventeen at the beginning of the period, fourteen in 1521 and only twelve in 1524. The four laymen added to the choir in 1529 as the result of a grant from Bishop Sherburne were required to have special skill in singing, and we know that some were married since an unusual provision allowed Dorothy Somer to continue receiving the stipend allocated to her husband, Henry, following his death, so long as she remained single, or even if she later married another singing man.[32] There were supposed to be twenty-seven vicars choral at Lichfield, although the full number was not always maintained. Lichfield was unusual in not permitting vicars to hold other offices (for instance as chantry priests) and this probably reduced the value of vicars' positions to the point where it was hard to recruit new singers.[33]

At most of the cathedrals, vicars choral were required to be in holy orders. At Exeter all twenty-four had to be priests.[34] It was more normal for a handful of vicars to be priests while the others remained in minor orders, as deacons, subdeacons, or even acolytes. Two laymen were admitted at Wells in 1489 on condition that they take holy orders as soon as possible.[35] In some cathedrals there were clear distinctions between vicars who were priests and those who were not. The priests at Lincoln, for instance (in 1501 there were fifteen, out of a total of twenty-five vicars choral), were called the vicars of the first form and sat above the vicars of the second form, who had so far taken only minor orders.[36]

As the attachment of the vicars to individual canons gradually weakened during the later Middle Ages, the vicars acquired residences and

[30] Matthews and Atkins, St. Paul's, p. 110; see also Stanford E. Lehmberg, "The Reformation of Choirs: Cathedral Musical Establishments in Tudor England," in Tudor Rule and Revolution, ed. D. J. Guth and J. W. McKenna (Cambridge: Cambridge University Press, 1982), p. 47.

[31] Nicholas Orme, "The Early Musicians of Exeter Cathedral," Music and Letters 59 (1978): 396; Philip Barrett, The College of Vicars Choral at Hereford Cathedral (Hereford: Friends of Hereford Cathedral, 1980), p. 7.

[32] W. D. Peckham, Chichester Chapter Acts, pp. 21, 32; idem, "The Vicars Choral of Chichester Cathedral," Sussex Archaeological Collections 78 (1937): 139.

[33] VCH, Stafford, 3: 164.

[34] Nicholas Orme, "The Medieval Clergy of Exeter Cathedral: 1. The Vicars and Annuellars," Transactions of the Devonshire Association for the Advancement of Science 113 (1981): 82.

[35] Liber Ruber, fol. 27 (HMC, Wells, 2: 116).

[36] Maddison, Vicars Choral, p. 5.

1. Vicars' Court, Lincoln.

incomes of their own.[37] The earliest residential accommodation was the famous Bedern at York. Here thirty-six small houses or sets of chambers were erected near the east end of the minster as a result of the bequest provided by one of the canons as early as the 1240s. In the fourteenth century the vicars were able to add their own chapel and a common dining hall, and at the end of the century a pedestrian bridge was built to link the Bedern and the cathedral gatehouse, so that vicars would not face danger or inconvenience in having to cross a busy road. The Bedern no longer exists, although foundations of its buildings were exposed in the 1970s when the area was redeveloped, but its activities during the sixteenth century are unusually well documented and will be considered again below.[38] At Lincoln a hall, kitchen, and some chambers for vicars choral were erected in 1309, on the bishop's order.[39] Some of these early buildings survive in what is now called Vicars' Court (see fig. 1). They are of interest architecturally because a number of chambers (originally six in the best of the

[37] See K. Edwards, *Secular Cathedrals*, pp. 273–291, and Lehmberg, "Reformation of Choirs," pp. 48–49.

[38] Aylmer and Cant, *York Minster*, pp. 90–91; Frederick Harrison, *Life in a Medieval College: The Story of the Vicars-Choral of York Minster* (London: John Murray, 1952), pp. 29–42. I am grateful to Claire Cross for taking me to see the excavations in 1979.

[39] Maddison, *Vicars Choral*, p. 8.

surviving houses) opened off a central staircase. Such a plan was to become common in the colleges of Oxford and Cambridge, but the work at Lincoln probably antedates that at the universities. This arrangement was not adopted elsewhere, however; in other places vicars choral had individual small houses with separate entrances.

Vicars' closes survive intact at Wells, Hereford, and Lichfield. The vicars' college at Wells was founded and endowed by Bishop Ralph of Shrewsbury in 1348 so that the vicars "might be freer to serve God, live more respectably and nearer the church, attend divine service constantly, and meet together for meals in a companionable way, but without idle and scurrilous gossip."[40] Forty-two small houses, facing one another along two sides of an enclosed street, provided ample accommodation (see figs. 2 and 3). A chapel and library terminate the close at its north end; an attractive refectory, with a large fireplace, was built at the south, and in 1457 Bishop Beckington ordered the construction of a covered way over the Chain Gate, linking the refectory directly to the cathedral, as at York. The quadrangle now known as the Cloisters at Hereford (fig. 4) was constructed just after 1472. Here there were twenty-seven small two-roomed houses, a hall with a kitchen, and a chapel; the cloister was connected to the southeast transept of the cathedral so that vicars would not be troubled by inclement weather.[41] At Lichfield the Vicars' Close, similar in appearance, consisted of sixteen houses built in the fifteenth century adjoining an older hall that was reconstructed in 1458 (fig. 5).[42]

Similar arrangements existed at the other secular cathedrals. The minor canons of St. Paul's had a hall by 1272 and houses in the 1350s.[43] At Exeter the vicars choral had acquired buildings comparable to those in Wells by the end of the fourteenth century. These were on the west side of the close, in Kalendarhay, an area that had belonged to a religious guild called the Kalendar brethren before being transferred to the vicars. Twenty houses were still standing in 1850; the vicars' hall remained until World War II but was destroyed by the bombing of 1942.[44] The Vicars' Close at Chichester (fig. 6) was under

[40] Colchester, *Wells*, p. 38. The buildings are described at length by Warwick Rodwell, pp. 212–226.
[41] Barrett, *Vicars Choral*, p. 9. See also Marcus Binney, "Hereford Cathedral Close," *Country Life* 168 (25 September 1980): 1026–1029.
[42] Thomas Harwood, *The History and Antiquities of the Church and City of Lichfield* (Gloucester: Jos. Harris, 1806), pp. 257, 264, 291–292.
[43] K. Edwards, *Secular Cathedrals*, pp. 282–283.
[44] See Orme, "Medieval Clergy," p. 86; J. F. Chanter, *The Custos and College of the Vicars Choral of the Choir of the Cathedral Church of St. Peter, Exeter* (Exeter: W. Pollard, 1933), pp. 4–13; Vyvyan Hope and L. J. Lloyd, *Exeter Cathedral* (Exeter: Exeter Cathedral, 1973), p. 41. There is some suggestion that things were still not complete in the early sixteenth

2. Vicars' Close, Wells. View from the cathedral tower, with the refectory at the bottom, the chapel and library at the top.

3. Refectory of the vicars choral, Wells.

construction by 1400, and the hall was already in use then. One side of this close remains; a local antiquarian has attacked the conversion of the other half to shops, fronting on South Street, as an early twentieth-century act of urban vandalism.[45] Salisbury was the last of the secular cathedrals to acquire a vicars' dining hall. Evidence of this comes only in 1409, and it seems that the vicars choral of Salisbury never had their own individual houses.[46]

By the beginning of the Tudor period the vicars choral of the secular cathedrals had acquired a remarkably large degree of independence from the Dean and Chapter. They had their own officers, their own statutes, and their own revenues (the income came from lands

century: in 1508 the chapter wrote to John Arundel, bishop of Lichfield and a former bishop of Exeter, asking for assistance toward establishing the vicars in the buildings newly erected for them, since Mr. Silk, who had promised to help, changed his mind on his deathbed (MS. 3498, no. 54, Exeter Cathedral Library).

[45] Ian C. Hannah, "The Vicars' Close and Adjacent Buildings, Chichester," *Sussex Archaeological Collections* 56 (1914): 92–109; Peckham, "Vicars Choral of Chichester," p. 133.

[46] K. Edwards, *Secular Cathedrals*, p. 284.

4. The Cloisters, Hereford.

5. Vicars' Close, Lichfield.

6. Vicars' Close, Chichester.

and rents just as that of the Dean and Chapter did, and from obits and other payments for services). In some places they also maintained their own bakehouse and brewery. These arrangements changed little during the Reformation, at least until the later years of Elizabeth's reign, when the marriage of most vicars choral dictated an end to their communal life. All of this will be considered later, as will some severe problems in discipline and morality during the later Middle Ages.[47]

The polyphonic music sung at vespers, the Lady mass, and the high mass on festive occasions also required boys with unchanged treble voices. The number of choristers did not vary greatly from place to place. Everywhere there were fewer boys than one would find in a modern cathedral choir. Salisbury and Exeter had fourteen choristers apiece; York, Lincoln, and Lichfield, twelve. There were ten at St. Paul's, eight at Chichester, six at Wells, and only five at Hereford.[48]

As early as the twelfth century, St. Paul's arranged to have its cho-

[47] See Chapter 8, below.

[48] Figures taken from the manuscript financial records of the cathedrals; see also Maddison, *Vicars Choral*, pp. 21–22; Nicholas Orme, "Education and Learning at a Medieval English Cathedral: Exeter, 1380–1548," *Journal of Ecclesiastical History* 32 (1981): 266–269; and K. Edwards, *Secular Cathedrals*, pp. 313–324.

risters live in the almonry, under the care of the official called the almoner, but this arrangement was borrowed from monastic houses and was not repeated in any of the other secular cathedrals. A different pattern was established at Lincoln, where the bishop in 1264 provided endowments, a choristers' house, and regulations for the boys' life and instruction. This plan was followed at Salisbury and Wells, where a master of the choristers was appointed, serving under the supervision of one of the residentiary canons.[49] Hereford and Exeter placed the boys in the care of the succentor. By the later fifteenth century the role of organists had become important; sometimes the organists also served as masters of the choristers, but sometimes the two positions remained separate. Schoolmasters were appointed as well, to teach in the song schools and grammar schools associated with the cathedrals. Surviving records make it possible to gain a fairly detailed knowledge of the choristers' lives; this will be discussed in the general account of the cathedral musicians and their work (Chapter 8 below).[50]

Two further groups of men were included in the staff of the secular cathedrals. Both were involved in serving chantries, the endowments that provided masses and prayers for the repose of the souls of the dead. In cases where prominent persons had given large revenues to the cathedral, there might be separate chantry chapels with a priest whose principal duty was the celebration of a daily mass at the chantry altar. Smaller bequests provided for obits, in which persons would be remembered on the anniversary of their death.[51]

[49] The house used by the choristers of Salisbury survives at the northwest corner of Choristers' Green; it is now called Hungerford's Chantry. A choristers' house was built in Lichfield as late as 1531, but it was rented to Lord Paget in 1550, and the choristers seem to have lived in various houses without a common hall (Harwood, *Lichfield*, pp. 181, 283; Act Book 5, fol. 35, Lichfield Joint Record Office). At Hereford, too, the choristers were being boarded in the homes of canons rather than in a choristers' house as late as 1525; an entry in the Act Book requires canons who leave the city to board their choristers with another canon, paying him 10*d.* per week, and one of the canons is criticized for taking choristers to his prebendal manor of Putson—an unsuitable place because of the long and dangerous crossing of the Wye (Act Book 1, fol. 37, Hereford Cathedral Library).

[50] See K. Edwards, *Secular Cathedrals*, pp. 313–324; Dora H. Robertson, *Sarum Close* (London: Jonathan Cape, 1938), pp. 64–127.

[51] I have not found evidence of confraternity or guild chapels in the cathedrals, though they may have existed. Financed by contributions from numerous individuals rather than by a single bequest, these existed in many parish churches and, like chantries, provided prayers for the dead. We know that they were growing in importance in some places, for instance Boston in Lincolnshire, during the sixteenth century. At Exeter, and probably elsewhere, there were guilds of lay people who made annual contributions of a penny to

7. Speke Chantry Chapel, Exeter Cathedral.

Many of the chantries traced their origins to the thirteenth and fourteenth centuries. For some reason fewer seem to have been founded during the fifteenth century, but the early Tudor period witnessed a rebirth of interest in these establishments, particularly notable since it occurred only a few years before they were dissolved and made illegal by acts of Parliament. Most of the secular cathedrals have some remains of early Tudor chantry chapels; one of the most splendid is that of Sir John Speke at Exeter (see fig. 7). Speke, who died in 1518 at the age of seventy-seven, had long been interested in the Church. He had gone on pilgrimage to Rome and the Holy Land while a young man. In later years he was closely associated with a num-

the cathedral in return for prayers by the cathedral clergy. At one time more than three hundred persons were members. But these guilds do not appear to have had a designated chapel or specific chaplain. See Nicholas Orme, *Exeter Cathedral as It Was* (Exeter: Devon Books, 1986), p. 60.

ber of cathedral clergy; the fact that he chose to display their coats of arms on his chantry chapel suggests that he held bishops Peter Courtenay (d. 1487), Richard Fox (d. 1492), and Hugh Oldham (d. 1519) in special esteem, as well as Dean John Veysey (promoted to bishop in 1519) and Canon John Ryse (treasurer of the cathedral from 1518 to 1531). Bishop Oldham erected a chantry chapel for himself at the same time that Speke's chapel was under construction, and the architectural style is so similar that the chapels must have been planned by the two men together. They remain as beautiful examples of Perpendicular architecture, enriched with statues and heraldry, and as evidence of the intimate relationship that might exist between cathedral clergy and prominent members of the local gentry or civic oligarchy.[52]

Other chantries were being founded as late as the 1540s, just before Reformation theology and royal greed combined to bring about the confiscation of their property. Among the last foundations were the chantries of William Silk, Richard More, and William Horsey at Exeter; there are also a number of magnificent chantry chapels built to commemorate bishops, including John Alcock (d. 1500) and Nicholas West (d. 1533) at Ely, Edmund Audley (d. 1503) at Hereford, and John Longland (d. 1547) at Lincoln (fig. 8), as well as Oldham at Exeter. Chantries were important to faithful lay people because they ensured that masses would be celebrated throughout all the early morning hours, when the laity would be able to attend. At Lincoln, for instance, there were continuous celebrations from 5 A.M. until 11 every day but Good Friday, "so that the faithful will not lack services."[53]

The priests who served chantries were known by several names in the English cathedrals. Most often they were called cantarists or altarists. At Exeter chantry priests were termed annuellars (in Latin *annuellarii*), the word obviously being derived from the original practice of celebrating a mass for a person's soul on the "annual," or anniversary, of his or her death.[54] It was possible for those vicars choral who were priests to hold chantry appointments; indeed, this provided an essential income for many of them. But other clergy were needed as

---

[52] Nicholas Orme, "Sir John Speke and His Chapel in Exeter Cathedral," *Reports and Transactions of the Devonshire Association* 118 (1986): 25–41. I am grateful to Dr. Orme for sending me a copy of this article in advance of publication.

[53] R.E.G. Cole, ed., *Chapter Acts of the Cathedral Church of St. Mary of Lincoln, A.D. 1520–1536*, Lincoln Record Society, no. 12 (Horncastle, 1915), pp. 142–144. See also Bowker, *Secular Clergy*, p. 165; K. Edwards, *Secular Cathedrals*, p. 300; and Orme, "Medieval Clergy," pp. 93, 96.

[54] An alternative form was "annivellar" (*annivellarius*). Cf. Orme, "Medieval Clergy," p. 91; MS. 3551, Exeter Cathedral Library, passim.

8. Chantry Chapel of John Longland, Lincoln Cathedral.

well. At York in the 1540s, twenty-one vicars choral were serving nine-teen chantries, but a further twenty-four chantries were staffed by a separate group of cantarists. At Lincoln fifteen vicars held chantry ap-pointments, but there were thirty-five other cantarists. One of the vic-ars choral of Hereford resigned in 1517 to become a full-time chantry priest.[55] Fourteen out of the twenty-one chantries at Hereford and nine of the fourteen at Chichester were served by vicars choral. The situation in the other cathedrals was similar.[56] Cantarists had assis-tants, younger men who were not priests, to help them in the celebra-tion of their offices, particularly by ensuring that supplies of bread, wine, and wax were available as needed. These men were sometimes called clerks of the second form, or secondaries, since they sat in the second row of choir stalls, below the vicars choral and cantarists but

[55] Act Book 1, fol. 10, Hereford Cathedral Library.
[56] Edwards, *Secular Cathedrals*, pp. 296–297.

above the choristers. Rather confusingly, they are referred to as altarists at Salisbury and Wells—the term more commonly designated the
chantry priests themselves, not their helpers—and at Lincoln they are
called the poor clerks. Many of the secondaries had been choristers;
when their voices broke, they remained at the cathedral with modified
duties. Generally they were expected to attend the grammar school,
and they received modest stipends for doing so. At Lincoln and Hereford they were specifically admonished to be faithful in attending
school and not wander about as they had done.[57] They were supposed
to come regularly to at least some of the cathedral services, and very
likely they joined in singing them: at Lincoln they are sometimes
called the poor clerks choral.[58] Those who could not sing, perhaps
while their voices were unstable, could be assigned the duty of blowing
the organ, for this was one of the responsibilities of the poor clerks.[59]
Secondaries often had preference for appointment as vicars choral,
and when they were old enough to be ordained priests, they might be
named cantarists.[60]

Halls of residence were established for the cantarists at a number of
cathedrals, generally later than the houses for the vicars choral. St.
Paul's, which not surprisingly had more chantries than any other English cathedral, was the first to reserve chambers in the churchyard for
its cantarists; these became known as Presteshouses or St. Peter's College. A common hall of residence, called the Monterey College, was
provided at Wells in 1399. St. William's College at York was established in 1461 to provide a home for twenty-four chantry priests who
were not vicars choral and could not live in the Bedern. Substantial
parts of this building still survive. The fifteenth century also saw the
building of a house for the cantarists in the close at Lichfield. Although there had been talk of providing a home for the annuellars of
Exeter as early as the 1380s, a residence was not actually built until the
late 1520s. It was called Peter's House or New Kalendarhay.[61] Lincoln

[57] R.E.G. Cole, ed., *Chapter Acts of the Cathedral Church of St. Mary of Lincoln, A.D. 1536–1547*, Lincoln Record Society, no. 13 (Horncastle, 1917), p. 63; Act Book 1, fol. 72, Hereford Cathedral Library.

[58] R.E.G. Cole, ed., *Chapter Acts of the Cathedral Church of St. Mary of Lincoln, A.D. 1547–1559*, Lincoln Record Society, no. 15 (Horncastle, 1920), p. 145. Cantarists often sang also; at St. Paul's they could not take office until their voices were approved by the succentor and a senior member of the choir (K. Edwards, *Secular Cathedrals*, p. 298).

[59] Maddison, *Vicars Choral*, p. 27.

[60] An example is provided by the case of one Hamo Thwyng at Lincoln. He was a poor clerk prior to 1491, when he was appointed a vicar choral and promised to be diligent in learning the organ, descant, and grammar. He was ordained subdeacon in 1497, deacon in 1501, and priest later in the same year. He died in 1510 (ibid., pp. 68, 76–78).

[61] K. Edwards, *Secular Cathedrals*, pp. 306–308; Colchester, *Wells*, p. 37; Orme, "Medi-

was the only cathedral to have a common hall and common endowments for its clerks of the second form. There were thus four separate houses or colleges at Lincoln, accommodating the choristers, poor clerks, junior vicars choral, and senior or priest vicars.[62]

❖

It is not easy to work out the details of cathedral finance during the years before the Reformation. Since income was often paid directly to individuals (cathedral officers and prebendaries) or to groups (like the colleges of vicars choral), there was no single person responsible for handling money and keeping accounts. Fragmentary records of certain types of transactions do survive at some of the secular cathedrals, and they yield information of some interest, especially regarding unusual expenditures. But it is impossible to put together any sort of full accounting of cathedral revenues from these sources.

We are fortunate, however, in having the information that was gathered by commissioners for Henry VIII in 1536, when the government was beginning to collect the clerical tenths formerly paid to the pope and needed an accurate evaluation of all the positions in the church. The resulting *Valor Ecclesiasticus* states a great deal of specific, and probably quite reliable, information about the income of the cathedrals and all the individuals associated with them.[63]

While the *Valor* does not directly give the total revenue of the cathedrals, it is not difficult to calculate cathedral income using the figures included in the survey. The results are quite interesting; they reveal very substantial differences in wealth, as shown in table 1.1.

The great wealth of Lincoln is immediately apparent. In fact, Lincoln was even richer than these figures indicate, for the income of twenty-eight of the prebendaries is not listed as part of the statistics for the cathedral, since their properties were located in other places and were taxed there. It is not possible to ascertain what the total value of such endowments was, but it can hardly have been less than £300 or £400. The revenues of Lincoln and the members of its staff were

---

eval Clergy," pp. 98–99; Aylmer and Cant, *York Minster*, pp. 97–98. In 1527 the annuellars specifically asked for scaffolds and pulleys to be used in building their close (MS. 3551, fol. 45, Exeter Cathedral Library).

[62] Cole, *Lincoln Chapter Acts, 1520–1536*, p. xvi; K. Edwards, *Secular Cathedrals*, p. 313.

[63] *Valor Ecclesiasticus*, 6 vols. (London: Record Commission, 1810–1834). Figures for the cathedrals are scattered throughout the six volumes, which are arranged by dioceses. The monetary symbols £, *s.*, and *d.* are used, as usual, for pounds, shillings, and pence. Fractions of a penny have been rounded off in the tables that follow. The figures used here are for net income, after some deductions have been allowed. The gross revenues are slightly higher.

CHAPTER 1

TABLE 1.1
Revenues of the Secular Cathedrals

Lincoln	£3,426	7s.	9d.
Salisbury	2,569	9s.	11d.
York	2,455	1s.	1d.
St. Paul's	2,344	11s.	10d.
Wells	2,239	4s.	10d.
Exeter	2,125	7s.	1d.
Lichfield	1,408	8s.	4d.
Hereford	1,006	11s.	11d.
Chichester	986	0s.	7d.

thus more than £1,000 greater than those of the second-ranking secular cathedral, Salisbury.

Five of the cathedrals are clustered together with similar incomes ranging from £2,000 to about £2,500. One might have expected that York and St. Paul's would rank higher than they do, because of York's special role as seat of an archbishop and St. Paul's unique position in London. Lincoln surpassed them largely because of the great size of the diocese before the 1540s, when the new sees of Oxford and Peterborough were carved out of it. The relative poverty of the cathedrals at Lichfield, Hereford, and Chichester, evident from other sources, is fully borne out by the statistics in the *Valor*.

Revenues assigned to the Dean and Chapter, drawn from lands, rents, tithes, and fees, were generally divided among the residentiary canons. Figures in the *Valor* make it clear why these positions were so lucrative. The *Valor* also lists the revenues associated with the individual prebends; the total of these is set out in table 1.2.

Several items in the table call for comment. Once again the revenue of prebendaries at Lincoln is understated by several hundred pounds. The unusual situation at Exeter, where the bulk of the revenues was received by the Dean and Chapter jointly with only a small sum allocated to individual prebendaries, is clearly revealed. The poorest cathedrals stand by themselves, as in the previous table, but all the others have quite similar resources available for their canons.

The income of the chief officers of these cathedrals varied enormously in relation to the wealth of the foundation (see table 1.3). In a few cases, specific revenues were received by the subdean. At Lincoln he had the large sum of £215 10s. 11d.; at York just over £50; at both Wells and Exeter about £22. Generally all of these officers were resi-

26

TABLE 1.2
Revenues of the Dean and Chapter

Cathedral	Dean and Chapter (total)	Prebends (total)	Grand total
Lincoln	£ 511 16s. 10d.	£395 3s. 10d.[a]	£ 907 0s. 8d.[a]
Salisbury	601 12s. 0d.	711 9s. 5d.	1,312 1s. 5d.
York	434 2s. 6d.	854 14s. 9d.	1,288 19s. 3d.
St. Paul's	725 7s. 10d.	443 15s. 4d.	1,169 3s. 2d.
Wells	729 3s. 4d.	446 0s. 10d.	1,175 4s. 2d.
Exeter	1,180 6s. 3d.	96 0s. 0d.	1,276 6s. 3d.
Lichfield	562 3s. 6d.	390 1s. 11d.	952 5s. 5d.
Hereford	423 17s. 2d.	234 5s. 0d.	658 2s. 2d.
Chichester	310 14s. 6d.	302 8s. 10d.	613 3s. 4d.

[a] Incomplete.

TABLE 1.3
Income of Chief Officers

Cathedral	Dean	Precentor	Chancellor	Treasurer
Lincoln	£368 3s. 1d.	£188 11s. 3d.	£235 10s. 4d.	£191 2s. 3d.
Salisbury	204 10s. 0d.	99 6s. 8d.	56 5s. 9d.	101 3s. 0d.
York	307 10s. 7d.	96 4s. 2d.	85 6s. 8d.	—
St. Paul's	210 12s. 1d.	46 7s. 3d.	33 0s. 0d.	37 0s. 0s.
Wells	295 14s. 1d.	24 6s. 3d.	40 5s. 0d.	62 2s. 2d.
Exeter	158 0s. 0d.	99 13s. 4d.	59 0s. 0d.	32 17s. 3d.
Lichfield	40 0s. 0d.	26 13s. 4d.	26 13s. 4d.	56 13s. 4d.
Hereford	38 6s. 1d.	21 19s. 5d.	14 4s. 4d.	15 8s. 0d.
Chichester	58 9s. 4d.	35 0s. 5d.	27 7s. 0d.	62 6s. 8d.

dentiary canons and shared in the distribution of the income of the Dean and Chapter. Archdeacons, who were cathedral clergy only in a limited sense, are listed along with them in most of the *Valor*'s entries. Here the variations are enormous (see table 1.4); they reflect different numbers of archdeacons (the largest not surprisingly being at Lincoln) as well as differing levels of income assigned to each.

The *Valor Ecclesiasticus* also gives figures of considerable interest for the vicars choral, chantry priests, and, in a few cases, choristers. These

TABLE 1.4
Income of Archdeacons (Total)

Lincoln	£660 17s. 10d.
Salisbury	347 11s. 3d.
York	249 19s. 4d.
St. Paul's	185 13s. 4d.
Wells	253 5s. 7d.
Exeter	149 0s. 3d.
Lichfield	—
Hereford	74 8s. 8d.
Chichester	77 18s. 2d.

TABLE 1.5
Revenues of Vicars Choral, Chantry Priests, and Choristers

Cathedral	Vicars choral	Cantarists	Choristers
Lincoln	£259 13s. 10d.	£196 15s. 6d.	£33 13s. 4d.
Salisbury	236 11s. 6d.	98 5s. 11d.	35 17s. 8d.
York	136 5s. 6d.	138 19s. 2d.[a]	
St. Paul's	245 18s. 10d.[b]	416 17s. 2d.	
Wells	208 12s. 7d.	83 15s. 10d.	
Exeter	204 10s. 3d.	74 0s. 0d.	
Lichfield	173 18s. 2d.	99 14s. 3d.	25 12s. 4d.
Hereford	106 18s. 1d.	77 6s. 1d.	
Chichester	31 12s. 0d.	78 12s. 4d.	

[a] Incomplete; this is the figure for St. Sepulchre's Chapel only.
[b] This figure is for the minor canons; there is no entry for the vicars choral.

are set out in table 1.5. In cases where there were no revenues allotted specifically to the choristers, the boys were supported by general revenues of the Dean and Chapter or by funds channeled through the precentor or succentor.

Composite figures such as those in the *Valor Ecclesiasticus* give a good idea of the status of cathedrals as institutions and help explain their place in Tudor society. It is helpful to compare the income of a cathedral with that of an ordinary parish church. While there was considerable variation among parishes, too, the income of rectors or vicars generally fell in the range between £5 and £30. Relatively few parish priests received more than £20. Their status was clearly lower than that of canons and prebendaries, though they may have been better off than many of the chantry priests at the cathedrals.

Sometimes the fragmentary accounts surviving in cathedral libraries give a better idea of the actual income of individuals, and sometimes they help fill gaps in the *Valor*. Choristers' accounts for Salisbury show them receiving about £55 in 1496, mainly from tenements in the city. By 1501 their income had fallen to £44, and by 1504 to £41. Payments included stipends to the master of the choristers and to their instructor, the cost of new gowns (called "togas"), and small sums for repairs to the choristers' house.[64] At Chichester each chorister was paid 13s. 4d. a year, every vicar choral twice that sum (£1 6s. 8d.).[65] The master of the choristers at Hereford was given £18 to pay for the boys' food in 1530; until this time they had still been fed by the residentiary canons.[66] Organists never figure in the *Valor*'s accounts, but we know that the organist at Salisbury received £6 11s. 8d. in 1538, while his counterpart at Wells had a mere £2 (probably in addition to income as a vicar choral and, perhaps, chantry priest) and the right to occupy a house worth 26s. 8d. a year.[67]

The most important financial officer of each cathedral was its treasurer of the common fund, often called the communar or collector of common rents. Communars' accounts frequently survive. At Lincoln there are records of the treasurer of the common fund for virtually the entire sixteenth century.[68] They list payments to all the members of the chapter, including nonresidents, stipends paid to chantry priests, schoolmasters, and organists, and such other expenses as gowns for the choristers. Income remaining after such charges had been met was distributed annually among the residentiary canons; in 1515, for instance, the sum remaining was £125 9s. 3d., or £20. 8s. 2d. for each of the six residents. A number of the rolls kept by the collector of the common rents at Hereford survive as well; since these are scattered throughout the Tudor period, they give a good idea of the chapter's changing status. Here again there are payments, including a number for choristers, with the remainder forming the dividend distributed among the residentiaries. In 1492, eight residentiary canons received 19s. each; in 1509, 17s. was paid to each of six residents; six

---

[64] Choristers' Accounts, 1/6–1/18, Salisbury Cathedral Library.

[65] Peckham, *Chichester Chapter Acts*, pp. 100, 105.

[66] Act Book 1, fol. 65, Hereford Cathedral Library.

[67] Christopher Wordsworth and Dora H. Robertson, "Salisbury Choristers: Their Endowments, Boy-Bishops, Music Teachers, and Headmasters," *Wiltshire Archaeological and Natural History Magazine* 48 (1937): 216–218; Liber Ruber, fol. 151 (HMC, *Wells*, 2: 208).

[68] Archives of the Dean and Chapter of Lincoln Cathedral, MSS. BJ. 3. 3–6, Lincolnshire Record Office.

shared a dividend of £4 9s. 6d. in 1538, receiving 14s. 10d. apiece.[69]
The great officers of Salisbury were entitled to double dividends,
which were confirmed in 1547 after some contention.[70]

The chamberlains' accounts at York are similar to those of the communars at other cathedrals, although they appear to be more general
and to cover a wider variety of expenses.[71] Payments to canons, chantry priests, vicars choral, choristers, and organ players are included.
York also possesses a few accounts of St. Peter's Portion, a sum equal
to a residentiary's dividend, which was set aside for common use and
to meet emergencies.[72]

There are only a few scattered accounts of other officers. Hereford
holds several of the rolls kept by the collector of mass pence, who received payments for obits and other memorial masses and distributed
them to the priests according to the number of masses said. In 1492,
for instance, £59 4s. 7d. came in from such endowments as manors,
glebes, and tithes; this was distributed to the dean and eighteen other
priests, one of whom received 19s. ½d. for 368 masses.[73] The clavigers
(there were two appointed each year) received money from four manors and some other miscellaneous sources; after payments for the choristers and for the repair of chancels in parish churches where the
rectorial tithes belonged to the cathedral, sums approximating £100 a
year were free for distribution to the residentiaries.[74] There are interesting fabric accounts at Hereford, Salisbury, Wells, and York, but
only for the period after the Reformation.

Some cathedrals received regular offerings from householders and
parish churches within their dioceses. At Lichfield it was customary to
have a Whitsun procession of clergy and lay people from neighboring
parishes, bringing contributions called Chad farthings; we know about
the matter only because of a dispute over precedence and the privilege
of carrying crosses within the close. Farthings from householders
within the city and diocese of Exeter were also collected by the cathedral there. A royal proclamation of November 1538 orders the continuation of this "goodly and commendable custom" and says that the
funds are to be used for maintenance of the cathedral fabric. We do

[69] R170–198, Hereford Cathedral Library.
[70] Act Book, MS. 80, pp. 22–23, Salisbury Cathedral Library.
[71] Accounts, E1/60–107, York Minster Library.
[72] Accounts, E2/21–30, York Minster Library. These accounts are of a later date, but
the Portion was in existence as early as the thirteenth century and is referred to in the
statutes of 1291.
[73] R522–582, Hereford Cathedral Library.
[74] R584–589, Hereford Cathedral Library.

not know how common this practice was, or how large the revenues were. Probably they were relatively insignificant.[75]

Bequests and offerings at shrines also provided incidental income for the cathedrals. The frequency with which early Tudor testators remembered their cathedral churches, as well as their own parishes, is surprising. Lincolnshire wills, for instance, often provide for the payment of small sums to "our mother church of Lincoln"—an interesting bit of evidence about the way in which cathedrals were perceived by the laity—or, more specifically, to the high altar, "our Lady's altar," the "Lady wark," or the cathedral fabric. Some of these funds were used to provide for the "works chantry" located in the south transept. Bequests to the cathedral were generally small, ranging from 6d. to 6s. 8d. They did not decline in frequency or size until 1533; in 1532 they produced £38; six years later, only £5 4s. 1d., and thereafter "nulla."[76]

Income from shrines was probably greater, at least until the 1520s. The most famous shrines, which attracted pilgrims in large numbers, were those of St. Erkenwald at St. Paul's in London, St. William at York, St. Hugh at Lincoln (fig. 9), St. Richard at Chichester, St. Chad at Lichfield, and St. Thomas Cantilupe at Hereford (fig. 10). In all of these places the faithful made offerings, in part at least because of the miracles attributed to the intervention of the saints.[77] Unfortunately we have little hard evidence about such oblations. A few figures that survive suggest no decline in offerings in the first decades of the sixteenth century. Early in Henry VIII's reign, for instance, the shrine of St. Chad at Lichfield was still said to bring in £400 a year.[78] It may be that belief in miracles was beginning to evaporate by the 1520s. We know that the Dean and Chapter of Hereford were troubled by a grave decrease in revenue as early as 1525; they were able to persuade the bishop to unite the profitable hospital of St. Ethelbert to the cathedral as a partial solution to the crisis. By 1532 alms and oblations at

[75] Act Book 4, fols. 97, 104; Lichfield Joint Record Office; H. E. Savage, *Lichfield Cathedral: The Cathedral and the Chapter, 1530–1553* (Lichfield: Johnson's Head, 1927), pp. 12–13; Paul L. Hughes and James F. Larkin, eds., *Tudor Royal Proclamations*, 3 vols. (New Haven: Yale University Press, 1964–1969), 1: 269–270.

[76] C. W. Foster, ed., *Lincoln Wills*, 3 vols., Lincoln Record Society, Horncastle (5, 1914; 10, 1918; 24, 1930), see esp. 1: 32, 63, 113, 122, 137, 145, 250; 3: 106, 230; Bowker, *Secular Clergy*, p. 93. For a general study of religious bequests in early Tudor wills, see J. J. Scarisbrick, *The Reformation and the English People* (Oxford: Blackwell, 1984), pp. 2–12.

[77] Shrines in the monastic cathedrals were generally of greater importance than those in the secular ones; see below, Chapter 2. Gifts to the shrines sometimes took the form of jewels and other objects to enrich the shrine itself, not money that could be spent by the Dean and Chapter. On the related question of pilgrimages, Scarisbrick (*Reformation*, pp. 54–55) concludes that the evidence is insufficient to support generalizations but notes that the shrine at Walsingham, at least, continued to attract pilgrims to the end.

[78] *VCH, Stafford*, 3: 168.

9. Shrine of St. Hugh, Lincoln Cathedral.

the shrine of St. Thomas Cantilupe had declined so disastrously that the cathedral was threatened with decay and dilapidation, and canons entering into residence were ordered to pay 100 marks (£67) to the fabric fund.[79]

It may be that another reason for growing financial problems was the policy of leasing manors, farms, tenements, and other property for long periods of time at fixed rents, which could not be altered with changing economic conditions. In a way the problem was not new; we know that there was concern about long leases at Lichfield as early as the thirteenth century, when the bishop ordered that farms were to be leased for not more than five years at a time.[80] But it became more

[79] Act Book 1, fols. 33, 68–69, Hereford Cathedral Library. In 1307 the shrine of St. Thomas Cantilupe had more than five hundred rings of silver and gold, some including precious stones, but only fifteen were left in 1538; the remainder had gone to pay cathedral expenses. For a detailed account of the history of this shrine and an examination of healings attributed to its curative powers, see Ronald C. Finucane, *Miracles and Pilgrims* (London: J. M. Dent, 1977), pp. 173–188.

[80] *VCH, Stafford,* 3: 146.

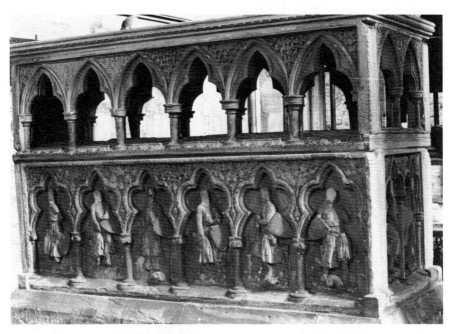

10. Shrine of St. Thomas Cantilupe, Hereford Cathedral. The heads of the statues
were probably defaced during Henry VIII's campaign
against shrines and images, 1538.

severe in the 1530s, as inflation began its steady onslaught, and cathedrals, like individuals living on fixed incomes, found themselves unable to keep up with rising prices and costs.

Large numbers of leases survive in cathedral archives; they would
enable a student of economic history to undertake a detailed examination of ecclesiastical estate management. Failing that, it is of some
interest to take a superficial look at selected leases. Those at Chichester and Hereford happen to be easily accessible. During the period
between 1500 and 1550, we do find a few leases for ninety-nine years
or three lives, the maximum legal periods. But such long terms are
unusual; most were for periods between thirty and fifty years, with
forty being about average. It may be that this represents an increase,
however. In the 1480s several of the leases granted at Chichester were
for periods as short as seven, ten, or thirteen years. After 1520 the
shortest lease was for eighteen years, and during the years between
1530 and 1547 there were none shorter than twenty-one years.[81] It is

[81] Peckham, *Chichester Chapter Acts*, passim; Archives of the Hereford Cathedral Library, misc. leases (1485–1547), e.g., nos. 1254, 376, 1883, 1978, 1905, 1979, 2902, 1775,
3175, 1987.

33

TABLE 1.6
Revenues of Welsh Cathedrals

St. David's	£344 6s. 1d.
Llandaff	338 12s. 10d.
St. Asaph	262 5s. 7d.
Bangor	194 0s. 10d.

interesting to note that the only rent charged at Hereford for the use of a pasture was one red rose each year, perhaps as a token of allegiance to the Crown.[82] There must have been special circumstances here; ordinarily money rents are clearly stated.

ALL four of the Welsh cathedrals were secular in organization. They were much smaller and poorer than their English counterparts. The *Valor Ecclesiasticus* gives the figures in table 1.6 for their annual income.

Some further details are recorded as well. At St. David's and Llandaff the dean's resources are not listed separately. Revenues available to the Dean and Chapter were £72 15s. 4d. at St. David's and £87 12s. 10d. at Llandaff, the latter figure including £22 17s. designated for repair of the fabric.[83] The dean of St. Asaph received £45 1s. 4d. annually; the dean of Bangor, £22 17s. 2d. The precentor of St. David's was allowed £20 6s. 10d., and the treasurer there £24 18s. 6d. The poorer Welsh cathedrals were bound to allocate large portions of their revenues to archdeacons: the single archdeacon at St. Asaph received £74 15s. 7d., while three archdeacons at Bangor were given £48 6s. 2d., £58 10s. 6d., and £13 3s. 3d., respectively.[84] We know that there were four vicars choral at St. Asaph, each being paid £6 14s. 6d. a year, and only two at Bangor, dividing £17 0s. 2d. equally between them. But by the early eighteenth century, and probably earlier, these were joined by four lay singing men and ten poor children, from whom so-

[82] Act Book 1, fol. 31, Hereford Cathedral Library. For a fuller discussion of long leases, see below, Chapter 7.

[83] At St. David's the bishop theoretically stood in place of the dean, although the precentor acted as head of the chapter; see Glanmor Williams, *Welsh Reformation Essays* (Cardiff: University of Wales Press, 1967), p. 116. The situation at Llandaff seems to have been similar; see Browne Willis, *An Survey of the Cathedral-Church of Landaff* (London: R. Gosling, 1719), p. 30.

[84] Two of the archdeaconries were regularly held by the bishop himself in later years; see Browne Willis, *A Survey of the Cathedral Church of Bangor* (London: R. Gosling, 1721), p. 44.

called singing boys were chosen.[85] There were eight vicars choral, organized as a corporation with their own seal for making leases, and four choristers at St. David's; about 1717 Browne Willis saw the ruins of their houses and common hall, which he likened to that at Hereford.[86]

It is interesting to note that building continued at the Welsh cathedrals in the early Tudor period, despite the poverty of these sees. Towers were erected at both Llandaff and Bangor. Henry VII's uncle, Jasper Tudor, was responsible for putting up the tower at Llandaff, about 1490. Bishop Skeffington built the tower at Bangor; it was originally planned to be twice as high, but construction stopped with the bishop's death in 1533. The upper stage of the tower at St. David's dates from the early sixteenth century, too, as does the roof of the nave and eastern chapel.[87] St. David's also has the chantry chapel of Bishop Vaughan (d. 1522), one of the finest pieces of Perpendicular architecture in Wales.[88] All of the Welsh cathedrals except St. Asaph served as parish churches; this was appropriate enough, since they stood in small though beautiful villages. With such limited resources, elaborate sung services could hardly be maintained. Indeed Browne Willis commented in 1719 that Llandaff showed "very small Signs of its being the Mother-Church of so wealthy and populous a Diocese," and he blamed the people of Cardiff for beautifying their parish church while neglecting the cathedral.[89]

WHAT, generally, was the condition of the secular cathedrals on the eve of the Reformation? The answer is not easy, and the verdict must be mixed.

Certainly there were problems. Most of them simply reflected human frailty and lack of devotion. Vicars choral were charged with incontinence, quarreling, living outside their assigned quarters, and ab-

[85] Ibid., pp. 43–44. The vicars choral at Bangor had had houses, which had been turned into stables by Browne Willis's time.

[86] Browne Willis, *A Survey of the Cathedral-Church of St. David's* (London: R. Gosling, 1717), p. 29. The College of the Blessed Virgin Mary, a chantry at St. David's, was supposed to have twenty-seven vicars choral and eight choristers at the end of the fifteenth century, but it is hard to believe that such a large establishment actually existed. See Glanmor Williams, *The Welsh Church from Conquest to Reformation* (Cardiff: University of Wales Press, 1962), p. 282.

[87] Richard Morris, *Cathedrals and Abbeys of England and Wales* (New York: W. W. Norton, 1979), pp. 239, 259, 268.

[88] Williams, *Welsh Church*, pp. 430–431.

[89] Willis, *Landaff*, p. 89.

sence from service with what may seem shocking frequency.[90] Secondaries are found wandering the streets rather than attending the grammar school; chantry priests neglect their duties; canons are non-resident; services are sometimes perfunctory or slipshod; buildings are occasionally allowed to decay.

A list of complaints presented at York in 1519 is typical of such charges. Some are petty: the missal lacks a clasp, "wherby a fayre boke is nye lost." Sometimes the candles on the high altar are not lighted. "The goodly reyredewse [reredos] is so full of dust and copwebbes that by lyklyode it shalbe shortly lost [unless] it be clensed & better keppte than it hathe bene." Hangings in the choir are covered with wax, and "dogges pysses of thame."[91] More serious complaints about the clergy were lodged in 1544: "The qwere is evill servid because the nowmbre of vicars ar so fewe, & so many of theyme are so sickle: and thoes that are in heilthe woll not take the more paynes in doyng theire dewties." There is "much confabulation" among the canons and vicars choral, and chantry priests do not adhere to the scheduled hours for their masses. Copes and vestments are decayed, and the minster "nedith reparacions in dyvers and sundrie places."[92] When Bishop Sherburne took office at Chichester in 1509 he complained that he found the cathedral in a state of "ancient squalor," with "most damnable customs by which eminent men were deterred from coming into residence." As a partial remedy to the situation he provided endowments for four new "Wiccamical" prebends (these were to be filled by graduates of Winchester College and New College, Oxford, the famous fourteenth-century foundations of William of Wykeham) and four singing men, to be called the Sherburne clerks.[93]

On the other hand, there are numerous instances of cathedrals that were being adorned and enriched even as Henry VIII was severing England's ties with the papacy—a good example is Hereford, where the magnificent north porch, including a Lady Chapel above the covered entrance, was added by Bishop Booth (see fig. 11)—and of chantries that were founded only months before an act of Parliament ordered their suppression. The famous Italian humanist Polydore Vergil, who was archdeacon of Wells throughout almost the entire reign of Henry VIII, included a favorable account of the cathedral in

[90] For details, see below, Chapter 8.
[91] *The Fabric Rolls of York Minster*, Surtees Society, no. 35 (Durham, 1859), p. 267.
[92] Ibid., p. 273.
[93] F. G. Bennett, R. H. Codrington, and C. Deedes, eds., *Statutes and Constitutions of the Cathedral Church of Chichester* (Chichester: Charles Knight, 1904), pp. 77–78; Bishop Sherburne's foundation charters, cap. 1/13/3, 1/13/5, 1/14/1, 1/14/3, West Sussex Record Office.

36

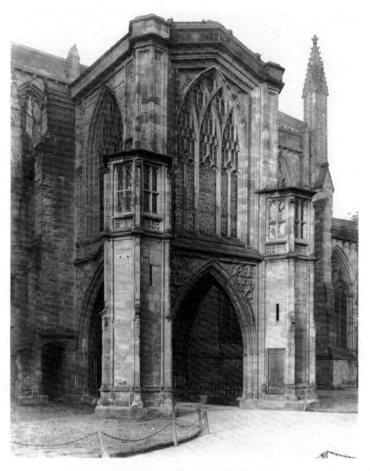

11. North Porch, Hereford Cathedral.

his *Anglica Historia*. At Wells, he wrote, "there flourished a famous college of priests, men of honest behaviour and well learned; wherefore
I account it no small worship that I myself, fourteen years archdeacon
of Wells, was elected one of that college."[94] Travelers came, even from
abroad, to marvel at the size and beauty of the great buildings, and
pilgrims thronged to their shrines, laden with offerings and intercessions. The secular cathedrals were an old, established, accepted
part of English society, still adhering to their traditional values and
performing their traditional services even as change loomed on the
horizon.

[94] Quoted in Colchester, *Wells*, p. 43.

37

2

THE END OF THE OLD ORDER:
THE MONASTIC CATHEDRALS

TEN OF the early Tudor cathedrals were monastic in organization. Canterbury, Durham, Winchester, Worcester, Ely, Norwich, Rochester, Bath, and Coventry were Benedictine priories, while the cathedral at Carlisle was staffed by Augustinian canons.[1] Cathedral and monastic functions and traditions were blended in these houses; the story of their last years forms one of the most interesting chapters in the history of English religious orders.

The early development of these houses need concern us only briefly. Although monasticism was an important aspect of the Celtic church, cathedrals were not, and no institutions date back to that period. The idea of cathedral monasteries first came to England with Augustine and his followers in 597, but it did not last long, if indeed it was actually established. The Viking invasions devastated a number of the religious houses, so that monastic life according to the rule of St. Benedict had virtually ceased to exist by the time of King Alfred. We know that Canterbury was staffed for several centuries by secular canons under the leadership of a dean, not a prior, and that a similar situation existed elsewhere.

The revival of monasticism was inspired by St. Dunstan, and to a lesser extent by Ethelwold and Oswald, in the tenth century. During the closing years of the Anglo-Saxon period Winchester, Worcester, Ely, and Canterbury came to be organized as cathedral monasteries.[2] It was the Norman Conquest, however, that marked the beginning of

---

[1] The Augustinian canons followed a rule similar to that of Benedict but somewhat looser, for (according to an early English customary) Augustine "had no wish to confine his disciples within an iron fence beyond what they could bear, but, by the help of a less severe rule, to induce them to enter the harbor of salvation as lovers of spiritual beauty." They were freer than the Benedictines to undertake parochial work and live outside the cloister. See J. W. Clark, *The Observances in Use at the Augustinian Priory of S. Giles and S. Andrew at Barnwell, Cambridgeshire* (Cambridge: Macmillan and Bowes, 1897), p. 35.

[2] The classic study of English monasticism is Dom David Knowles, *The Monastic Order in England* (Cambridge: Cambridge University Press, 1940), continued in idem, *The Religious Orders in England*, 3 vols. (Cambridge: Cambridge University Press, 1948, 1955, 1959). A useful brief summary of monastic history can be found in David Knowles and R. Neville Hadcock, *Medieval Religious Houses: England and Wales* (London: Longmans, Green, 1953), pp. 1–55.

a new epoch in English monastic history. The monastic cathedrals at Rochester, Durham, Norwich, and Bath were founded between 1080 and 1100, with Coventry following in 1102 and Carlisle in 1133. These establishments were to remain essentially unchanged until the time of the Reformation. Attempts were made to convert several more secular cathedrals, including Lincoln, to monastic houses, but these were unsuccessful. It is interesting to note that monastic cathedrals were a uniquely English phenomenon; secular organization prevailed elsewhere. The only other examples appear to have been Monreale in Sicily, where the abbey was made a bishop's see in 1176, perhaps with the English precedent in mind, and Downpatrick in Ireland, which was colonized by monks from Chester in 1188.[3]

In organization, the monastic cathedrals were quite different from their secular counterparts. For one thing, they housed much larger numbers of people. Seventy was often regarded as the ideal number of monks for a large Benedictine house, and the greater cathedral priories often approximated that size. Like other Benedictine houses they seem to have reached their peak shortly before the disaster of the Black Death in the fourteenth century but to have recovered substantially by 1485 or 1500.[4]

The monastic population of Durham is unusually well documented and has been studied with unusual care by Alan Piper. His statistics, unfortunately not published, suggest that the number of monks varied between eighty and a hundred during the years between 1274 and 1348. There were fifty-two deaths from the plague in 1349, leaving only thirty-nine monks in 1350, but the population soon returned to about seventy and remained there until 1539.[5]

It is difficult to collect comparable figures for the other cathedral monasteries; records are usually incomplete, and what survives has generally not been analyzed. One can set out some figures for the early sixteenth century, but many of them represent the situation just before the Dissolution in 1539, when trouble clearly lurked around the corner and monastic populations declined rapidly. The numbers

---

[3] Kathleen Edwards, *The English Secular Cathedrals in the Middle Ages* (Manchester: Manchester University Press, 1949), p. 10 n. 3.

[4] See figures gathered by Hadcock in Knowles and Hadcock, *Religious Houses*, p. 359.

[5] The average for the entire period 1274–1539 is 79. I am grateful to Mr. Piper for permission to quote from his work.

TABLE 2.1
Monks in Cathedral Priories

Cathedral and date	Number	Cathedral and date	Number
Canterbury		Norwich	
1534	70	1533	39
1537	58	1538	18
Durham		Bath	
1530	76	1525	22
1539	70	Coventry	
Winchester		1539	13
1501	40	Rochester	
1540	45	1534	20
Worcester		Carlisle	
1534	41	1540	27
Ely			
1532	37		
1539	25		

in table 2.1 therefore often underestimate the normal size of these houses.[6]

Not all of the monks enumerated in this list actually lived in their mother house, for several of the priories had smaller communities or cells dependent on them. Durham led the way, with seven of these so-called handmaids as well as a college at Oxford. The largest and most flourishing of the Durham cells—Finchale—was only three miles north of Durham and had come, by this period, to be a place of rest and refreshment for monks from the cathedral. (The prior's manor of Bearpark—more correctly named Beaurepaire—was even closer to the city and served a similar function.) Jarrow, Monkwearmouth, Holy Island, and Farne were much smaller, and were evidently maintained primarily because of their historical associations with saints of earlier centuries; Farne sometimes housed a single hermit. In addition there was the priory of Lytham on the Lancashire coast and St. Leonard's, near Stamford in Lincolnshire. Durham College, Oxford, will be discussed later. Of the seventy monks regarded as the normal complement at Durham, forty generally resided in the cathedral priory itself

[6] Except in the case of Durham, these numbers are drawn from Knowles and Hadcock, *Religious Houses*, pp. 59–81, 132, and sources cited there. Figures for Durham include monks in dependent cells and at Oxford.

and thirty in the dependencies.[7] Norwich had five such dependencies, other houses smaller numbers, of which the most important was probably Dover priory, a daughter of Christ Church, Canterbury.[8] Secular cathedrals might control hospitals but otherwise had nothing comparable to these dependent houses.

Monastic cathedrals also differed from their secular counterparts so far as officials and finance were concerned. Monastic cathedrals had no deans, for the chief officer of the monastery ruled the cathedral as well. These houses were called priories, not abbeys. Normally, large monasteries were presided over by an abbot, but in the case of the cathedrals, the bishop theoretically filled the abbot's place. Since he was seldom a monk and never resident within the monastic community, the second officer—the prior—assumed the actual rule of the house.

The priors of the great cathedral monasteries were rich, prominent men. For several centuries they had enjoyed their own separate establishments within the walls of the monastery: they had their own dining halls and kitchens, their own living quarters and servants. Generally they held country estates as well and might live there like country gentlemen. The duties of the prior were enormous: he was ultimately responsible for the buildings, the worship, and the finance of the cathedral, and for the education, discipline, and salvation of the monks under him. He was also drawn into local politics and national affairs, since he was accepted as the equal of the feudal lords of neighboring lands. The prior of Coventry even had the right of being summoned to the House of Lords in Parliament, a curious tradition since the heads of larger and richer cathedral monasteries did not enjoy that privilege.[9]

Large numbers of subordinate officers assisted the prior. There was always a subprior, who could perform the prior's duties when he was absent. Large houses like Durham had a third prior, who assumed responsibility when both of his superiors were away, while Canterbury and Winchester even had a fourth prior.[10]

[7] R. B. Dobson, *Durham Priory, 1400–1450* (Cambridge: Cambridge University Press, 1973), pp. 52–54, 299–316. An additional dependency—Coldingham—lay in Scotland, nine miles north of Berwick; after many difficulties associated with the Anglo-Scottish wars, it was abandoned in 1462.

[8] The Norwich dependencies are listed in Knowles and Hadcock, *Religious Houses*, p. 72.

[9] See Stanford E. Lehmberg, *The Reformation Parliament, 1529–1536* (Cambridge: Cambridge University Press, 1970), pp. 41n, 44.

[10] For descriptions of the duties of the various officers see R. B. Dobson, *Durham Priory*, pp. 66–67; R.A.L. Smith, *Canterbury Cathedral Priory* (Cambridge: Cambridge University

Officers with more specialized duties, placed in charge of specific aspects of monastic life, were called obedientiaries. Simply noting their titles and functions gives one an idea of the complexity of monastic organization. The sacristan, or sacrist, had custody of all relics, ornaments, vestments, and service books; everything that bore on the order and decency of worship was entrusted to his care. The precentor was responsible for music, as in the secular cathedrals. An officer called the *circa* (or, in English, the "roundabout") patrolled the cathedral cloisters and precincts, admonishing gossiping loiterers or collecting vestments and books that had been left behind. The anniversarian was in charge of obits and annual commemorations of benefactors; he also had to provide wine, beer, or other rewards to those who took part in them. The clerk of the works (*custos operum*) was charged with maintenance and repair of the buildings.

The receiver, as his name implies, gathered in revenues from the monastic estates. The hordarian had charge of the "hoard" of food for the monastic kitchens, while the cellarer (one of the most important officers) actually supplied the monks with food and drink, sometimes assisted by a kitchener (*coquinarius*). The refectorarian, or refectorer, maintained the dining hall or refectory in decent order. Clothing, shoes, and bedding were provided for the monks by the chamberlain. An infirmarer, or infirmarian, ran the infirmary, where the sick could be nursed, the aged cared for as they awaited death, and the healthy permitted to enjoy special food and a respite from their normal duties as they underwent periodic bleedings. There might be a gardener, a fruiterer, a porter or doorkeeper, a garnerer (in charge of the granary for wheat), a bartoner (responsible for the priory's home farm), and a pittancer (to distribute small gifts and treats on feast days). The almoner, an important officer found everywhere, was generally charged with operating a school for poor boys as well as with the distribution of relief. Finally, the guest master, or hosteler, provided shelter and hospitality for travelers, for those who needed to transact business with the monastery, and for persons who came to attend special services—the consecration of a new bishop, for instance, or an occasional royal wedding or aristocratic funeral. Most of the obedientiaries had assistants, and several had clearly designated subordinates, like the subsacrist or the succentor.[11]

Press, 1943), pp. 37–49; G. W. Kitchin, ed., *Compotus Rolls of the Obedientiaries of St. Swithun's Priory, Winchester*, Hampshire Record Society, no. 7 (London, 1892), pp. 39–82.
[11] Information about obedientiaries is drawn from a variety of sources. There is an early sixteenth-century list of the duties and obligations of the obedientiaries of Worces-

In all, as many as twenty-five men might hold office as obedientiar-ies.[12] The more important ones came to have separate establishments, like the prior's but less elaborate. At Canterbury we know that the subprior, the sacrist, the cellarer, the infirmarian, and the almoner all had private households by the end of the fourteenth century, with servants, cooks, and chaplains. Their responsibilities no doubt required that they be free to transact business and to deal with members of the outside world in ways that were forbidden to ordinary cloistered monks, but some loss in spirituality must have gone along with absence from the full round of choir services, and some loss of community inevitably followed departure from the dormitory and refectory.

Numerous lay persons, too, lived within the monastic cathedral precincts. It has been estimated that there were twice as many servants as monks at Canterbury.[13] There were boys, educated in the monastic schools that will be considered shortly. There were also the so-called corrodians, generally older men who were maintained for life upon nomination by the king, the prior, or occasionally the pope. R.A.L. Smith has likened them to retired civil servants and suggested that their "stories of court life, of adventure, and of intrigue, would certainly come as a welcome relief" from the monotony of the monastic routine.[14]

THE more important obedientiaries received income directly from manors and other properties and kept their own accounts, usually in the form of rolls. Large numbers of these obedientiary rolls survive at Canterbury, Durham, Norwich, Winchester, and Worcester. Some have been studied, and a few of the Winchester rolls have been published, but these are mainly from the fourteenth and fifteenth centuries.[15] Apart from a set of accounts for 1521–1522 at Worcester, published in 1907, the records of the early Tudor period await systematic examination.[16]

Worcester Cathedral Library holds an unusually full and accessible

---

ter in the Registers of the Prior and Convent, vol. 6, pt. 2, fol. 32, Worcester Cathedral Library.

[12] Carlisle, like the Benedictine houses, had obedientiaries; if its organization was comparable to that of the Augustinian house at Barnwell, near Cambridge, there were seventeen of them (Clark, *Augustinian Priory*, p. xxxiii).

[13] R.A.L. Smith, *Canterbury*, p. 50.

[14] Ibid., p. 52.

[15] See sources cited in n. 10 above.

[16] J. M. Wilson, ed., *Accounts of the Priory of Worcester for the Year 13–14 Henry VIII*, Worcestershire Historical Society, no. 24 (Worcester, 1907).

TABLE 2.2
Worcester Obedientiary Rolls

Officer	Date	Receipts	Disbursements
Cellarer	1503	£374 4s. 2d.	£466 8s. 5d.
Kitchener	1503	169 17s. 1d.	175 0s. 3d.
Sacrist	1508	153 18s. 9d.	155 18s. 0d.
Almoner	1505	83 14s. 9d.	71 19s. 9d.
Chamberlain	1502	66 19s. 2d.	73 7s. 0d.
Pittancer	1502	48 5s. 7d.	48 5s. 1d.
Keeper of the Lady Chapel	1504	26 0s. 2d.	25 19s. 7d.
Precentor	1502	10 7s. 8d.	10 15s. 8d.
Hosteler	1504	4 10s. 0d.	4 7s. 1d.
Refectorer	1502	3 2s. 6d.	3 3s. 0d.

collection of obedientiaries' accounts. A sample of them for the beginning of the sixteenth century reveals the figures in table 2.2.[17]

Specific items listed among the disbursements deserve brief mention. The cellarer's overdraft included more than £150 of debts run up by Prior More, about whose sumptuous life more will be said in a moment; this indebtedness had, however, been reduced by £300 from the previous year's figure of £450. The kitchener's expenses are broken down week by week, each week identified by the beginning of the appropriate Latin Collect (e.g., "Inclina," "In voluntate," "Gaudete," "Puer natus"); the usual figure of 40s. or 50s. rose to 68s. during the Christmas festivities. The sacrist made payments to singers and bell ringers for celebrating holy days, and he paid for the chalice and censer bought by Prior More in London. The chamberlain gave a shilling to thirty-eight monks, and larger sums to the prior and subprior, for the singing of the antiphon "O Emmanuel"—the practice of requiring obedientiaries to reward their colleagues on special occasions, when monastic ceremonial demanded that the officer sing a set, suitable prayer, was common to many of the monasteries.[18]

Several obedientiaries contributed to the maintenance of a young monk of Worcester as a scholar at Oxford: the cellarer paid £6 for

[17] Monastic records, c.48–49, c.102–106, c.161–168, c.209–212, c.238–240, c.287–291, c.344–350, c.387–394, c.423–424, c.426–430, Worcester Cathedral Library. Fractions of a penny have been disregarded in all of the following tables.
[18] See Kitchin, *Compotus Rolls*, pp. 61–62.

bread and ale, the chamberer 30s. for commons, the kitchener 30s. for meat, and other officers smaller sums totaling £3. 2s. 9d. The hosteler was charged with special payments whenever monks were ordained to the priesthood and celebrated their first mass. No sixteenth-century accounts survive for the infirmarian or for the *tumbarius* (keeper of the shrines and tombs), but the Worcester archives do contain rolls maintained by the subcellarer, recording receipts of grain rather than money, and by the sheep reeve (*magister bercarius*), a lay employee who was overshepherd of all monastic flocks.

If one adds the figures given by these obedientiaries' rolls, it becomes evident that something approaching £1,000 passed through the hands of the monastic officers each year. One must be careful about such calculations, however, for some entries represent transfers from one obedientiary to another rather than new income. A further complication is introduced by the fact that some foodstuffs were received in kind, not in cash. But the most important deficiency in these documents stems from the fact that they do not record the income of the prior, who was the direct beneficiary of revenues from a considerable number of manors.

Since the prior was not himself an obedientiary, he was not bound to account before his monks, and often less is known about his financial dealings than about those of the religious house itself. Once again we are especially fortunate to have unusual materials at Worcester, for the great William More, prior from 1518 until 1536, ordered the compilation of master accounts recording his own dealings alongside those of his subordinates. The roll for 1532 is summarized in table 2.3.[19] These records, more complete than the separate rolls cited earlier, show that the Worcester cathedral priory had annual resources exceeding £1,260.

The *Valor Ecclesiasticus* contains figures for the monastic cathedrals that agree with these very closely (see table 2.4). They emphasize the great wealth of Canterbury and the relative poverty of such smaller houses as Coventry, Rochester, and Carlisle.[20]

Even the richer houses experienced financial difficulties in the later Middle Ages. The thirteenth century had seen monastic incomes

[19] Monastic records, c.414c, Worcester Cathedral Library.

[20] *Valor Ecclesiasticus*, 6 vols. (London: Record Commission, 1810–1834). The entry for Winchester (2: 2–3) is especially interesting because it sets out the revenue of the prior and the individual obedientiaries separately. The prior is credited with revenues in excess of £1,000, but this evidently includes funds that supported the cellarer as well as the prior's own establishment. As in Chapter 1, the numbers given represent net income. In the case of monasteries with daughter houses, the figure includes the revenues of the cells; the income of the Durham cathedral itself, for instance, was £1,366 10s. 9d.

TABLE 2.3
Worcester Accounts, 1532

Officer	Receipts	Disbursements
Prior	£254 15s. 1d.	£278 15s. 2d.
Pittancer	58 6s. 7d.	56 10s. 8d.
Kitchener	163 4s. 6d.	198 8s. 11d.
Cellarer	515 16s. 3d.	514 7s. 9d.
Almoner	92 3s. 1d.	93 4s. 5d.
Chamberlain	80 0s. 6d.	74 7s. 4d.
Master of the Chapel	31 6s. 9d.	29 18s. 3d.
Precentor	10 10s. 6d.	11 13s. 7d.
Tombkeeper	15 2s. 3d.	14 0s. 0d.
Hosteler	7 14s. 4d.	6 16s. 9d.
Master of the common table	21 18s. 2d.	26 11s. 2d.
Refectorer	2 16s. 6d.	2 16s. 11d.
Infirmarer	13 13s. 0d.	14 16s. 4d.

TABLE 2.4
Revenues of the Monastic Cathedrals

Canterbury	£2,449 8s. 6d.
Durham	1,575 12s. 10d.
Winchester	1,507 17s. 2d.
Worcester	1,299 12s. 9d.
Ely	1,084 6s. 9d.
Norwich	874 14s. 7d.
Bath	617 2s. 3d.
Coventry	538 4s. 0d.
Rochester	486 11s. 5d.
Carlisle	418 3s. 5d.

reach their highest point, with sheep very profitable and a system of what has been called high farming under which large acreages of pasture were run directly by monks, as part of the demesne, rather than leased out to laymen. This system decayed in the fourteenth century, especially after the Black Death. We know that Canterbury was frequently in debt, and that Durham never again enjoyed an income approaching the £4,500 it had collected in 1308.[21] But the financial situation at Durham appears to have been improving in the priory's last years, partly as a result of exploitation of salt pans.[22] Canterbury, too, seems to have enjoyed a season of calm before the storm of the Reformation.

A VIVID picture of the life of a prior, if not of an entire cathedral monastery, can be found in the journal maintained for William More of Worcester between 1518 and 1536.[23] This formed the basis of one of David Knowles' beautifully etched cameos, although it is clear that he did not really admire More: the prior possessed neither "holiness of life [nor] intellectual or practical ability," and "his inclusion in a gallery of portraits [was] due primarily to the aptness with which his career at all points illustrates the trend of the age."[24]

More, or Peers as he was originally named, was probably born in the hamlet called le More near Tenbury in Worcestershire. His parents, for whom he provided gifts and care after his advancement, were of middling social status. William took vows at sixteen, served as kitchener while still a young man, was named subprior in the opening years of the sixteenth century, and survived to see his whole way of life threatened by the impending Reformation. The income from fifteen manors, (one-quarter of the revenue of the entire priory) was assigned to Prior More, who lived most of the year as a country gentleman on his estates at Battenhall, Crowle, and Grimley, all within a five-mile ride of the cathedral. More did come to Worcester for the great liturgical festivals of Christmas, Easter, and Whitsunday, and he usually spent about a month each year in London, mending political fences and purchasing luxury items not available in the provinces.

His journal describes some of these in tantalizing detail. More patronized the finest craftsmen in the country, including the vestment maker William Dysse and the goldsmith John Cranks. The latter made him not only a great chalice "selver & gylt with many stones in ye futt" and a crosier or "croystaff" but also a lavish miter embellished with

[21] R.A.L. Smith, *Canterbury*, pp. 190–205; Lionel Butler and Chris Given-Wilson, *Medieval Monasteries of Great Britain* (London: Michael Joseph, 1979), pp. 90–93.

[22] Information kindly communicated by Alan Piper.

[23] MS. A.11, Worcester Cathedral Library, edited by Ethel S. Fegan as the *Journal of Prior William More* (Worcester: Worcestershire Historical Society, 1914). This is the only such journal to survive from this period.

[24] Knowles, *Religious Orders*, 3: 108–126.

embroidery, pearls, and dozens of jewels, costing in all nearly £50.[25] Dysse was responsible for "a sewte of vestaments of clothe of Golde" purchased in 1521 for £90; this included two copes, a chasuble, two tunicles, albs, stoles, and maniples.[26] He probably provided the cope of blue velvet with ostrich feathers mentioned in an inventory of More's household stuff as well.[27]

Other disbursements recorded in Prior More's journal are equally fascinating. The young Princess Mary Tudor visited him at Worcester and at his manor of Battenhall for long periods in 1525 and 1526, possibly attracted to the cathedral because her uncle, Prince Arthur, was entombed there in an elaborate chantry chapel decorated with the armorial symbols of Catherine of Aragon as well as those of the Tudors; she gave More a half-noble in gold (3s. 4d.) for singing mass at the high altar, and he gave her servants £7 13s. 4d. when they departed.[28] Singers, jugglers, tumblers, players, and Wolsey's minstrels were also rewarded, as was the messenger who brought news of Anne Boleyn's coronation in 1533. The bailiffs and citizens of Worcester were treated to wine after evensong on Christmas Day, 1524; on New Year's Day, 1525, More received gifts himself, including a peacock from the almoner. When a monk was granted his divinity degree at Oxford, he was sent a present of 40s., and later £4 was paid for his expenses in London, while another monk, William Wolverley, was given 3s. 4d. for "pricking" (writing out: presumably composing) an Exultavit in five parts.

More also spent considerable sums on books, generally acquired during his visits to London. In his earlier years these were mainly the works of the church fathers (Jerome, Gregory, and Ambrose) or literary and historical writers (Bede, Cyprian, Seneca, and Philo). In 1527 More bought Henry VIII's defense of the seven sacraments, *Assertio septem sacramentorum*, published in 1521.[29] Once the Reformation Parliament began its sessions, More invested in several volumes of statutes and records of General Councils. He also bought a "pointed" mass book (a missal with chant settings), and he paid a maker of illuminated manuscripts, one Arthur of Evesham, for "lymyng and florusshyng of grete letters in my grayle," another service manual. At least thirty printed volumes were acquired by More, probably in-

[25] Fegan, *Journal of Prior More*, pp. 163–164.
[26] Ibid., p. 137. Descriptions of these traditional vestments can be found in Christa C. Mayer-Thurman, *Raiment for the Lord's Service* (Chicago: Art Institute of Chicago, 1975), pp. 25–41.
[27] ADD. MS. 145, p. 67, Worcester Cathedral Library (a transcription of MS. A.12).
[28] Fegan, *Journal of Prior More*, pp. 37, 224.
[29] Ibid., p. 240.

tended less for his own use than for the cathedral library, which was already rich in manuscripts.

The final assessment by Knowles is apt. More's life, he wrote, "though it may have had little of the monastic in it, was morally blameless. His expenses, if occasionally large, . . . were not ruinous or prodigal." He was a good administrator, "open-handed but alert. In all respects, he was a child of his age. . . . He followed, in fact, both for good and for evil, the way of the world."[30]

CATHEDRALS that were organized as Benedictine monasteries maintained the full round of monastic offices that had been sung in houses of the Black Monks since the time of Lanfranc. In organization these differed little from the services celebrated in the secular cathedrals: the mass and the eight daily offices. Monastic cathedrals generally had three great masses each day: the morning mass, the chapter mass, and the mass honoring the Blessed Virgin Mary, sung in the Lady Chapel with more elaborate polyphonic music than was thought appropriate for other monastic services.[31] Services sung by the Augustinian canons at Carlisle were similar. Chantry masses and obits were celebrated as well.

Shrines and services held at their altars were even more important in the monastic cathedrals than in their secular counterparts. In part this is true simply because the greatest shrines, especially those at Canterbury and Durham, happened to be in cathedral priories. It is probable, too, that the larger population of monks made services at monastic shrines more impressive than those celebrated by smaller numbers of canons in secular cathedrals. The best description of a monastic shrine comes from the so-called *Rites of Durham*.[32] This volume was not written until 1593, but its author was obviously present at the cathedral in the 1530s, perhaps attending a monastic school if not himself a monk, and his picture may be trusted as one drawn by an original observer. His tone makes it clear that he loved the beauty of Durham's

[30] Knowles, *Religious Orders*, 3: 126.

[31] The hours and arrangement of these services varied from summer to winter; see the table in Frederick Bussby, *Winchester Cathedral, 1079–1979* (Southampton: Paul Cave, 1979), pp. 64–65.

[32] *A Description or Breife Declaration of all the Ancient Monuments, Rites, and Customes belonginge or beinge within the Monastical Church of Durham before the Suppression*, ed. James Raine, Surtees Society, no. 15 (Durham, 1842), reprinted with additional editorial material by J. T. Fowler, Surtees Society, no. 107 (Durham, 1903).

ancient shrines and ceremonies and that he deplored the reforms and spoliation of later years.

Some of the most moving services at Durham took place at the shrine of St. Cuthbert, erected between the choir and the Chapel of the Nine Altars. The author of the *Rites* describes this in some detail.

His sacred shrine was exalted with most curious workmanshipp of fine and costly green marble all limned and guilted with gold hauinge foure seates or places conuenient under the shrine for the pilgrims or lame men sittinge on theire knees to leane and rest on, in time of theire deuout offeringes and feruent prayers to God and holy St. Cuthbert, for his miraculous reliefe and succor which beinge neuer wantinge made the shrine to bee so richly inuested, that it was estimated to bee one of the most sumptuous monuments in all England, so great were the offerings and Jewells that were bestowed upon it, and no lesse the miracles that were done by it, euen in theise latter dayes.

In the time of diuine seruice they were accustomed to drawe upp the couer of St. Cuthbert's shrine beinge of Wainescott wherevnto was fastned vnto every corner of the said Cover to a loope of Iron a stronge Cord which Cord was all fest [fastened] together over the Midst over the Cover. And a strong rope was fest vnto the loopes of bindinge of the said Cordes which runn upp and downe in a pully under the Vault which was aboue over St. Cuthbert's feretorie [tomb] for the drawinge upp of the Cover of the said shrine, and the said rope was fastned to a loope of Iron in the North piller of the ferretory: haueing six silver bells fastned to the said rope, soe as when the cover of the same was drawinge upp the belles did make such a good sound that itt did stirr all the peoples harts that was within the Church to repaire unto itt and to make ther praiers to God and holy St. Cuthbert, and that the behoulders might see the glorious ornaments therof.[33]

Pilgrims visiting St. Cuthbert's shrine, or those merely traveling in the north, could be accommodated in the guest hall, "a famouse house of hospitallitie" where no one was turned away. Its entertainment was "not . . . inferior to any place in Ingland, both for the goodness of ther

[33] *Rites*, 1903 ed., pp. 3–5. The last miracle to occur at St. Cuthbert's shrine is said to have taken place in 1502; St. Cuthbert's banner, incorporating a relic of the saint, was supposed to have been responsible for English victories over the Scots, including that at Neville's Cross in 1346, and was carried by the rebels in the Pilgrimage of Grace. See Mervyn James, *Family, Lineage, and Civil Society: A Study of Society, Politics, and Mentality in the Durham Region, 1500–1640* (Oxford: Clarendon Press, 1974), p. 56.

diete, the sweete and daintie furneture of there Lodginges, and generally all thinges necessarie for traveillers."[34]

Beautiful as St. Cuthbert's shrine must have been, it was far less imposing than Thomas à Becket's tomb at Canterbury. Here a golden reliquary was concealed beneath a wooden cover, which was itself hidden under an elaborate canopy; as at Durham there were ropes and a pulley, so that the shrine could be uncovered once or twice a day for viewing by pilgrims. Henry VIII, Catherine of Aragon, and Charles V paid homage at the shrine during Charles' first visit to England in 1520.[35] The emperor's reaction is not recorded, but we do have the comments of the Venetian ambassador, who wrote the doge about 1500 that

> the magnificence of the tomb of St. Thomas the Martyr . . . surpasses all belief. This, notwithstanding its great size, is entirely covered over with plates of pure gold, but the gold is scarcely visible from the variety of precious stones with which it is studded, such as sapphires, diamonds, rubies, balas-rubies, and emeralds, and on every side that the eye turns, something more beautiful than the other appears. And these beauties of nature are enhanced by human skill, for the gold is carved and engraved in beautiful designs, both large and small, and agates, jaspers and carnelians set in relievo, some of the cameos being of such size that I do not dare to mention it, but everything is left far behind by a ruby, not larger than a man's thumbnail, which is set to the right of the altar. The church is rather dark, and particularly so where the shrine is placed, and the weather was cloudy, yet I saw that ruby as if I had it in my hand. They say that it was a gift of the King of France.[36]

Indeed another account relates that the ruby had miraculously leaped from Louis XII's finger to its place on the shrine.

An equally famous visitor was Erasmus, who came with his friend John Colet to view the relics at Canterbury in 1513. The episode is described in one of his most famous colloquies, "A Pilgrimage for Religion's Sake." "The church sacred to St. Thomas rises to the sky so majestically that it inspires devotion even in those who see it from

---

[34] *Rites*, 1903 ed., pp. 89–90, 8, 12–13, 43–44, 89–90; 1842 ed., p. 14.

[35] The duke of Buckingham and the French ambassador attended services in the cathedral with other members of the official entourage; see Barbara J. Harris, *Edward Stafford, Third Duke of Buckingham, 1478–1521* (Stanford: Stanford University Press, 1986), p. 169.

[36] Quoted in Francis Woodman, *The Architectural History of Canterbury Cathedral* (London: Routledge and Kegan Paul, 1981), pp. 221–22.

afar," he wrote. Once inside, and no doubt armed with appropriate introductions, the two scholars were shown the site of the martyrdom, with its Altar of the Sword's Point,[37] and then the crypt, where Becket's skull was exhibited, together with "the hair shirt, the girdle, and the drawers, by means of which the Archbishop subdued the flesh; the very sight of them striking us with horror." On the north side of the choir they saw a multitude of "choice treasures: . . . skulls, jaws, teeth, hands, fingers, entire arms." Midas and Croesus were mere beggars compared to this cathedral, with its gold and silver ornaments for the altars. "Ye Gods! What a show was there of silken vestments, what a power of golden candlesticks. I saw there the pastoral staff of St. Thomas."

Still more magnificent was the shrine itself, where the saint's body was said to lie. Once the wooden cover was drawn up, "treasures beyond all calculations [were] displayed. The most worthless thing there was gold, every part glowed, sparkled and flashed with rare and large gems, some of which were bigger than a goose egg." Erasmus and Colet knelt in devotion, along with the monks standing by, but the Dutch humanist's comments make it apparent that he had doubts about the value of relics and pilgrimages, and reservations about the wealth displayed at Canterbury. "I never saw any place more overloaded with treasures," he concluded.[38]

Other cathedrals had their own shrines, not of course so famous as that which drew pilgrims to Canterbury, but regional sites of veneration, prayer, and oblation. St. Swithun's shrine at Winchester, St. Wulfstan's at Worcester, and St. Etheldreda's at Ely were perhaps the best known. Henry VIII and Charles V visited Swithun's shrine during the emperor's second trip to England, in 1522.[39] There was also the peculiar case of St. William, a baker from Perth, said to be so pious that he attended mass daily and so charitable that he gave every tenth loaf to the poor. He resolved to visit the Holy Land and set out in 1201, accompanied by a young companion whom he had adopted as a foundling. After spending the night at the priory of Rochester, William was found dead by the roadside, presumably murdered by his foster son. His body was brought back to the cathedral for burial, miracles began to occur at his tomb, and soon the poor priory had its own martyr's shrine and offerings to swell its coffers.[40] The gifts of pious

[37] Destroyed under Henry VIII, this was reconstructed in the 1980s.
[38] *The Colloquies of Erasmus*, trans. Craig R. Thompson (Chicago: University of Chicago Press, 1965), pp. 285–312.
[39] Butler and Given-Wilson, *Medieval Monasteries*, p. 391.
[40] Anneliese Arnold, *St. William of Perth and Rochester* (a pamphlet published by Roch-

pilgrims seem to have reached their peak in the fourteenth century—Canterbury took in more than £800 in 1350, and as much as £644 in 1420. But this was exceptional—1420 was a year of jubilee attended with a general pardon. In 1455 offerings amounted to only £25, and in 1532 to a mere £13.[41] Inadequate evidence suggests that belief in miracles had declined by the early Tudor period, although pilgrimages to some shrines remained popular. Those who still made trips to see cathedral treasures may have resembled modern tourists more than medieval suppliants.

BUILDING activities continued at the monastic cathedrals during the earlier decades of the Tudor period; surviving work, often of great beauty, can be seen at Winchester, Ely, Norwich, Rochester, Durham, and Bath.[42] The finest achievements, however, are at Canterbury, where the central tower and gate to the precincts date from the years immediately preceding the Reformation.

The tower acquired its traditional name, "Bell Harry," when that bell was hung in 1498. Earlier it had been called the Angel Steeple. After a hiatus in construction no doubt caused by the Wars of the Roses, Prior William Sellyng and Archbishop John Morton initiated the campaign to complete the Perpendicular tower. It is a glorious piece of work; as Canterbury's architectural historian has written, "its success is two-fold. It forms an almost perfect grouping with the short nave and west towers, while at the same time its mass is sufficient to balance the disordered sprawl of the choir."[43] It has been called the noblest tower in Christendom (see fig. 12).[44]

Two building account rolls—one from autumn, 1492, and the other from Easter, 1494, to Michaelmas, 1497—provide details of the construction. More than £350 was expended during the second of these

---

ester Cathedral), based on the Nova Legenda printed in 1516. The money received at St. William's shrine was used to rebuild the choir of the Norman church in the Early English style.

[41] Woodman, *Architectural History*, p. 221. For additional information about the decline in income of shrines, see Ronald C. Finucane, *Miracles and Pilgrims* (London: J. M. Dent, 1977), p. 193. Finucane makes the very interesting point that devotion to Mary and to Christ himself grew during the later Middle Ages as belief in the curative efficacy of traditional saints' shrines declined (pp. 195–197), but the sites of the newer veneration, like Walsingham and Hailes, were not cathedrals.

[42] The enormous quantity of church building in the fifteenth and early sixteenth centuries has been pointed out by J. J. Scarisbrick, *The Reformation and the English People* (Oxford: Blackwell, 1984), pp. 12–15.

[43] Woodman, *Architectural History*, p. 199.

[44] Ibid.

12. Crossing Tower ("Bell Harry"), Canterbury Cathedral.

periods, most of it a gift from Morton, whose rebus and cardinal's hat are carved all the way up the exterior turrets. The last phase of the work, including the supremely lovely fan vault that crowns the interior of the tower, was supervised by John Wastell, the greatest early Tudor architect, who was soon to design the vaults of King's College Chapel in Cambridge.[45]

When Cardinal Morton died in 1501 he left 1,000 marks for further building at the cathedral. Some of his legacy was spent on Christ Church Gate, which—much restored—still guards the entrance to the cathedral precincts from the streets of Canterbury (fig. 13). Full of coats of arms carried by angels and Tudor armorial symbols surmounted by crowns, it was constructed between 1504 and 1521. A bequest from Prior Goldstone, who died in 1517, was applied to the work, which was overseen by his successor, Thomas Goldwell, the last prior before the Dissolution. The gate is of special interest architecturally because it combines classical motifs and antique capitals with Perpendicular Gothic tracery and battlements. Since these features are also characteristic of King's College Chapel, one might have thought that Wastell's hand lay behind them. But Francis Woodman sees here a different style, and thinks that the gate may have become a royal project for which Henry VII provided his own master mason, Robert Vertue.[46]

One would have thought that the works at several other cathedrals were enough to prove the vitality of these houses in the early Tudor era, were they not overshadowed by the building at Canterbury. At Durham the highest stage of the crossing tower was added about 1490 by a master mason named John Bell. It may, as Pevsner commented, add a decisive accent in a place where the original builder (the Norman bishop William of St. Carileph) would not have wanted it, but it adds a great deal to the visual impact made by the cathedral as seen from afar (see fig. 14).[47] Norwich also boasts a tower, or rather a spire, raised by Bishop James Goldwell in the very last years of the fifteenth century (fig. 15); 351 feet in height, it is the second highest spire in England, and in the flat countryside of East Anglia, it can be seen for miles around.[48]

Remodeling of the east end, which changed the appearance of Win-

[45] Ibid., pp. 199–211.

[46] Ibid., pp. 211–217.

[47] Nikolaus Pevsner, *The Buildings of England: County Durham* (Harmondsworth: Penguin Books, 1953), p. 83.

[48] Butler and Given-Wilson, *Medieval Monasteries*, p. 312. The fine lierne vaults in the chancel and transepts at Norwich were also erected in the early Tudor period.

13. Christ Church Gate, Canterbury. This photograph is
of interest because it was taken before the
restoration of the 1930s.

chester from Norman to Perpendicular Gothic, was completed after
1485, and the great stone screen behind the high altar, originally filled
with dozens of statues, was erected by the rich and powerful Bishop
Fox between 1500 and 1528.[49] Ely has the chantry chapels of Bishop
Alcock (d. 1500) and Bishop West (d. 1533). The Alcock Chapel (fig.
16) is all Late Gothic, "with canopy piled on canopy and pinnacle upon
pinnacle, accomplished by almost breathtaking feats of undercutting"
of the local hard chalk stone, but the vaulted ceiling of Bishop West's

[49] Ibid., p. 395.

14. General view of Durham Cathedral, showing the crossing tower.
The cloister and monastic buildings can be seen to the south of the nave.
The cathedral's dramatic site, surrounded on three sides by the river Wear
and adjacent to the castle, is evident in this aerial photograph.

15. General view of Norwich Cathedral, showing the crossing tower
and early Tudor spire.

chantry (fig. 17), like the gate at Canterbury, combines Gothic features
with details borrowed from the Italian Renaissance.[50] At Rochester a
new Lady Chapel was completed in 1492. A large rectangular space
with tall Perpendicular windows, it was inserted at the angle of the
nave and north transept, an unusual location probably chosen to avoid
disturbing the east end. A fan vault was intended but never actually
built.[51]

[50] Donald Purcell, *The Building of Ely Cathedral*, pamphlet (Ely: Dean and Chapter of
Ely Cathedral, 1973), pp. 14–15.
[51] W. H. St. John Hope, *The Architectural History of the Cathedral Church and Monastery of
St. Andrew at Rochester* (London: Mitchell and Hughes, 1900), p. 87.

16. Bishop Alcock's Chapel, Ely Cathedral, showing canopies.

Bath Abbey, the only cathedral building to be undertaken from the ground up while the Tudors ruled England, was begun in 1499, after Bishop King, Henry VII's secretary, had a dream in which he saw angels ascending and descending a ladder from heaven. The bishop thought that he had heard a voice saying, with delightful ambiguity, "Let a King restore the church," and he was able to call in Henry VII's chief masons, the brothers Robert and William Vertue. The Norman church was torn down and its Perpendicular successor begun (see fig. 18), but the abbey remained incomplete at the time of the Dissolution, and its fan vaults were not erected until the seventeenth century—

17. Bishop West's Chapel, Ely Cathedral, vaulted ceiling.

indeed the nave vault was not finished until the 1800s.[52] Glazing, statuary, and other adornments are also found as part of the early Tudor architectural heritage in the monastic cathedrals.

ALL the monastic cathedrals maintained schools. These were of three sorts. Internal schools for young monks must have existed since the

[52] Nikolaus Pevsner, *The Buildings of England: North Somerset and Bristol* (Harmondsworth: Penguin Books, 1958), pp. 100–101.

18. General view of Bath Abbey, from the east.

beginning of the houses; by the period under discussion these had become grammar schools, which could fit the brightest young men for study at the universities and their less academically inclined brethren for service within the monastery. Almonry schools had been founded, many in the early fourteenth century, to provide an elementary education for younger boys, generally orphans or other poor children who were entrusted to the care of the monks. Almonry boys were expected to assist the monks at their private masses, much like the secondaries or poor clerks who served the chantry priests in the secular cathedrals. Their presence was so essential that it was occasionally necessary to reduce the number of private masses for want of boys to serve. As Knowles suggests, many of the almonry boys must have gone on to become monks themselves, although records do not survive to demonstrate that this was the case.[53]

The third type of school, the song school, was for choristers and

53 Knowles, *Religious Orders*, 3: 294–297.

paralleled the choristers' houses in the secular cathedrals. No doubt these boys were taught some Latin—one hopes that they understood the meaning of the liturgical texts they had to sing!—but their training was chiefly musical, and it must have been quite advanced, since the elaborate polyphonic masses of the late fifteenth century, such as those by Robert Fayrfax and John Taverner, are demanding works. We know that the master of the song school at Durham was required to teach the boys "pleynsange, priknot, faburden, dischaunte et countre." Here six children were instructed in a building adjacent to the Chapel of the Nine Altars, "fynely bourded within" for warmth; they had their meals with the children of the almonry school, while their master dined in the prior's hall.[54] Eight boys are recorded at Winchester in 1482, taught music by one Edward Pyngbrygge and his assistant, Thomas Goodman.[55] It is said that these choristers, together with boys from Hyde Abbey, presented a religious drama called "Christ's Descent into Hell" for the entertainment of Henry VII when he visited Winchester for Prince Arthur's baptism in 1486.[56] Other cathedrals had comparable establishments.

Not all young monks, of course, aspired to the priesthood, and not all priests could boast a university education. But the monastic cathedrals did send significant numbers of students to Oxford and Cambridge during the later Middle Ages. We read of monks from Durham and Worcester at Oxford as early as 1290 and of three men from Canterbury studying there in 1331. For a time these students were attached to what came to be called Gloucester College, which accepted young men from all of the Benedictine houses. In 1363, however, Canterbury College, Oxford, was founded, with a warden and fellows who were monks of Christ Church, Canterbury, and varying numbers of "sojourners," including some secular persons as well as monks. Several of the monastic cathedrals sent scholars to Canterbury College, with stipends from the monastery and with the expectation that these more highly educated monks would return to provide intellectual and administrative leadership within their communities.[57] At the time of

[54] *Rites,* 1842 ed., p. 54; Knowles, *Religious Orders,* 2: 296n. In addition to the boys educated in these organized schools, there were occasionally young noblemen sent to be pages in the prior's house and to receive a sort of courtly training there; cf. Knowles, *Religious Orders,* 2: 297.

[55] *VCH, Hampshire,* 2: 259–260.

[56] John Crook, *A History of the Pilgrims' School and Earlier Winchester Choir Schools* (Chichester: Phillimore, 1981), p. 6.

[57] See W. A. Pantin, *Canterbury College, Oxford,* 3 vols. (Oxford: Clarendon Press for Oxford Historical Society, 1947), esp. 1: v–vii; *VCH, Kent,* 2: 118; Michael Craze, "Worcester Cathedral Monastic Life" (unpublished paper, Worcester Cathedral Library, 1985).

the Dissolution the site of Canterbury College was absorbed into Christ Church—an appropriate carrying over of the name of the priory—and the connection is still reflected in Canterbury Quad there.

The most important monastic establishment at Oxford, however, was Durham College. Originally small and loosely organized, this had been turned into a full-fledged college on the site still occupied by its successor, Trinity College, in 1381. In addition to a legacy from Bishop Hatfield, Durham College enjoyed the revenues from four churches and had, from the fifteenth century, a stable annual income of about £175. Its grounds were large, including a grove of three thousand trees, and its buildings included a chapel, residential quarters, and an exceptionally attractive library, furnished with a good collection of books. Most students read philosophy or theology, not canon law, and only a few, mainly those who remained at the College as fellows, proceeded to the doctorate. Piper's statistics show that, throughout the fifteenth century, there were usually about twenty monks of Durham who had experience at Oxford, out of a total population of about seventy. Fourteen members of the community in 1485 had attended the university; three held bachelors' degrees in theology, and one had received the doctorate. In the early sixteenth century these numbers rose: by 1520, twenty-four monks had been to Oxford, of whom four had been granted bachelors' degrees and four doctorates. Of the twenty-one former students at the time of the Dissolution in 1540, five held bachelors' degrees and five held doctorates.[58] It seems appropriate to stress the importance that the monks of Durham attached to university education in general and to the holding of a degree in particular; it was the graduates who were called to positions of leadership within the monastery, and they were also in demand at convocation and at Benedictine gatherings.[59] In all, as many as 350 monks and friars are known to have studied at Oxford between 1505 and 1538.[60]

The other priories seem to have been less committed to higher education than Durham and Canterbury were. Fewer students went to Cambridge than to Oxford, and there was no Cambridge college comparable to Durham or Canterbury. Ely, it is true, had established a hostel at Cambridge under the famous Prior Crauden (d. 1341). Originally located on the site of what is now Trinity Hall, it housed two

[58] Unpublished information kindly made available by Mr. Piper, Prior's Kitchen, Durham.

[59] On Durham College, see R. B. Dobson, *Durham Priory*, pp. 343–359.

[60] Research by A. G. Little, cited in *The English Reformation*, by A. G. Dickens (London: Batsford, 1964), p. 54.

students from Ely and possibly a few monks from other Benedictine houses. But the monastic cathedrals in eastern England, which would normally send young men to Cambridge rather than Oxford, seem in fact to have sent few monks anywhere. Norwich had at one time been distinguished for theological study, but this enthusiasm had vanished by 1492, when Bishop Goldwell complained that the cathedral had failed to support students at the university. He ordered that two were to go immediately—rather surprisingly, they were sent to Gloucester College, Oxford, rather than to Cambridge.[61] In 1538 there were two students at Cambridge, each receiving an allowance of 26s. 8d.[62]

The most learned monk of the early Tudor period was probably William Sellyng, prior of Christ Church, Canterbury, from 1472 until his death in 1494. Educated in the monastic school and at Canterbury College, Oxford, he studied also in Italy, receiving his doctorate from Bologna in 1466. He was one of the earliest Englishmen to teach Greek and to prepare translations from that language into Latin. Indeed, the school at Canterbury, according to a long and probably accurate tradition, was one of the first places where the Greek tongue was taught in England; Thomas Linacre was probably one of Sellyng's pupils there. While the interests of most monks remained medieval, Sellyng's outlook marks him as one of the earliest exponents of classical studies and shows that at least one of the monastic schools could adapt itself to the New Learning.[63]

The libraries of the cathedral priories generally surpassed those of the secular cathedrals. Because of the Dissolution, one might have supposed that fewer of the books from the monastic libraries would remain in place. In fact the reverse is true: the largest collection of medieval books and manuscripts to be found in any English cathedral is at Durham, where over three hundred medieval works survive. In addition, more than two hundred manuscripts and printed books from the monastic library at Durham have found their way into other collections; curiously enough, these appear to have been alienated in the seventeenth century rather than in the 1540s. It is interesting to note that many of the books at Durham were given by individual monks, generally at their death, rather than purchased for the library directly. We know of twenty-three monks who donated books during the years between 1485 and 1540; eight of these men left more than a

[61] Knowles, *Religious Orders*, 3: 73–74.

[62] Liber Miscellaneorum 2, DCN, R226A, accounts for 20 Hen. 8 (not paginated), Norfolk Record Office.

[63] See Roberto Weiss, *Humanism in England during the Fifteenth Century* (Oxford: Blackwell, 1957), pp. 153–159; Knowles, *Religious Orders*, 3: 87–90.

single volume. Most of the donors had studied at Oxford and probably acquired their books there.

The second largest holdings—more than two hundred fifty volumes—are to be found at Worcester. A few of these books are among those purchased by Prior More. Only twenty-one books from the library of Christ Church are still at Canterbury, but nearly three hundred more survive, scattered among thirty modern libraries. We know that the monastic library at Canterbury held nearly two thousand volumes, and that there were nearly three hundred more at Canterbury College; surviving catalogs and lists of books to be repaired enable us to know the titles of most of the volumes.[64] The other cathedral libraries were probably smaller, but they, too, must have held impressive collections of theological, literary, and historical manuscripts and early printed books. Because the survival of these works is so largely a matter of chance, it is hard to estimate the original size of the cathedral holdings.[65]

The existence of these libraries, which were rivaled only by the combined collections of the colleges at Oxford and Cambridge, points up the important role played by cathedrals as centers of learning. It may be true that the books were not actually used very much in the early Tudor period; library resources, like fields, sometimes lie fallow. Nevertheless they were there, and a handful of scholars able to interpret them was also present in the cathedrals. Especially in parts of England distant from London, Oxford, or Cambridge, the pre-Reformation cathedrals were significant centers of learning; as R. B. Dobson has suggested, we would be well advised to question the conventional view that the monks of Durham lived in an intellectual backwater.[66]

ANY judgment about the state of the monastic cathedrals and their contribution to English society in the half-century preceding the Dissolution must be subtly drawn; an unbiased observer will see varying shades of gray rather than pure black and white. It is easy enough to

[64] M. R. James, *The Ancient Libraries of Canterbury and Dover* (Cambridge: Cambridge University Press, 1903), pp. xliv–lvi, 7–172.

[65] Peterborough, not yet a cathedral, is said to have had a very large library with 1,700 books. See *Catalogi Veteres Librorum Ecclesiae Cathedralis Dunelm*, Surtees Society, no. 7 (Durham, 1838), p. xxxiii.

[66] On these libraries, see N. R. Ker, *Medieval Libraries of Great Britain*, 2d ed. (London: Royal Historical Society, 1964), pp. x–xv, 252–261, 317–320; R. B. Dobson, *Durham Priory*, pp. 360–386.

agree with the reformers that some of the old rites were superstitious, and many will share Erasmus's distaste for dubious relics and overrich shrines. We should be more skeptical of some harsh modern judgments, for instance that which characterizes Norwich cathedral as "a singularly useless institution . . . whose last years were notable mainly because of a long sustained strife between the monks and the townspeople."[67] Perhaps we should exercise caution, too, in accepting the view that contrasts the genuine spirituality of monks in the High Middle Ages with the worldliness of their early Tudor successors. The evidence for such inward matters is never adequate, and most of the historians of monasticism have themselves been medievalists, more likely to see good in their favorite centuries than in other periods. If we had fuller knowledge of the thirteenth century, we might well find as many examples of lukewarm belief and slipshod ceremony in it as in the early 1500s.

Whatever can be said against the rites and shrines of the monastic cathedrals in pre-Reformation England should be balanced by an acknowledgment that they brought warmth, color, and drama into the otherwise cold and drab lives of many people. Once again David Knowles' prose captures exactly the right tone. No matter how mediocre the spirituality of the monks at Durham, he wrote,

> the beauty of the setting remained, and the display on high days and holy seasons of the treasures of artists and craftsmen that the centuries had accumulated. The lights still "did burne continually both day and night" in the great cressets before the high altar, "in token that the house was always watchinge to God," and the sound of bells at midnight "in the lanthorne called the new worke," clear in the magical silence of midsummer or borne fitfully across the Wear in winter storms, gave assurance to the townspeople and the countryside "in the deep night that all was well."[68]

[67] *VCH, Norfolk*, 2: 326–327.
[68] Knowles, *Religious Orders*, 3: 136–137; the quotations are from *Rites*, 1903 ed., pp. 14, 22.

3

HENRY VIII: THE REFORMATION
BEGINS

THE earliest stages of the Reformation affected the cathedrals relatively little. Some of the clergy may have wished to read the writings
of Luther and Tyndale, which were denounced as heretical and prohibited in England as early as 1528.[1] A few may have been included
among the heretics, like those within the diocese of Lincoln ("no small
number," according to Henry VIII) whom Bishop Longland was ordered to suppress.[2] But the surviving records of the cathedrals themselves contain no trace of the coming religious upheaval.

Even the earlier sessions of the Reformation Parliament had little
direct impact. It is certainly true that cathedral canons were affected
by the limitation of pluralism and nonresidency demanded by Parliament in 1529. Like other clergy, they were charged in 1531 with violating the Statute of Praemunire, and they were forced to pay large
sums for their pardon. They were included in the Supplication against
the Ordinaries, which was discussed by Parliament and Convocation
in 1532, and they were affected by the Submission of the Clergy, in
which the whole English church lost its power of making canon law
without reference to the monarchy.[3] The long-range implications of
these acts were enormous, for through them the English clergy was
stripped of its ability to resist changes ordered by the king. At the
time, however, they were little felt and perhaps little understood.

As is well known, the issue that precipitated this crisis in relations
between Church and State was Henry VIII's wish to divorce his first
wife, Catherine of Aragon, motivated partly by his desire for a male
heir and partly by his love for Anne Boleyn. After six years of fruitless
negotiation with Pope Clement VII, Henry finally took affairs into his
own hands, allowing his chief advisor, Thomas Cromwell, to draft legislation that would not only permit the English church to grant the
divorce without reference to Rome but also totally extinguish papal
jurisdiction in England. The resulting Act in Restraint of Appeals,

[1] See the documents printed in David Wilkins, *Concilia Magnae Britanniae et Hiberniae*,
4 vols. (London: R. Gosling, 1737), 3: 706, 727–737.

[2] Ibid., 3: 698.

[3] See Stanford E. Lehmberg, *The Reformation Parliament, 1529–1536* (Cambridge: Cambridge University Press, 1970), pp. 92–94, 107–116, 138–153.

passed with little debate in the spring of 1533, really marks the beginning of the English Reformation; it is the most significant statute in the entire constitutional history of the church within England.[4]

Although the cathedrals were not singled out or sent individual directives, they were included in the royal proclamation that made it illegal to pray for Catherine of Aragon as queen or give her any title other than that of princess dowager, to which she was entitled as the widow of Henry's older brother, Prince Arthur. Praemunire charges, with their accompanying confiscation of all property, could be brought against whose who refused to comply or denied the style of Queen to Anne Boleyn.[5] The Act of Supremacy, passed in 1534, carried with it an oath to be sworn by all clergy, acknowledging royal supremacy over the church and renouncing the jurisdiction of the papacy.[6] We know that the clergy of Worcester were notified of the acts of supremacy and succession; presumably similar statements were sent to the other cathedrals.[7] The submission of the Dean and Chapter of St. Paul's is duly recorded in a document signed by the minor canons, vicars choral, and chantry priests as well as the canons.[8] At Chichester the cathedral clergy renounced the pope and affirmed their support of supremacy and Queen Anne in July 1535.[9] A circular letter addressed to all sheriffs and justices of the peace in the same year urged these secular officials to see that the bishops enforced the king's order that prayers invoking the name of the pope cease and that all references to him be erased from service books.[10] The Dean and Chapter of Wells even asked the king to give them new statutes in 1536.[11] Evidently they believed that their existing constitution was invalidated by the break with Rome. The government does not seem to have agreed, for their request was ignored.

[4] See ibid., pp. 161–176.

[5] Paul L. Hughes and James F. Larkin, eds., *Tudor Royal Proclamations*, 3 vols. (New Haven: Yale University Press, 1964–69), 1: 209–210.

[6] Lehmberg, *Reformation Parliament*, pp. 202–203.

[7] Muniments, A.6 (ii), fol. 182, Worcester Cathedral Library.

[8] Wilkins, *Concilia*, 3: 774.

[9] W. D. Peckham, ed., *The Acts of the Dean and Chapter of Chichester, 1472–1544*, Sussex Record Society, no. 52 (Lewes, 1952), p. 45.

[10] Hughes and Larkin, *Proclamations*, 1: 229–232. Although Hughes and Larkin printed this as a royal proclamation, G. R. Elton has shown that it is in fact a circular letter rather than an actual proclamation; see his *Policy and Police* (Cambridge: Cambridge University Press, 1972), p. 239. As late as 1540 there was complaint that the names of the pope and Thomas à Becket had not been erased from a "legend" at Carlisle. See *Letters and Papers, Foreign and Domestic, Henry VIII*, 21 vols. (London: HMSO, 1862–1932), vol. 15, nos. 619, 633.

[11] HMC, *Calendar of the Manuscripts of the Dean and Chapter of Wells*, 2 vols. (London, 1907, 1914), 2: 250, calendaring Ledger Book D for December 6, 1536, Wells Cathedral Library.

Cathedral finance was affected by parliamentary action of 1534 ordering that clerical annates (first fruits and tenths) be paid to the king rather than the pope.[12] This annual tax was supposed to equal the entire first year's profits from church offices and a tenth of the income received subsequently. A royal order of 1535 commanded all churches to reveal the true value of their possessions to the king's commissioners, who then compiled the *Valor Ecclesiasticus* to form the basis for assessment and collection.[13] It has been pointed out that the clergy in fact paid considerably larger sums to the king than they had previously remitted to the pope, for papal collections had been based on low, outdated valuations.[14] Few laymen seem to have regretted the beginning of the government's attack on the wealth of the church; when there were rumors of even more drastic action against the clergy, an English observer wrote Lord Lisle, the king's deputy in Calais, that "many be glad and fewe bemone them."[15]

THE first actual attack on the cathedrals themselves was motivated by theological and political considerations as well as the government's greed. This was the campaign against shrines and images.[16] Both skeptical humanists and early Protestant reformers had denounced belief in shrines and miracles. In 1536 they were joined by Thomas Cromwell, whose Injunctions ordered the clergy not to "extol any images, relics, or miracles, . . . nor allure the people to the pilgrimage of any saint."[17] His Injunctions of 1538 went further; a section condemning "feigned images . . . abused with pilgrimages or offerings" ordered that such objects of idolatry be taken down without delay. No candles or lights were to be set before images or pictures, although some images might be allowed to remain if the people were instructed that they "serve for no purpose but as to be books of unlearned men" and reminders of the lives of the saints. Should clergy have "heretofore

---

[12] Lehmberg, *Reformation Parliament*, pp. 190–191, 205–207; Wilkins, *Concilia*, 3: 783.

[13] Wilkins, *Concilia*, 3: 799–802.

[14] W. E. Lunt, *Financial Relations of the Papacy with England, 1327–1534* (Cambridge: Harvard University Press, 1962), p. 445.

[15] SP 3/5, fol. 16, PRO; Lehmberg, *Reformation Parliament*, p. 185.

[16] For a general account, see John Phillips, *The Reformation of Images: Destruction of Art in England, 1535–1660* (Berkeley and Los Angeles: University of California Press, 1973). Phillips limits this study to theological and political issues; there is no detailed listing of the specific works destroyed or the circumstances under which they were attacked. The destruction of the shrines is also described in Ronald C. Finucane, *Miracles and Pilgrims* (London: J. M. Dent, 1977), pp. 203–216.

[17] W. H. Frere and W. M. Kennedy, eds., *Visitation Articles and Injunctions*, 3 vols., Alcuin Club, nos. 14–16 (London, 1910), 2: 5.

declared to [their] parishioners anything to the extolling or setting forth of pilgrimages, feigned relics, or images, or any such superstition," they shall "now openly . . . recant and reprove the same," showing them to be abuses that crept into the church through the "avarice of such as felt profit by the same."[18]

This attack on images was paralleled by a denunciation of Thomas à Becket, whose shrine at Canterbury had been the most popular focus of pilgrimages during the Middle Ages. The ludicrous process began in April 1538, when a citation ordering Becket to appear before the King's Council was read at his tomb. As prescribed by law, thirty days were allowed to elapse, but the "holy blissful martyr" failed to materialize at the judicial proceedings, and sentence was duly pronounced against him. During his life, it was said, he had disturbed the realm, and his own crimes were the cause of his death. He was therefore declared to be no martyr; his bones were to be taken up and burned publicly, and the treasures of his shrine confiscated by the king.[19] Continuing the same line, a proclamation of November 1538 insisted that Becket was a stubborn cleric who had stuck against "the wholesome laws established against the enormities of the clergy by the King's highness' most noble progenitor, King Henry II." His death, which resulted from a scuffle, was "untruly called martyrdom; . . . and further . . . his canonization was made only by the Bishop of Rome because he had been a champion to maintain his usurped authority." Since all this was now acknowledged, Becket should no longer be reckoned a saint, and his images and pictures were to be torn down throughout the realm. His name was to be erased from all service books and his feast day no longer celebrated.[20]

Before the end of the year, the great shrine at Canterbury, so much marveled at by Erasmus, had been demolished. It produced nearly three hundredweight of gold, the same amount of silver, almost twice as much silver gilt, and innumerable precious stones. This spoil filled two great chests, so heavy that six or seven strong men could barely carry one out of the church.[21]

[18] SP 6/3/1, PRO, calendared in *Letters and Papers*, vol. 13, pt. 2, no. 281, printed in Frere and Kennedy, *Visitation Articles*, 2: 38–39. Cf. Stanford E. Lehmberg, "The Religious Beliefs of Thomas Cromwell," in *Leaders of the Reformation*, ed. Richard L. DeMolen (Selinsgrove, Pa.: Susquehanna University Press, 1984), pp. 136–137.

[19] Wilkins, *Concilia*, 3: 835–836; *Letters and Papers*, vol. 13, pt. 2, no. 133.

[20] Hughes and Larkin, *Proclamations*, 1: 275–276. When the pope heard of this "cruelty and impiety" against Becket, he appointed cardinals Campeggio and Ghinucci, both of whom had English connections, and two other members of the Curia to investigate the situation; in December he issued a bull denouncing Henry's excesses (*Letters and Papers*, vol, 13, pt. 2, nos. 684, 1087).

[21] Francis Woodman, *The Architectural History of Canterbury Cathedral* (London: Routledge and Kegan Paul, 1981), p. 226.

Other shrines soon met the same fate, even though they were dedicated to saints who could not be charged with having opposed the monarchy. Thomas Wriothesley, who with Richard Pollard had supervised the spoliation at Canterbury, reported that Bishop Gardiner approved of the destruction of Becket's tomb and would welcome similar action at the shrine of St. Swithun in his own cathedral at Winchester.[22] In fact the royal agents were already on their way; St. Swithun's shrine was demolished at 3 A.M. on Saturday, September 21, 1538. Pollard and Wriothesley claimed that there was "no gold, nor ring, nor true stone in it, but all great counterfeits," but they exaggerated. The silver alone amounted to 2,000 marks (£1,333), and there were also several great chalices and crosses (one studded with emeralds). The commissioners seem to have gone beyond their instructions, for they took down part of the high altar as well as the shrine; its lower stage was covered with gold plates garnished with stones, while the upper was covered with embroidery incorporating numerous pearls. The mayor, eight or nine of his brethren, and the bishop's chancellor are said to have assisted in this work and praised the king for it.[23]

On December 14 the king issued a commission to Sir William Goring and William Ernley, ordering them to demolish the shrine of St. Richard at Chichester and destroy any other idolatrous images in the cathedral.[24] They did their work on the twentieth, carting off a ship's coffer filled with fifty-five images of silver and gilt, St. Richard's coffin full of fifty-seven more pieces of gold and silver, three chests of broken silver, thirty-one rings, fifty-one jewels, and some other treasures, all destined for the Tower.[25]

Comparable information about the despoiling of other cathedrals in 1538 does not exist. If there were more royal commissions, they do not survive, and local documents, such as the act books of the Dean and Chapter, seldom mention such things; they are more likely to record routine business—such as the leasing of lands—than truly momentous matters. Tangential evidence is tantalizing but imprecise. In

[22] *Letters and Papers*, vol. 13, pt. 2, no. 442.
[23] Ibid., no. 401. The inventory, printed as no. 402, is undated but evidently refers to items removed at this time. A gold and emerald cross from Winchester is listed among the articles delivered to the master of the king's jewels in 1538; see William Dugdale, *Monasticon Anglicanum*, 6 vols. (London: James Bohn, 1846), 1: 63, a copy of MS Bodley e Museo 57 from the Bodleian Library, Oxford.
[24] *Letters and Papers*, vol. 13, pt. 2, no. 1049; Wilkins, *Concilia*, 3: 840.
[25] *Letters and Papers*, vol. 13, pt. 2, no. 1103. A few years later the chapter paid its mason 15d. for "amending the Tumbe in the Lady Chapel that was broken up when the commissioners were here from the Council to search for treasure" (Chichester Accounts, cap. I/23/2, fol. 66, West Sussex Record Office).

London, for instance, Sir Richard Gresham heard of Cromwell's campaign against images from Dr. Robert Barnes, a friend of the secretary whose views were much influenced by Luther. Since Gresham was already dining with Bishop Sampson of Chichester, he took the cleric with him; they notified the dean of St. Paul's, and the three of them together removed the images that same night (August 23).[26] Just what they removed, we cannot tell. Most likely they concentrated on a famous statue of St. Wilgefort, popularly called St. Uncumber because she could dispose of unwanted husbands if wives offered prayers and, according to one version of the tradition, oats at her shrine.[27] If St. Erkenwald's shrine was not sacked then, it must have gone soon thereafter; we know that an image of St. Erkenwald, probably from the shrine, was delivered to the master of the king's jewels in October.[28]

The image of Our Lady at Worcester, according to Edward Hall, disappeared in September, along with other idolatrous statues in monasteries that were not cathedrals.[29] Hugh Latimer, the bishop of Worcester, praised this removal in a letter to Cromwell and revealed his reforming spirit when he attributed the idleness of local people to excessive veneration of the Virgin: "Now that she is gone, they be turned to laboriousness, and so from ladyness to godliness."[30] Were the shrines of St. Oswald and St. Wulfstan sacked at the same time, or were they allowed to remain until the monastery was dissolved two years later? We cannot be sure. An undated list of articles removed from Hereford Cathedral probably belongs in 1538; it includes chalices, censers, a pax, a holy water stoup, and an intriguing "image of the Trinity, of gold with a diadem on his head."[31] It may have been at this time that a sixteenth-century processional cross, several small crucifixes, fragments of alabaster carvings, and remnants of an elaborate fourteenth-century shrine were hidden in the groined vault of the central tower; these were discovered by the dean during a survey of the fabric in 1841.[32]

It was probably in 1538 that the shrine of St. Chad at Lichfield was

[26] *Letters and Papers*, vol. 13, pt. 2, no. 209.

[27] See Thomas More, *Dialogue concerning Tyndale*, ed. W. E. Campbell (London: Eyre and Spottiswood, 1927), pp. 166–167.

[28] Dugdale, *Monasticon*, 1: 65.

[29] Edward Hall, *Hall's Chronicle* (London: J. Johnson, 1809), p. 826.

[30] Hugh Latimer, *Sermons and Remains*, Parker Society, no. 28 (Cambridge, 1845), pp. 402–404. It may be of interest to note that these statues were frequently clothed. St. Uncumber was described as wearing a "gay gown" and silver shoes, and Our Lady of Worcester turned out to be a tall statue of some bishop once her robes were removed (Latimer, *Sermons*, p. 402n; *Letters and Papers*, vol. 13, pt. 1, no. 1393).

[31] *Letters and Papers*, vol. 13, pt. 2, no. 1208.

[32] See F. G. Havergal, *Fasti Herefordenses* (Edinburgh: R. Clark, 1869), pp. 146–147.

demolished. According to an earlier sacrist's roll, the relics here included bits of Golgotha, Calvary, and the rock on which Jesus wept over Jerusalem, as well as part of the bones of the eleven thousand virgins. Some of these objects were surreptitiously carried away by a conservative canon, Arthur Dudley; eventually they found their way to St. Chad's Roman Catholic Cathedral in Birmingham.[33]

Documentation about the destruction of St. Cuthbert's shrine at Durham is unsatisfactory. It may have taken place late in 1537, when Thomas Legh is known to have been demolishing shrines at Selby and William Blythman, another commissioner, doing the same at York, or it may have been delayed until December 1539, when Legh and other officials came to Durham to receive the surrender of the cathedral priory. When the visitors opened the shrine, they expected to find dust and bones, but instead saw the saint "lyinge hole vncorrupt with his face baire, and his beard as yt had bene a forth netts growth, & all his vestmentes vpon him as he was accustomed to say mess withall." The bystanders could not believe their eyes; they placed the body in an inner chamber until the king's pleasure could be known. Eventually it was buried below ground where the shrine had stood. Bede's shrine in the Galilee was defaced at the same time, and his body, too, was reinterred at the site of the shrine.[34] Gold weighing 344 ounces and 5,081 ounces of silver were confiscated from Ely in 1539.[35] Much if not all of this must have come from Etheldreda's shrine.

It was not until 1540 that a royal commission was issued for Lincoln. Here the king's agents were to dismantle St. Hugh's shrine (see fig. 19), sending the jewels to the Tower, and take down other monuments of superstition.[36] More than 2,620 ounces of gold and 4,280 ounces of silver from Lincoln, together with numerous pearls and precious

[33] J. Charles Cox, ed., *Catalogue of the Muniments and Manuscript Books Pertaining to the Dean and Chapter of Lichfield*, William Salt Archaeological Society, pt. 2, vol. 6 (London, 1886), pp. 207, 214.

[34] *A Description or Briefe Declaration of all the Ancient Monuments, Rites, and Customes belonginge or beinge within the Monastical Church of Durham before the Suppression*, ed. James Raine, Surtees Society, no. 15 (Durham, 1842), reprinted with additional editorial material by J. T. Fowler, Surtees Society, no. 107 (Durham, 1903), pp. 102–103, 284; *Letters and Papers*, vol. 14, pt. 2, no. 772. St. Cuthbert's body was probably in a mummified condition, as suggested by *Rites*, 1903 ed., pp. 284–285. The reburial in a plain tomb probably took place in 1542; see Mervyn James, *Family, Lineage, and Civil Society: A Study of Society, Politics, and Mentality in the Durham Region, 1500–1640* (Oxford: Clarendon Press, 1974), p. 58.

[35] *Letters and Papers*, vol. 14, pt. 2, no. 777.

[36] R.E.G. Cole, ed., *Chapter Acts of the Cathedral Church of St. Mary of Lincoln, 1536–1547*, Lincoln Record Society, no. 13 (Horncastle, 1917), p. 35; Margaret Bowker, *The Henrician Reformation: The Diocese of Lincoln under John Longland, 1521–1547* (Cambridge: Cambridge University Press, 1981), pp. 92–95.

19. Shrine of St. Hugh, Lincoln Cathedral,
showing one of the defaced statues.

stones, were in the King's Jewel House by June 1540, as were Becket's staff from Canterbury and miscellaneous items from churches and cathedrals in the west country.[37] There is a persistent story that Henry Litherland, the treasurer of Lincoln Cathedral, threw down his keys and resigned his office when the commissioners carried off his precious articles, saying angrily, "Now that the treasure is seized, the duties of treasurer come to an end."[38] This cannot be literally true, for Litherland had been executed in August 1538 on charges that he was involved in the Pilgrimage of Grace in Yorkshire, where he held the vicarage of Newark on Trent, and had preached favoring the pope, the veneration of the Virgin Mary, and the continued use of images.[39]

[37] Dugdale, *Monasticon*, 1: 63–67.
[38] Henry Bradshaw and Christopher Wordsworth, eds., *Statutes of Lincoln Cathedral*, 2 vols. (Cambridge: Cambridge University Press, 1892, 1897), 1: 103; Kathleen Edwards, *The English Secular Cathedrals in the Middle Ages* (Manchester: Manchester University Press, 1949), p. 220. Bradshaw and Wordsworth got Litherland's first name wrong, calling him John rather than Henry.
[39] Cole, *Lincoln Chapter Acts, 1536–1547*, pp. x–xi, and sources cited there. It looks as if

The Dean and Chapter of Lincoln, however, did not replace Litherland; ever since his death, the cathedral has been without a treasurer, the remaining duties of that office being performed by the sacrist.[40]

At Norwich the Dean and Chapter paid a mason named Robert Grene for his work in taking down St. William's tomb. More positively, they found room to install eleven altars that had been removed from the dissolved church of the Black Friars.[41] The destruction of St. William's shrine at York was supervised by Richard Layton, the notorious commissioner for the suppression of monasteries, who was named dean of the minster in 1539.[42] At Exeter the issue of images became enmeshed in a dispute between the chapter and the dean, the irascible reformer Simon Heynes, who had taken office in 1537 upon the resignation of Reginald Pole. An initial argument about the dean's powers was settled by compromise, but the feud erupted again in September 1540, when ten of the canons framed an indictment against Heynes. He was charged with destroying beautiful images of saints that for centuries had ornamented the church and had called the faithful to devotion. He had also lacerated the choir books and had extinguished the sanctuary lamp, a great scandal because it had burned without ceasing for two hundred years. Heynes departed from the cathedral in December 1541 and seldom resided thereafter, but his absence did not prevent his continued quarreling with the chapter, which lasted until his ouster under Queen Mary in 1554.[43]

One of the bitter ironies of this period is that Henry VIII himself appears to have admired some of the confiscated images, since he ordered a payment of £28 to his goldsmith, named Barnes, for "newe trymyng and garnishing" a dozen of them, including one of the Father

---

Litherland hid away some articles from the cathedral, including a silver gilt "Image of owr savyor" and a number of small crosses; some of these reappeared during the reign of Mary (Bowker, *Henrician Reformation*, p. 94).

[40] Edwards, *Secular Cathedrals*, p. 220. The office of treasurer at York disappeared a few years later under similar circumstances.

[41] Liber Miscellaneorum 3, DCN, R226A, accounts for 31 Hen. 8 (not paginated), Norfolk Record Office.

[42] Claire Cross, *York Clergy Wills, 1520–1600: I. Minster Clergy* (York: Borthwick Institute, 1984), p. 57.

[43] MS. 3552, fols. 1–44, Exeter Cathedral Library for a printed calendar, not entirely reliable, see Herbert Reynolds, ed., *The Use of Exeter Cathedral* (London: Church Printing Co., 1891), pp. 22–38. In 1543 Heynes spent some time in the Fleet, charged with evil opinions in religion during a phase when the government was dominated by conservatives; see Stanford E. Lehmberg, *The Later Parliaments of Henry VIII, 1536–1547* (Cambridge: Cambridge University Press, 1977), p. 185. One reason for Heynes' nonresidence is that he was president of Queens' College, Cambridge, and for a time vice-chancellor of the university. Cf. G. R. Elton, *Star Chamber Stories* (London: Methuen, 1958), p. 74n. For more on Heynes, see Nicholas Orme, *Exeter Cathedral as It Was* (Exeter: Devon Books, 1986), pp. 95–101. I am grateful to Dr. Orme for sending me a copy of this chapter in advance of publication.

of Heaven. Evidently things that were thought to inspire idolatry in ordinary people were acceptable when viewed by the sophisticated eyes of the king and his courtiers.[44]

It is particularly unfortunate that we do not know the exact circumstances in which the great reredoses at Winchester and Durham lost their statues. The beautiful Perpendicular Gothic screen behind the high altar at Winchester was nearly new, for it had been erected by Bishop Fox shortly before his death in 1528; it contained dozens of statues of saints (see fig. 20, 21).[45] The Neville Screen at Durham was earlier, a gift of Lord Neville about 1380. Before the Reformation it supported 107 statues, some surrounding the high altar, facing the choir, and some facing east toward St. Cuthbert's shrine, which was behind the altar. All of these were richly painted and gilded; none survive, and the screen has held empty niches ever since the sixteenth century, probably since 1538 (see fig. 22). York Minster was more fortunate. Here the stone screen (fig. 23) divides the nave and choir rather than standing behind the high altar. Built between 1475 and 1500 and adorned with fifteen statues, it was allowed to remain, presumably because these depicted the kings of England from William the Conqueror to Henry VI rather than saints. We know that the reredos at Lichfield, which may have survived intact because it did not contain images, was regilded in 1543, and that the "mappe" of the Crucifixion that hung in the middle of the high altar at Chichester was repainted in the same year.[46]

FOR some of the secular cathedrals, the destruction of the shrines and images was the heaviest blow of Henry VIII's reign. For the monastic cathedrals, however, it was of far less importance than the dissolution of the religious houses.

The story of the suppression of the monasteries in England has

[44] Dugdale, *Monasticon*, 1: 64.

[45] Lionel Butler and Chris Given-Wilson, *Medieval Monasteries of Great Britain* (London: Michael Joseph, 1979), p. 395. The screen now contains Victorian statues and so, at least from a distance, looks much as it originally did. In the seventeenth century the reredos was hidden by Jacobean paneling, with the Decalogue over the altar. By 1808 some of the canopied niches had been uncovered and were filled with urns; a painting, "The Raising of Lazarus," filled the central space. The screen was restored to its original form by 1910. See Gerald Cobb, *English Cathedrals: The Forgotten Centuries* (London: Thames and Hudson, 1980), pp. 136–137, where these stages are illustrated by reproductions of early prints.

[46] H. E. Savage, *Lichfield Cathedral: The Cathedral and the Chapter, 1530–1553* (Lichfield: Johnson's Head, 1927), p. 14; Chichester Communar's Accounts for 1543, cap. I/23/2, fol. 64, West Sussex Record Office.

20. Choir reredos, Winchester Cathedral, as restored in the
nineteenth century to approximately its original appearance.
Fragments of some of the original statues have recently been
found hidden in the gallery of the cathedral.

been told often and well; there is no need to recount it in detail here.[47]
It is helpful, however, to understand the context in which the cathedral priories met their end.

There were precedents, both within England and on the Continent,
for the closure of religious houses and the assignment of their re-

[47] See Dom David Knowles, *The Religious Orders in England*, 3 vols. (Cambridge: Cambridge University Press, 1948, 1955, 1959), vol. 3; G.W.O. Woodward, *The Dissolution of
the Monasteries* (London: Blandford, 1966); Joyce Youings, *The Dissolution of the Monasteries*
(London: George Allen and Unwin, 1971).

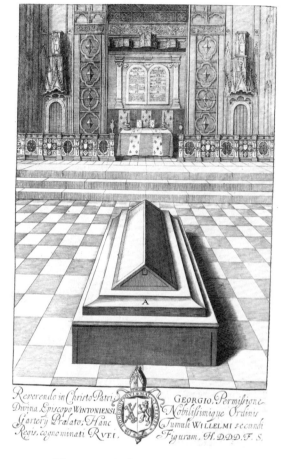

21. The east end of Winchester Cathedral
after the Reformation, with the
Ten Commandments displayed above the simple
communion table. Engraving from Sandford's
Kings and Queens of England (1677).

sources to other uses. At home, the most notable instances were
Bishop Alcock's conversion of St. Radegund's nunnery at Cambridge
into Jesus College, at the end of the fifteenth century, and Wolsey's
later suppression of St. Frideswide's at Oxford and some twenty further monasteries for the endowment of his new colleges at Oxford and
Ipswich.[48] On the Continent, parallel events that seem less well known

[48] Knowles, *Religious Orders*, 3: 157, 161.

22. Neville Screen, Durham Cathedral, following demolition
of statues. This photograph shows the east side of the
screen, which faced St. Cuthbert's Shrine.
The west side of the screen faces the high altar.

by English historians include the dissolution of religious houses in Lutheran parts of Germany and Scandinavia (including the convent of
Wittenberg itself), beginning in the 1520s.[49] Acting on this base, and
armed with a finely tuned sense of public opinion and political oppor-
tunism, Thomas Cromwell conceived his plans for a far more thorough attack. While the evidence is inconclusive, it seems probable that

[49] See ibid., 3: 165–172.

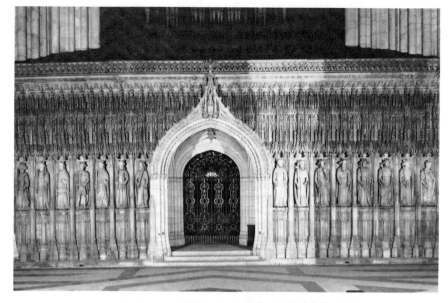

23. Choir screen with statues of kings, York Minster.

he had decided, as early as the beginning of 1535, to seek the dissolution of all religious houses—the extinction of monasticism in England.[50]

It was probably in order to justify such drastic action that Cromwell
sent commissioners—Richard Layton, Thomas Legh, John ap Rice,
and John Tregonwell—to visit the religious houses, compiling descriptions of their condition and lists of any failings that might exist.[51] Unfortunately for us, the commissioners did not examine all of the monastic cathedrals, and their comments on those priories they did visit
are not especially revealing. At Carlisle, for instance, they found seven
monks guilty of sodomy and three, including the prior, incontinent.
(Sexual lapses take up a large part of the commissioners' *comperta*, or
findings, and the validity of their charges has been questioned for centuries.) Carlisle also had some dubious relics: a fragment of the True
Cross, the sword with which Thomas à Becket was martyred, and the

[50] See Lehmberg, *Reformation Parliament*, pp. 223–228. Not all historians agree with my
view that Cromwell determined on a total Dissolution as early as this—indeed I have
debated the issue with three generations of scholars, ranging from Professor Knowles to
my own graduate students—but reexamination of the evidence has not led me to change
my mind.
[51] For biographical information about these visitors, see Knowles, *Religious Orders*, 3:
270–274.

girdle of St. Bride.[52] At York the visitors complained only of pilgrimages to St. William's shrine, at Lichfield of the veneration of St. Chad.
Further sexual irregularities were noted at Norwich.[53]

During the weeks before the Reformation Parliament met for its
final session in February 1536, Cromwell and his helpers were busy
drafting an act for the dissolution of the monasteries. By this time the
secretary had decided on a gradual approach to the suppression,
probably in the conviction that this would arouse less opposition than
immediate closure of all the houses. There was talk of shutting down
only those monasteries and nunneries housing fewer than twelve persons, but the statute as finally framed used a financial criterion, ordering the suppression of all houses with annual incomes of £200 or less.
Monks and nuns from such small houses were allowed to transfer to
other, larger institutions that would survive, or, if they preferred, renounce their vows and receive pensions from the government. The
property of the dissolved houses was turned over to the king, to be
managed by a new financial bureau, the Court of Augmentations.

Since all the monastic cathedrals had revenues substantially greater
than £200, they were not affected by the first dissolution statute. They
were soon caught up, however, in the second stage of Cromwell's campaign, which involved the negotiated surrender of the larger houses.[54]
Within the next several years, two of the monastic cathedrals were dissolved altogether, the remaining eight transformed into secular institutions, and six new cathedrals founded in order to utilize some of the
greatest of the monastic buildings.

THE first monastic cathedral to be converted into a secular foundation
was Norwich. Surviving records do not tell exactly why it received special treatment, but there is reason to think that it was the least well run
of the cathedral priories, and we know that Bishop Repps (or Rugg),
originally a monk himself, was a timeserver who acceded to every demand of the government, finally having to resign his see in 1549 because he had given away too much and was no longer able to manage
diocesan finance. A royal charter dated May 2, 1538, converted Norwich into a secular cathedral. The last prior, William Castleton, became the first dean; five monks were named prebends, with a sixth

[52] *Letters and Papers*, vol. 10, no. 364.
[53] Ibid.
[54] These were confirmed by a second dissolution statute passed in 1539; see Lehmberg,
Later Parliaments, pp. 61–64.

prebendal stall assigned to John Salisbury, the suffragan bishop of Thetford. Sixteen more monks were named canons. This was a peculiar arrangement, for the terms *prebendary* and *canon* were ordinarily used interchangeably, and these men were not referred to as minor canons, a separate, lower classification of priests found in a number of the cathedrals. When these canons died they were not replaced, and it has been suggested that the category was created for temporary use as a way of giving former monks a life office and stipend.[55] The Dean and Chapter were authorized to make their own statutes (they did not get around to doing so until the seventeenth century) and were allowed to allocate revenues for the support of the clergy and singers as they saw fit.[56]

The government's hand fell next on the cathedral priories at Coventry and Bath. These were special cases, for both of them were co-cathedrals for bishops who enjoyed a seat in a secular cathedral as well as a place in these monastic houses. They were therefore not needed as diocesan centers and (to use modern terminology) could be considered redundant. After 1539 the bishop of Coventry and Lichfield had to be content with his cathedral at Lichfield, although he still used the dual title, and the bishop of Bath and Wells had to be satisfied with Wells Cathedral. The priory at Coventry surrendered to the king's commissioner, John London, on January 15, 1539, with Bath following suit on the twenty-seventh.[57] The building at Coventry soon fell into ruin, and nothing now remains of it (the cathedral that was destroyed by bombing in World War II was a medieval parish church raised to cathedral status in 1918); the church at Bath, which was noted earlier because it was the only cathedral building erected primarily in the Tudor period, became the principal parish church of the city, perhaps an indication that it was already the chief place of worship for the laity there.

The remaining monastic cathedrals were destined to survive as secular establishments, but they were not actually refounded until 1541 or January 1542. Winchester received royal letters patent establishing its secular status on March 28, 1541, with Canterbury following in

[55] A. Hamilton Thompson, ed., *The Statutes of the Cathedral Church of Durham*, Surtees Society, no. 143 (Durham, 1929), pp. xxvi–xxxi.

[56] Ibid.; *VCH, Norfolk*, 2: 258; *Letters and Papers*, vol. 13, pt. 1, no. 867. A copy of Henry VIII's letters patent founding the secular cathedral is in the Liber Miscellaneorum 2, DCN R226A, fols. 23–53, Norfolk Record Office. Early in the reign of Edward VI, letters patent were issued to bring Norwich in line with the other cathedrals of the new foundation. Letters of endowment followed on November 9, 1547. See Thompson, *Statutes of Durham*, p. lii.

[57] *Letters and Papers*, vol. 14, pt. 1, nos. 69, 148.

April, Carlisle and Durham in May, Rochester in June, and Ely in September. The last of these cathedrals to be dealt with was Worcester, reestablished by a document issued on January 24, 1542.[58] While it is not entirely clear what happened at these places during the interim (usually more than a year) between the dissolution and the new foundation, it looks as if some members of the monastic community at Worcester stayed on, acting as caretakers of the fabric and probably maintaining services as well.[59] At Carlisle the last prior was guardian of the buildings until a new cathedral chapter was formed.[60] Similar provisions, perhaps informal, were probably made elsewhere.

The royal letters patent appoint the dean and prebendaries by name. Generally the last prior became the first dean. This arrangement, obviously a convenience and one that helped overcome any opposition that the monks might have expressed at the dissolution, was followed at Durham, Ely, Rochester, Winchester, Worcester, and Carlisle as well as at Norwich. The only outsider appointed to head a refounded cathedral was Nicholas Wotton, a learned courtier and diplomat, later secretary of state under Edward VI. He was named dean of Canterbury in 1541. Three years later he was made dean of York as well. Generally nonresident in both places, he continued to hold these offices through all the religious changes down to his death in 1567.

Not all the monks were so fortunate as their priors, for the new foundations were smaller than the old and many of the religious had to be satisfied with pensions. At Durham, sixty-six of the last monks have been traced. Of these, twenty-seven were given office in 1541, and one more was appointed later.[61] David Marcombe, who has made a careful study of the Durham chapter, regards those who stayed on as the most articulate and intelligent members of the monastic community.[62] Former monks, however, did not have a monopoly on prebendal posts; secular canons were appointed as well. Some other cathedral functionaries, as well as the monks, were occasionally given pensions; when the monastery at Winchester was dissolved, for in-

[58] Thompson, *Statutes of Durham*, pp. xxxii–xxxiii. For summaries of the letters patent, see *Letters and Papers*, vol. 16, nos. 678 (53), 779 (6), 878 (15, 25), 947 (35), 1226 (11).

[59] See the Visitation Act Book of Bishop John Bell (ca. 1520–1541), B.A. 2764/802, fols. 188, 215, Worcester Record Office.

[60] C.M.L. Bouch, *Prelates and People of the Lake Counties: A History of the Diocese of Carlisle, 1133–1933* (Kendal: Titus Wilson, 1948), p. 179; *Letters and Papers*, vol. 15, no. 619.

[61] S. L. Greenslade, "The Last Monks of Durham Cathedral Priory," *Durham University Journal* 41 (1948–1949): 107–113.

[62] David Marcombe, "The Durham Dean and Chapter: Old Abbey Writ Large?" in *Continuity and Change*, ed. Rosemary O'Day and Felicity Heal (Leicester: Leicester University Press, 1976), p. 127.

stance, provision was made for four singing men, eight choristers, and four bell ringers.[63] One imagines that they stayed in place, and very likely continued performing their usual duties, pending the introduction of new conditions.

Rearrangement of the living quarters associated with the monastic cathedrals was obviously necessary. It was relatively easy to convert the prior's lodgings into a deanery, since these were self-contained apartments of some luxury. We know that this was done at Durham and Worcester, and doubtless in most other places. At Worcester the sub-prior's house and the home of the master of the guest hall were assigned to prebendaries, while at Durham twelve houses for the canons were formed out of the monastic buildings. Refectories could easily be converted into dining halls for the minor canons and singing men; we know that this was done at Canterbury, Ely, and Worcester. After 1560 the monks' refectory at Worcester found a new use as a schoolroom; it is still the College Hall of the King's School.[64] Rochester was less fortunate. Here most of the monastic buildings were taken over by the king, who planned to use them as a residence when traveling between London and Dover. There was considerable rebuilding in 1541. In 1551 the property was granted to Lord Cobham, who returned it to the Dean and Chapter in 1558.[65]

THE most positive aspect of the dissolution of the monasteries was the accompanying foundation of six new cathedrals. A scheme for creating new bishoprics, probably originally Wolsey's, had been in the king's mind for some time. At one stage it was suggested that there should be a bishop—and a cathedral—in every county, a logical notion that can be traced back to King Alfred. Such new foundations really became feasible only with the confiscation of monastic endowments, which could be used to support the work of new dioceses, and monastic buildings, some of which were already of cathedral proportions.

Two sets of papers that survive in the Public Record Office show the government toying with the idea of establishing as many as fifteen new

---

[63] *Letters and Papers*, vol. 15, no. 139.

[64] Michael Craze, *King's School, Worcester, 1541–1971* (Worcester: Baylis, 1972), pp. 29–31; *Rites 1903 ed.*, pp. 159–160.

[65] W. H. St. John Hope, *The Architectural History of the Cathedral Church and Monastery of St. Andrew at Rochester* (London: Mitchell and Hughes, 1900), pp. 203–212. The monastic orchard became the King's Orchard, a term still used to describe the grounds adjoining the Deanery.

cathedrals.[66] Another document now among the Cottonian Manuscripts in the British Library reveals a plan to create sixteen bishoprics
with their cathedral churches, each diocese being allocated £1,000 out
of the revenues of dissolved religious houses.[67] Exact arrangements
had not yet been decided when Parliament met in 1539; nonetheless,
Cromwell was determined to introduce a bill giving the king authority
to create an indefinite number of new bishoprics, altering diocesan
boundaries as necessary and of course naming the new bishops himself. An aspect of the measure that is interesting constitutionally is the
clause stating that royal letters patent naming bishops shall have the
force of statute. Even more fascinating is the preamble, written by
Henry VIII himself and of importance because it is the only extant
example of such royal drafting. This notes the "slothful and ungodly
life which hath been used among all those sorts which have borne the
name religious folk." Now that the religious houses were dissolved,
their endowments could be "turned to better use . . . whereby God's
word might better be set forth, children brought up in learning, clerks
nourished in the universities, old servants decayed to have livings,
almshouses [provided] for poor folk to be sustained in, Readers of
Greek, Hebrew, and Latin to have good stipends, [and] daily alms to
be administered." All of these responsibilities (and even the maintenance of highways) could be assigned to the new bishops and
cathedrals.[68]

In the end, the early grand designs were abandoned and only six
new cathedrals were founded. No doubt the first thoughts were too
expansive—too costly and too disruptive of the existing order. We do
not know what sort of discussions took place behind the scenes, but it
may well be that bishops whose jurisdiction and revenues would have
been reduced if new dioceses were carved out of their territories

[66] These would have been at Westminster, Waltham, Gloucester, St. Albans, Oxford,
Peterborough, Burton-on-Trent, Chester, Shrewsbury, Dunstable, Colchester, Bristol,
Bodmin, Gisburne, and Fountains. The intention was probably to join Gisburne and
Fountains together as cathedrals for a single new diocese. Thornton, also mentioned in
the papers, was probably meant to be a college rather than a cathedral. The documents
are E 315/24, fols. 1–34 and 37–80, PRO, calendared in *Letters and Papers*, vol. 14, pt. 2,
no. 429. The second set is in the hand of Bishop Sampson of Chichester, and an endorsement states that it came from the bishop of Winchester (Stephen Gardiner). Possibly
there had been some thought of creating bishoprics without cathedral chapters; a "short
remembrance" by Bishop Sampson argues that "a buysshop . . . neyther having dignities
prebendes nor benefices in his disposition . . . shall neyther haue lerned men with hym
nor commissarie officiall or ony other person meate to serue" (E 315/24, fols. 35–36).

[67] Cottonian MS Cleopatra E. IV, fols. 312–455, BL, calendared in *Letters and Papers*, vol.
14, pt. 2, no. 428.

[68] See Lehmberg, *Later Parliaments*, pp. 66–67, 302. The statute, which passed with exceptional speed, is 31 Hen. 8, cap. 9.

joined the king's financial advisors in opposing truly drastic change. New Henrician cathedrals were created only at Westminster, Gloucester, Peterborough, Chester, Bristol, and Oxford.[69]

All of these were based on great monasteries, four of them Benedictine and two (Bristol and Osney, which was to serve as the cathedral for Oxford) houses of Augustinian canons, as at Carlisle. Several of them made possible the continuing use of monastic churches that were among the finest buildings in the realm. Indeed the government probably paid too much attention to the available structures and too little to the size and shape of the dioceses created. Gloucester and Oxford formed adequate centers for the administration of a bishopric, but Peterborough was far from the center of its long, narrow diocese, while Chester became the cathedral church of a huge territory that was calculated to provide an income for the bishop with little regard for the fact that personal oversight of such a diocese was impossible.[70] Even more absurd geographically was the arrangement that created the diocese of Bristol out of the city and a few parishes as far away as Dorset.[71] Westminster presented still greater difficulties. It was obvious that such a wealthy foundation, long associated with the monarchy and containing many royal tombs, could not be allowed to fall into ruin, and conversion into a cathedral must have seemed the easiest way of preserving it. But the division of greater London into two dioceses did not work well and did not last long. The position of bishop of Westminster was apparently offered to bishop Sampson,[72] but in the end he was translated from Chichester to Coventry and Lichfield rather than Westminster, and another conservative, Thomas Thirlby, was appointed to the new see. He has the distinction of being the only bishop of Westminster in Anglican history. No successor was appointed when he was translated to Norwich in 1550, to pick up the pieces left in disarray by Repps, and for six years the diocese of London had two cathedrals, St. Paul's and Westminster. In 1556 Queen Mary restored monastic life at the Abbey; when Elizabeth finally dissolved the monastery three years later, Westminster attained its pres-

[69] The foundation charters are summarized in *Letters and Papers*, vol. 16, nos. 379 (30), 1135 (4), 1226 (2, 6); vol. 17, nos. 71 (28), 443 (9), 881 (3).

[70] This is one of the chief reasons that Puritanism and recusancy flourished in Cheshire during the coming century, with relatively little support for the Anglican establishment. See R. C. Richardson, *Puritanism in North-West England* (Manchester: Manchester University Press, 1972); K. R. Wark, *Elizabethan Recusancy in Cheshire* (Manchester: Chetham Society, 1971); Christopher Haigh, "Finance and Administration in a New Diocese: Chester, 1541–1641," in *Continuity and Change*, pp. 146–147.

[71] Thompson, *Statutes of Durham*, pp. xxxi–xxxii.

[72] This is stated in E 315/24, fols. 35–36, (Sampson's "remembrance"), PRO.

ent status as a "royal peculiar," operating much like a cathedral but not attached to a bishop or diocese.[73] An anonymous writer, offering suggestions for reforms to be enacted by the Elizabethan Parliaments, proposed the creation of a bishopric to serve the queen's court out of the merged deaneries of Westminster and Windsor—an interesting idea, but abortive.[74]

The diocese of Oxford, originally named Osney and Thame, may have been viable, but Osney, across the river west of Oxford, proved an unsatisfactory site for its cathedral. In 1546 the cathedral was transferred to its present location, as an integral part of Christ Church within Oxford itself. A fine historic structure (in part Norman) was available here, too, for Wolsey had dissolved St. Frideswide's, another house of Augustinian canons, in 1524 and had incorporated its buildings into those of his new college.[75] The last abbot of Osney, Robert King, was the first bishop of Oxford, while John London, who had been the government's chief agent in the suppression of monasteries in Oxfordshire, was the first dean of the cathedral at Osney. When he died in 1544 he was succeeded by Richard Cox, who may have been instrumental in suggesting the move to Christ Church. Four canons from the Osney chapter came to Oxford with him.[76]

The most successful of the new dioceses, and the possessor of the finest building, was probably Gloucester; it is hard to believe that this magnificent church, with one of the largest and most beautiful east windows in the land, was not always a cathedral.[77] Bristol, too, inherited a marvelous edifice: the choir, with its tall aisles and unique vaulting pattern, is one of the masterpieces of the Decorated style, and the fine Perpendicular tower had been completed only at the beginning

[73] On Westminster Abbey, see C. S. Knighton, "Collegiate Foundations, 1540 to 1570, with Special Reference to St. Peter in Westminster" (Ph.D. thesis, Cambridge University, 1975).

[74] G. R. Elton, *The Parliament of England, 1559–1581* (Cambridge: Cambridge University Press, 1986), p. 279. The original document is SP 12/107, fols. 96–98, PRO.

[75] St. Frideswide's shrine had been broken up in 1538, but many of the carved stone arches were recovered later, and the shrine was reconstituted in the nineteenth century. A watching loft overlooking the shrine, built of timber in the fifteenth century, surprisingly survives as well. The Abbey of Osney was originally more celebrated than St. Frideswide's; the view of it, across the water meadows, was one of the glories of Oxford, and travelers commented on its stately towers, shrines, fine windows, and ring of bells, one of which eventually found its way to Christ Church and gave its name to Tom Tower. See C. E. Mallet, *A History of the University of Oxford,* 3 vols. (London: Methuen, 1924–1927), 2: 67–68.

[76] *Letters and Papers,* vol. 17, no. 881 (3); vol. 21, pt. 2, no. 476 (9); *VCH, Oxfordshire,* 2: 27–32, 90, 97; 4: 365, 369. Furnishings, bells, and roofing lead were moved from Osney to Christ Church in 1546.

[77] See David Welander, *The Stained Glass of Gloucester Cathedral* (Gloucester: Gloucester Cathedral, 1985).

TABLE 3.1
Financial Arrangements: Monastic Cathedrals

	Former income	Income from new endowment
Canterbury	£2,450	£2,542
Durham	1,576	1,227
Winchester	1,508	1,492
Ely	1,084	996
Worcester	1,300	1,249
Norwich	875	[875]
Rochester	487	800
Carlisle	418	654

NOTE: Figures for income of the monasteries are from *Valor Ecclesiasticus*, 6 vols. (London: Record Commission, 1810–1834); figures for new endowment are those proposed in E 315/24, fols. 37–72, PRO. All figures have been rounded off to the nearest pound; those for the monasteries represent net revenue and include the income of cells. Norwich is not included in either of the PRO drafts, no doubt because it had been refounded before these documents were produced, but it is said to have been given the full endowment of the cathedral priory (Dugdale, *Monasticon*, 4: 8).

of the sixteenth century. The Norman nave was being rebuilt at the time of the Dissolution, but this project was abandoned and whatever had been done was torn down. The present nave, which copies the style of the choir, is Victorian.

FINANCIAL arrangements for the new cathedrals, and for the secularized monastic cathedrals as well, were quite generous. Tables 3.1 and 3.2 compare the income of these houses before the Dissolution and after their refoundation. In the case of the new cathedrals the number of monks present in the dissolved monasteries is also shown.

It is evident that some leveling of resources was thought desirable; the revenues of Durham and Westminster were reduced substantially, while those of the poorest houses (Rochester, Carlisle, and Oxford) were increased.[78] This was appropriate in view of the fact that large

[78] Carlisle was given the revenues of the Benedictine priory of Wetheral, Cumberland, formerly a dependency of St. Mary's, York; its income at the time of the Dissolution was £117. See Knowles and Hadcock, *Religious Houses*, p. 80; J. E. Prescott, *The Statutes of the Cathedral Church of Carlisle* (London: Elliot Stock, 1903), p. 3. The cathedrals were better treated financially than the new bishoprics, which were inadequately funded. See Felicity Heal, *Of Prelates and Princes: A Study of the Economic and Social Position of the Tudor Episcopate* (Cambridge: Cambridge University Press, 1980), pp. 116–117.

TABLE 3.2
Financial Arrangements: New Cathedrals

	Former income	Income from new endowment	Number of monks
Westminster	£3,470	£2,598	43 (1534), 25 (1539)
Gloucester	1,430	721	36 (1534)
Peterborough	1,679	836	42 (1534), 40 (1539)
Chester	1,103	883	11 (1540)
Bristol	670	661	19 (1534), 12 (1539)
Oxford:		825	
Osney	654		25 (1520), 13 (1539)
St. Frideswide's	220 (1524)		9 (1520)

NOTE: Figures for monastic income and number of monks from David Knowles and R. Neville Hadcock, *Medieval Religious Houses* (London: Longmans, Green, 1953); figures for cathedral endowment are those proposed in E 315/24, fols. 37–72, PRO, except in the case of Westminster, where the figure represents the precise sum actually allocated.

numbers of monks had been supported at Canterbury and the Abbey, while the staff required in a cathedral of the new foundation was considerably smaller. Cathedrals of middling status had the bulk of the previous endowments transferred to them intact.

It is of some interest to note the number of positions and the specific stipends allocated to these cathedrals. Westminster and Canterbury may be taken as examples (admittedly not typical) of a new cathedral and a refounded cathedral priory.

At Westminster the proposed allocations can be traced through two government drafts and two "erection books," the last representing the final establishment. These are summarized in table 3.3.[79] It will be noted that the dean, whose salary as originally proposed would have been far lower than that of deans in cathedrals of the old foundation, was actually given an income comparable to that of deans at Salisbury, Wells, and St. Paul's. The number of scholars to be supported while studying in the cathedral school was reduced from sixty to forty, but the annual allowance for each remained at about £3. Choristers received the same amount. Minor canons were to be paid £10 a year,

[79] First draft: E 315/24, fols. 5–6, PRO; second draft: E 315/24, fols. 37–38, PRO; first erection book, ADD. MS. 40061, fols. 2–5, BL; second erection book, WAM. 6478, fols. 1–5, Westminster Abbey Muniment Room; cf. Knighton, "Collegiate Foundations," p. 16. Figures from the first erection book have been omitted in the table; they differ little from those in the second.

TABLE 3.3
Allocations for the Cathedral at Westminster

Position	Number	First draft	Second draft	Erection Bk. II
Dean	1	£ 50	£232 10s. 0d.	£232 10s. 0d.
Canons	12	480	339	339
Scholars	60	200		
	40		133 6s. 8d.	133 6s. 8d.
Headmaster	1	20	20	20
Undermaster	1	10	10	10
Students	20	200	166 13s. 4d.	166 13s. 4d.
Minor canons	8	80		
	12		120	120
Singing men	12	80	96	96
Choristers	10	33 6s. 8d.	33 6s. 8d.	33 6s. 8d.
Master of the choristers	1	10	10	10
Gospeler	1	6	10	10
Epistoler	1	5	10	10
Sextons	2	13 6s. 8d.	13 6s. 8d.	13 6s. 8d.
Almsmen	12	80	80	80

singing men £8 in the later drafts, almsmen £6 13s. 4d. each. Twenty students were to be maintained at Oxford and Cambridge, each receiving a bit more than £8. In addition to the items listed in the table, there was provision for readers at the universities, in Greek, Hebrew, Latin, civil law, and physic (medicine); for porters, butlers, cooks, and an auditor; and for alms and repairs to the buildings.

The situation at Canterbury was similar. Here the first refoundation proposal allowed for a dean (called provost), twelve prebendaries, six preachers (an office peculiar to Canterbury, probably indicating that the prebendaries could not be trusted to preach reformed doctrine), eight minor canons, twelve lay clerks or singing men, ten choristers, sixty scholars to be taught Latin and Greek in the grammar school, twenty students at Oxford and Cambridge, five readers of divinity, physic, and civil law, a master of the choristers, and two masters of the grammar school.[80] In the final settlement the dean was paid £300 a

[80] E 315/24, fols. 1–2, PRO.

year, the canons £40 each, the preachers £24 2s. 2½d., fourteen minor canons (an increased number) £10 each, the singers £8, fifty "gramaryans" £4, and twenty-four scholars in the universities (half at Cambridge and half at Oxford) £6 or £8 depending on their status.[81]

The other foundations varied in size and cost. Durham and Winchester, as one would expect, remained large and rich. At the other end of the scale is Carlisle, which was allowed four prebendaries, eight minor canons, four singing men, and six choristers. The normal complement of musicians was eight or ten boys and six or eight men. Winchester, Worcester, and Ely, as well as Westminster and Canterbury, were originally given endowments for the support of university students, but these did not last long. They were taken over by the government in 1545, and the cathedrals were relieved of any responsibility to support higher education.[82]

As noted above, the Dean and Chapter of Norwich were given authority to make their own statutes. The other new foundations, however, had statutes imposed on them from without; the letters patent creating these new institutions stated that they were to be operated "according to the ordinances, rules and statutes to be specified ... hereafter."[83] These were delivered in 1544 (see fig. 24).[84]

We are fortunate in knowing who the actual compilers of the statutes were. Cromwell was of course not involved, since he had been executed in 1540. Cranmer and Gardiner, who led the reforming and conservative wings of the church, may have been consulted, but the detailed work was left to Nicholas Heath, bishop of Worcester; George Day, bishop of Chichester; and Richard Cox, archdeacon of Ely. It is possible that the three were chosen to represent divergent factions in the church, for Heath and Day were staunch conservatives, destined to be deprived of their sees under Edward VI but restored by Mary,

[81] M.A. 40, Canterbury Cathedral Library.
[82] G. W. Kitchin and F. T. Madge, eds., *Documents Relating to the Foundation of the Chapter of Winchester* (Winchester: Hampshire Record Society, 1889), p. 168; Craze, *King's School, Worcester*, p. 21; Knighton, "Collegiate Foundations," p. 312.
[83] Thompson, *Statutes of Durham*, pp. xxxviii–xxxix.
[84] For some reason, the statutes for Carlisle were delayed until 1545. They are unusual in having been issued under the Great Seal. The statutes for Durham and Westminster do not survive, but there is some evidence that they once existed. See ibid., p. xl; Knighton, "Collegiate Foundations," p. 69; Act Book, 1542–1609, fol. 38, Westminster Abbey Library. Statutes for Oxford do not seem to have been issued, probably because of the uncertain status of the cathedral there.

24. Statutes of Ely Cathedral, drawing showing
Henry VIII presenting statutes to the Dean and Chapter.
From EDC 1/E/12, Ely Cathedral Archives,
Cambridge University Library.

whereas Cox was a leading Protestant, later to be dean of both Westminster and Oxford, theological tutor to Edward, a Marian exile, and
finally the Elizabethan bishop of Ely.

Although there are some local variations in the wording of the statutes, they share a basic common text. This is divided into chapters (the
number of these ranges from thirty-eight to forty), beginning with
provisions for the election and duties of the dean and canons. Then
follow clauses regulating the choice and responsibilities of the subdean, receiver, and treasurer. (These, together with the dean, are the
only statutory officers drawn from the cathedral chapter.) Several sections of the statutes relate to the extracapitular members of the foundation: the minor canons, vicars choral, choristers, precentor, sacrist,
organist and master of the choristers, teachers in the grammar school,
almsmen, and servants (porters, butlers, and cooks). The statutes conclude with general comments on order and discipline.

The constitutional arrangements laid down by the statutes are of some significance. It is interesting to note, for instance, that the bishop had no place in the operation of these cathedrals; since two bishops were involved in drafting the statutes, one might have expected that they would emphasize episcopal jurisdiction in some way. (Bishops were directed to hold a visitation every three years; otherwise they could act only at the invitation of the Dean and Chapter.) The dean was given greater authority to govern the cathedral than in the old secular cathedrals (now often referred to as cathedrals of the old foundation), but legal jurisdiction resided in the corporation of the Dean and Chapter, the latter including all the canons or prebendaries. The canons had no individual rights apart from their collective voice within the chapter. Unlike the prebendaries in cathedrals of the old foundation, they did not hold estates individually either; for that reason they should properly be called canons rather than prebendaries, though the terms continued to be used almost interchangeably. The appointment of deans and canons was placed securely in the hands of the monarch, not the bishop or any other authority. The Dean and Chapter were to act jointly in electing minor canons, vicars choral, and choristers; only the cathedral servants could be appointed (and presumably removed) by the dean alone. The vicars choral were made subject to the Dean and Chapter, and were not to hold property independently, as did the vicars choral in cathedrals of the old foundation.

The dean and canons were to have separate houses within the cathedral precinct and were to maintain hospitality, although there was no demand that they incur the heavy burdens of entertaining laid earlier on some residentiaries. The minor canons, singing men, choristers, and grammar masters might live separately but were supposed to dine together in the common hall, the precentor presiding: minor canons, the master of the choristers, and the headmaster of the school were to sit at the high table, lay clerks and the undermaster at the second, and the choristers at the third.

The statutes contain only brief references to the services of the church. What is said is quite conservative. Masses are still to be celebrated daily at the altars, and the obits of founders and benefactors are to be observed. Midnight matins, however, are dispensed with— quite understandably, these had always presented problems, and permission for absence from them was often granted long before they were abandoned altogether.

Of the local variations, the most important relate to Canterbury and

93

Worcester. Canterbury was unique in having constitutional provision for its six preachers, whose appointment and responsibilities are duly defined. The grammar school at Worcester was the subject of special comment there; the statutes even included provisions for its curriculum, all in Latin, with Aesop being read in the second form, Terence in the third, and Erasmus by sixth-form boys. It is possible that the hand of Bishop Heath lay behind this statute, as well as a few other clauses that seem to relate directly to specific conditions within his cathedral.[85]

The old secular cathedrals had no need for new statutes.[86] There was at least one proposal, however, that they, too, might be reformed along more Protestant lines. This emanated from the troublesome dean of Exeter, Simon Heynes. The chief officer in a cathedral, he suggested, should be called its pastor, not dean. The prebendaries should be renamed preachers, while the chancellor might be transformed into a lecturer in theology. Some changes in educational arrangements could be made as well. As one might expect, these advanced notions did not receive a favorable hearing.[87]

CARLISLE cathedral possesses a fascinating artistic monument to its refoundation. This is the wooden screen, enclosing part of the choir, erected about 1541 by Lancelot Salkeld, the last prior and first dean (see fig. 25). The carving, of superb quality, incorporates early Renaissance design such as that seen in the screen placed in the chapel of King's College, Cambridge, a few years earlier. The designs at the top of the side facing the choir are ecclesiastical, with the shield of Carlisle priory and the initials *LSDK* (Lancelot Salkeld Decanus Karleolensis). All of the devices on the outer side of the screen are secular. The royal

[85] On all of this, see Thompson, *Statutes of Durham*, pp. xxxviii–lii. Many of the cathedral statutes have been printed; to Thompson's list (pp. xviii–xx) should be added the statutes of Peterborough in *Northamptonshire Record Society* 13 (1940): 75–104. There are useful materials, not limited to Lincoln, in Bradshaw and Wordsworth, *Statutes of Lincoln*. I have also consulted manuscript statutes, both originals and later copies, which survive in most of the cathedral libraries or repositories to which their muniments have been transferred.

[86] An act passed in 1559 (1 Eliz. 1, cap. 22) gave the queen authority to provide new statutes and ordinances for cathedrals as well as colleges and collegiate churches (see Elton, *Parliament of England*, p. 196), but so far as the cathedrals were concerned she did not avail herself of the power.

[87] Nicholas Orme, *Education in the West of England, 1066–1548* (Exeter: University of Exeter, 1976), p. 54.

25. Salkeld Screen, Carlisle Cathedral, showing Tudor
symbols and the ostrich feathers of the Prince of Wales.

arms, flanked by Tudor symbols, are placed on the cresting. Below,
the center compartment has the feathers of the Prince of Wales and
the inscription *GSPE*, presumably meaning "God Save Prince Edward." Panels at the bottom of the screen contain finely carved profiles
of human heads (fig. 26); the significance of these is uncertain. The
screen's general meaning, however, is clear enough. Salkeld must have
wished to celebrate his own continuing appointment and his success in
converting the cathedral to its new status. In addition he may have
hoped to curry favor with the king, who had so greatly desired a male

26. Salkeld Screen, Carlisle Cathedral, detail showing portrait heads.

heir, and with Prince Edward, whose accession to the throne could not be far off.[88]

THE factional strife between conservatives and reformers, so evident at court during the later years of Henry VIII's reign, was mirrored in dissension at some of the cathedrals. The most serious case arose at Canterbury, where in 1543 it culminated in the famous Prebendaries' Plot against Archbishop Cranmer.

Cranmer had been unable to secure the refoundation of Canterbury cathedral along the lines he himself favored. His vision of it as a great center of Protestant worship and teaching was not realized; his attempt to have a reformer appointed dean failed, and seven of the twelve prebendaries of the new foundation were conservative former

[88] For comments on the Salkeld screen, see C. G. Bulman, "The Gondibour and Salkeld Screens in Carlisle Cathedral," *Cumberland and Westmorland Antiquarian and Archaeological Society Transactions*, n. s., 56 (1955): 104–127; C.M.L. Bouch, "The Salkeld Screen in Carlisle Cathedral: Its Date and Motive," ibid., 57 (1956): 39–43. The only similar screen containing devices of Prince Edward was erected at Bristol about 1543; it is made of stone, not wood. Cf. R. H. Warren, "Bristol Cathedral: The Choir Screen," *Transactions of the Bristol and Gloucestershire Archaeological Society* 27 (1904): 127–130.

monks hostile to his views. Only three members of the original chapter (Nicholas Ridley, Richard Champion, and Hugh Glazier) were sympathetic to the Reformation, and only three of the six preachers were reformers. (When questioned about this, Cranmer replied that Henry VIII would have it so—probably an accurate statement, in view of the king's proclivity for giving office to political rivals, trusting that the monarch could hold the balance between them.)

Factional struggles at the cathedral filled the years between 1541 and 1543 and had repercussions outside the cathedral close, since both prebendaries and preachers appeared in rural churches rallying support, while a number of the conservative clergy enjoyed close ties with the gentry of Kent. Cranmer urged the prebendaries to live in Christian charity, but he must have realized that they were unlikely to do so. Indeed, he acknowledged the existence of an unfriendly faction at the cathedral, telling one of the prebendaries, "You be there knit in a bond among you which I will break."

Instead, the prebendaries nearly broke Cranmer. They collected evidence, much of it no better than gossip, linking the archbishop with theological opinions so radical they could be considered heretical, and saw that it was presented to the king, possibly through the agency of Bishop Gardiner. The outcome forms one of the most revealing episodes in Henry's reign, with the king telling Cranmer, "Ah, my chaplain, I know now who is the greatest heretic in Kent" and agreeing to appoint commissioners to investigate the charges, only to confound the conservatives by naming Cranmer himself head of the commission. Thus the attempt to send Cranmer to the Tower failed, and the king tried to make peace, ordering the conservative councilors to shake hands with the archbishop and Cranmer to entertain them at dinner. But peace in Canterbury did not come easily, nor did the triumph of Protestantism there. A decade later, there was general rejoicing when the old liturgies were revived under Mary Tudor.[89]

SINCE the four Welsh cathedrals were not monastic, they were not affected by suppression and refoundation. At St. David's, however, the

[89] On the Prebendaries' Plot, see Jasper Ridley, *Thomas Cranmer* (Oxford: Clarendon Press, 1962), pp. 229–245; John F. Davis, *Heresy and Reformation in the South-East of England, 1520–1559* (London: Royal Historical Society, 1983), pp. 90–95; and Peter Clark, *English Provincial Society from the Reformation to the Revolution* (Hassocks; Sussex: Harvester Press, 1977), pp. 63–65. Our knowledge of the episode derives primarily from John Foxe and from the enormous quantity of interrogatories and depositions obtained by the government in examining the charges against Cranmer. Now MS. 128 at Corpus Christi Col-

chapter found itself embroiled in a bitter quarrel with the bishop, William Barlow. A Protestant protégé of Cromwell and of Anne Boleyn, through whose favor he gained appointment in 1536, Barlow has been characterized as "fanatical, iconoclastic, rash, and often unscrupulous, but a courageous and not insincere innovator."[90]

His most intriguing innovation would have ended St. David's status as a cathedral and moved the see to St. Peter's, Carmarthen. This was not entirely unreasonable, for Carmarthen was the largest town in Wales, well served by roads and a much more convenient administrative center than St. David's, which Barlow accurately described as lying in "the most barren angle of the diocese." But Barlow's plan was based as much on theology as geography; he detested the superstitious atmosphere at St. David's, redolent of false relics and popish shrines.

Naturally enough, the clergy of St. David's resisted Barlow's attempts at change. Their animosity was increased by the bishop's demand for greater jurisdiction within the cathedral itself. Here an unusual situation applied. St. David's had no dean. By tradition and prescriptive right, the precentor acted as head of the chapter, but the bishop could lay a vague claim to the deanery. When Barlow attempted to exercise this authority, he found himself locked in a bitter feud with Thomas Lloyd, the precentor, which led to charges, countercharges, and finally a Star Chamber suit. Rather surprisingly, Cromwell did not support Barlow, even though the bishop offered to make Cromwell or his son steward of the bishopric's lands. After Cromwell's fall, Barlow had little influence at court, and his reforming campaign had no effect other than the removal of images and relics. In 1548, when Protestants were clearly in the ascendant, Barlow was translated to the English bishopric of Bath and Wells; the cathedral remained at St. David's.[91]

As the reign of Henry VIII drew to a close, there were some signs that liturgical and theological reforms were coming soon. Sensitive observers, especially those committed to Protestant views, may have understood the implications of the proclamation issued in 1541 ordering the English Bible to be set up, available to lay persons, in every

lege, Cambridge, this volume of documents is calendared in *Letters and Papers*, vol. 18, pt. 2, no. 546 (pp. 291–378).

[90] Glanmor Williams, *Welsh Reformation Essays* (Cardiff: University of Wales Press, 1967), p. 111.

[91] The episode is described in ibid., pp. 111–124, with sources listed on pp. 135–139.

church[92] as well as the king's order that Cranmer's English Litany—a foretaste of the English Prayer Book—be used beginning in 1544.[93] The English Primer, which included the Litany as well as other vernacular prayers, was authorized in 1545 and carried the movement toward worship in the vernacular a step further.[94]

In the main, however, the services of the English church and its cathedrals remained traditional so long as Henry lived. A proclamation of 1538 tried to end the "difference, strife, and contention" regarding such old ceremonies as creeping to the Cross on Good Friday or bearing candles on the Feast of the Purification (popularly called Candlemas) by ordering that they remain in use as good and laudable customs, even though no one ought to place trust of salvation in them.[95] Three years later another royal proclamation insisted that the feasts of St. Luke, St. Mark, and St. Mary Magdalene should continue to be celebrated—some people had argued that they should be abrogated because the first two fell within the law terms at Westminster, while the last came during harvest season. St. Mark's Day was clearly identified as a feast, not a fast day, thus ending local variations; perhaps as a sop to the reformers, the "superstitious and childish observances" of special days for St. Nicholas, St. Catherine, St. Clement, and the Holy Innocents were abolished.[96] Account books kept by the cathedrals themselves confirm that age-old customs continued. At Chester, four men were paid a penny apiece for carrying the canopy for the Palm Sunday procession in 1545, and almonds, raisins, spiced cake, spiced ale, and wine were provided for the Maundy Thursday supper. The bells were rung on Christmas and Corpus Christi Day, and new altar cloths were still being provided.[97] Shortly before Henry VIII's death, a gilt candelabrum was purchased at Worcester.[98]

When the king died in January 1547, a solemn dirge must have

[92] Hughes and Larkin, *Proclamations*, 1: 296–298.

[93] Wilkins, *Concilia*, 3: 869. A "Rationale," or "Book concerning Ceremonies," was prepared in the early 1540s, but since it was essentially an explanation of existing Latin services, it soon became irrelevant and was not published. There is a modern edition: C. S. Cobb, ed., *The Rationale of Ceremonial*, Alcuin Club, no. 18 (London, 1910). The Register of Nicholas Heath, bishop of Worcester, includes his order that processions be sung in English, according to the form newly set forth, and his charge to preachers to explain the change, so that the people will accept it in godly fashion. Worcester Diocesan Registry, MS. 2648/b716.093/9(ii), fol. 13, Worcester Record Office. For further information about the Litany, see William P. Haugaard, "The English Litany from Henry to Elizabeth," *Anglican Theological Review* 51 (1969): 177–203.

[94] Hughes and Larkin, *Proclamations*, 1: 349–350.

[95] Ibid., 1: 270–276.

[96] Ibid., 1: 301–302.

[97] Account Book 1, fols. 76, 144, 163, 180, Chester Cathedral Library.

[98] Accounts, A204, Worcester Cathedral Library.

been sung in all the cathedrals. Occasionally there is a specific reference to this in the accounts: at Chester, for instance, 12*d.* was paid to the singers who helped honor the king's memory.[99] The obsequies would have included the Latin mass that Henry had long known and loved.

For the cathedrals, as for the church generally, the reign of Henry VIII had brought profound constitutional and financial changes. The Henrician Reformation, however, had been almost entirely a political one. The adoption of Protestant theology and an English liturgy remained ahead.

[99] Account Book 1, fol. 149, Chester Cathedral Library.

4

EDWARD VI: THE PROTESTANT
ASCENDANCY

THE DEATH of Henry VIII removed the chief obstacle to further reform in the church. His successor, the nine-year-old male heir whose
birth he had so greatly desired, had been taught by Protestant tutors,
including Richard Cox, and had become convinced that he was di-
vinely destined to bring true religion to the land, sweeping away the
last vestiges of popery and superstition. Surrounded by such Protestant churchmen as Archbishop Cranmer and such Protestant ministers as his uncle, Protector Somerset, Edward VI supported a Protestant ascendancy that soon ushered in the most drastic changes of the
century for the cathedrals.

The new regime started with the promulgation in July 1547 of royal
injunctions concerning religious reform. In the main, these echo
Henry VIII's orders, emphasizing royal supremacy and the extirpa-
tion of papal jurisdiction. Images, relics, shrines, and pilgrimages are
denounced in several of the injunctions, with preachers commanded
to instruct the people that there is "no promise of reward in Scripture"
for honoring them. But the new orders go beyond the old in directing
deans to destroy utterly all shrines, tables, candlesticks, pictures, paintings, and other monuments of idolatry and superstition, even images
found in stained glass windows. No torches or other lights are allowed
except for two candles on the altar, "for the signification that Christ is
the very true light of the world." The Bible and Erasmus's *Paraphrases*
are to be set up in all churches; sermons shall be preached regularly,
and one of Cranmer's newly issued *Homilies* shall be read each week if
an authorized preacher is not available. "To avoid all contention and
strife which heretofore" had arisen during processions, the new English Litany was not to be said as the clergy and choir processed, but
rather as they knelt "in the midst of the church." It was to be used
more frequently than before: under Henry the Litany was to be sung
on Wednesdays and Fridays, but the Edwardian injunctions mandate
its regular use before high mass. The Epistle and Gospel of the mass
are to be read in English rather than Latin, and the portions of Scripture for matins and evensong are also to be in the vernacular. But the

"laudable ceremonies of the church . . . as yet not abrogated" must still be observed without dissension, and chantry priests still remain in place, now exhorted to be diligent in teaching the young to read and write.[1]

These general orders were supplemented by a set of royal injunctions aimed specifically at the cathedrals. The most interesting of these direct all cathedrals to fit up a library containing the standard patristic works together with the writings of Erasmus and other good, presumably modern, writers; to make yearly inventories of all their vestments, ornaments, jewels, and plate; to establish free grammar schools if these do not already exist; and to support former choristers studying at a grammar school for five years with an annual stipend of £3 6s. 8d. Further injunctions were given to some cathedrals individually. Those for Canterbury attempt to clarify ambiguities in the constitutional position of the dean by reiterating his authority to make appointments so long as he is within the realm, just as if he were physically present at the cathedral. They also mandate the creation of a common garden and the allocation of suitable chambers to minor canons and vicars choral. The wearing of copes was forbidden at Winchester, while at Lincoln ministers below the degree of prebendaries were ordered not to wear habits or black hoods, but only surplices. At York Minster there was to be but one mass each day, celebrated at the high altar at 9 A.M., and the singing of dirges and some other services was discontinued so that the clergy might spend their time in study and contemplation of God's Holy Word.[2]

These injunctions were to be enforced by a general visitation of the church. Cranmer and Somerset evidently did not trust the bishops to see that the reforming orders were actually obeyed—indeed their fear was justified, for at least one-third of the bishops were conservatives who felt no enthusiasm for enforcing change.[3] So normal episcopal powers of visitation were inhibited while visitors named by the government made their way throughout the realm. For this purpose, the kingdom was divided into six sections; thirty visitors were appointed, of whom two-thirds were laymen, generally lawyers of staunch Prot-

[1] Paul L. Hughes and James F. Larkin, eds., *Tudor Royal Proclamations*, 3 vols. (New Haven: Yale University Press, 1964–1969), 1: 393–403, also printed in W. H. Frere and W. M. Kennedy, eds., *Visitation Articles and Injunctions*, 3 vols., Alcuin Club, nos. 14–16 (London, 1910), 2: 114–130. On the use of the Litany under Edward VI, see William P. Haugaard, "The English Litany from Henry to Elizabeth," *Anglican Theological Review* 51 (1969): 181–187.

[2] Frere and Kennedy, *Visitation Articles*, 2: 135–170.

[3] For an analysis of the early Edwardian episcopate see W. K. Jordan, *Edward VI: The Young King* (Cambridge: Harvard University Press, 1968), pp. 130–131.

estant or Erastian views.[4] When Gardiner and Bonner, the chief of the conservative bishops, opposed this infringement of their authority, they were packed off to prison. Both were deprived later in the reign.

The visitors were given a set of seventy-four articles that were to serve as the basis for interrogation of appropriate clergymen and lay people.[5] None of the articles relates solely to cathedrals, but several would have an impact there. The campaign against images and shrines continued, as clergy were asked whether they knew of any shrines "or other monuments of idolatry, superstition, and hypocrisy" that had not been destroyed and whether they had taught the people the true use of images, "which is only to put them in remembrance of the godly and virtuous lives of them that they do represent: and . . . if [they] . . . use the images for any other purpose, they commit idolatry to the great danger of their souls."

Another set of articles reveals the growing concern for the use of English in the services of the church. Priests were asked "whether they have counselled or moved their parishioners rather to pray in a tongue not known than in English," and they were interrogated about their use of the English Litany. It is interesting to find lay persons asked whether matins and evensong, as well as the mass, are kept at due hours in the church, for these were to be the main non-Eucharistic services set forth in the Prayer Book which Cranmer was preparing but which had not yet been published or put into use. In view of the movement to dissolve chantries that would shortly be the focus of governmental activity, it is interesting, too, to find five articles for chantry priests. The visitors were to ascertain whether they were resident, what benefices they held in addition to their chantries, whether they assisted in the administration of the sacraments, whether they were of honest conversation and behavior, and whether they performed all the deeds of charity mandated by their chantry foundations.[6]

Local sources confirm the effect of these policies. At Hereford, the chapter act books record the receipt in March 1547 of a letter requiring that any remaining images be pulled down.[7] Some further jewels

[4] Ibid., p. 164. Inhibition of episcopal jurisdiction was not a novelty. The most notorious previous episode had come while Cromwell was Henry VIII's vicegerent in spirituals; see Stanford E. Lehmberg, "Supremacy and Vicegerency: A Re-examination," *English Historical Review* 81 (1966): 225–235.

[5] They are printed in Frere and Kennedy, *Visitation Articles*, 2: 103–113.

[6] At the time the articles were issued, Cranmer probably hoped to reform the chantries, not to abolish them. See Alan Kreider, *English Chantries: The Road to Dissolution* (Cambridge: Harvard University Press, 1979), pp. 188–189.

[7] Act Book 1, fol. 98, Hereford Cathedral Library. The Edwardian campaign against images is discussed in John N. King, *English Reformation Literature: The Tudor Origins of the Protestant Tradition* (Princeton: Princeton University Press, 1982), pp. 144–160.

27. Lady Chapel, Ely Cathedral, showing
one of the numerous decapitated statues.

and plate from Canterbury were sent on their way to the mint in July.[8]
Despite Bonner's opposition, all the images at St. Paul's were demolished in September, and the rood, crucifix, tombs, and even altars followed in November. Those who still sympathized with the old religion did not fail to note that two of the workmen engaged in these sacrilegious acts were killed.[9] It is likely that the tragic defacement of the fourteenth-century statues in the Lady Chapel at Ely (see fig. 27) occurred at about the same time.[10] The order to clear away all images was received at Lichfield in March 1548 and was honored by the removal of statues from the high altar and throughout the church. To

[8] Lit. MS. E. 37 (unpaginated note of an order from the council), Canterbury Cathedral Library.

[9] J. G. Nichols, ed., *Chronicle of the Grey Friars of London*, Camden Society, no. 53 (London, 1852), p. 55; W. R. Matthews and W. M. Atkins, eds., *A History of St. Paul's Cathedral* (London: John Baker, 1957), p. 123; Jordan, *Young King*, p. 163.

[10] As Nikolaus Pevsner wrote, "Not one figure, not one scene is as it should be, and what remains makes one feel sad about it" (*The Buildings of England: Cambridgeshire* [Harmondsworth: Penguin Books, 1954], p. 286).

prevent further losses, the resident canons divided the altar ornaments, copes, and other vestments among themselves in October.[11] In
1549 the Chapter of Westminster agreed to sell two lecterns of brass
and several candlesticks adorned with gilt angels "by cause they be
monymentes of Idolatre and supersticyon"; the proceeds of the sale
were to be spent on books for the cathedral library.[12] The conservative
dean of Wells, John Goodman, offered up four large brass candlesticks and two brass images of bishops but seems to have been able to
avert any thoroughgoing iconoclastic activity there for the time
being.[13]

WHAT threatened to be one of the heaviest blows of the century to
cathedral finance came late in 1547 with the act for the dissolution of
the chantries. After a stormy session, this was finally passed by Edward's first parliament on Christmas Eve.[14]

Previous discussion has shown how important the chantries were,
especially in cathedrals of the old foundation, where many of the vicars choral gained supplementary employment and badly needed income as chantry priests. The confiscation of chantry endowments
would severely reduce the revenues available to singing men just at
the time when they were being allowed to marry; many of them were
already experiencing financial pressures as they attempted to support
families in an era of rising prices on stipends that had been barely
adequate for celibate clerics.[15] There was even a threat to the continued existence of the organized colleges of vicars choral, which might
be suppressed along with the colleges of chantry priests.

Theologically the movement against chantries, indeed against all
prayers for the dead, can be traced back to Luther's doctrine of Justification by Faith, which had been accepted by many of the English
reformers. If salvation did depend solely upon one's faith, prayers for
the departed were of no avail; indeed they might be worse than useless, since they could create the illusion that salvation can be pur-

[11] H. E. Savage, *Lichfield Cathedral: The Cathedral and the Chapter, 1530–1553* (Lichfield: Johnson's Head, 1927), pp. 18–19.

[12] Act Book, 1542–1609, fol. 48, Westminster Abbey Library.

[13] L. S. Colchester, ed., *Wells Cathedral: A History* (Shepton Mallet: Open Books, 1982), p. 149, based on the fabric rolls.

[14] For an account of the act's passage, see Kreider, *English Chantries*, pp. 186–208.

[15] The conservative Act of Six Articles (1539), which insisted on the maintenance of celibacy, was repealed in 1547, and a further act passed in 1549 (2 & 3 Edw. 6, cap. 21) stated specifically that there was no impediment to the marriage of priests.

chased. Most of the reformers came to reject the doctrine of purgatory as being a popish invention, devised purely as a means of extracting money from the faithful. That some laymen, too, had come to reject prayers for the dead was made clear in a visitation at Gloucester in 1540, when one Humphrey Grynshall had affirmed "that there is no moo places wherein christen soules departed maye be, but only hell & heven, and therefore he sayde that he wolde haue no prayers sayde for his sowle when so euer he shall dye, . . . [for] suche prayers & suffragyes did nothinge prevayle nor helpe soules departed."[16]

The attack on chantries had begun in the last years of Henry's reign, when an act passed by Parliament in 1545 gave the government authority to dissolve chantries, colleges, hospitals, and guilds, just as it had done in the case of the monasteries.[17] This act, which was justified in terms of financial necessity rather than theology, was applied selectively, only a few chantries actually being suppressed by 1547. Because the power to appoint commissioners and confiscate properties was thought to lapse with the old king's death, a new bill was put before Parliament in 1547, this time adorned with a preamble alleging that "a great part of superstition and errors in Christian religion hath been brought into the minds and estimation of men by reason of the ignorance of their very true and perfect salvation through the death of Jesus Christ, and by devising and phantasying vain opinions of purgatory and masses satisfactory to be done for them which be departed." The act then speaks of the king's desire to convert chantry endowments to more suitable educational and charitable purposes.[18]

Armed with this legislation, commissioners were once again sent around the country, this time to list all chantry foundations, set valuations on their endowments and fixed properties, and state whether the incumbent priests served any purpose other than that of memorializing the departed. The certificates of these commissioners were returned to two young financial administrators, Sir Walter Mildmay and Robert Keilway, who made the final decisions about confiscation, continuation, or reassignment of revenues and, through the Court of Augmentations, handled pensions for displaced priests.[19]

[16] Visitation Act Book of Bishop John Bell (ca. 1520–1541), B.A. 2764/802, fol. 137, Worcester Record Office.

[17] 37 Hen. 8, cap. 4; see Stanford E. Lehmberg, *The Later Parliaments of Henry VIII, 1536–1547* (Cambridge: Cambridge University Press, 1977), pp. 221–223.

[18] 1 Edw. 6, cap. 14.

[19] Cf. Stanford E. Lehmberg, *Sir Walter Mildmay and Tudor Government* (Austin: University of Texas Press, 1964), pp. 19–24; and Walter C. Richardson, *History of the Court of Augmentations, 1536–1554* (Baton Rouge: Louisiana State University Press, 1961), pp.

Although surviving documentation is incomplete and ambiguous, it appears that in fact some cathedrals succeeded in retaining chantry endowments, now turning the revenues to the support of cathedral services rather than prayers for the dead. The commissioners who reported on the situation at York in 1546 had been very generous, even recommending that the College of St. William, which housed twenty-four chantry priests, should be allowed to continue as a residence for the petty canons who would still minister in the choir and say mass at their several altars.[20] A second set of reports, submitted in 1548, also proposes the exemption of many cathedral properties. In the end, St. William's College was confiscated and the property sold in 1549.[21] But the Bedern, or college of vicars choral, was allowed to remain; its continuation was ratified by the government in 1552.[22] Some chantry properties "annexyd to the same vicares choralles, and always used and taken for parcell of th'augmentacion of theyre lyvyng" may have been retained as well. The total revenues of the chantries at York, after some deductions were allowed, were given by the commissioners as £627. Even if all of these were confiscated, the sum was not large in comparison to the total income of the cathedral, which had been stated as £2,455 in the *Valor Ecclesiasticus*.[23]

At Chichester there is an Elizabethan list of the cathedral chantries that had not suffered expropriation, together with a note that states that the Edwardian statute did not apply to the endowments of chantries within the cathedrals so long as these were used for the maintenance of services.[24] Ironically, the vicars choral of Lichfield had sought a charter of incorporation in 1528, but without success. Had it been

---

170–177. The certificates of the chantry commissioners are in E 319/1, files 1–25 and rolls 1–14, PRO.

[20] William Page, ed., *The Certificates of the Commissioners Appointed to Survey the Chantries, Guilds, Hospitals, etc., in the County of York*, 2 vols., Surtees Society, nos. 91–92 (Durham, 1894–1895), 1: 7–41.

[21] Ibid., 2: 428–450. See also D. M. Palliser, *The Reformation in York, 1534–1553* (York: St. Anthony's Press, 1971), pp. 24–25; Claire Cross, "Priests into Ministers: The Establishment of Protestant Practice in the City of York, 1530–1630," in *Reformation Principle and Practice*, ed. Peter Brooks (London: Scolar Press, 1980), p. 213; Frederick Harrison, *Life in a Medieval College: The Story of the Vicars-Choral of York Minster* (London: John Murray, 1952), pp. 194–205. At least twenty chantry priests at York lost their jobs; the more fortunate were able to move to appointments in parish churches within the city; see Claire Cross, *York Clergy Wills 1520–1600: I. Minster Clergy* (York: Borthwick Institute, 1984), p. ix.

[22] The document is printed in Frederick Harrison, *Medieval College*, pp. 203–204.

[23] See above, Chapter 1. The government did confiscate a good deal of plate, mainly chalices, which had been used in the chantries and in the Bedern; see William Page, ed., *The Inventories of Church Goods for the Counties of York, Durham, and Northumberland*, Surtees Society, no. 97 (Durham, 1897), pp. 115–116.

[24] Cap. 1/4/7/9, West Sussex Record Office.

granted, their college might have been dissolved. As it was, the Court of Augmentations ruled that the vicars choral were not independent but part of the cathedral community, and they escaped trouble.[25] At Hereford, too, the vicars choral were able to claim that their endowments (and the choristers') formed an integral part of the cathedral establishment. This was later confirmed by a royal charter granted in 1587.[26]

At Lincoln the number of senior or priest vicars seems to have fallen from twenty-five to twelve at about this time, although there is no mention of such a reduction in the chapter acts. Four vicars choral were granted annuities and presumably pensioned off in 1549.[27] But it is not certain that these changes had anything to do with the dissolution of the chantries; the number of young men who sought ordination had been declining since the 1530s, and a general movement toward lay vicars is a more likely explanation.

One suspects that a number of the cathedrals found themselves in the same situation as Exeter. Here it was held that the cathedral's chantry property did fall within the scope of the chantry act, so it was seized by the Crown. All the chantry priests, or annuellars, were pensioned off. But little of the property was actually alienated during Edward's reign, and most of the endowments were eventually returned to the cathedral in exchange for an annual payment of £145. Queen Elizabeth confirmed such a grant in 1585.[28]

In the end, then, it seems likely that most cathedrals survived the dissolution of the chantries without catastrophic blows to their revenues or disastrous losses of personnel. Nowhere were the vicars choral forced to vacate their courts or closes. Chantry priests in the cathedrals were less likely to be involved in teaching than those attached to parish churches, so the grammar schools associated with the cathedrals do not seem to have suffered.[29] Obviously there were changes, often quite visible: the chantry chapels, many of them great architectural monuments, stood empty, despoiled of their ornaments. Cathe-

[25] Savage, *Lichfield Cathedral*, p. 19.
[26] Archives 4254, Hereford Cathedral Library.
[27] R.E.G. Cole, ed., *Chapter Acts of the Cathedral Church of St. Mary of Lincoln, A.D. 1547–1559*, Lincoln Record Society, no. 15 (Horncastle, 1920), pp. xxiii, 40.
[28] Nicholas Orme, "The Dissolution of the Chantries in Devon, 1546–8," *Transactions of the Devonshire Association for the Advancement of Science* 111 (1979): 84; idem "The Medieval Clergy of Exeter Cathedral: I. The Vicars and Annuellars," in ibid., 113 (1981): 99.
[29] There has been considerable debate among historians regarding the effect of the dissolution of the chantries on education. For opposing views, see A. F. Leach, *English Schools at the Reformation, 1546–1548* (London: Constable, 1896); Joan Simon, *Education and Society in Tudor England* (Cambridge: Cambridge University Press, 1966), esp. pp. 223–244.

drals came to operate with smaller staffs, as those chantry priests who held no other office departed. Many of their young assistants, the poor clerks or secondaries, also disappeared from the scene, although a number of them received stipends to remain as students in the cathedral schools. Prayers for the departed no longer formed one of the reasons for the existence of the cathedrals or one of their ties to local families that had founded chantries or endowed obits. Even those who applauded the end of belief in purgatory and "masses satisfactory" may have felt passing melancholy at the thought that the great men and women of earlier ages now had no memorial.[30]

A RENEWED campaign of iconoclasm was ushered in by the dissolution of the chantries. In virtually every cathedral one can find a chantry chapel that suffered mutilation. Dates are seldom recorded, but spoliation at the time of the dissolution seems most likely. There was probably considerable local variation in the timing and the severity of the destruction.

Possibly the most interesting instance, and one that is important because of its royal connotations, is provided by Prince Arthur's chantry at Worcester. Here the body of Henry VIII's older brother was entombed soon after Arthur's death at Ludlow in 1502. The chantry chapel, which stands to the right of the high altar, was erected by Henry VII; its exterior is decorated with heraldic devices illustrating the union of the houses of Lancaster and York. In addition, there are symbols of Arthur's wife, Catherine of Aragon: the bunch of arrows emblematic of Catherine's mother, Isabella, and the pomegranate of Granada, Catherine's former home. The arms of England and France are supported by the greyhound and the Welsh dragon of Cadwallader. The garter, the Tudor rose and portcullis, and the ostrich feathers of the Prince of Wales are also represented in stone (see fig. 28).

Inside the small chapel itself, an altar is surmounted by a reredos bearing five large statues (fig. 29). The central figure is a Christ of pity,

---

[30] The dissolution of the chantries in the church generally (there is no specific reference to the cathedrals) has been studied with some care by W. K. Jordan, *Edward VI: The Threshold of Power* (London: George Allen and Unwin, 1970), pp. 181–203. Here as elsewhere, Jordan's view of the chantries is excessively negative; he held that the chantries "were in fact not institutions making any significant charitable contribution. . . . One can . . . argue with considerable force that a chantry endowment was by definition the most narrowly selfish of all possible outlays" (p. 197). See also Kreider, *English Chantries*, and K. L. Wood-Legh, *Perpetual Chantries in Britain* (Cambridge: Cambridge University Press, 1965).

28. Prince Arthur's Chantry, Worcester Cathedral, showing
symbols of the Tudors and of Catherine of Aragon.

supported by angels. St. George and the Dragon are depicted at the
south end, and the two crowned figures are probably Edward the Confessor and Edmund, King and Martyr. The figure at the extreme
north, carrying a long scroll, remains unidentified. Between these
large statues are four small representations of saints; the upper pair
are bishops, one of them probably Becket, while the lower two are
ladies, undoubtedly St. Margaret and possibly either St. Catherine or
Elizabeth of Hungary. All of these exquisite carvings were defaced,
most likely in 1548. It is possible that animosity against Catherine of
Aragon as a staunch Catholic was coupled with distaste for chantries
as a motive for this work. Many of the eighty-eight small statues, how-

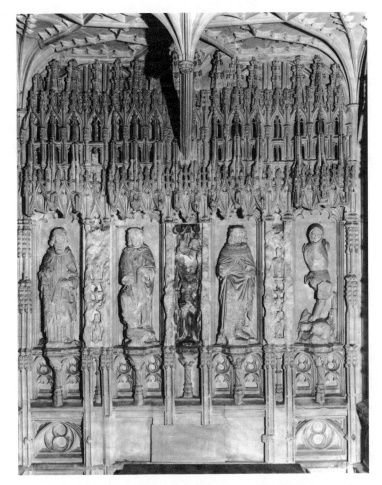

29. Prince Arthur's Chantry, Worcester Cathedral,
reredos with mutilated figures.

ever, escaped the hammer and chisel and remain as beautiful examples of the Tudor mason's craft.[31]

Prior to Queen Elizabeth's visit in 1575, the east wall of the chapel
was plastered over to conceal the mutilated statues, and the royal arms
and "Vivat Regina" were painted there. Only in 1788 was the plaster
removed. Here in microcosm we see a representation of the last years
of chantries and of their destruction.

[31] I am indebted to Pamela Tudor-Craig, Lady Wedgwood, for assistance with the iconography of the reredos.

111

At Wells the elaborate cruciform Lady Chapel that had been built by Bishop Stillington less than a century earlier was demolished. It had lost its revenues to the chantry commissioners, and in 1552 it was made over to Sir John Gate, the king's collector of lead, who not only stripped off the roof but took down the entire building. According to John Harington, "such was their thirst after lead (I would they had drunke it scalding) that they tooke the dead bodies of Bishops out of their leaden coffins, and cast abroad the carkases skarce throughly putrified."[32] A bit earlier the chronicler John Stowe recorded a peculiar bit of demolition at St. Paul's, the destruction of a cloister that must have resembled the famous Campo Santo of Pisa. In 1549

> the cloister of Paul's church in London, called pardon churchyard, with the dance of death, commonly called the dance of Paul's about the same cloister costly and cunningly wrought, and the chapel in the midst of the same churchyard were begun to be pulled down. Also the charnel-house of Paul's with the chapel there (after the tombs and other monuments of the dead were pulled down, and the dead men's bones buried in the fields) were converted into dwelling houses and shops.[33]

THE most positive aspect of religious change under Edward VI was the introduction of the Book of Common Prayer. As has been noted, Cranmer wished to have the people worship in their own tongue, not in an ancient language that only the learned could understand. His English Litany had foreshadowed a liturgical revolution even before the death of Henry VIII. With the accession of Edward VI, and with a political leader like Protector Somerset who shared his desire for reform, the archbishop was free to proceed rapidly. He was probably already at work on the first Book of Common Prayer in 1547 and was able to see it through the press and into use throughout the church by 1549.[34]

There had been some experimentation with the use of English in

[32] John Harington, *Nugae Antiquae*, quoted in Colchester, *Wells*, p. 151. See also Warwick Rodwell, *Wells Cathedral: Excavations and Discoveries* (Wells: Friends of Wells Cathedral, 1979), pp. 11–12.

[33] Quoted in Barrett L. Beer, "John Stowe and the English Reformation, 1547–1559," *Sixteenth Century Journal* 16 (1985): 261.

[34] The texts of the Prayer Books of 1549 and 1552 are conveniently available in *The First and Second Prayer Books of Edward VI* (London: Everyman's Library, 1910). The standard history of the Prayer Book is Francis Procter and W. H. Frere, *A New History of the Book of Common Prayer* (London: Macmillan, 1902).

services other than the Litany ever since the beginning of the new reign. On Easter Monday, 1547, compline was sung in English at the Chapel Royal.[35] Westminster Abbey, no doubt because of its close connection with Parliament and the Crown, was a center for trial usages. We know that the Gloria in Excelsis, the Credo, Sanctus, Benedictus, and Agnus Dei were all sung in English at the mass that marked the beginning of Parliament in November 1547. A similar polyglot service was held to celebrate Henry VIII's obit in May 1548.[36] The musical settings used for these sung portions of the mass may survive in the so-called Wanley Part Books, where a few of the texts clearly antedate the Prayer Book versions.[37]

At St. Paul's the Epistle and Gospel, as well as the Litany, were read in English in February 1548; the Chronicle of the Grey Friars says that "after Ester beganne the servis in Ynglyche at Powles at the commandment of the dene at the tyme, William May."[38] At Lincoln the Injunctions of 1548 directed:

> They shall from hensforthe synge or say no Anthemes off our lady or other saynts but only of our lorde, And them not in laten but choseyng owte the best and moste soundyng to cristen religion they shall turne the same into Englishe, settyng therunto a playn and distincte note, for euery sillable one, they shall singe them and none other.[39]

The legal basis for the use of the English Prayer Book was laid by the Act of Uniformity passed early in 1549 by Edward's second parliament. Here the preamble noted that the medieval English church had not possessed a common liturgy, for there were local variations, including the uses of York, Bangor, and Lincoln as well as Salisbury, home of the Sarum rite, which enjoyed the greatest popularity. Further alternate forms had crept in during recent years, as reformers

[35] Henry Bradshaw and Christopher Wordsworth, eds., *Statutes of Lincoln Cathedral*, 2 vols. (Cambridge: Cambridge University Press, 1892, 1897), 2: 855.

[36] Charles Wriothesley, *A Chronicle of England*, 2 vols., Camden Society, vol. 1: n.s. 11 (London, 1875); vol. 2: n.s. 20 (London 1877), 1: 187; 2: 2. Cf. C. S. Knighton, "Collegiate Foundations, 1540 to 1570, with Special Reference to St. Peter in Westminster" (Ph.D. thesis, Cambridge University, 1975), pp. 126–27.

[37] See Peter Le Huray, *Music and the Reformation in England, 1549–1660* (London: Herbert Jenkins, 1967), pp. 172–181. Another early Edwardian reform, involving actions rather than words, permitted lay people to receive Communion in both kinds, ending the normal medieval practice of withholding the cup from the laity. This was the subject of a statute (1 Edw. 6, cap. 1) and a proclamation (Hughes and Larkin, *Proclamations*, 1: 417–418).

[38] Nichols, *Chronicle of the Grey Friars*, p. 55.

[39] Bradshaw and Wordsworth, *Statutes of Lincoln*, 2: 592.

began to use new liturgies despite the government's warning that these should not be introduced until a common order was provided. Now, to end these differences and divisions, the Book of Common Prayer was to be published and to be used uniformly throughout the realm.[40]

The Act of Uniformity mandated the introduction of the Prayer Book by the Feast of Pentecost, which in 1549 fell on June 9. But copies of the book seem to have been available earlier, at least in London, and in some places the new services came into use before Easter. The last Latin mass at St. Paul's was sung on the second Sunday in Lent; Coverdale preached, and after the service, the dean "commandyd the sacrament at the hye autre to be pullyd downe."[41]

Once the Prayer Book was in use the continued performance of Latin services became illegal, except in cases where people were familiar with the tongue. (This allowed the continued use of Latin in college chapels.) To ensure that old service books were abandoned, the government ordered their destruction; a proclamation issued on Christmas Day, 1549, commanded subjects to give up any hope that the Latin services would ever be brought back (for they were "but a preferring of ignorance to knowledge and darkness to light"). The old books, including "all antiphoners, missales, grayles, processionales, manuelles, legendes, pies, portiases, journalles, and ordinalles," were to be delivered into the hands of the bishops, who were directed to destroy or deface them.[42]

The relatively small number of service books that survives testifies to the success of this campaign. Among the lost volumes were many that included illuminated initials or musical settings. In a few cases manuscripts were sold, not for their contents but for the parchment that could be used in stiffening bindings.[43] The books that remain were probably hidden away in 1549; these include the famous Worcester Antiphoner, which contains the music for a whole range of services, another manuscript antiphoner from Gloucester, the Winches-

---

[40] 2 & 3 Edw. 6, cap. 1. Jordan has a careful account of the act's consideration by Parliament (*Young King*, pp. 313–318). It is particularly interesting to note that the principal opposition to the bill came from the conservative bishops in the House of Lords, eight of whom voted against the measure.

[41] Nichols, *Chronicle of the Grey Friars*, p. 58.

[42] Bradshaw and Wordsworth, *Statutes of Lincoln*, 2: 856; Hughes and Larkin, *Proclamations*, 1: 485–486, where several of these words are given inappropriate modern equivalents.

[43] We know that this happened at Lichfield, where old choir books were sold for 2 marks in 1550; see Savage, *Lichfield Cathedral*, p. 20; and Act Book 4, fol. 158, Lichfield Joint Record Office.

ter Troper, an antiphoner and a gradual from Salisbury, and a missal according to the use of Hereford, printed in 1502.[44]

There must have been an urgent scramble to provide suitable musical settings for the new English services. Occasionally this is reflected in the financial records of the cathedrals. At Canterbury, for instance, twenty-six "psalters of the gretter sort for the quere" were purchased in 1550.[45] Psalters were also bought at Chester.[46] At Wells the organist, William Parsons, was given 16s. 4d. "for divers songs and books by him made and to be made."[47] Expenses at Christ Church, Oxford, included 12s. 8d. for ten Psalters as well as 2s. 8d. "for pryckyng of the buriall seruice eight tymes in sundry places," while the Dean and Chapter of York paid 4s. 4d. for a service book in 1551.[48]

In 1550 John Marbeck, the firmly Protestant organist of St. George's, Windsor, published his *Boke of Common Praier Noted*, in which simplified plainsong—unison and monosyllabic—was set to the new English texts. The Edwardian church was fortunate in its composers; among those writing English church music at this time were Christopher Tye, Thomas Tallis, William Mundy, John Shepherd, Richard Farrant, and Osbert Parsley, all of whom are still represented in the repertory of cathedral choirs. Nevertheless it must have been difficult throughout Edward's reign to perform the new services with dignity and artistic integrity; not until the Elizabethan church became firmly established would adequate musical settings be readily available. Despite proclamations and injunctions to the contrary, Latin anthems, if not Latin settings of the mass or of the canticles for morning and evening prayer, must still have been used in many cathedrals, particularly those with conservative deans and bishops, located in remote areas. Even in London there may have been diversity in musical practice just as there was about holy days—the Grey Friars' Chronicle testifies that "at the Assumpcion of our Lady was soche devision thorrow alle Lon-

[44] W. H. Frere studied several of these manuscripts; see *The Winchester Troper* (London: Harrison, 1894), *Antiphonale Sarisburiense* (London: Plainsong and Medieval Music Society, 1902), and *Graduale Sarisburiense* (London: B. Quaritch, 1894); The Worcester volume is in the cathedral library there; the Gloucester manuscript has migrated to Jesus College, Oxford; the Hereford missal, which includes some plainsong, is in the Gloucester Cathedral Library. Additional service books that survive are listed in N. R. Ker, *Medieval Manuscripts in British Libraries*, 2 vols. (Oxford: Clarendon Press, 1969).

[45] MS. M.A. 40 (not paginated), Canterbury Cathedral Library.

[46] Account Book 1, fol. 210, Chester Cathedral Archives.

[47] HMC, *Calendar of the Manuscripts of the Dean and Chapter of Wells*, 2 vols. (London, 1907, 1914), 2: 274; Ledger Book E, Wells Cathedral Library. Cf. Le Huray, *Music and the Reformation*, pp. 377–378.

[48] Disbursement Book for 1548, Archives, Christ Church, Oxford; E1/82, York Minster Library.

don that some kepte holy day and some none. Almyghty God helpe it when hys wylle ys! for this was the second yere, and also the same devision was at the fest of the Nativitie of our Lady."[49]

ALTHOUGH the 1549 Prayer Book still referred to altars, the movement to demolish stone altars because of their association with the popish doctrines of transubstantiation and the mass as a sacrifice started almost immediately after its introduction. Thus began a further round of iconoclasm. In May 1550, less than a month after his installation as bishop of London, the reformer Nicholas Ridley ordered his clergy to remove their old altars, arguing that a table was "more meet" for the Lord's Supper. The required change was made at St. Paul's in June.[50] Later, in 1552, "alle the goodly stoneworke that stode behynde the hye alter," together with the seats of the priests and the dean and the subdean, was hacked away. Only a command from the council saved John of Gaunt's tomb from similar treatment.[51]

In November the council ordered all the bishops to follow Ridley's example. Most of them must have complied rapidly; we know that the removal of the altar at Hereford was undertaken in December 1550.[52] The Chester accounts for this year record the payment of 5s. 6½d. for taking down stone altars and 2s. 9d. for making a wooden communion table.[53] The bishop of Chichester, George Day, refused to enforce the removal of altars or to preach against them, although he would have been willing to see their form changed. He explained his precise position in a letter to William Cecil:

> I stick not at the alteration either of the usual form of the altar, either of the situation thereof, either of the matter (as stone or wood) whereof the altar was made, [for] I . . . take these things to be indifferent, and to be ordered by them that have authority.

[49] Nichols, *Chronicle of the Grey Friars*, p. 67.

[50] A. G. Dickens, *The English Reformation* (London: Batsford, 1964), p. 247. See also G.W.O. Addleshaw and Frederick Etchells, *The Architectural Setting of Anglican Worship* (London: Faber and Faber, 1947), pp. 22–29. I am grateful to Peter Burman for calling my attention to this source.

[51] Matthews and Atkins, *St. Paul's*, p. 127; Nichols, *Chronicle of the Grey Friars*, p. 70. Stowe confirms that the place "where the high altar stood, was broken down and all the choir thereabout" (Beer, "John Stowe," p. 264).

[52] Act Book 1, fol. 105, Hereford Cathedral Library.

[53] Account Book 1, fol. 210, Chester Cathedral Archives. When Laud set up a stone altar once again in 1635, it was discovered that the top of the old altar had been buried, not smashed, and could be reused; see R.V.H. Burne, *Chester Cathedral* (London: SPCK, 1958), pp. 118–119.

But the commandment, which was given to me to take down all altars within my diocese and in lieu of them to set up a table, implying in itself (as I take it) plain abolishment of the altar (both the name and the thing) from the use and ministration of the Holy Communion, I could not with my conscience then execute.[54]

When Day remained adamant, he was summoned to appear before the council, imprisoned in Fleet Prison, and ultimately deprived. At Worcester the choir stalls and bishop's throne were taken down in 1551, and further clearing out was undertaken by John Hooper, the zealous reformer who became bishop when the conservative Nicholas Heath was deprived. "Our Churche ys greatly defaced," the Dean and Chapter were later to write Cardinal Pole, "owr quear pulled down, owr belles and organns be broken, owr Altars and Chapelles are by Hoper violated and overthrowne."[55] Westminster Abbey, evidently suffering from the pressures of inflation, was forced to sell plate and ornaments in 1550 and again in 1552 in order to pay salaries.[56] Lawrence Stone has shown that whole shiploads of religious statuary were exported to France in the 1550s, and one of the illustrations in the 1570 edition of Foxe's *Book of Martyrs* (fig. 30) depicts just such a scene.[57]

The financial crisis in which the Edwardian government found itself was responsible for further losses and confiscations. In March 1550, "forasmuche as the Kinges Majestie had neede presently of a masse of mooney," it was ordered that commissioners be sent into every county to take into the king's hands such church plate as remained in the parishes and cathedrals.[58] In general the policy seems to have been to allow parish churches to retain a single chalice and paten, cathedrals being permitted to keep two.[59] In many cases actual expropriation did not take place until the last months of the young king's life and was in fact incomplete at the time of Mary's accession.[60]

[54] Quoted in Lacey Baldwin Smith, *Tudor Prelates and Politics* (Princeton: Princeton University Press, 1953), pp. 268–269, from Lansdowne MS. 11, no. 53, fol. 121, BL.

[55] MS. D.71, Worcester Cathedral Library; Michael Craze, *King's School, Worcester, 1541–1971* (Worcester: Baylis, 1972), p. 35; *VCH, Worcestershire*, 4: 396. The letter dates from about 1557.

[56] Knighton, "Collegiate Foundations," p. 127; Act Book, 1542–1609, fol. 72, Westminster Abbey Library.

[57] Lawrence Stone, *Sculpture in Britain: The Middle Ages* (Harmondsworth: Penguin Books, 1955), p. 1.

[58] *Acts of the Privy Council*, 32 vols. (London: HMSO, 1890–1907), n.s., 3: 228.

[59] We know, however, that Canterbury still had five in 1563; see C. E. Woodruff and William Danks, *Memorials of the Cathedral and Priory of Christ in Canterbury* (London: Chapman and Hall, 1912), p. 297.

[60] Jordan, *The Threshold of Power*, pp. 389–392.

30. Images being pulled down and burned or shipped abroad.
The lower scenes depict Edward VI and a simple
communion table as arranged during his reign.
Woodcut from John Foxe's *Book of Martyrs* (1570 ed.).

Often the commissioners did not limit themselves to removal of
plate; it was common for them to carry off vestments and other ornaments in addition. At Lichfield, the royal agents removed a large
number of vestments in January 1553, selling them for the meanest
price ("pro vilissimo pretio"). Later, in May, one of the commissioners
returned with a wagon and carried off the best copes and miters as
well as all the silver vessels, pouring the consecrated oil from three
cruets on the ground before the eyes of two horrified canons.[61]

The losses recorded at York are staggering, and must be typical of
those suffered at the greater cathedrals. Among the articles taken
away were chalices of gold and silver, bread boxes, censers, gold and
silver basins, sconces, cruets, paxes, pectoral crosses of gold and silver
set with precious stones, candlesticks, standing cups, and holy-water

[61] Savage, *Lichfield Cathedral*, pp. 21–22; Act Book 4, fols. 158–159, Lichfield Joint Record Office. This was not the only tragedy at Lichfield, for the bell tower had been shat-
tered by lightning in 1550.

pots; silver basins, ewers, goblets, and ale pots belonging to the individual canons; nearly fifty red and purple copes, dozens of green, blue, black, and white copes and sets of vestments, altar cloths and curtains, fringes, hangings, canopies, cloths of tissue, turkey carpets, and miters decorated with diamonds, sapphires, and pearls.[62]

At Chester, an example of a much poorer cathedral, the commissioners sent the best vestments to the King's Wardrobe and sold the rest for £5 11s. 3d. They left two chalices and patens, a pair of organs, and five bells; the government was distressed to learn that the Dean and Chapter had already sold another great bell and applied the money to their stipends, and that income from the sale of a cross and two silver censers had been used to pay for repairs to their houses.[63] It is tragic to think of the finest artistry of medieval gold- and silversmiths, now melted down and lost forever, and of the gorgeous embroidered vestments that might have been saved as a part of the country's artistic heritage even if there was no desire to have them worn by clergy in the reformed church.[64]

THE last great religious measure of Edward VI's reign was the introduction of the second Book of Common Prayer in 1552. By this time Protector Somerset had fallen and his place as chief minister had been taken by John Dudley, duke of Northumberland. Whatever Northumberland's religious views may have been—he is usually pictured as a *politique* but may in fact have been a convinced, advanced Protestant—Archbishop Cranmer retained his primacy in determining ecclesiastical policy, urged on more and more by the young king himself as Edward grew in years and in understanding of politics.

Cranmer seems to have been dissatisfied with his first Prayer Book soon after its introduction. Perhaps it never really represented his own

[62] Fabric Rolls, York Minster Library, cited in G. E. Aylmer and Reginald Cant, eds., *A History of York Minster* (Oxford: Clarendon Press, 1977), p. 200. An inventory of 1540 shows that Canterbury had a hundred white copes, fifty green ones, fifty red, and thirty-seven blue. Fifty of these, a surprisingly large number, still survived in 1563, as did eight out of forty chasubles (Woodruff and Danks, *Memorials of Canterbury*, pp. 297–298).

[63] Burne, *Chester Cathedral*, pp. 22–23.

[64] Cf. J. J. Scarisbrick, *The Reformation and the English People* (Oxford: Blackwell, 1984), pp. 85–108. The Syon Cope and other examples of "Opus Anglicanum" now displayed at the Victoria and Albert Museum give one some idea of what was lost, though few of the vestments can have been of this quality. Some vestments could have been turned into coverings for altars and holy tables; see Addleshaw and Etchells, *Architectural Setting*, p. 32. A medieval dalmatic at Rochester is one of the very few vestments to survive in the cathedrals themselves.

theological convictions: he may well have produced a more conservative and more ambiguous book than he wanted in the hope of avoiding dissension. Such zealous English reformers as Ridley and Hooper as well as Protestant émigrés from the Continent, among them Martin Bucer and Peter Martyr, soon convinced him that ambiguity was unacceptable in any cause as vital as religious belief. Hence the Prayer Book had to be revised, to eliminate any remaining hint of popish superstition and to make clear the Protestant complexion of the English church.

While there are numerous differences between the 1549 volume and its successor, the most significant can be found in the Communion service and in the funeral liturgy. Communion, no longer called the mass, is now celebrated in remembrance of the Last Supper, not because of Christ's sacrifice on the Cross, and belief in the Real Presence is no longer appropriate. All prayers for the dead are deleted from the burial office despite their acknowledged antiquity, a final acceptance of the logic behind Justification by Faith and the dissolution of the chantries.[65]

Use of the new Prayer Book beginning in November 1552 was ordered by a new Act of Uniformity.[66] This was carefully drafted so as to make it appear that the 1549 book had merely been revised, not supplanted because of inherent defects; the revision had been intended to remove "divers doubts for the fashion and manner of administration of the authorized worship" that had arisen, because of which "a great number of people, . . . following their own sensuality, and living without knowledge or due fear of God, do wilfully and damnably . . . refuse to come to their parish churches." Penalties are now prescribed for those who absent themselves from the authorized services and for any who persist in worshiping according to other rites.[67]

St. Paul's was one of the first cathedrals to bring in the new liturgy. The account in the Grey Friars' Chronicle emphasizes the simplified vestments that were required by a rubric in the new book—no albs or copes, but plain white surplices for priests and rochets for bishops.

Item on Alhallon day began the boke of the new servis of bred and wyne in Powlles, . . . and the byshoppe [Ridley] dyd the servis hymselfe, and prechyd in the qwere at the mornynge servis, and

[65] Cf. Jordan, *The Threshold of Power*, pp. 342–353; Dickens, *English Reformation*, pp. 247–249; Procter and Frere, *Book of Common Prayer*.
[66] 5 & 6 Edw. 6, cap. 1. Three lay peers and two bishops (Thirlby and Aldrich) voted against the act in the House of Lords.
[67] An associated act, 5 & 6 Edw. 6, cap. 3, specifies the holy days that are still to be kept and mandates continuation of fasting in Lent and on Fridays and Saturdays.

dyd it in a rochet and nothynge elles on hym. And the dene with alle the resydew of the prebentes went but in their surples and left of[f] their [h]abbet of the universyte [hoods]; and the byshope prechyd at afternone at Powlles crosse, and stode there tyll it was nere honde v. a cloke, and the mayer nor aldermen came not within Powlles church nor the crafftes as they were wonte to doo, for because they were soo w[e]ary of hys longe stondynge. . . .

Item after Allhollanday was no more communyon in no place but on the sondayes.[68]

Morning and evening prayer were now more important than the Eucharist, and preaching more vital than the sacraments.

Local sources tell little about the reception of the second Prayer Book. Several of its rubrics must have proved as important as its changes in wording. The destruction of altars is recognized by a rubric directing that the Lord's Supper shall be administered at a table covered with a fair white linen cloth, placed in the body of the church (the nave) or in the chancel, not necessarily where the old altar had been. The priest was directed to stand at the north side of the table, which would have been positioned with its longer dimension east and west, not "altar-wise" north and south; the priest's eastward stance, with his back to the congregation, was ruled out.

The order for simplified vestments reflected the reformers' dislike of the old, elaborate "popish rags" as well as the fact that most of these had already been confiscated or destroyed. Two more rubrics of some interest regulated the administration of the Communion. This was not to be celebrated unless four persons, or at least three, were present to communicate with the priest—there could be no more private masses, and there was obviously no expectation that every priest would celebrate daily. In cathedrals all priests and deacons were to receive Communion each Sunday, unless they had reasonable excuses; lay persons were to communicate at least three times a year, always including Easter. The famous Black Rubric, added by the council after the other rubrics had already been printed in red ink, stated that communicants should still kneel but that this was done for the preservation of order, not because anyone should adore or venerate the bread and wine.

As Edward's brief reign drew to its end the cathedrals, like the rest of the English church, reached the most Protestant point in their long

[68] Nichols, *Chronicle of the Grey Friars*, p. 76.

history. The sweeping reforms of these six years must have been be-
wildering in their rapidity and variety. No area was left untouched, as
change affected liturgy, theology, finance, staffing, living conditions,
music, vestments, images and ornaments, even the very altars at which
the sacred liturgy of the church had been celebrated time out of mind.
It would have taken years for most people to digest the reforms and
to gain an appreciation of the new manner of worship and belief presented by the Edwardian leaders. Alas for the reformers, this time was
not theirs. Edward was already ill when the new Prayer Book came
into use; he died on July 6, 1553, three months short of his seventeenth birthday. With him died the radical Protestant experiment in
the Anglican church and its cathedrals.

5

MARY TUDOR: THE CATHOLIC
REACTION

As HE lay dying Edward VI had accepted the so-called device for the succession presented to him by Northumberland and Cranmer. This would have guaranteed the continuation of Protestant practices by excluding both of Edward's half-sisters, Mary and Elizabeth, from succession and passing the throne instead to his cousin, Lady Jane Grey. But Lady Jane was scarcely known outside the closed circle of ministers and courtiers, while Mary was remembered as the older daughter of Henry VIII and the next in line for the crown according to Henry's will and an act of Parliament, as well as normal hereditary right. That she was an ardent Catholic who would be bound to rescind all the reforms of Edward's reign must have been generally understood but evidently seemed less important than adherence to the accepted order. So Jane found few supporters, and Mary was acknowledged to be the lawful sovereign on July 19, less than two weeks after Edward's death. Seldom has a change on the throne implied such a profound reaction for the church.

Mary's reign appeared to begin mildly, with a proclamation issued on August 18 acknowledging that she could not "hide that religion which God and the world knoweth she hath ever professed from her infancy hitherto." She would "be glad the same were of all her subjects quietly and charitably embraced," and yet "she mindeth not to compel any her said subjects thereunto unto such time as further order by common assent may be taken." So for the time being existing laws should be obeyed, and subjects should leave "those new-found devilish terms of papist or heretic, and such like; and . . . live in the fear of God."[1]

[1] Paul L. Hughes and James F. Larkin, eds., *Tudor Royal Proclamations*, 3 vols. (New Haven: Yale University Press, 1964–1969), 2: 5–8. The best general accounts of Mary's reign are D. M. Loades, *The Reign of Mary Tudor* (London: Macmillan, 1979); H.F.M. Prescott, *Mary Tudor* (London: Eyre and Spottiswoode, 1940); Jasper Ridley, *Mary Tudor* (London: Weidenfeld and Nicolson, 1973). For an account of these years by a distinguished Roman Catholic historian, see Philip Hughes, *The Reformation in England*, 3 vols. (London: Hollis and Carter, 1950–1954), 2: 181–330. Mary's bishops have been studied by Angelo J. Louisa, "The Marian Bishops: A Study of the Backgrounds and Ecclesiastical Activities of the Marian Episcopate" (Ph.D. diss., University of Minnesota, 1985).

Despite these conciliatory words the work of replacing Protestant leaders with those loyal to the old faith began almost immediately. Indeed it had already started, for Edmund Bonner, the former bishop of London, was released from prison on August 5; he made his way to St. Paul's dressed in full pontifical vestments, and (according to the Grey Friars' Chronicle) all the people bade him welcome. As many women as could kissed him. The cathedral's bells were rung for joy as the bishop knelt on its steps to pray.[2] His place in prison was taken by Richard Cox, the Protestant dean of Westminster, who was thus barred from officiating at Edward VI's funeral three days later.[3] Bishops Gardiner, Tunstall, Day, and Heath were shortly freed, as was the duke of Norfolk; Northumberland was beheaded, while Cranmer, Ridley, Latimer, and Barlow were sent to the Tower.

A revolution in personnel had thus taken place well before Mary's coronation, which was celebrated in Westminster Abbey on October 1. Gardiner officiated, joined by a large choir and as full a procession of mitered bishops as could be gathered; services at St. Paul's were suspended so that all might be present at the great event. The bishops of Lincoln and Hereford, John Taylor and John Harley, withdrew at the beginning of the mass, which they felt in conscience they could not attend.[4]

Mary's first parliament convened on October 5. The Convocation of the Clergy, always held concurrently, began on the seventh with a solemn Mass of the Holy Ghost sung in St. Paul's by Bishop Bonner. This was the first mass (the former Grey Friar noted) to be celebrated there since 1549, and the high altar was set up again for the occasion.[5] Parliament's main business was the passage of Mary's first Act of Repeal, which extinguished all the religious legislation of Edward's reign, thus disposing of the Prayer Book and officially bringing back the Latin services of the old church.[6] The change was to become effective on December 20, prior to Christmas but allowing some time for the gathering of missals and music books.

One of the Edwardian statutes now abrogated was that which permitted the marriage of the clergy. Since one of the queen's most firmly held beliefs demanded celibacy, the campaign against those who had

[2] J. G. Nichols, ed., *Chronicle of the Grey Friars of London*, Camden Society, no. 53 (London, 1852), p. 82.

[3] The service was conducted according to the 1552 Prayer Book, as Edward would have wished; Mary herself attended a private mass in the Tower.

[4] Both were deprived in 1554.

[5] J. G. Nichols, *Chronicle of the Grey Friars*, p. 85.

[6] The act is 1 Mary, sess. 2 (the second session of this Parliament began on 24 October, after a brief recess), cap. 1.

taken wives was fast and, probably, thorough.[7] The full effect of this action so far as the cathedral clergy are concerned will be considered later. Here a few examples will illustrate the magnitude of the issue. At Lichfield the dean, two prebendaries, and two vicars choral were deprived.[8] The married dean of Bangor was ejected. The dean of York remained in office, but seven married canons and three vicars choral were turned out.[9] At Hereford the precentor and three prebendaries were deprived, and there was trouble about the proposed admission of a chorister and, later, a vicar choral who acknowledged that they were the sons of priests.[10] The succentor of Salisbury was ousted in 1554, probably because of his marriage, and six prebendaries of Canterbury were deprived for this reason in 1553.[11]

A set of royal injunctions promulgated by proclamation in March 1554 ordered bishops and other appropriate officers to proceed "with all celerity and speed" in depriving those "who contrary to the state of their order and the laudable custom of the Church have married and used women as their wives, or otherwise notably and slanderously disordered or abused themselves." Moving on to ceremonies, the injunctions commanded the restoration of processions, holy days and fasting days, and in general the "laudable and honest ceremonies which were wont to be used" in the church.[12]

MANY of the cathedral clergy and musicians—those who had reluctantly acquiesced in the changes of Edward's reign as well as the conservatives once ejected and now restored—must have welcomed the return of traditional forms of worship. We know, for instance, that a splendid procession was held in 1554 at St. Paul's to honor St. Paul's Day, January 25. Fifty priests were clad in copes of cloth of gold,

[7] We are not sure of the overall effects of the deprivation, for full statistics are available only for London and Norwich. In these dioceses a quarter of the clergy lost their livings. See Loades, *Mary Tudor*, p. 157.

[8] H. E. Savage, *Lichfield Cathedral: The Cathedral and the Chapter, 1530–1553* (Lichfield: Johnson's Head, 1927), p. 17.

[9] A. G. Dickens, *The Marian Reaction in the Diocese of York* (York: Borthwick Institute, 1957), pt. 1, pp. 23–29; G. E. Aylmer and Reginald Cant, eds., *A History of York Minster* (Oxford: Clarendon Press, 1977), p. 202.

[10] Act Book 1, fols. 125, 148, 154, Hereford Cathedral Library.

[11] Act Book, MS. 80, fol. 42, Salisbury Cathedral Library; C. E. Woodruff and William Danks, *Memorials of the Cathedral and Priory of Christ in Canterbury* (London: Chapman and Hall, 1912), p. 297.

[12] Hughes and Larkin, *Proclamations*, 2: 37.

somehow found for the occasion; all sang the traditional processional hymn "Salve Festa Dies."[13]

Even grander ceremonial marked the queen's marriage to Philip II of Spain. This was solemnized by Bishop Gardiner in his own cathedral at Winchester, not at Westminster Abbey: it may be that disruptions were feared in London, which had already been the scene of a rebellion protesting the Spanish alliance,[14] but it is also possible that Winchester was thought to be more convenient because of its proximity to Southampton, where Philip landed, and because of its association with Gardiner. Philip was initially welcomed to Winchester on July 23, 1554; there was a procession of civic and ecclesiastical dignitaries, and the choir sang a Te Deum. The wedding itself was held two days later, on St. James's Day, a date chosen to honor the patron saint of Spain.

The cathedral had been prepared most elaborately for the event. A scaffold had been erected, three feet high, running down the length of the nave. Flanking this, twelve Flemish tapestries were suspended from hooks on the nave pillars; these had just been woven to commemorate the victory of Philip's father, Charles V, over the infidel at Tunis in 1535. Five bishops in full pontificals and the combined choirs of the English and Spanish royal chapels as well as the cathedral choir helped lend splendor to the occasion. There were also ceremonial trumpeters. Just before the ceremony began a herald announced that Philip had been created king of Naples (he had not yet inherited the Spanish crown), so that the marriage could unite sovereigns of equal rank.[15] Large numbers of Spanish grandees, as well as English noblemen, attended.[16]

In London, bells were rung and bonfires lighted to celebrate the union. A few days later the king and queen made their ceremonial entry into the capital, where pageants and displays had been prepared along the royal route. This was the famous occasion on which a painter depicted Henry VIII holding a volume inscribed *Verbum Dei* (the Word of God); when some functionary realized that the Catholic rulers might be distressed by this reference to Henry's religion, the

[13] H. H. Milman, *Annals of St. Paul's Cathedral* (London: John Murray, 1868), pp. 233–239.

[14] This was Wyatt's Rebellion; see D. M. Loades, *Two Tudor Conspiracies* (Cambridge: Cambridge University Press, 1965), as well as idem, *Mary Tudor*, pp. 124–129.

[15] As a king Philip was entitled to have a sword carried in front of him, and there was some delay in the service while one was found.

[16] J. G. Nichols, ed., *The Chronicle of Queen Jane and Queen Mary*, Camden Society, no. 48 (London, 1850), pp. 167–172; Frederick Bussby, *Winchester Cathedral, 1079–1979* (Winchester: Paul Cave, 1979), pp. 100–104. Following the wedding the tapestries were sent to Spain, where they survive.

sign painter was summoned, interrogated, and finally made to paint a pair of gloves over the offending book.[17] A Te Deum was again sung at St. Paul's. On St. Luke's Day (October 18) Philip returned to the cathedral to hear mass sung by a Spanish priest. By this time the rood had been reinstated.[18]

With Philip at her side, Mary was ready for the final stages in the restoration of the Catholic faith. The parliament that met in November 1554 passed a second Act of Revocation, annulling all the religious legislation of Henry VIII's reign, back to the beginning of the Reformation Parliament in 1529.[19] This very long bill confirmed the confiscations of Henry and Edward, so that persons who had acquired church lands need not fear that they would lose their property. It also acknowledged the existence of Henry VIII's new bishoprics. The charge of treason that had been laid by Henry against his Catholic kinsman Cardinal Pole was now lifted, in order that Pole could enter England again after his long exile in Italy and assume the post of archbishop of Canterbury to which Mary intended to name him once Cranmer had been deprived.

Pole's arrival and his ceremonial absolution of the entire realm from the sins of heresy and schism that had been committed in the years since 1533 provided the occasion for what must have been the most splendid and, for some, the most moving event of the century at St. Paul's. On December 2, the second Sunday in Advent, the king and cardinal attended high mass. The mayor, alderman, and members of the City guilds were present in their finest liveries, as were a hundred English, a hundred Spanish, and a hundred German guards of honor. The choir of the Chapel Royal joined the musicians from the cathedral in singing the service. It is said that such an audience was never before seen at St. Paul's, and that all listened in profound silence as Gardiner preached on the text, "Brethren, now is the time to awake out of sleep."[20]

THE work of refurbishing cathedrals, providing ornaments appropriate for Catholic worship, and restoring old customs proceeded rapidly and has left traces in most of the surviving accounts or chapter act books. The queen herself gave jewels for a new screen at Westminster

[17] J. G. Nichols, *Queen Jane and Queen Mary*, pp. 78–79.
[18] J. G. Nichols, *Chronicle of the Grey Friars*, p. 91; W. R. Matthews and W. M. Atkins, eds., *A History of St. Paul's Cathedral* (London: John Baker, 1957), p. 128.
[19] 1 & 2 Phil. & M., cap. 8.
[20] Matthews and Atkins, *St. Paul's*, p. 130.

Abbey.[21] Eight stops were added to the organ there, some new music was written for the coronation, and old service books were bought back from singing men who had taken them away during Edward's reign. Five quarts of muscatel were provided "accordyng to the old custome" for the choir and readers of the Passion on Palm Sunday, 1555, when candles, incense, and baskets of flowers to be strewn by the choristers were also purchased.[22]

The accounts for Canterbury list an exceptionally large number of expenses associated with the revival of traditional worship. Missals, psalters, antiphoners, ordinals, pontificals, and other service books were acquired, some of them in London. John Marden, a singing man, was paid for "pricking" a Gloria in Excelsis, Sanctus, and Agnus Dei. His colleague, Robert Colman, received 5s. "for prycking of four bookes to set forthe the olde Seruice," while a priest, George Frevell, was given 12d. for writing out a legend of St. Thomas. A new organ was erected in the Lady Chapel, and other organs were repaired with calf skins and glue for their bellows. A chalice and paten, cruet, pax, monstrance, and Sanctus bell were provided. Among the new vestments and hangings were copes, tunicles, albs, and frontals (with fringe). A new rood was made, with statues of Mary and John as well as Christ on the Cross, all painted and gilded. The Easter sepulcher and paschal candle were reinstated.[23]

Some of the refurbishing at Canterbury was probably undertaken in preparation for a visit by the queen and Cardinal Pole in 1557. Additional organs appear to have been borrowed for this great occasion, since four laborers were paid 8d. "for feching and carydg of a paire of organs from St. Georges & thether againe." When the queen departed she was given £10 in a purse of crimson velvet ornamented with gold and lace. Perhaps it was at this time that Pole presented a gold and silver miter to his cathedral church. He also fitted up the old almonry chapel for his private use.[24]

York was fortunate in receiving ornaments as gifts. In 1556 an alderman, George Gale, provided money for an altar frontal of purple,

[21] C. S. Knighton, "Collegiate Foundations, 1540 to 1570, with Special Reference to St. Peter in Westminster" (Ph.D. thesis, Cambridge University, 1975), pp. 147–148.

[22] Ibid., p. 150; WAM 37437, 37634, 37646B, Westminster Abbey Library.

[23] MSS. M.A. 39, 40, accounts for 1553–1558 (not paginated), Canterbury Cathedral Library. It is interesting to note that one of Pole's articles of inquiry directed in 1557 to all churches within the diocese of Canterbury asked whether the buildings were sufficiently garnished and adorned, and specifically whether there was a rood with representations of Mary and John. See W. H. Frere and W. M. Kennedy, eds., *Visitation Articles and Injunctions*, 3 vols., Alcuin Club, nos. 14–16 (London, 1910), 2: 424.

[24] Woodruff and Danks, *St. Paul's*, pp. 302–303.

red, and blue velvet with the Resurrection embroidered on it in gold, and a year later Sir Leonard Beckwith presented a red and green canopy under which the Sacrament might be carried in procession. The cathedral's own funds paid for repainting the high altar and replacing statues of the Virgin and St. John, presumably as a rood loft. The fabric rolls record the payment of 4s. 8d. for old glass, probably panels that had been removed from the windows because they contained images but had been hidden away to avoid destruction. Some of the windows were releaded, and 4d. was paid "for settinge uppe of an ymage." Other expenses include making a tabernacle and scouring candlesticks.[25]

At Wells fourteen great tapers were supplied for the Easter sepulcher at a cost of 2s. 8d., while £18 was paid to Richard Roberts of London, probably an embroiderer, for twelve silk copes and six dalmatics and tunicles.[26] The Dean and Chapter of Chichester bought copes, tunicles, albs, antiphoners, processionals, hymnals, and books of music for the Lady Chapel; they paid for repairing bells and raising and lowering the great paschal candle.[27] Although no local records provide proof, it may be that some cathedrals were able to take back gold copes and other vestments that were still stored at Whitehall, for Machyn's diary says that the "good qwyne Mare" ordered them to be returned to churches that could identify their former property.[28]

It appears that some service books, a chasuble, two tunicles of blue velvet, and a needlework cushion had been hidden away at Lichfield; they were now returned to the cathedral.[29] The dean of Hereford presented a new cope to his church—probably quite a plain one, since it cost only 40s.[30] At Chester, a conservative cathedral where the return to the old religion was generally welcomed, twelve pounds of wax was provided for tapers at Candlemas, and wine and ale were allowed on Maundy Thursday; a painted cloth with velvet embroideries and silk fringe was placed on the Jesus altar (presumably the high altar), and a pax and censer were purchased for the altar dedicated to Our

[25] *The Fabric Rolls of York Minster*, Surtees Society, no. 35 (Durham, 1859), pp. 112–113; Aylmer and Cant, *York Minster*, p. 202.

[26] Communar's Paper Book, 1557–1558, Wells Cathedral Library; HMC, *Calendar of the Manuscripts of the Dean and Chapter of Wells*, 2 vols. (London, 1907, 1914), 2: 280–281; L. S. Colchester, ed., *Wells Cathedral: A History* (Shepton Mallet: Open Books, 1982), p. 151. Twenty-one yards of dowlas (a coarse linen) were also purchased, to be made up into albs.

[27] Cap. 1/23/3, fols. 1–23 (accounts for 1553–1558), West Sussex Record Office.

[28] J. G. Nichols, ed., *The Diary of Henry Machyn*, Camden Society, no. 42 (London, 1848), pp. 165–166.

[29] Act Book 4, fol. 158, Lichfield Joint Record Office.

[30] Act Book 1, fol. 142, Hereford Cathedral Library.

Lady.[31] At Durham, where the reconciliation with Rome was celebrated with feasting, bonfires, and minstrels, repairs were made to the
bells and windows, wainscot was placed around the altar, and a "cayse"
of ironwork was made for the Sacrament reserved there.[32]

MONASTIC life at Westminster Abbey was revived in 1556. For the first
three years of Mary's reign the Abbey had continued to operate as a
cathedral, sharing this status in the diocese of London with St. Paul's.
But Mary was personally devoted to the idea of religious orders; while
recognizing that it was impossible to reestablish all the monasteries or
to return the endowments confiscated from them, she was eager to see
the institution of monasticism reborn and to provide for the restoration of at least a few religious houses.[33]

On September 7, 1556, letters patent for the dissolution of the existing foundation at Westminster and the erection of the new abbey
were issued. The Dean and Chapter resigned on September 26, and
the monastery received its endowments on November 10. Additional
chalices, bells, and vestments were purchased, together with £40 worth
of choir books and £13 in missals and service manuals.[34] The singing
men and choristers remained, now probably performing services at
the high altar although they had sung only in the Lady Chapel prior
to the dissolution.

By the end of November 1556 about twenty-six monks had returned to the Abbey. Only two of them were from the old community
at Westminster; the others came from different Benedictine houses.
There were also at least two Cistercians and two Augustinian canons.
By the end of the reign some fifty men had come to the Abbey, and
several had died while wearing the habit. The Marian abbot, John
Feckenham, was a sincere and able man who had been sent to the

[31] R.V.H. Burne, *Chester Cathedral* (London: SPCK, 1958), p. 33, based on the account
book.

[32] ADD. MS. 31983, BL, a treasurer's book that has migrated from Durham (photostat in
the Prior's Kitchen, Durham); Treasurer's Book 1, fols. 18–20, Prior's Kitchen; David
Marcombe, "The Durham Dean and Chapter: Old Abbey Writ Large?" in *Continuity and
Change*, ed. Rosemary O'Day and Felicity Heal (Leicester: Leicester University Press,
1976), p. 129.

[33] Seven were actually reestablished; in addition to the Abbey, they were houses at
Greenwich (Franciscan Observants), St. Bartholomew's, Smithfield (Dominicans), Sheen
(Carthusians), Syon (Bridgettines), and King's Langley and Dartford (Dominican nuns).
See Dom David Knowles, *The Religious Orders in England*, 3 vols. (Cambridge: Cambridge
University Press, 1948, 1955, 1959), 3: 438–440; Louisa, "Marian Bishops," pp. 86, 99.

[34] WAM 37727, Westminster Abbey Library; Knighton. "Collegiate Foundations," pp.
154–164.

Tower during Edward's reign.[35] Freed by Mary, he was dean of St. Paul's during her earlier years on the throne and was well qualified to oversee the refounding of the monastery. But he was realistic and worldly, not a fanatic about monkish observances; many years later a writer who had known some of Feckenham's monks wrote that he did "not insist . . . much upon monastick regularities . . . but . . . contented himself to have sett up there a disciplin much like to that he saw observed in cathedral churches, as for the Divine Office; and as for other things he brought them to the laws and customs of colledges and inns of court."[36]

Some of the records for this period have been lost (or perhaps they were never generated by the monks), so we know relatively little about the exact state of affairs at the Abbey during the Marian restoration. C. S. Knighton, who has made a careful study of the history of the Abbey, thinks that the church was little affected by the changeover from secular to monastic status, and that most lay officials remained in place during the later years of Mary's reign.[37] It does appear, however, that the choir saw its worst days under Mary. There were only eight boys in 1553, and the allocation for choristers' expenses was reduced from £33 6s. 8d. to £27 18s. 4d. It was suggested that the number of lay singing men be cut in half, from twelve to six. This was not done, but the choir remained small, with only eight men and five boys at the time of Mary's death.[38] It would be interesting to know just how the polyphony of these trained voices was mixed with the plainsong chanted by the monks themselves, but the surviving sources do not say.

A SIGNIFICANT number of Protestants fled to the Continent during Mary's reign. Some, no doubt, feared persecution and possible death if they remained in England; others were moved by conscience and the determination to worship according to the dictates of a reformed church. In either case, the motives must have been strong, for the dis-

---

[35] Knowles, *Religious Orders*, 3: 424–441; Edward Carpenter, ed., *A House of Kings* (London: Westminster Abbey, 1972), pp. 121–126.

[36] *Memorials of Father Augustine Baker*, ed. J. McCann and R. H. Connolly, Catholic Record Society, no. 32 (London, 1933), pp. 95–96, quoted in Loades, *Mary Tudor*, p. 354.

[37] Knighton, "Collegiate Foundations," p. 164.

[38] Stanford E. Lehmberg, "The Reformation of Choirs: Cathedral Musical Establishments in Tudor England," in *Tudor Rule and Revolution*, ed. D. J. Guth and J. W. McKenna (Cambridge: Cambridge University Press, 1982), p. 59; WAM 33604, 37646B, 37716, 3319E, Westminster Abbey Library.

location of family life and the distress of financial uncertainty would have been enough to stay the fainthearted.

Nearly 800 Marian exiles can be traced. Of these, a number were wives, children, and servants; we have the names of 472 adult males, of whom 67 were priests.[39] In 1553 or shortly thereafter, 30 persons who had served the cathedrals in some capacity left England for Frankfort, Strasbourg, Geneva, Zurich, or some other refuge.

The exiles included six deans: Thomas Cole of Salisbury, Robert Horne of Durham, Thomas Sampson of Chichester, William Turner of Wells, Bartholomew Traheron of Chichester, and Richard Cox, who had held both Westminster and Oxford. Several of these, most notably Horne and Turner, were such radical Protestants that they had been involved in disputes with their own chapters prior to Mary's accession. The five exiled archdeacons included Thomas Cranmer's brother Edmund (who took the archbishop's son under his care), John Aylmer and Thomas Bullingham from the diocese of Lincoln, the future bishop John Jewel of Chichester, and Guy Heton of Gloucester.

Four of the eighteen exiled canons or prebendaries had held positions at Westminster (the group included a future archbishop, Edmund Grindal); there were also men from Canterbury, York, St. Paul's, Salisbury, Oxford, Lichfield, Peterborough (Edwin Sandys, the future archbishop of York), St. David's (Thomas Young, the precentor and effective head of the cathedral), and Wells (William Thynne, brother of Sir John, the builder of Longleat). Two of the six preachers who had been appointed according to the statutes at Canterbury fled (they were Richard Beeley and John Joseph). The roster of exiles was completed by Alexander Nowell, headmaster of Westminster School and future dean of St. Paul's, and, rather surprisingly, a former chantry priest, John Staunton from Hereford.[40]

PATHETIC as the plight of the exiles often was, the sufferings of those who were imprisoned and martyred were infinitely greater. In all,

[39] Christina H. Garrett, *The Marian Exiles* (Cambridge: Cambridge University Press, 1938), pp. 32, 41. In addition to the priests, Garrett identified 166 gentry, 119 theological students, and 79 merchants or artisans (including 7 printers).

[40] List compiled from ibid., pp. 67–349, where biographical information about these men will be found. Garrett did not list John Emmanuel Tremellius, canon of Carlisle, a converted Jew from Ferrara, possibly because he was not an Englishman, and she did not note that Gaius Dixon was a prebendary of Wells. It is interesting to see that Christ Church, Oxford, gave permission to two students (Thomas Randolph and Henry Daubeney) to study overseas during Mary's reign, while receiving their normal stipends from the college (Act Book, 1549–1619, fols. 89, 92, Christ Church Archives), although neither

about three hundred men and women were executed between February 1555 and November 1558, and others died in custody, sometimes of starvation. Although most of the martyrs were husbandmen or artisans—weavers, glovers, or shoemakers, for instance—a significant minority were priests, several of whom had held office in one of the cathedrals.

The best-known Marian victims were of course the bishops, especially the Oxford martyrs, Ridley and Latimer (who were burned together) and Cranmer.[41] Curiously enough, these three had no special connection with Oxford; all had been educated at Cambridge, and they had held other bishoprics. No doubt many who witnessed the emotional scenes of fervor and distress as these men went to the stake were moved, but it was not because they had known the victims.

The burning of John Hooper at Gloucester may have been different, for he had been a zealous and controversial leader there. Indeed, he had also served as bishop of Worcester, for the two sees were amalgamated in 1552, only to be separated again when Hooper was deprived in 1555. Hooper was the only bishop to be executed in the precincts of his own cathedral; he was sent to the stake under a great elm tree near the college of priests at Gloucester in 1555. The priests are said to have watched his execution from a chamber over the gatehouse.[42]

Robert Ferrar, who had been named to the Welsh see of St. David's when his friend William Barlow was translated to Bath and Wells, met his death in 1555 at Carmarthen, the market town to which Barlow had tried to move the cathedral. Like Barlow, Ferrar had quarreled bitterly with the chapter of St. David's; indeed, they had brought a suit against him and he had been imprisoned in 1552, partly because he had no friend at court after the fall of Protector Somerset. According to Foxe he died well, but since he did not speak Welsh, there were probably few who understood his last words, and there may have been some gloating among the conservatives at the fate of their antagonist.[43]

Some of the other bishops survived by going into exile; this group includes Ferrar's patron Barlow, John Ponet of Winchester, Miles Cov-

man held a cathedral appointment. Randolph is noted by Garrett (pp. 267–268) but Daubeney is not.

[41] See Loades, *The Oxford Martyrs* (New York: Stein and Day, 1970).

[42] John Foxe, *Acts and Monuments*, ed. S. R. Cattley, 8 vols. (London: Seeley and Burnside, 1838), 6: 636–675. See also F. Douglas Price, "Gloucester Diocese under Bishop Hooper, 1551–3," *Transactions of the Bristol and Gloucestershire Archaeological Society* 60 (1938): 51–151.

[43] Foxe, *Acts and Monuments*, 7: 1–27; Glanmor Williams, *Welsh Reformation Essays* (Cardiff: University of Wales Press, 1967), pp. 124–135.

erdale of Exeter, John Scory of Chichester, and Robert King, the first bishop of Oxford. Two others, John Taylor of Lincoln and Robert Holgate, archbishop of York, died before the persecution could reach them.

Among the cathedral canons to meet their deaths by execution, pride of place belongs to John Rogers, the earliest of all the victims of the Marian purge. A prebendary of St. Paul's, Rogers was especially disliked because of his association with Tyndale in preparing the English translation of the Bible; he was burned at Smithfield, not far from the cathedral, in 1555. John Bradford of St. Paul's was also executed there in 1555. Rowland Taylor, another prebendary of St. Paul's who is depicted by John Foxe as the "lively image or pattern of all those virtuous qualities described by St. Paul," had spent most of his ministry at Hadleigh in Essex and was executed on a nearby common. John Cardmaker, alias Taylor, a former friar who had married and become a prebendary of Wells, was consigned to the fires of Smithfield, while Laurence Saunders, a reader at Lichfield and prebendary of York, was burned in Coventry.

A number of the burnings of lay people took place in cathedral cities. Generally we do not know exactly where the fires were set, but since cathedral closes provided a suitable open space, it may be that many of the martyrs met death in the shade of cathedral towers. The persecution was largely concentrated in south and east England, so it is not surprising that there should have been large numbers of executions in Kent and East Anglia. Foxe tells of twenty-seven persons who were burned at Canterbury, where an additional five perished in prison. Two more were killed in Rochester. The deans of Ely and Norwich as well as Bishop Thirlby of Ely and his suffragan, Nicholas Shaxton, were active in prosecuting laymen and were responsible for two deaths at Ely and six at Norwich. Perhaps because the north and northwest were generally conservative areas, they remained relatively quiet. But seventeen Protestants were executed at Chichester, eleven at Lichfield, five at Bristol, and one (a "godly woman") at Exeter.[44] Only a few cathedrals escaped some sort of involvement in the Marian tragedy.

ANYONE who has pored over Foxe's *Book of Martyrs* or looked at the engravings with which most editions are illustrated will find it hard to

---

[44] Foxe, *Acts and Monuments*, 6: 591–611, 676–704, 7: 77–85, 6: 612–637, and passim.

hold any mental image for Mary's reign other than that of persecution and horror. So far as the cathedrals are concerned, however, there are more positive aspects of these years that should be put alongside accounts of deprivation and death.[45]

Recent studies have shown that a number of the Marian bishops were able men, dedicated to the restoration of what they regarded as the true faith. Several of the Marian deans, too, appear to have been intelligent and constructive, introducing improvements in the organization and finance of their cathedrals. Among those who stand out are Thomas Watson of Durham, John Christopherson of Norwich, Thomas Reynolds of Exeter, Feckenham of St. Paul's and Westminster Abbey, and Henry Cole (dean of St. Paul's after Feckenham's departure).[46] One of the achievements of these leaders was a great increase in the number of young men ordained to the priesthood and to lesser orders, especially in the dioceses of London, Oxford, and Chester. Ordinations, together with matriculations at Oxford and Cambridge, had fallen severely during the unsettled decade of the 1540s. Now, at Oxford, ordination lists for Mary's reign contain nearly five times as many names as those for Edward's, while the increase in Chester was even more dramatic, as many as seventy priests being ordained in Mary's last year alone. This number was far higher than that for any earlier year in the history of the diocese.[47]

Dean Watson may have been at least partly responsible for new statutes that were granted to Durham cathedral in 1555. The issuance of these had been prompted by unusual circumstances. During Edward's reign, Bishop Tunstall had been imprisoned and later deprived. No successor was appointed, and an act passed by Edward's last parliament proposed that the diocese be divided into two halves, with a second cathedral to be established at Newcastle. The cathedral at Durham was to continue, but with revenues reduced to 2,000 marks a year (£1,333), while the Dean and Chapter of Newcastle were to be granted 1,000 marks.

Edward's advisors had intended to translate Ridley from London to the diminished bishopric of Durham. But the king died before these plans could be put into effect, and Mary disliked them. Her first parliament repealed the Edwardian statute, thus confirming the tradi-

---

[45] For an example of a sympathetic, balanced account of Mary's reign, see Elizabeth Russell, "Marian Oxford and the Counter-Reformation," in *The Church in Pre-Reformation Society*, ed. Caroline M. Barron and Christopher Harper-Bill (Woodbridge, Suffolk: Boydell Press, 1985), pp. 212–227.

[46] Louisa, "Marian Bishops," pp. 91, 102–103.

[47] Ibid., pp. 92–93; Christopher Haigh, *Reformation and Resistance in Tudor Lancashire* (Cambridge: Cambridge University Press, 1975), p. 200.

CHAPTER 5

tional arrangements.[48] The see was reconstituted by letters patent early in 1554, and a full set of statutes, unusual in being issued under the Great Seal, was delivered to the cathedral in March 1555. They had been drawn up by Heath, the new archbishop of York, Tunstall (now restored to Durham), Bonner, and Thirlby.

While based on the Henrician statutes issued for cathedrals of the new foundation, the Marian code for Durham was carefully reworked. Some of the changes were chiefly stylistic, adding clarity or removing superfluous phrases. Others, like that requiring the dean to be of sound Catholic faith, reflected the complexion of the Marian establishment. A new section defined the role of the bishop in relation to the cathedral: in processions and other ceremonies, he was to take precedence over the dean and canons, and he was to be allowed to preach in the cathedral whenever he saw fit. He was still, however, not a member of the chapter. Another new section clarified and strengthened the authority of the dean. A statute defining the requirements of residence allowed the dean to spend up to forty days a year at his manor of Bearpark (the old monastic house of rest and recreation). Provision was made for a procession and mass each year on October 1, celebrating the anniversary of the queen's coronation, and for observance of royal obits.[49]

Further efforts were made to strengthen the church in other parts of the realm. In May 1556 the archdeaconry of Wells, which had been suppressed by an Edwardian statute, was reestablished and reendowed.[50] At Chester and Durham the right of naming the prebendaries, formerly held by the Crown, was granted to the bishop, thus bringing these houses in line with the other secular cathedrals.[51] At Lincoln the poor clerks were revived. They and the junior vicars choral were to be housed in a new College, or School, of Thirty Poor Clerks, within the cathedral close. Here ten scholars between the ages of fifteen and twenty were admitted in 1556, and others probably came later.[52] In 1557 the minster school at York was refounded; fifty boys were to be taught grammar in the former hospital at the Horsefair. Dean Wotton and his colleagues in the chapter were quite specific about their hope that the men educated here would become militant

[48] 1 Mary, sess. 3, cap. 3.
[49] A. Hamilton Thompson, ed., *The Statutes of the Cathedral Church of Durham*, Surtees Society, no. 143 (Durham, 1929), pp. lii–lxi. The statutes are printed and translated on pp. 72–217. See also Marcombe, "Durham Dean and Chapter," pp. 130–133.
[50] Loades, *Mary Tudor*, p. 355.
[51] Burne, *Chester Cathedral*, p. 34; Marcombe, "Durham Dean and Chapter," p. 133.
[52] R.E.G. Cole, ed., *Chapter Acts of the Cathedral Church of St. Mary of Lincoln, A.D. 1547–1559*, Lincoln Record Society, no. 15 (Horncastle, 1920), pp. xxiii, 131.

136

shepherds who could "put to flight the rapacious wolves, that is devilish men, ill-understanding the Catholic faith, from the sheepfolds of
the sheep entrusted to them."[53]

THE melancholy events of Mary's later years held profound implications for the cathedrals. Stephen Gardiner, the greatest conservative
statesman of the century, died halfway through the reign, in November 1555. His loss was severe, for he had been Mary's lord chancellor
and closest advisor as well as her bishop of Winchester. The queen's
isolation and loneliness were made worse by her husband's absence.
After Charles V abdicated the Spanish throne, Philip found it essential
to be in Spain, and there was no suggestion that Mary should accom-
pany him. Even the pope abandoned Mary at the end. As part of a
campaign against the Hapsburgs, he withdrew his legates from all of
Philip's territories, including England, thus denying Pole's position as
archbishop of Canterbury. Mary refused to accept Pole's deprivation
or the pope's nomination of the eighty-year-old former friar William
Peto in his place, but the idea of quarreling with the papacy after her
struggle to restore papal jurisdiction in England was heart-rending.

A further tragedy was more personal and, if possible, even more
poignant. On several occasions Mary believed that she was pregnant,
bearing the child who would assure the continuation of the true faith
in England. There had even been Te Deums of rejoicing and peals of
bells at St. Paul's, prompted by rumors that a boy had been born. But
"on the morrow it turned out otherwise to the pleasure of God"; the
queen was not with child, but was suffering from delusion and ultimately from the disease that would end her life.[54] The loss of Calais,
just as her health failed, was a final bitter blow.

Within the church the absence of leadership became increasingly
apparent. It was hard to find new bishops who shared the queen's
views, so bishoprics were left vacant, often for a year or more. Among
the sees that suffered were Winchester, Chichester, Lincoln, Peterborough, and Carlisle. Salisbury, Oxford, and Bangor were without bishops at the time of Mary's death. And there were financial problems:

[53] Aylmer and Cant, York Minster, p. 203.

[54] Matthews and Atkins, St. Paul's, pp. 130–131. At Hereford prayers had been offered
for the queen's supposed pregnancy in 1555 (Act Book 1, fol. 136, Hereford Cathedral
Library).

in the summer of 1558 Tunstall complained that he did not have enough money to meet his pension obligations at Durham.[55]

Mary's brief reign ended with her death early in the morning of November 17, 1558. Cardinal Pole followed her later the same day. The queen's funeral at Westminster Abbey was conducted with all the pomp that such a bastion of Catholicism could muster: the hearse was met by four bishops and the abbot, mitered and in copes, and a procession of a hundred poor men bearing long torches. John White, who had succeeded Gardiner as bishop of Winchester, preached the sermon, after which Mary's officers followed the coffin into Henry VII's chapel, broke their staffs of office, and threw them into the grave. The royal trumpeters blew a blast as the entourage departed.[56] This was the last great Latin requiem mass to be sung in the Abbey, an appropriate symbol for the end of an era in the church.

[58] Loades, *Mary Tudor*, p. 438.
[59] Nichols, *Diary of Henry Machyn*, pp. 183–184.

6

THE ELIZABETHAN SETTLEMENT

PAGEANTS enacted on the eve of Elizabeth's coronation gave dramatic visual form to the realization that her accession would bring a reversal of religious policy. Naturally enough those who prepared the displays favored change. Thus the queen was greeted, as she rode along her route near St. Paul's Cathedral, with a living tableau showing the Virtues trampling on Vices: "Pure religion," we are told, "did tread vppon Superstition and Ignoraunce." Another pageant contrasted Mary's "ruinous Republic," where the "decayed common weale" was characterized by "want of the feare of God," with the "well instituted Republic" or flourishing common weal, where a wise prince, learned rulers, and obedient subjects lived peaceably in awe of the Almighty.[1]

Although religious changes affecting the entire realm had to wait until the assembly of Elizabeth's first parliament, the queen proceeded to institute limited reforms in her own chapel almost immediately after her accession. According to an unsubstantiated rumor, she was using the English Litany as early as December 17, only a month after her accession.[2] Shortly thereafter, on Christmas Day, she demonstrated that she did not believe in transubstantiation by ordering that the elevation of the Host be omitted. When Bishop Oglethorpe, who was celebrating, refused to comply, the queen simply left the chapel prior to the consecration.[3]

Far more important, since they were great public ceremonies, were

[1] Sydney Anglo, *Spectacle, Pageantry, and Early Tudor Policy* (Oxford: Clarendon Press, 1969), pp. 348–350.

[2] A proclamation issued on December 27 permitted subjects to use the Epistle and Gospel, Creed, Ten Commandments, Lord's Prayer, and Litany in English, as was the practice in the queen's chapel, pending further direction by Parliament. Another proclamation, dated March 22, 1559, allowed communion in both kinds. Paul L. Hughes and James F. Larkin, eds., *Tudor Royal Proclamations*, 3 vols. (New Haven: Yale University Press, 1964–1969), 2: 102–103, 109–111.

[3] Norman L. Jones, *Faith by Statute* (London: Royal Historical Society, Studies in History, 1982), pp. 43–44. Cf. William P. Haugaard, "The English Litany from Henry to Elizabeth," *Anglican Theological Review* 51 (1969): 191–201. It is interesting to see the elevation of the Host still being specifically forbidden in Bishop Middleton's Injunctions for St. David's as late as 1583, on the grounds that it gives rise to "horrible idolatry." See W.P.M. Kennedy, *Elizabethan Episcopal Administration*, 3 vols., Alcuin Club, nos. 25–27 (London, 1924), 3: 146.

the coronation and the subsequent opening of the parliament of 1559. Both involved religious actions that implied a good deal about Elizabeth's own beliefs. There has been some disagreement among historians about just what happened during the celebration of the mass at the coronation, but it appears that Oglethorpe now managed to swallow his misgivings and omit the elevation. The Epistle and Gospel were read in English after they had been sung in Latin, and the consecration was probably intoned in English as well. It is significant that a bishop from the relatively obscure diocese of Carlisle officiated at such an important event. There was of course no archbishop of Canterbury in office, but one would have expected Archbishop Heath of York or another prominent episcopal leader to participate. It must have been painfully evident that all of them refused to accede to the queen's demands.[4]

The ceremonial opening of Parliament on January 25 presented another opportunity for the queen to manifest her Protestantism. On this occasion the monks of Westminster were rebuffed. When the queen arrived at the Abbey,

> the Abbot, robed pontifically, with all his monks in procession, each of them having a lighted torch in his hand, received her as usual, giving her first of all incense and holy water; and when her Majesty saw the monks who accompanied her with the torches, she said, "Away with these torches, for we see very well;" and her choristers singing the litany in English, she was accompanied to the high altar under her canopy.[5]

It has usually been assumed that she was protesting the monastic procession with its smoking lights, but William P. Haugaard may well be right in suggesting that her chief desire was to be accompanied by her young choristers, wearing white surplices and singing the English Litany, rather than elderly monks clad in black, chanting Latin. There could hardly have been a clearer visual symbol of the new order. Richard Cox, newly returned from exile, preached the sermon, inveighing against the monks as authors of the Marian persecution and urging Elizabeth to waste no time in reforming the church.[6]

The parliament itself presented serious problems. The new govern-

---

[4] Jones, *Faith by Statute*, pp. 45–46, and sources cited there. Our most reliable account of the coronation comes from the Venetian agent Il Schifanoya.

[5] Il Schifanoya, quoted in Haugaard, "English Litany," p. 197.

[6] Il Schifanoya, in *Calendar of State Papers, Venetian 1202–1603*, 9 vols. (London: HMSO, 1864–1898), 7: 22–23.

ment was caught between the conservative Marian bishops together with the abbot of Westminster, who were still members of the House of Lords, and the reformers, including the "wolves coming out of Geneva" and other former exiles, who had a few seats and a larger number of friends in the Commons.[7] There is no need to consider the parliamentary maneuverings in detail here—the subject is a vexed one, with J. E. Neale's ingenious but highly hypothetical reconstruction now challenged quite convincingly by Norman Jones and Winthrop Jordan.[8] The parliament is poorly documented, and we will probably never know precisely what went on or why.

When the long session ended on May 8 the final outcome was clear enough: the statutes assented to by the queen included an Act of Supremacy, granting her the title Supreme Governor of the Church, and an Act of Uniformity, restoring the Book of Common Prayer to use throughout the realm. Elizabeth's title thus differed from that claimed by her father and brother, who had held Supreme Headship, but it was still to be enforced by an Oath of Supremacy that could be used as a vehicle for depriving papists of their positions in the church. The Prayer Book of 1559 was based on the second, more Protestant version of Edward's reign—contrary to Neale, it now appears that virtually everyone expected the revival of the 1552 volume—but with a few changes of considerable significance, all of them tending toward moderation, ambiguity, and toleration, probably insisted on by the queen herself. The English services were introduced in the Chapel Royal immediately, on May 12,[9] and came into compulsory use everywhere on June 24.

ROYAL articles and injunctions, together with a royal visitation of the church, were needed to put the Elizabethan Settlement into effect. Elizabeth's visitation articles are based on those set out at the beginning of Edward VI's reign, although the situation was somewhat dif-

    [7] J. E. Neale, *Elizabeth I and Her Parliaments, 1559–1581* (London: Jonathan Cape, 1953), pp. 40, 57. It was Bishop White, in his sermon at Mary's funeral, who had referred to the exiles as wolves, an unfortunate phrase that was to earn him imprisonment in the Tower.

    [8] Ibid., pp. 51–84; Jones, *Faith by Statute*, passim; Winthrop S. Hudson, *The Cambridge Connection and the Elizabethan Settlement of 1559* (Durham, N.C.: Duke University Press, 1980), pp. 90–146.

    [9] J. G. Nichols, ed., *The Diary of Henry Machyn*, Camden Society, no. 42 (London, 1848), p. 197.

ferent: Edward's government was innovating, while Elizabeth's was in essence restoring a form of religion that had existed earlier but had been interrupted by Mary's accession.

As under Edward, several of the visitation articles dealt with images, shrines, relics, and other forms of "vain and superstitious religion." These were to be abandoned once again, both in churches and in private homes. The visitors were to inquire whether any persons "contemn and abuse" priests and other ministers of the church, whether any talked or caused disruption during services, whether any were drunkards, adulterers, brawlers, sorcerers, or rumormongers, and whether any secretly held masses or other services prohibited by law. An article new in Elizabeth's reign inquires whether the English Litany came into use when the queen commanded it by proclamation; another orders the compilation of lists of those who died or were imprisoned for the sake of religion.[10]

The Injunctions of 1559 begin with the command that deans, archdeacons, and parish clergy obey the laws extinguishing all foreign jurisdiction in the church and preach quarterly sermons showing "that the queen's power within her realms and dominions is the highest power under God, to whom all men, within the same realms and dominions, by God's law owe most loyalty and obedience." Processions must be abandoned, because they lead to quarrels about precedence and because prayers said in procession cannot be heard distinctly, but the Litany is retained and, indeed, given greater prominence by the order that it shall be said or sung in the midst of the church before the beginning of the Communion.

Two injunctions that were to prove of special importance dealt with marriage of the clergy and with church music. In both cases the queen's own tastes and preferences were involved. As is well known, Elizabeth was not enthusiastic about clerical marriage, and Sir William Cecil had to argue as "stiffly" as he could to keep her from outlawing it altogether. (He realized, perhaps earlier than the queen did, that the reconstructed church would have to rely on ministers who had married under Edward.) If she could not go that far, Elizabeth was determined to place as many obstacles in the path of married clergy as she could. The Injunctions of 1559 therefore contains a clause intended

[10] W. H. Frere and W. M. Kennedy, eds., *Visitation Articles and Injunctions*, 3 vols., Alcuin Club, nos. 14–16 (London, 1910), 3: 1–7 (vol. 3 was actually edited by Frere alone and will hereafter be cited with his name). The articles and injunctions are also printed in Henry Gee, *The Elizabethan Clergy and the Settlement of Religion* (Oxford: Clarendon Press, 1898), pp. 46–70.

to prevent unsuitable marriages by ordering that prospective wives should be examined and approved by the diocesan bishop and two local justices of the peace. Even this demeaning requirement did not satisfy the queen; two years later she issued a supplementary order banning the wives and children of deans, prebendaries, and other members of cathedral and collegiate foundations from living within the precincts of the college or cathedral. It was said that their presence violated the intention of founders and, worse, was a hindrance to study and learning.[11] Copies of the queen's order were written into the act books at several cathedrals, as was a letter from Archbishop Parker to the Dean and Chapter of Lincoln urging compliance.[12] Fortunately for the married ministers, none of the bishops undertook a drastic campaign to enforce the rule. Many of them must have shared the views of Bishop Cox, who wrote, "in these vast cathedral churches with their rooms plenty and several, on what ground should this be ordained? I have but one prebendary continually resident in Ely Church. Turn him out, and daws and owls may dwell there for any continual housekeeping."[13]

The famous injunction regarding singing reflects the queen's own love of church music; it must reveal, too, that demands for extreme simplification were already being felt. Elizabeth was clearly thinking of the cathedrals among the places where "there hath been livings appointed for the maintenance of men and children to use singing in the church, by means whereof the laudable science of music hath been had in estimation, and preserved in knowledge." This tradition was to continue. In the hope of satisfying the reformers, the queen ordered that the new English services be sung with "modest and distinct song, . . . so that the same may be as plainly understanded, as if it were read without singing"; but "for the comforting of such as delight in music," she permitted the singing of a more elaborate hymn or song at the end of morning or evening prayer, "in the best sort of melody and music that may be conveniently devised." Were it not for this clause, we might be deprived of the glorious anthems that fill the large volumes of *Tudor Church Music*.[14]

---

[11] Edward Cardwell, *Documentary Annals of the Reformed Church of England*, 2 vols. (Oxford: Oxford University Press, 1839), 1: 273–274; cf. William P. Haugaard, *Elizabeth and the English Reformation* (Cambridge: Cambridge University Press, 1968), pp. 200–205.

[12] Lincoln Chapter Acts, A/3/7, fol. 23, Lincolnshire Record Office; Norwich Chapter Book 1, fol. 55, Norfolk Record Office.

[13] Quoted in R. W. Dixon, *History of the Church of England*, 6 vols. (Oxford: Clarendon Press, 1902), 5: 310.

[14] 10 vols. (Oxford: Oxford University Press, 1923–1929).

Several additional orders were appended to the injunctions. "An Admonition to Simple Men Deceived by Malicious" was intended to satisfy at least some of the conservatives by putting a broad interpretation on the Oath of Supremacy, indicating that the allegiance required was no greater than that acknowledged to be due to the queen's father or brother. More important for the cathedrals was a statement of policy regarding "the Tables in the Church." This commanded that no more altars be destroyed. In cases where they had been taken away, a wooden table might remain, but it should be placed where the altar had stood except during the actual administration of Communion, when it might be moved temporarily to a more convenient location, still within the chancel. Here again the queen attempted to define a via media and to introduce that "mediocrity in religion" which she wished to characterize her reign.[15]

No general set of injunctions for cathedrals was prepared, as had been done early in Edward's reign. Instead, the royal visitors delivered separate injunctions to the Dean and Chapter of each cathedral as they examined them beginning in August 1559. The injunctions for Salisbury, Wells, Exeter, Worcester, and Peterborough survive, as do the answers made by the clergy of Canterbury to the visitors' queries. The issues are mainly the same as those dealt with in the earlier royal injunctions. In addition, there are some unique clauses. At Salisbury a divinity lecture was to be read each week, the lecturer being appointed by the chancellor and paid £20 a year; all prebendaries and other ministers of the church were to attend. Provision was made for choristers whose voices break: formerly employed as altarists, they were now to be given the same stipends but to spend their time studying in the grammar school. Vicars choral, whether married or not, were required to live within the cathedral close or lose their appointments. At Worcester the visitors insisted that the common hall should continue, with all the petty canons, "inferior ministers," schoolmasters, and children being taught grammar or music eating together; a sufficient amount of the produce from cathedral lands was to be reserved for this purpose. The injunctions for Peterborough include a requirement that the scholars admitted to the grammar school be "apt for learning and the poorest of birth," chosen without regard for friendship, kindred, or bribery.

The normal round of services is specified more clearly than usual at Exeter. Here the day was to begin at 6 A.M. with the Litany and a New Testament Lesson, followed by morning prayer at 7:45. At 9 A.M. on

[15] Frere, *Visitation Articles*, 3: 8–29.

Monday, Wednesday, and Friday the chancellor was to provide a divinity lecture, with one of the vicars choral reading a paraphrase of the Epistle and Gospel on Tuesday, Thursday, and Saturday. All the vicars and singing men were expected to participate in the Communion at 10 A.M., though we know from other sources that they actually received the bread and wine much less frequently. Interestingly enough the Dean and Chapter at Canterbury denied that they were required to have a divinity lecture (although they acknowledged that the staff was still to include the six preachers), and therefore said that they could not be bound to attend it.[16]

Some further orders issued between 1560 and 1562 complete the first phase of the Settlement. The Ornaments Rubric printed in the new Prayer Book required ministers to wear the vestments in use during Edward VI's second year. (Evidently the intention was to bring back the vestments prescribed by the Prayer Book of 1549, even though this was not actually issued until Edward's third year; that would include albs, chasubles—commonly referred to simply as "vestments" during this period—and copes at Communion, white linen surplices at other services.) A supplementary royal injunction regulating the outdoor garb of the clergy perhaps added confusion by referring to the garments commonly worn at the end of Edward's reign. An interpretation issued by the bishops said very directly that there was to be "only one apparel" throughout the land: "the cope in the ministration of the Lord's Supper, and the surplice at all other ministrations."[17] As shall be seen, this requirement faced considerable opposition from the Puritans, who refused to don vestments that smacked of popery and superstition, and soon led to one of the most bitter confrontations of Elizabeth's reign.

A proclamation issued in 1560 complained of the destruction or defacing of ancient monuments and tombs in churches and cathedrals. This "barbarous" practice was to cease, and those who were guilty of it, if they were known and still alive, were to restore the monuments.[18] A royal order of 1561 deals with rood lofts and related matters. In many places the figures so recently set up under Mary were taken down by overzealous reformers at the beginning of the new reign; the

[16] Ibid., 3: 30–53. The injunctions for Peterborough were not printed by Frere, who does not seem to have known of their existence. They are in MS. 30, fols. 1–6, Peterborough Cathedral Archives, Cambridge University Library. The commissioners visited Peterborough on August 28, 1559.

[17] Frere, *Visitation Articles*, 3: 61. Archbishop Parker's Injunctions for Canterbury added that the prebendaries should wear their academic hoods over their surplices, as was done at Oxford and Cambridge (ibid., 3: 78).

[18] Hughes and Larkin, *Tudor Royal Proclamations*, 3: 146–148.

roods, "with Mares [Marys] and Johns and odur emages," made two great bonfires in London.[19] Elizabeth herself would have been pleased to see the roods remain, but (uncharacteristically) she finally gave ground on the issue, and the order confirmed that they should be removed. Their place could be taken by a "convenient crest" if desired— this led to occasional taunts that the "lion and dog" flanking the royal arms had replaced the religious images.[20] Some sort of partition between the nave and the choir, such as that which the old roods had provided, was said to be appropriate. Fonts were not to be moved from their accustomed places, nor was there to be any further damage to bells, steeples, or porches. The Ten Commandments were to be displayed on the wall behind communion tables; a printed form was suitable for parish churches, but cathedrals were to have "the said precepts . . . more largely and costly painted out, to the better shew of the same."[21] Finally, the linguistic situation in Wales was at last acknowledged in injunctions that provided for the reading of the catechism as well as the Epistle and Gospel in Welsh.[22]

THE Elizabethan Oath of Supremacy was used as an instrument for ejecting from the church those ministers who refused to support the Settlement. At the episcopal level the revolution was virtually total; there was a greater break in continuity than at any other time in the history of the English church. Ten sees were vacant in 1559, so only sixteen bishops were required to subscribe. Fifteen of them declined to do so and were deprived. Oglethorpe, having accommodated the queen earlier, now obeyed his conscience and joined his colleagues in refusing submission; he died at the end of December 1559. The only Marian bishop who was not put out was the octogenarian Anthony Kitchin of Llandaff, a weak reed on which to support a church, and even he did not actually swear, merely submitting a curious paper in which he promised conformity to the new course of religion mandated by the government.[23]

In filling the vacancies created by this purge, Elizabeth relied heav-

[19] J. G. Nichols, *Diary of Henry Machyn*, p. 207.

[20] Cf. Dixon, *Church of England*, 5: 311–313; Haugaard, *Elizabeth*, p. 185; G.W.O. Addleshaw and Frederick Etchells, *The Architectural Setting of Anglican Worship* (London: Faber and Faber, 1947), p. 101.

[21] Frere, *Visitation Articles*, 3: 108–110.

[22] Ibid., 3: 111–114.

[23] See Philip Hughes, *The Reformation in England*, 3 vols. (London: Hollis and Carter, 1950–1954), 3: 36.

ily on men who had been Marian exiles and, earlier, scholars and administrators at Cambridge and Oxford. Matthew Parker, the new archbishop of Canterbury, had been dean of Lincoln and master of Corpus Christi College, Cambridge. He preferred the study of Anglo-Saxon history to involvement in theological controversy; more than any other prominent cleric of the reign he shared the queen's own moderate, generally tolerant views. Many of the other new bishops were dedicated reformers with advanced beliefs. These included Edmund Grindal, who was made bishop of London. Richard Cox was sent to Ely, Edwin Sandys to Worcester, and John Jewel to Salisbury. William Barlow, whom we have met as bishop of St. David's and, later, Bath and Wells, was now given Chichester, while John Scory, the Edwardian bishop of Chichester, was named to Hereford.[24] These men, and others like them, soon came into contact—and often conflict—with the cathedrals.

Most of the cathedrals also witnessed a substantial turnover of clergy. In all, twelve deans, twenty-five archdeacons, and just over a hundred prebendaries were deprived or replaced between 1558 and 1564.[25] A few examples, some of them especially interesting, will illustrate the situation. At Worcester the Catholic dean, Seth Holland, who had spent Edward's reign on the Continent, was replaced by John Pedder, a Marian exile and intransigent Puritan; five of the ten canons were ejected.[26] John Ramridge, the zealous papist dean of Lichfield, voluntarily left England at the time of Elizabeth's accession, only to be murdered in Flanders. He was succeeded by Laurence Nowell, a Marian exile, eminent antiquarian, and (like Parker) an Anglo-Saxon scholar.[27] Laurence's older brother, Alexander Nowell, who had been master of Westminster School and a prebendary of the Abbey before fleeing to Frankfurt, became dean of St. Paul's.

Another exile, the learned physician and botanist William Turner, was restored to the deanery at Wells—the Marian dean, John Goodman, was ejected, as he had been once before under Edward VI. Turner was soon in trouble: too much a Calvinist precisian to comply with the moderate Settlement, he was suspended for nonconformity in 1564, and his writings were banned.[28] At Hereford, John Ellys sup-

[24] These deprivations and appointments are discussed in ibid., 3: 36–47.
[25] See the lists in Gee, *Elizabethan Clergy*, pp. 271–287.
[26] See Michael Craze, *King's School, Worcester, 1541–1971* (Worcester: Baylis, 1972), p. 37; Accounts, A211a and A211b, Worcester Cathedral Library; and Christina H. Garrett, *The Marian Exiles* (Cambridge: Cambridge University Press, 1938), p. 246.
[27] Thomas Harwood, *The History and Antiquities of the Church and City of Lichfield* (Gloucester: J. Harris, 1806), pp. 182–183.
[28] After 1564 Turner lived in London rather than Wells, but he seems to have received

planted the Marian dean, William Daniel, and several of the prebends changed hands.[29] One of Queen Mary's secretaries of state, John Boxall, was sent from the deanery of Peterborough to the Tower of London; his place was filled by William Latimer, who was also a prebendary of Westminster.[30]

Religious change was of course especially evident in London. At St. Paul's five archdeacons (one of them the notorious John Harpsfield) and perhaps as many as twelve prebendaries were deprived.[31] Harpsfield and his brother Nicholas, who lost his own archdeacon's position at Canterbury, were both imprisoned for their strenuous opposition to the Protestant Settlement. Nicholas Wotton, more prominent as a diplomat than as a dean (though he held that post at both Canterbury and York), possessed a pliable conscience that enabled him to hold his preferments from the 1540s until his death in 1567, but about half the members of the chapter at York were displaced at the beginning of Elizabeth's reign.[32] In addition to Harpsfield, four prebendaries were deprived at Canterbury.

More remote areas were more immune to revolution. At Carlisle, Lancelot Salkeld, the former prior who presented the screen, took the oath but seems to have been deprived nonetheless. He soon accommodated Elizabeth by dying, and Sir Thomas Smith, the layman who was to be one of her principal secretaries, was restored to the deanery that he had held under Edward.[33] But the chancellor and all four prebendaries (one of them a former monk, and all of them probably conservative) remained in office. At Chester two archdeacons were deprived, but the four canons named by Mary stayed in place.[34] Hugh Turnbull, appointed dean of Chichester a few months before Mary's

---

the revenues of the deanery until his death in 1568. See *Dictionary of National Biography* s.v. "Turner, William"; Garrett, *Marian Exiles*, pp. 314–315; L. S. Colchester, ed., *Wells Cathedral: A History* (Shepton Mallet: Open Books, 1982), pp. 152–153.

[29] Act Book 1, fols. 152–155, Hereford Cathedral Library.

[30] W. T. Mellows, ed., *The Foundation of Peterborough Cathedral*, Northamptonshire Record Society, no. 13 (Northampton, 1941), pp. xxviii–xxix.

[31] Gee, *Elizabethan Clergy*, pp. 279–280; lower figures, probably incomplete, are given in W. R. Matthews and W. M. Atkins, eds., *A History of St. Paul's Cathedral* (London: John Baker, 1957), p. 132.

[32] G. E. Aylmer and Reginald Cant, eds., *A History of York Minster* (Oxford: Clarendon Press, 1977), pp. 204–205.

[33] See Mary Dewar, *Sir Thomas Smith* (London: Athlone Press, 1964), pp. 30, 75, 82, 117. Smith insisted that he had never resigned under Mary and demanded reinstatement. Salkeld is said to have signed the oath "voluntarie et bono animo"; see Gee, *Elizabethan Clergy*, pp. 80, 263, 273.

[34] R.V.H. Burne, *Chester Cathedral* (London: SPCK, 1958), p. 37; Gee, *Elizabethan Clergy*, p. 274.

death, retained that position until he died in 1567. But as many as twelve prebendaries of Chichester appear to have been ejected.[35]

Even where there was change, the tone might remain conservative. A good example is provided by Durham, which saw the deprivation of Mary's dean, Thomas Robertson, and the return of his Edwardian predecessor, Robert Horne. Nine of the prebendaries originally refused to subscribe—one of them said quite clearly, "the Pope hath and ought to have the jurisdiction ecclesiastical and not the Queen"—but several eventually persuaded themselves that accommodation to the new order was possible, and only five were actually deprived. Eight minor canons who originally declined the oath also submitted in the end. The result was a chapter that was dominated by conservatives for a decade or more, a situation common in other cathedrals as well.[36] Although five or six canons were deprived at Lincoln, the dean, Queen Mary's former chaplain Francis Mallet, was allowed to stay on, and that chapter, too, resisted change for several years.[37]

Since so many prominent Protestants had fled from England under Mary, it was not surprising that Elizabeth turned to Marian exiles in staffing her church. In all, we know of nineteen men who had held positions in the cathedrals before 1553 and returned to an office (not necessarily the same one) after 1558. An additional thirty-eight exiles, not previously employed in a cathedral, were given posts under Elizabeth. Most of them became canons, but we can count at least four exiles appointed to deaneries at the beginning of the reign and five more named after 1561.[38]

CHANGES in the physical appearance of the cathedrals made the coming of the new order clear for all to see. Entries in account books often tell just what was done, and when. At Salisbury the unusually full fabric account for 1559 includes payments for taking down altars, laying

[35] Gee, *Elizabethan Clergy*, pp. 274–275; W. D. Peckham, ed., *The Acts of the Dean and Chapter of the Cathedral Church of Chichester, 1545–1642*, Sussex Record Office, no. 58 (Lewes, 1959), pp. 29–55. The fact that the act book does not record the deprivations or all of the installations is a warning that such records cannot be used for this purpose without confirmation from other sources.

[36] David Marcombe, "The Dean and Chapter of Durham 1558–1603" (Ph.D. thesis, Durham University, 1973), pp. 165–171. Dean Robertson subsequently lived in York, where he said mass for Lord Dacre.

[37] R. B. Walker, "Lincoln Cathedral in the Reign of Queen Elizabeth I," *Journal of Ecclesiastical History* 11 (1960): 186–188.

[38] Information mainly from Garrett, *Marian Exiles*, passim. For other sources, see below, Chapter 9.

altar stones, setting twenty-three feet of new glass in the chapel on the north side of the church, and procuring a large printed Bible for the choir as well as copies of the Prayer Book and Psalter.[39] The charges for painting and erecting the Ten Commandments are recorded at Winchester ("to Addams for painting vpp ye X Commaundyments where the altar stoode," 20s.), Chichester (the purchase of canvas and paint), and Chester (a mere 14d. "to my Lord Busshops man" who did the work).[40] Three tables of the Commandments were set up at Wells in 1561, at a cost of only 4s., but this was evidently a temporary expedient, and a year later a painter from Gloucester received 53s. 4d. "for writing off the x commandementes and other thinges upon the wall within the quier."[41]

Payments for communion cups are found in several places. Probably there was a general order, issued about 1560, commanding that pre-Reformation chalices no longer be used, because of their association with the popish mass. No copy of such an injunction seems to have survived,[42] but local records show its being put into effect nonetheless. It is not clear exactly how the new cup was to differ from the old chalice; no doubt it was to be larger, since it was intended to hold wine for the whole congregation, not just for the priests. Certainly this was the case at Canterbury, where two chalices were melted down to make one communion cup and an additional sum of 39s. 7d. was paid, presumably for more silver. At the same time an hourglass was provided for the pulpit in an obvious attempt to regulate the length of sermons.[43] Communion cups also figure in the accounts at Durham, Carlisle, and Chichester,[44] and the bishops ordered that they be provided at Rochester, Norwich, York, and Winchester.[45] At Lincoln the holy table was

---

[39] Fabric Account, 1559, Salisbury Cathedral Library.

[40] Treasurer's Book, 1561, Winchester Cathedral Library; Chichester Accounts (1560–1561), cap. I/23/3, fol. 48, West Sussex Record Office; Account Book 2, fol. 25, Chester Cathedral Library. Winchester also paid a stonemason from Oxford £13 6s. 8d. "for making and filling vpp the wall where the hie altar stoode," and a joiner was paid "to stopp vp a hole in the hie alter" with a board adorned with a painting of a rose.

[41] Colchester, *Wells*, pp. 152–153; Communar's Accounts, 1560–1561 and 1561–1562, Wells Cathedral Library.

[42] See Frere, *Visitation Articles*, 3: 155.

[43] Miscellaneous Accounts, MS. M.A. 40, accounts for 1562–1563 (not paginated), Canterbury Cathedral Library.

[44] Durham paid £11 0s. 6d. for two communion cups (Treasurer's Book, 1569–1570, Prior's Kitchen, Durham). A silver communion cup with a cover (probably used as a paten) is listed in the inventory of 1571 at Carlisle; see J. E. Prescott, *The Statutes of the Cathedral Church of Carlisle* (London: Elliot Stock, 1903), pp. 106–107. The "great standing cup" at Chichester, "double gilt," weighed 22 oz. and cost £7 16s. 6d. (Chichester Accounts, cap. I/23/3 [1563], West Sussex Record Office).

[45] Frere, *Visitation Articles*, 3: 155, 199, 275, 377.

to be covered with "a comely table cloth"; there were to be two "handsome Communion cups, and a decent paten of silver to minister the Lord's bread upon, and also two comely pots of pewter to fetch wine to serve the Lord's table, reserved and kept clean to that use, being no tavern pots."[46]

During a later visitation at Worcester, the sexton testified that the plate and jewels had been taken away by the prebendaries at the beginning of Elizabeth's reign and divided among them, "but to what vse they did employ the same he saith, that he cannot tell. And the Copes, Vestmentes, and suche ornamentes were conuerted, some of them to the making of cushens, and to some suche other vses belonging to the Churche, and the rest thereof conuerted, he knoweth not to what vses."[47] Some years later, Dean Goodwin of Canterbury was accused of dividing and selling £1,000 worth of plate and ornaments, but he insisted that the division had occurred at the beginning of the reign, when Wotton was dean, so that "not a tenth" remained when Goodwin took office.[48] At Peterborough, Bishop Scambler inquired whether any persons had sold vestments, ornaments, or plate, or had converted them to their own private uses without his permission.[49] One would have expected the use of incense to disappear after 1559, with thuribles being melted down or hidden away, but the accounts record payments to "thuriblers" at York as late as 1562.[50] Throughout the 1570s injunctions issued by the bishops and archbishops frequently ordered the destruction of any remaining popish books or articles, and as late as 1581 Bishop Chaderton still thought it necessary to inquire whether such "monuments of superstition and idolatry" as missals, antiphoners, vestments, paxes, sacring bells, censers, or crosses and candlesticks remained in the diocese of Chester.[51]

Account books also record the purchase of books necessary for performing the new services. We know that Psalters were bought at Wells, Salisbury, Chester, and Canterbury, where a "table of Psalms" was painted up and erected to remind the vicars which ones were appointed for each service. The treasurer at Chester was evidently not fond of the new English texts, for he recorded the purchase of a considerable quantity of paper "for prickyeng of dyvers strange songs to

[46] Ibid., 3: 371 (Bishop Cooper's articles for Lincoln diocese, 1574).
[47] MS. A25, fol. 147–148, Worcester Cathedral Library.
[48] Dixon, *Church of England*, 6: 204–205.
[49] MS. 30, fol. 42, Peterborough Cathedral Archives, Cambridge University Library.
[50] El/81/3, York Minster Library. Incense is said to have been used at Ely until 1830.
[51] Kennedy, *Episcopal Administration*, 2: 12, 48, 99, 112.

the quyre." But at Wells the communar noted the payment of 13*d*. "to Mr. Lyde for a good songe, viz. Te Deum in Englishe."[52]

THE cathedral at Durham was deeply involved in the Northern Rising, or Rebellion of the Earls, in 1569.[53] As old aristocrats and adherents to the old faith, the earls of Westmorland and Northumberland were out of step with the Elizabethan government and were ignored by the queen and her council. Thus isolated, they came to believe that many of their neighbors in the north of England shared their convictions and would rise under their banner if they sought to restore Catholicism and gain recognition for Mary, Queen of Scots, as Elizabeth's legitimate successor. Indeed enough rebels did gather in Yorkshire and the county of Durham to frighten the government badly—their number was said, at its peak, to exceed five thousand.[54]

A force of five hundred horsemen entered the city of Durham on November 14, 1569. Dean Whittingham had suggested that the church mobilize the tenants on its estates to oppose the rebels, but Bishop Pilkington refused to do so and the riders were not challenged. Making straight for the cathedral, they smashed the communion table and destroyed Protestant books, proclaiming in the name of the queen herself that the Catholic faith had been restored. Westmorland's uncle, Cuthbert Neville, was left in charge while the earls and most of their followers moved south. Under his direction laborers reerected several altars and replaced holy water stoops. The Latin mass was restored in the cathedral; especially splendid services were held on St. Andrew's Day (November 30) and the following Sunday, December 4, when the preacher inveighed against Protestantism and pronounced the reconciliation of the faithful to Rome. This state of affairs continued for a month. Only on December 16 were the rebels driven out of the city. For eight days there were no services in the cathedral. Finally

---

[52] Communar's Accounts, 1559–1560 and 1560–1561, Wells Cathedral Library; Fabric Account, 1559, Salisbury Cathedral Library; Account Book 2, fols. 2, 38–39, 43–44, Chester Cathedral; MS. M.A. 40, accounts for 1562–1563 (not paginated), Canterbury Cathedral Library.

[53] For general accounts see Hughes, *Reformation in England*, 3: 265–271; and Wallace T. MacCaffrey, *The Shaping of the Elizabethan Regime* (Princeton: Princeton University Press, 1968), pp. 330–371. A recent specialized study is Mervyn James, "The Concept of Order and the Northern Rising of 1569," *Past and Present* 60 (1973): 49–83, reprinted in his book, *Society, Politics and Culture* (Cambridge: Cambridge University Press, 1986), pp. 270–307.

[54] Hughes, *Reformation in England*, 3: 270, and sources cited there.

the Prayer Book was brought back into use and the Anglican Settlement was reestablished.[55]

Once the rebellion had been suppressed the government set about determining what had happened and fixing punishment. Just over two hundred were executed in the county of Durham, and another eighty in the city itself—a tenth of the adult male population. Depositions were taken from various members of the cathedral staff. A lay clerk admitted that he

> came to masse, matens, evensong, procession, and like idolatrous service, therat knelling [kneeling], bowing, knocking, and shewing such like reverent gesture, used praying on beades, confession or shriving to a priest, toke holy water and holye breade; and did also then and ther heare false and erroneouse doctrine against God and the churche of England preached by one W. Holmes in the pulpit, and, subjecting him selve to the same doctrine, and to the Pope, did, among other like wicked people knowen to him, knell down and received absolution under pope Pius name, in latin; falsely terming this Godly estate of England to be a schism or heresy.[56]

When the dean attempted to correct three more lay clerks before allowing them to receive communion, they insisted that he had no jurisdiction over them (the Dean and Chapter might have, but not the dean alone) and that the cathedral was legally bound by its Marian statutes, which commanded the use of the Latin services. George Clyffe, a prebendary, spoke nostalgically about hearing the Advent anthem "Gaude, Virgo Christopara," but denied that he had received "the Poop's absolution." A minor canon admitted that he had sung "Ora pro nobis" out of a processioner delivered to him by the chanter, a significant indication that old service books had not been destroyed, and John Brimley, the aging organist, confessed that he had "played at orgaines, and dyd dyvers tymes help to singe salveas at mattins and evensonge . . . and went in procession, as other dyd, after the Crosse." At the command of Neville and Northumberland he had also instructed the choristers in the use of the old services, which the boys would of course not have heard before. Several laborers, when exam-

---

[55] Marcombe, "Dean and Chapter of Durham," pp. 171–177. Regarding Whittingham and Pilkington, see Mervyn James, *Family, Lineage, and Civil Society: A Study of Society, Politics, and Mentality in the Durham Region, 1500–1640* (Oxford: Clarendon Press, 1974), pp. 146–147.

[56] Printed in J. G. Nichols, ed., *Depositions and Other Ecclesiastical Proceedings from the Courts of Durham*, Surtees Society, no. 22 (Durham, 1845), p. 131.

ined, stated that they had set up five altars and helped roll and lift two large stones into place for the high altar, but they insisted that they were forced to do so and had acted against their will.[57] This is again interesting evidence, suggesting that pieces of altars had been hidden away in the hope that they would one day be wanted.

Four conservative minor canons were deprived following the rebellion. Fourteen others known to have been involved were permitted to retain their positions. Protestant members of the chapter complained that they had lost books and furniture, and Dean Whittingham, who had fled to the south before the rebels arrived, said that his house had been entered and spoiled, his books "rent in peices . . . in such sort and abundance as was pityfull to beholde," and cattle and corn stolen from his manors.[58]

CONSERVATIVE rebels, like the earls and their followers, could be dealt with by military action and, if necessary, execution. The reformers who mounted left-wing opposition to the Settlement could not be handled in that way, and they proved far more difficult for the queen and her ecclesiastical leaders to manage.

Puritan dissatisfaction with the Elizabethan church hardened around several issues. Perhaps the first of these to become evident involved music. In December 1559, when the Settlement was less than a year old, a group of townspeople from Exeter, probably urged on by zealots from London, invaded the choir of Exeter Cathedral, usurped the places of the lay clerks, and began singing metrical Psalms at the early morning service. In doing so they were attempting to introduce the simplified, unaccompanied congregational singing favored by Calvin in Geneva and adopted by the more advanced Marian exiles. The clergy tried to drive the singers out, but when an appeal was made to royal visitors, including Bishop Jewel, they lost their case, for the visitors admonished them to permit these "godly doings" to continue. In a further appeal to the ecclesiastical commissioners, the Dean and Chapter pointed out that they were merely trying to enforce the Act

---

[57] Ibid., pp. 133–149.

[58] Marcombe, "Dean and Chapter of Durham," p. 176; *Life of Mr. William Whittingham, Dean of Durham*, Camden Society, no. 104 (London, 1870), pp. 24–25. Rebellion threatened to break out in Lancashire as well as in Northumberland, the county of Durham, and Yorkshire; see J. J. Scarisbrick, *The Reformation and the English People* (Oxford: Blackwell, 1984), pp. 145–147. Cf. C.M.L. Bouch, *Prelates and People of the Lake Counties: A History of the Diocese of Carlisle, 1133–1933* (Kendal: Titus Wilson, 1948), p. 204, on the sympathetic views at Carlisle.

of Uniformity by forbidding liturgical actions not sanctioned by the Prayer Book, but this, too, was unsuccessful, and the Puritan singers won the day.[59]

The issue came to a head in the Convocation of 1563. In preparation for this the Puritan leaders had drafted a set of "General Notes" that proposed, among other things, that "the use of organs and curious singing be removed." An expansion of this demand, found in the more detailed "Seven Articles," said that the Psalms should be sung "distinctly by the whole congregation," or, if that were not convenient, be said by the minister alone. Had such a petition prevailed, the long tradition of church music in the English cathedrals would have been terminated, the organs silenced, and the choirs disbanded. Several prominent churchmen, including Dean Nowell of St. Paul's, supported the radical position, which came close to gaining the endorsement of the Lower House. In the end a somewhat more tolerant view prevailed, and the deputies of the clergy merely requested that organs be removed but that otherwise the queen's broad-minded injunction regarding music be put in execution. Vicars choral throughout the land, if they knew what was going on in London, must have rejoiced when the Genevan propositions failed. Most organists, too, probably realized that their positions were safe enough so long as they enjoyed the support of the dean or bishop.[60]

Local sources make it abundantly clear that the traditional sung services continued everywhere, and that organs were repaired, tuned, and in some cases enlarged or rebuilt. Choral singing of the traditional Prayer Book canticles was confirmed in an agreement with the new organist appointed at Lincoln after William Byrd left the cathedral to take up duties in the Chapel Royal: the Te Deum and "Canticum Zacharie" (the Benedictus) were to be used at matins, with Magnificat and Nunc Dimittis at evensong, and the services were to include "Le anthem."[61]

Still, there were occasional Puritan outbursts. In 1570 the queen, obviously distressed at rumors emanating from Norwich, ordered Bishop Parkhurst to inquire into the activities of certain prebendaries who were said to have broken down the organs and committed other outrages in the choir. Parkhurst's reply does not exist, but his injunc-

[59] Frere, *Visitation Articles*, 3: 42n; MS. 3552, fol. 145, Exeter Cathedral Library. See also Nicholas Temperley, *The Music of the English Parish Church*, 2 vols. (Cambridge: Cambridge University Press, 1979), 1: 39–49.

[60] Haugaard, *Elizabeth*, pp. 168–170; Patrick Collinson, *The Elizabethan Puritan Movement* (London: Jonathan Cape, 1967), pp. 65–66.

[61] Lincoln Chapter Acts, A/3/7, fol. 86, Lincolnshire Archives Office.

tions for the cathedral, issued in 1571, suggest that he was in two minds about the matter: he said that "no ditties nor notes of psalms" were to be used without authority but betrayed his sympathy by referring to them as "godly songs."[62] Troubles at Norwich may well have continued, however, for George Gardiner, who was probably one of the offending prebendaries, was named dean in 1573.[63]

The activities of the Puritan dean of Durham, William Whittingham, will engage our attention later. We know that he wrote metrical versions of several of the Psalms, and also of the Ten Commandments, but his love of music led him to support the continued use of organs and anthems.[64] While he was dean of York, Matthew Hutton regularly purchased additional copies of the Genevan Psalter.[65] Bishop Horne's injunctions for Winchester Cathedral (1571) suggest that he, too, favored the Puritan position on music, for he commanded

> that in the quire no note shall be used in song that shall drown any word or syllable, or draw out in length or shorten any word or syllable otherwise than by the nature of the word it is pronounced in common speech, whereby the sentence cannot well be perceived by the hearers. And also the often reports or repeating of notes with words or sentences whereby the sense may be hindered in the hearer shall not be used.[66]

This was clearly more restrictive than the queen's order.

For the church at large, although not for the cathedrals, the issue of vestments gave rise to more bitter division than the matter of music. The Ornaments Rubric and the bishops' interpretation of it—copes for Communion, surplices for all other services—had never pleased the reformers, whose "gloss upon this text" was "that we shall not be forced to use them."[67] We know that copes were used in some places; a statement of custom at Canterbury made in 1563, for instance, says that the epistler and gospeler, in addition to the celebrant, wore them.[68] But practice varied, and if there was one thing that the queen could not tolerate it was outward, visible lack of uniformity in her church.

[62] Frere, *Visitation Articles*, 3: 317.
[63] *Calendar of State Papers, Domestic, 1547–1580*, p. 393; *VCH, Norfolk*, 2: 267n.
[64] Marcombe, "Dean and Chapter of Durham," pp. 201–208.
[65] Aylmer and Cant, *York Minster*, p. 208.
[66] Frere, *Visitation Articles*, 3: 319.
[67] Sandys to Parker, quoted in Haugaard, *Elizabeth*, p. 184.
[68] C. E. Woodruff and William Danks, *Memorials of the Cathedral and Priory of Christ in Canterbury* (London: Chapman and Hall, 1912), p. 304.

The surprisingly moderate Puritan proposals regarding copes made in the Convocation of 1563 would have softened the requirements by allowing the surplice for all services. These failed to pass in the Lower House by a single vote; even if they had been adopted they would have been rejected by the queen as going too far and by the real reformers as not going far enough. Parker seems to have been able to persuade Elizabeth to give ground, by agreeing that she would not oppose some relaxation of the order even though she would not give it her official sanction. Thus the archbishop's "Advertisements" of 1566 make a distinction between cathedrals, where copes shall continue to be worn by the chief ministers at Communion, with surplices for all other services and hoods for preachers, and parish churches, where "a comely surplice with sleeves, to be provided at the charges of the parish," is to be the attire for all services.[69] With this lower standard as the basis on which uniformity was to be enforced, the issue was joined between those ministers who flatly refused to wear the surplice, for them an important symbol of continued belief in popery and darkness, and those whose consciences permitted them to satisfy the queen and acquiesce in the archbishop's command.

The first confrontation between these opposing forces came at Oxford, where two leading Protestant divines, Thomas Sampson, the dean of Christ Church, and Laurence Humphrey, president of Magdalen College, continued their longstanding campaign against the surplice. As early as 1549, when Sampson had been ordained by Bishop Ridley, he had refused to wear the popish garb and had been granted a dispensation. Appointed dean of Chichester shortly before Edward's death, Sampson had spent Mary's reign imbibing the pure Protestant waters of Geneva and Zurich. He was offered the bishopric of Norwich in 1560 but turned it down, accepting instead a canonry at Durham and, in 1561, his appointment at Oxford. Here he made a bonfire of popish articles that Machyn termed "grett reches" that might have been turned to other uses.[70] For a time Sampson was permitted to preach in a doctoral gown rather than a surplice, but in March 1565 he was called before the Ecclesiastical High Commission, refused to conform, and was deprived. He thus has the distinction of being the first man ejected from the English church for nonconformity.

Humphrey's case was similar. A great scholar and linguist, educated at both Cambridge and Oxford, he was a Marian exile but on his re-

[69] Frere, *Visitation Articles*, 3: 175.
[70] Nichols, *Diary of Henry Machyn*, p. 266.

turn was named regius professor of divinity at Oxford and president of Magdalen College. He, too, was deprived in 1564.[71]

The Vestiarian Controversy reached its climax a year later, when Parker, on the queen's order, required the clergy to promise that they would wear the surplice. A petition signed by twenty leading churchmen, including deans Nowell of St. Paul's and Whittingham of Durham, requested the ecclesiastical commissioners to renounce any attempt at enforcement, but this plea did not gain acceptance. The campaign against nonconformity was now centered primarily in London; some ministers simply feigned illness and absented themselves from gatherings at which they would be asked to subscribe, but quite a number had the courage of their convictions and were driven out of the church for their refusal to comply.[72] This episode marks the real beginning of organized nonconformity in England.

So far as we know, the cathedrals were affected relatively little, for many of their officers were either conservative or Erastian. Grindal said that he disliked the order but would comply—he was willing to wear a surplice at St. Paul's but did not promise to do so everywhere.[73] Bishops Jewel, Cox, Horne, and Guest, though they might have private scruples, conformed publicly and encouraged others to do the same. At Durham both Bishop Pilkington and Dean Whittingham abhorred the surplice—with fine literary flair Whittingham wrote Leicester, "How can God's glory be advanced by those garments which superstitious men and Antichrist have invented for the maintaining and beautifying of idolatry?"—and both were brought before the High Commission on charges of failing to wear it. In the end they promised to conform and doubtless did so on occasion, but Whittingham may well have continued to conduct services in a black gown rather than a surplice, and it is said that he did not celebrate Communion after 1563 in order to avoid putting on a cope. In 1567 three of the Durham prebendaries were brought before the High Commission for vestiarian offenses, and two of them were deprived. Documentary sources do not reveal exactly what the normal practice was, but several paintings show the surplice being worn at Durham, and one may assume that this was the custom by the 1570s.[74]

Elsewhere a few adamant Protestants were deprived. The irrepres-

[71] See the articles on Sampson and Humphrey in the *Dictionary of National Biography*; also Dixon, *Church of England*, 6: 60–64.

[72] For fuller accounts, see Dixon, *Church of England*, 6: 89–135; and Collinson, *Elizabethan Puritan Movement*, pp. 71–83.

[73] Collinson, *Elizabethan Puritan Movement*, p. 74.

[74] Marcombe, "Dean and Chapter of Durham," pp. 186–196.

sible William Turner of Wells, who supposedly trained his dog to snatch the square cap off the head of a bishop dining with him, lost a lectureship in Middlesex but was allowed to retain the profits of his deanery,[75] and Robert Crowley, perhaps the most vocal of all the recalcitrant clerics, whose appointments had included a prominent London parish as well as an archdeaconry at Hereford and a canonry at St. Paul's, was imprisoned and forced to beg the Privy Council for mercy.[76] A conciliatory line was taken by Bishop Horne in his injunctions of 1571 for Winchester, which stipulated that copes worn in the cathedral should be plain, "without any images."[77] But this cannot have made much difference; if Horne imagined that the opposition was limited to the embroidered orphreys on the copes, he did not understand his adversaries very well.

In the later years of the queen's reign the issue of vestments generated less heat, and the government tacitly permitted black Geneva gowns in place of the white surplices. Sampson, for instance, was allowed to officiate outside Oxford without wearing offensive vestments, a practice he continued at St. Paul's after being named a prebendary there in 1570. Humphrey became dean of Winchester in 1580, evidently still adhering to his earlier views. But in 1589 Bishop Freake exhorted the dean and prebendaries of Worcester to wear surplices and hoods.[78] We will never know precisely what the situation was in all the cathedrals, but the chances are that they presented a motley sight: the choristers and singing men probably wore surplices,[79] but a number of the higher officials may have succeeded in officiating without them.[80]

Another issue that separated the Puritans from their more conservative colleagues was the relative importance of preaching and sacraments. Zealous Protestants had always set great store by sermons, through which the people could be instructed in religion and ex-

[75] John Strype, *The Life and Acts of Matthew Parker*, 3 vols. (Oxford: Oxford University Press, 1821), 1: 301; Colchester, *Wells*, p. 153.

[76] Haugaard, *Elizabeth*, pp. 226–227.

[77] Frere, *Visitation Articles*, 3: 320. An inventory made at Carlisle in 1571 confirms that the cathedral still possessed a cope of blue damask with images on the orphreys, as well as a plain cope of "tissue" (J. E. Prescott, *Statutes of Carlisle*, pp. 106–107).

[78] Kennedy, *Episcopal Administration*, 2: 253.

[79] They were required to do so by Bishop Bancroft's articles for St. Paul's, 1599, which go so far as to insist that the choristers' surplices be clean and not tattered and torn (ibid., 3: 306, 315).

[80] The cathedral financial records contain few references to the purchase of vestments during Elizabeth's reign. We do know that some new vestments were acquired at Salisbury in 1582, but not whether they included surplices and copes (Act Book, MS. 81, p. 97, Salisbury Cathedral Library).

horted to godly living, while the more conservative wing of the church continued to believe in the importance and efficacy of the Eucharist. On this matter the reformers' point of view prevailed more and more as the sixteenth century wore on, with frequent sermons and infrequent Communions becoming the rule, even in the cathedrals.

One can follow the decline in frequency of Eucharistic celebrations in episcopal injunctions and in the record books of the cathedrals themselves. The Royal Injunctions of 1559 for Exeter Cathedral seem to anticipate a daily Communion, but this was unusual. At Winchester a weekly celebration was required. One set of orders for Rochester mentions Communion every Sunday and on holy days, but another speaks of celebration every three weeks.[81] That was in 1565; by 1571 monthly Communion was the norm.[82] At Wells the queen's visitors required one of the residentiary canons to celebrate Communion on the first Sunday of each month, with all the canons and vicars receiving the elements.[83] Similar orders refer to monthly celebrations at St. Paul's, Canterbury, Salisbury, and York. The matter should have been settled by Parker's Advertisements of 1566, which required that Communion be administered in cathedrals and colleges on the first or second Sunday of each month; the dean, prebendaries, and other clerks were to receive monthly, and other members of the cathedral staff at least four times a year.[84] This was a significant decline from the standard weekly celebration anticipated by the rubrics in the 1559 Prayer Book.[85] But even this modest requirement was not always observed. Archbishop Grindal's injunctions for cathedrals in the province of Canterbury, issued in 1576, refer merely to a yearly reception, as do Bishop Howland's for Peterborough (about 1584).[86] At Wells two vicars choral were suspended in 1581 because they had not communicated in four years. In 1596 the vicars there were admonished to receive Communion at least three times a year, but not all complied and two vicars had to be threatened with deprivation in 1599 if they continued to fail to communicate.[87]

Preaching, on the other hand, grew in importance.[88] Weekly ser-

[81] Frere, *Visitation Articles*, 3: 43, 135, 319, 148, 152.

[82] Kennedy, *Episcopal Administration*, 2: 28.

[83] Frere, *Visitation Articles*, 3: 37, 79, 94, 116, 347; Kennedy, *Episcopal Administration*, 2: 84.

[84] Frere, *Visitation Articles*, 3: 175.

[85] Cf. Haugaard, *Elizabeth*, p. 214.

[86] Kennedy, *Episcopal Administration*, 2: 18; 3: 160.

[87] Act Book H, fols. 15, 168, and Act Book, 1591–1607, fol. 140, Wells Cathedral Library.

[88] For analysis of Elizabethan sermons, see J. W. Blench, *Preaching in England* (New York: Barnes and Noble, 1964), and Irvonwy Morgan, *The Godly Preachers of the Eliza-*

mons were required almost everywhere. The orders for Winchester, set out in 1562 and 1571, are especially clear; they charge the prebendaries with providing sermons each Sunday, either preaching in person or by deputy. Each prebendary had to preach at least one sermon a year himself. Fines of 20s., to be used for poor relief, were to be levied for any failure to deliver the sermons, which were to deal with such topics as royal supremacy, the end of the pope's usurpation, and the "enormities" of private masses. The dean, prebendaries, and other ministers are to attend all of these sermons, unless they are prevented from doing so by a "just, urgent, and lawful cause." Grindal's injunctions for York Minster (1572) include a schedule showing clearly which officer is responsible for preaching week by week.[89] A rota for Bangor Cathedral was established by Grindal in 1576, and in 1577 Bishop Whitgift ordered a "table" of preachers to be set up at Worcester.[90] When Bishop Barnes visited Carlisle Cathedral in 1571 he "urged the importance of preaching and the need for a fuller provision of Sermons in the Cathedral Church," and he agreed to a scheme by which the bishop and dean would contribute four sermons a year each, the archdeacon two, and every major canon six.[91]

At Hereford the chapter ordered that all twenty-eight prebendaries, not just the residentiaries, should preach in order, so that there would be a sermon each Sunday. The dean was to preach on Christmas and Easter. A later fabric roll recorded the payment of £1 13s. 9d. to a carpenter "for making a backe for a new seate for the gentlemen of the citie, on promise that he make it lower, that the people may see the pulpit and heare the better."[92] The prebendaries of Peterborough were responsible for preaching once a quarter, but since this did not produce a weekly sermon, it was agreed that one of them, William Hills, would preach every second Sunday and receive an annual payment of £10.[93]

By the mid-1570s the chapter at Durham had changed character

---

bethan Church (London: Epworth Press, 1965). Neither book contains a separate study of preaching in cathedrals. The semiofficial sermons delivered at Paul's Cross have been studied by Millar MacLure, *The Paul's Cross Sermons, 1534–1642* (Toronto: University of Toronto Press, 1958).

[89] Frere, *Visitation Articles*, 3: 134–135, 318–319, 345, 352.

[90] Kennedy, *Episcopal Administration*, 2: 21–23, 66.

[91] Frere, *Visitation Articles*, 3: 338. Other orders and injunctions that require weekly sermons, each prebendary preaching at least quarterly, are in Kennedy, *Episcopal Administration*, 2: 33, 84, 102.

[92] Act Book 2, fol. 72 (1577), and R588 (fabric roll for 1587–1591), Hereford Cathedral Library.

[93] MS. 12 (not paginated) for October 28, 1587, Peterborough Cathedral Archives, Cambridge University Library.

and, surprisingly, had become the most Puritan group of cathedral clergy in the land. Much of the change was the work of two great Protestant deans, William Whittingham and his successor, Toby Matthew. Both were zealous preachers; we know that Dean Matthew personally preached twenty-eight sermons in the cathedral during 1585, nineteen in 1586, and twenty-seven in 1587.[94]

Divinity lectures, as noted above, were mandated by statute at many of the cathedrals. Even more than sermons, they provided an opportunity for Puritan teaching in the cathedrals. In 1562 Bishop Horne commanded the Dean and Chapter of Winchester to appoint a virtuous man, learned in divinity, to lecture twice a week at a stipend of £1 per lecture.[95] At Durham one of the prebendaries read a divinity lecture two or three times a week in the chapter house, for an annual salary of £20. Hugh Broughton, the lecturer in the late 1570s, was especially popular and is said to have attracted large crowds.[96] A lecturer named Thomas Hitchins was active at Chester in the 1580s, while at Peterborough Walter Baker was hired in 1588 to read a weekly lecture as well as to preach on alternate Sundays. His stipend was £20, to be taken from the wages formerly paid to two petty canons.[97] Bishop Scambler required the dean and prebendaries of Peterborough to lecture themselves, in turn, on Wednesday mornings; at Rochester the singing men were to be fined if they failed to attend lectures.[98] We know that a number of parish churches where Puritan feeling ran strong fulfilled the letter of the Anglican law by having Prayer Book services on Sunday mornings and Puritan lectures in the afternoons. The evidence for the cathedrals is not so clear, but it may

[94] Figures from MS. 18, York Minster Library; cf. Marcombe, "Dean and Chapter of Durham," p. 10. The anonymous author of the *Rites of Durham* charged Whittingham with ordering that the image of Cuthbert be "defaced and broken all in peaces, to thintent that there should be no memory nor token of that holie man," but enough of the shrine remained that it was a tourist attraction in the 1560s. See Marcombe, "Dean and Chapter of Durham," pp. 201–208; and *A Description or Briefe Declaration of all the Ancient Monuments, Rites, and Customes belonginge or beinge within the Monastical Church of Durham before the Suppression*, ed. James Raine, Surtees Society, no. 15 (Durham, 1842), reprinted with additional material by J. T. Fowler, Surtees Society, no. 107 (Durham, 1903), p. 68.
[95] Frere, *Visitation Articles*, 3: 134.
[96] Marcombe, "Dean and Chapter of Durham," p. 11.
[97] Account Book 3, fol. 3, Chester Cathedral Library; MS. 12 (not paginated), for October 26, 1588, Peterborough Cathedral Archives, Cambridge University Library. It may be noted that the prophesyings—the regional gatherings of clergy for practice in preaching, disliked by the queen as vehicles for the dissemination of Puritan views and defended by Archbishop Grindal, who was finally sequestered for the refusal to ban them—took place in parish churches, not in the cathedrals. See Stanford E. Lehmberg, "Archbishop Grindal and the Prophesyings," *Historical Magazine of the Protestant Episcopal Church* 34 (1965): 87–145.
[98] Kennedy, *Episcopal Administration*, 2: 40, 103.

be that some of them, too, used lectures as a means of satisfying the more zealous Protestants or inculcating reformed theology.

A final sign of Puritan influence, significant as a symbol rather than for its own sake, may be found in the contribution of £5 sent in 1590 by the Dean and Chapter of Ely to the city of Geneva, presumably a token of appreciation for spiritual leadership given at a time of need.[99]

THE later years of Elizabeth's reign were calmer than its beginning. Some accommodation with the Puritans had gradually been worked out, often tacitly rather than by official action. Years of familiarity with the Prayer Book produced acceptance and, for some at least, affection. Cathedral services settled comfortably into a routine; more and more they were enriched by new musical settings of unsurpassed beauty, written by such masters as William Byrd and Thomas Tallis. As preaching grew in importance it became clearer that cathedral churches were places of instruction for the laity, not merely houses where isolated clerics sang the praises of God or offered intercessions for the dead. To some extent the quiet was deceptive, as the events of the seventeenth century were to prove. The Puritans had gone underground, not died out, while on the other side there remained a few—they would eventually find a leader in William Laud—who felt that the church had abandoned too much of its medieval tradition, its "beauty of holiness" in ceremony and sacrament. But in 1603 the Puritan Revolution lay decades in the future. As the Tudor age closed, the cathedrals appeared to have weathered the storm of the Reformation and to have adjusted to new circumstances without compromising their essential character.

[99] EDC 3/1/1, Treasurer's Book 1587–1591, fol. 14, Ely Cathedral Archives, Cambridge University Library.

7

ELIZABETHAN CATHEDRAL FINANCE

THE MATTER of finance in the Elizabethan cathedrals presents problems of two sorts. It is clear that difficulties were perceived during the period itself: revenues were inadequate in most places, and arrangements for collecting them were complex. In addition, problems face the modern historian who seeks to unravel the mysteries of cathedral finance, for full documentation does not exist and even those papers which remain are little studied and not easy to understand. In this chapter I will attempt to lay out the chief issues and main lines of interpretation without claiming to offer a definitive examination of a topic that demands a detailed study of its own.

There is no nationwide accounting of ecclesiastic revenues for the years after the Reformation comparable to the *Valor Ecclesiasticus* for the earlier period. Perhaps the most useful general figure comes from the era of the Civil War in the seventeenth century, when the estates of the cathedral chapters were sold by the Commonwealth government for £455,621.[1] They were first offered for sale at twelve years' purchase (twelve times the anticipated annual income), but this was soon reduced to ten. If one adopts ten years' purchase as the basis of calculation, the yearly revenues of the cathedrals taken together should have been £45,562, so that the average income of a single cathedral would have been about £1,820 a year. Because—for reasons that will become apparent—income appears to have risen very little during the period after Elizabeth's accession, a figure not much less than this is probably typical of the later sixteenth century. Comparison with the average income of £1,539 that can be calculated from the *Valor* suggests stagnation in the revenues available to the cathedrals during a period of rapid price inflation.[2]

---

[1] See Christopher Hill, *Economic Problems of the Church from Archbishop Whitgift to the Long Parliament* (Oxford: Clarendon Press, 1956), p. 8.

[2] For figures from the *Valor Ecclesiasticus*, see above, Chapters 1 and 2. Hill quotes Sir Thomas Wilson's estimate that the total annual revenue of Dean and Chapter lands in 1600 was £4,500 a year, but this is a misinterpretation, for Wilson's figure actually refers only to the income of the deans themselves. See Thomas Wilson, *The State of England*, ed. F. J. Fisher, Camden Miscellany, no. 16 (London, 1936), p. 22. Income from sources other than lands and tithes seems to have been negligible. Offerings from householders and parishes, like those at Lichfield described in Chapter 1, probably continued, but tes-

TABLE 7.1
Income of the Dean and Chapter of Durham

Source	1559–1560	1601–1602
Temporalties, County Durham	£1,381 15s. 0d.	£1,414 1s. 10d.
Temporalties, Northumberland	31 19s. 7d.	31 19s. 7d.
Spiritualities, County Durham	294 1s. 0d.	294 14s. 4d.
Spiritualties, Northumberland	171 17s. 4d.	183 15s. 0d.
Spiritualties, Yorkshire	75 0s. 0d.	88 13s. 4d.
Miscellaneous	17 12s. 1½d.	26 10s. 0d.
TOTAL	£1,972 5s. ½d.	£2,039 14s. 1d.

Information for Durham and Worcester is somewhat fuller and more accessible than evidence for the other cathedrals, so they may be taken as examples, richer than the average but otherwise fairly typical. The Dean and Chapter of Durham were supported principally by landed estates lying within the county; these produced three-fourths of the cathedral's total income. In addition there was a smaller group of lands in Northumberland, as well as valuable tithes ("spiritualities," they are called in the records, as opposed to "temporal" revenue from lands) in County Durham, Northumberland, and Yorkshire. The cathedral also received small amounts of money from woods and forests, coal mines, lead and iron mines, quarries, fisheries, mills, and salt pans.[3] The Dean and Chapter were responsible collectively for administering this estate; their chief agents were the receiver and treasurer, who were members of the chapter, aided by a number of laymen, principally the clerk of the works and (after 1576) a full-time attorney.

Income from all of these sources remained virtually constant throughout Elizabeth's reign, as table 7.1 shows.[4]

Expenses also remained nearly constant, fluctuating between £1,725 and £2,173 a year, so that accounts came close to balancing. An exceptional surplus of more than £500 was recorded by the treasurer in 1572, but deficits characterized the years from 1574 to 1577. Gener-

tamentary bequests to mother churches appear (on the basis of inadequate evidence) to have disappeared almost altogether after 1540.

[3] David Marcombe, "The Dean and Chapter of Durham, 1558–1603" (Ph.D. thesis, Durham University, 1973), pp. 94–95, based on Dean and Chapter Registers A and B, Prior's Kitchen, Durham.

[4] Figures from Marcombe, "Dean and Chapter of Durham," pp. 361–363, based on Receivers' Books 7 and 26, Prior's Kitchen. Temporalties consisted mainly of rents from land; spiritualties were mainly tithes.

ally a sum of less than £100 remained on hand at the end of the accounting year.[5]

At Worcester receipts of £1,846 18s. 11d. in 1559–1560 had risen to just over £2,500 by 1586–1587. Payments made by the treasurer rose, too: they are listed as £1,120 in 1559–1560 and £1,410 in 1601–1602, having hit a high of £1,630 in 1597–1598.[6] In addition to the money paid by those who held its lands, the Dean and Chapter collected wood and corn from the cathedral estates; it is impossible to place a value on them. The cathedral received revenues from about twenty manors and ten parish churches, together with money referred to as "Godsilver, suretesilver, and Whitsun farthings."[7] It would thus appear that there was a small but comfortable surplus, but this may be illusory, for the receiver carried arrears forward as if they were income, while some payments may not have passed through the treasurer's hands. It is also likely that needed expenditures, particularly repairs to the cathedral fabric, were simply not made, as the cathedrals cut their coats to fit the available cloth.

A few more figures, these from poorer cathedrals, will help illustrate the problem of fixed income. At Peterborough—one of Henry VIII's new foundations—revenues were about £820 in 1542. Under Elizabeth they rose slightly, to £889 in 1563 and £928 in 1576, but they had fallen again to £887 in the last year of the reign.[8] The revenues of Chichester (the least well endowed of the old secular cathedrals) were £507 in 1555, £584 in 1558, and £535 in 1585.[9]

Stipends of those who served the cathedrals also remained fixed throughout the sixteenth century. The salaries paid to deans varied a good deal: a sampling shows £400 at Winchester, £333 at Peterborough, £300 at Canterbury, £266 13s. 4d. at Durham, £200 at Exeter, £133 6s. 8d. at Worcester, £120 at Ely, and £100 at Chester. But these figures must not be taken too literally, for the deans had additional sources of income; the dean of Exeter, for instance, received a further £158 from rectories and tithes, while the total income of the dean of Durham probably exceeded £1,000 a year in the 1590s.[10] The stipends

[5] Marcombe, "Dean and Chapter of Durham," pp. 365–368, based on York Book, fols. 14–18, Prior's Kitchen, Durham.

[6] Accounts, A211a, A234, A235, A235b, A238, Worcester Cathedral Library.

[7] See Accounts, A74, fols. 2–3, and A235b, Worcester Cathedral Library.

[8] MS. 50, Receivers' and Treasurers' Accounts, 1541–1602, Peterborough Cathedral Archives, Cambridge University Library.

[9] Chichester Accounts, cap. 1/23/3, Compotus Book, 1555–1558, West Sussex Record Office.

[10] MS. 3686, fol. 29, Exeter Cathedral Library; Marcombe, "Dean and Chapter of Durham," pp. 39, 53. Only the deans of Canterbury and York received more than the dean of Durham; his income exceeded that of several of the poorer bishops.

of prebendaries ranged from £40 at Canterbury to £20 at Ely, Chester, Worcester, and Peterborough. Again these figures do not reflect all payments, for a residentiary canon at Durham might receive as much as £800 and a nonresident prebendary £130. Petty canons were paid £10 almost everywhere, and had little opportunity to earn more; singing men generally received £6 13s. 4d. a year, although Canterbury and Norwich paid them £8. The normal allocation for choristers was £3 6s. 8d.[11]

Salaries for dignitaries other than the dean were often quite high. At Exeter, for instance, the precentor received £120, the chancellor £60, the treasurer £66 13s. 4d., and the three archdeacons £66, £53, and £50, respectively.[12] Minor officers and employees also figure in most of the accounts. Almost every cathedral supported almsmen, who were usually given £6 13s. 4d., the same stipend as vicars choral, in addition to being provided living accommodations. At Peterborough the master of the grammar school was paid £16 13s. 4d. and his assistant, called the usher, £8. Twenty scholars received £2 13s. 4d. each. The steward of cathedral lands was given £6 13s. 4d., the auditor £10, two porters £6 each, the butler, cook, and caterer also £6, and the undercook £3 6s. 8d.[13] A barber received £6 at Durham.[14] Fees allowed at Canterbury included £6 each to two vergers, two subsacrists, four bell ringers, and two janitors; the keeper of the clocks was paid £1.[15] An analysis of the accounts for 1576–1577 at Worcester reveals these categories of expenses: stipends, £700; fees, £68 6s. 8d.; alms, £90; pensions, £28 16s. 8d.; repairs, £107 2s. 5d.; extraordinary expenses, £39 2s. 3d.; miscellaneous expenses, £38 6s.; and the queen's subsidy, £185 4s. 10d.[16]

In cathedrals of the new foundation—the former monastic cathedrals as well as Henry VIII's new establishments—statutes provided that income should be received and disbursed centrally, with a single set of records maintained by the receiver and treasurer. Things were not so simple in the old secular cathedrals, where individual prebendaries continued to collect the revenues from their prebendal estates without having to enter them in any master account. Because of this situation

[11] Figures from the MS accounts of the several cathedrals.
[12] MS. 3686, fol. 32, Exeter Cathedral Library.
[13] MS. 55, Peterborough Cathedral Archives, Cambridge University Library.
[14] Treasurer's Book 3, Prior's Kitchen, Durham.
[15] MS. M.A. 40, Canterbury Cathedral Library.
[16] Accounts, A219, Worcester Cathedral Library.

it is more difficult to document the financial condition of the cathedrals of the old foundation. Things are made still more complex by the existence in these cathedrals of colleges of vicars choral, who handled their own revenues and kept their own accounts, virtually independent of the Dean and Chapter.

At Durham the Dean and Chapter took it upon themselves to make their constitution more like that of the cathedrals of the old foundation by assigning specific lands to the individual prebendaries as an augmentation of their stipends. Such properties, called "corpes lands," comprised many of the estates of the former monastery that had been managed by obedientiaries. Thus the dean obtained the delightful grounds of Bearpark as well as the manor of Holme in Billingham and other tenements and rectories, while members of the chapter engorged other choice morsels of property. There were some problems with this. In the 1540s the Dean and Chapter had leased out much of the land to relatives and friends, so that the estates were tied up at unrealistically low valuations. In 1567 suits were filed to void these leases, relying on a legal technicality (the precise name of the cathedral corporation had not been used properly on the original documents). The litigation was successful but costly, legal fees amounting to £1,000.

There were also "bye corpes," portions of tithes that were annexed to the various prebendal positions in 1567. Dean Whittingham had not been present when this allocation was made and later complained that it had not been done fairly. The process of doling out the tithes to individual prebendaries was referred to as a lottery; further lotteries were held in 1573 and 1575. The revenues involved in all this were substantial, generally much greater than the actual stipends paid to the prebendaries. Toby Matthew, dean in the 1580s, thought that they provided two-thirds of his living. Certainly the return was considerable: the dean paid £105 to the cathedral receiver as rent for his corpes lands and could expect a return of more than £500, while a prebendary, for a rent of £10, could receive £200.[17] The result of these procedures, of course, was to transfer income from the general funds of the cathedral to the pockets of the dean and prebendaries.

An unusual sort of revenue seems to have been collected only at

---

[17] These complicated financial dealings have been unraveled by Marcombe, "Dean and Chapter of Durham," pp. 122–160, from the accounts in the Prior's Kitchen. The cathedral's tenants objected to the lottery leases, apparently on the grounds that their entry fines were increased. See Mervyn James, *Family, Lineage, and Civil Society: A Study of Society, Politics, and Mentality in the Durham Region, 1500–1640* (Oxford: Clarendon Press, 1974), p. 82n.

TABLE 7.2
Burial Fees

Paid to:	Burial of a bishop	A dean	A canon
The dean	20s.	—	10s.
Each residentiary canon	13s. 4d.	10s.	6s. 8d.
Other prebendaries	10s.	6s. 8d.	5s.
Each vicar choral	6s. 8d.	5s.	3s. 4d.
Each chorister	3s. 4d.	2s.	12d.

Norwich. Called "cope silver" or "knowledge money," this was an assessment levied on farmers and stewards of manors belonging to the Dean and Chapter at the time of the installation of a new dean. The chapter acts record collections authorized in 1575, 1589, 1601, and 1602, as well as several from the early Stuart period; since these dates do not coincide perfectly with the appointment of new deans, we may suppose that the revenues were not sought with great efficiency and that they were relatively small supplements to the income that the dean received from other sources.[18]

It was probably more common for members of the cathedral staff to receive payments whenever prominent officials were buried in the cathedral. A list of fees to be paid when bishops, deans, and residentiary canons were interred at Lichfield happens to survive; its figures are set out in table 7.2. In addition, each deceased dean or canon left his best surplice and hood to his vicar, or made a payment of 40s. in lieu of the vestments.[19]

PROBLEMS involving the residence of canons or prebendaries arose almost everywhere. Cathedrals of the old foundation generally had quite large numbers of prebendaries, only a few of whom were actually in residence at the cathedral at any given time. Most of these

[18] J. F. Williams and B. Cozens-Hardy, eds., *Extracts from the Two Earliest Minute Books of the Dean and Chapter of Norwich Cathedral, 1566–1649*, Norfolk Record Society, no. 24 (Norwich, 1953), pp. 16–17, 41.

[19] Act Book 5, fol. 53, Lichfield Joint Record Office. This table dates from the time of George Boleyn, dean from 1576 to 1602. Before the Reformation the prior of Worcester had the right of appointing a number of parish priests; when one of these died the prior was to receive "hys hatt, his Typpett . . . his Rydyng gownne, his partous, his spurs and gurdull, his Rydyng boots with Spurris, a hanger, his knyffe, his bedis, his horse saddull and brydull with the harnes" (ADD. MS. 145, fol. 51, Worcester Cathedral Library).

men held other benefices that were of greater value than their prebends, and they lived in the places where they held these preferments, visiting the cathedral only occasionally to preach or take part in elections. The statutes of cathedrals of the new foundation provided for relatively small numbers of canons, but here, too, pluralism and nonresidence were common and most cathedrals were actually served by no more than three or four canons at any given time.

Residentiary canons were given supplementary allowances, sometimes called quotidians, for their daily expenses. At Durham these were fixed at 12s. 5d. a day for the dean and 1s. 4½d. for the residentiaries, provided that they attended at least one service.[20] In addition, they shared the money that was left in the treasurer's hands at the end of each quarter or accounting year; these distributions were generally called dividends. Since the sums involved were often quite substantial, the rewards of residence grew increasingly appealing in the later sixteenth century, and one finds numerous instances of canons requesting the privilege of residence and of cathedrals attempting to limit the number of residentiary canons in order to preserve the profits of those who were already there.

Some examples will illustrate the situation. In 1574 the chapter of Chichester ordered that there should be no more than four residentiaries besides the dean, since the revenues would not support a larger number. Here the burdens of residence were not great: residentiaries were actually required to live near the cathedral and "keep the old laudable hospitality" for only three months in the year. Prebendaries who wished to take up residence filed formal applications, called protestations, asking to be admitted at the next vacancy, but these were not always accepted, and it is common to find prebendaries making two or three such protestations without success. In 1585, a typical year, the accounting surplus was £124 11s. 8d.; £20 of this was kept in reserve and the rest divided among the dean and residentiaries (now five in number), producing a dividend of £20 15s. 3d. for each of them.[21]

At Wells, John Herbert, a layman who was dean from 1590 to 1602 as well as Elizabeth's master of requests, secured a new charter in the form of letters patent confirming the cathedral's endowments and redefining the constitution of the chapter. The existing number of prebendaries (forty-nine) was to continue, and the eleven residentiary

---

[20] The dean could also claim 6s. 8d. a day for expenses when engaged on chapter business (Marcombe, "Dean and Chapter of Durham," pp. 30, 35).

[21] F. G. Bennett, R. H. Codrington, and C. Deedes, eds., *Statutes and Constitutions of the Cathedral Church of Chichester* (Chichester: Charles Knight, 1904), p. 26; protestations, cap. 1/4/4/72–78, and accounts, cap. 1/23/3, fol. 202, West Sussex Record Office.

canons were allowed to retain their positions, but it was agreed that no further residentiaries would be admitted until the number fell to eight. (This took fifteen years.) In future the number of residentiaries was not to be less than six or more than eight, the dean being one if he so desired. Only the residentiaries were to constitute the chapter, so they and the dean formed the corporation in which was vested legal control of the cathedral and its estates; other prebendaries had no voice except in the formal election of a bishop. The residentiary canons were to reside at least three months a year, or four if they held an office—for instance, that of precentor, chancellor, or treasurer.[22]

At Hereford the chapter decided in 1576 to limit the number of residentiaries to seven, so that they could be paid decently and funds husbanded for the repair of the cathedral fabric.[23] The accounts for York refer to twenty-two residentiary canons in 1560, when £162 12s. 8d. was divided among them.[24] But it is hard to believe that such a large number of prebendaries were actually present, and one suspects that the reference is to petty canons, the lower-ranking clergy who did really reside and conduct most of the services. Certainly Lincoln, another rich cathedral, had few canons in residence. After 1565 their number rarely exceeded four, and approval by the Dean and Chapter was needed if any others desired to reside. As in other cathedrals, these residentiaries were allowed to be away from Lincoln for long periods: more than twenty-weeks' absence was permitted as early as 1467, to which an additional "Seney" day for each week in residence was added during Elizabeth's reign. Finally, in 1584, the Dean and Chapter resolved that each of them was to reside for at least a quarter of the year.[25]

In 1599 the vicars choral of Lincoln complained that the dean was improperly claiming the rewards of residence from the common fund, thus reducing the dividend in which the vicars might claim a share. At a meeting of the chapter later in that year, it was pointed out that the archdeacon of Lincoln and the subdean were receiving payment for residence even though they were not present for the required thirty-four weeks. These officers were able to produce special "graces" that permitted their absence on the grounds that they held other benefices. Arguments about the dean's residence continued, however. Finally the

[22] L. S. Colchester, ed., *Wells Cathedral: A History* (Shepton Malet: Open Books, 1982), pp. 153–155.

[23] Act Book 2, fol. 28, Hereford Cathedral Library.

[24] Accounts, E1/18/1, York Minster Library.

[25] R. B. Walker, "Lincoln Cathedral in the Reign of Queen Elizabeth I," *Journal of Ecclesiastical History* 11 (1960): 189–190.

CHAPTER 7

bishop of Lincoln entered the fray, urging the chapter to allow the dean's claim: the statutes did not intend "to seclude the deane of your churche owte of Residence, being a principall member theareof and by hys oathe bounde to ordinarie Residence theare. . . . Yt ys not one-lie Comlie but alsoe necessarie that he shoulde be one of your number." Even this did not settle the issue; the chapter was still unwilling to allow the dean to enter major residence in August 1601.[26] At Worcester, too, there was a complaint that the dean's quotidians were being divided among the residents.[27]

York was unique in setting aside a sum equivalent to the dividend of a residentiary in a special fund called St. Peter's Portion. The statutes of 1291 state that this money was to be used for emergency needs and for the common uses of the chapter. The earliest surviving account book for St. Peter's Portion begins in 1572; it records a number of payments, quite miscellaneous in nature.[28]

IT has often been suggested that the stagnation of cathedral revenues was due to a system of long leases, which made it impossible to raise rents as prices increased.[29] In some cases, it has been alleged, leases were made for terms as long as ninety-nine years; reversions were granted long before the expiration of these leases, giving a favored grantee the right to enter the property as soon as the existing lease fell in, often at the existing rent; in exchange for these advantageous leases, a high entry fine was required and often pocketed by a functionary instead of finding its way into the cathedral treasury.[30] All of these claims require examination.

[26] Lincoln Chapter Acts, A/3/9, fols. 6–7, 18, 20, Lincolnshire Record Office.
[27] Accounts, A25, p. 23, Worcester Cathedral Library.
[28] Accounts, E2/21–30, York Minster Library.
[29] See C. Hill, *Economic Problems*, pp. 35–38, 311–316, e.g. Occasionally one also meets the statement that cathedrals suffered from unequal exchanges of lands with the king or from other royal actions. While it is true that some bishoprics, especially Norwich, were milked in this way, I have found no evidence of exchanges or confiscations affecting the cathedrals. Such exchanges were generally ratified by a private act of Parliament, but a search of the private acts passed between 1529 and 1563 reveals none that relate to exchanges involving a cathedral. Cathedrals benefited from private acts passed in 1542 and 1543 to give the Dean and Chapter of Lichfield and of Wells full authority to make leases (they had formerly shared this power with Coventry and Bath, respectively), and an act of 1543 appropriated the revenues of a parsonage for the support of choristers at Lincoln.
[30] See, e.g., W. T. Mellows, ed., *The Foundation of Peterborough Cathedral*, Northamptonshire Record Society, no. 13 (Northampton, 1941), p. xxxv, where it is suggested that these undesirable practices were borrowed from the former monastery.

172

For cathedrals of the new foundation, the maximum length of leases was regulated by the Henrician statutes, which said quite specifically that lands were not to be leased for periods longer than twenty-one years. Urban houses and tenements might be let for longer terms of fifty or at most sixty years, presumably in order to give the occupier the security of tenure needed if he was to effect repairs or improvements. No reversions were to be granted until the existing lease had eight years or less to run.[31] These provisions were reiterated under Elizabeth; an act passed by Parliament in 1570 made the Henrician restrictions apply to all cathedrals, after complaining of the fraudulent conveyances made by "ecclesiastical persons" that prevented their successors from obtaining the revenues needed to keep their ancient palaces and manor houses in repair.[32] In several cases the act books maintained at the individual cathedrals refer to these limitations, making it clear that the Dean and Chapter knew what was legally required of them.[33]

A large number of leases are recorded in the archives of the several cathedrals, so it is not difficult to see what the length of leases actually was. Indeed, this is the sort of evidence most likely to have been retained, since it might have to have been produced in subsequent legal proceedings while other matters, more interesting to the historian, were not so likely to require documentation.

There is certainly some evidence of long leases and unreasonably distant reversions. Almost all of this comes from the old secular cathedrals, which were not affected by the Henrician statutes, and from the period before the Elizabethan act. At Lincoln it appears that Bishop Longland ordered the leasing of a great deal of prebendal land in the period between 1532 and 1541, most of it for terms between thirty-one and forty years, because he feared that it would be confiscated if left in the hands of the church. Much later, and for different reasons, the great musician William Byrd was granted a reversion in 1563, to take effect in 1582, and in 1558 the Dean and Chapter granted a sixty-year lease to begin in 1574.[34] Although unwise from the point of view

[31] A. Hamilton Thompson, ed., *The Statutes of the Cathedral Church of Durham*, Surtees Society, no. 143 (Durham, 1929), pp. 95–99; J. E. Prescott, *The Statutes of the Cathedral Church of Carlisle* (London: Elliot Stock, 1903), p. 31.

[32] 13 Eliz. 1, cap. 10. A subsequent act (18 Eliz. 1 cap. 11) prohibited the granting of reversions until the previous lease was within three years of expiration.

[33] E.g., EDC 2/1/1, Act Book of the Dean and Chapter of Ely, 1586, Ely Cathedral Archives, Cambridge University Library.

[34] Margaret Bowker, *The Henrician Reformation: The Diocese of Lincoln under John Longland, 1521–1547* (Cambridge: Cambridge University Press, 1981), pp. 97–98; Walker, "Lincoln Cathedral," p. 195, based on the chapter acts.

of the cathedral, such actions were not illegal. A similar situation applied at Norwich, a new foundation that (as we have seen) was unique in not being governed by Henrician statutes. Here we find (for instance) several manors leased for ninety-nine years in 1567, the grant to begin at some unspecified date when the existing lease ends.[35]

It appears that most cathedral chapters did in fact adhere to the limitations imposed on them by Parliament and their own statutes. A few examples, from the less well known cathedrals, may be of interest. All the leases of lands granted at Carlisle between 1579 and 1596 are for twenty-one years; virtually all the leases of urban properties ran for sixty years.[36] Chester also leased lands for twenty-one years, but it violated its statutes if not the Elizabethan act by renting out urban properties, mainly under Edward VI, for periods as long as ninety-nine, eighty-seven, and eighty years.[37] Several ninety-nine-year leases of tenements are to be found at Hereford, too, but almost all of these date from 1550–1551, not from Elizabeth's reign.[38]

The real problem with leases does not seem to have been their length but rather the fact that new leases were generally made at the same rent as the old. It is hard to understand why cathedral officials were so reluctant to raise rents. Obviously they were not knowledgeable about economics and estate management; probably they did not realize the extent of the inflation under which they were living, since their own stipends remained fixed. The result was something of a bonanza, or at least very generous treatment, for all who leased lands or houses from the cathedrals. Some of these persons, of course, were themselves members of the chapter, or friends and relatives of the canons; favorable treatment is perhaps not surprising under the circumstances. But the loss to the cathedral could be great. At Peterborough, for instance, two manors leased at the beginning of Elizabeth's reign for a rent of £54 were said in 1638 to be worth £560 a year more than the rent paid.[39]

---

[35] Williams and Cozens-Hardy, *Extracts*, p. 23.

[36] Chapter Registers, vol. 3, Carlisle Record Office.

[37] Lease Book, Chester Cathedral Library.

[38] Misc. leases, esp. nos. 1839, 1845, 1996, 3152, Hereford Cathedral Library. It is interesting to find the Privy Council interfering in lease arrangements occasionally; in 1580 they were angry about what they considered unfair treatment of George Freville at Durham; see Act Book, 1578–1583 (not paginated), for October 23, 1580, and April 4, 1581, Prior's Kitchen, Durham. Felicity Heal, in *Of Prelates and Princes: A Study of the Economic and Social Position of the Tudor Episcopate* (Cambridge: Cambridge University Press, 1980), app. 4, provides tables showing the lease lengths for eight of the episcopal sees; almost uniformly these show a peak, often to seventy years or so, during the period from 1535 to 1553. It may well be that cathedral leases followed the same pattern.

[39] Walker, "Lincoln Cathedral," p. 196.

The continuation of such unreasonably low traditional rents might have been justifiable if large entry fines had been levied whenever leases were renewed, provided that these fines were paid into the general treasury of the cathedral. But neither of these conditions appears to have been fulfilled. It is hard to gather statistics about entry fines, for most documents that record leases either ignore the fine or state that one was levied without telling what it was. There are, of course, a few exceptions. In 1584 the dean of Carlisle was willing to grant a twenty-one-year lease to the heirs of the former lessee at an annual rent of £10 16s. 8d., for a fine of £10. Five years later the chapter allowed one of the prebendaries to lease the tithes of St. Mary's, the parish church associated with the cathedral, for £18 13s. 4d. a year but made him pay a fine of £40. The dean, who was nonresident, sometimes allowed the chapter to make the best terms it could: he agreed to a twenty-one-year lease at £5 a year with a fine of 40 marks (about £27) "or more as ye company shall agree," and a few years later he thought it appropriate to lease a farm and tenement for three lives at a rent of £10 and a fine of £45 "or more as you can gitt."[40]

Such information as we have suggests that fines, like rents, were not increased substantially in this period. In most cases they seem to have been three or four times the annual rent, a sum not much different from the expectations of monastic officials before the Reformation.[41]

The situation for the cathedrals was made worse by the fact that fines were generally not paid into the common funds. Indeed, they usually disappear from the accounts altogether. In most cases they seem to have been shared by the residentiaries. This arrangement is clear at Lincoln, while at Chester it was stated in 1740 that fines were divided among the prebendaries, the dean being entitled to a double share.[42] Almost certainly this division was already in effect under Elizabeth, and most likely it applied in virtually all the cathedrals.

In general, then, local evidence supports the view that cathedral revenues remained fixed throughout the later sixteenth century. Although some long leases can be found, most were for twenty-one years or (in the case of urban properties) for terms not greater than sixty years, as permitted by statute. The real problem did not arise so much from the length of the leases as from the fact that rents were almost

---

[40] Chapter Registers, vol. 3, fols. 58, 67, 97, 119, Carlisle Record Office.

[41] This view is supported by Marcombe, "Dean and Chapter of Durham," p. 104.

[42] Walker, "Lincoln Cathedral," p. 194; R.V.H. Burne, *Chester Cathedral* (London: SPCK, 1958), p. 238. In later periods entry fines were raised, but rents were not. Thus in the early nineteenth century the rent that Chester cathedral received for the bailiwick was only £73 a year, but the entry fine for a twenty-one-year lease was £2,920 (Burne, *Chester Cathedral*, p. 238).

never raised when new ones were granted. Nor were entry fines increased as an alternate, if shortsighted, way of keeping pace with inflation. And such fines as were collected benefited only the prebendaries, not the entire cathedral establishment.[43]

SPECIAL signs of trouble are found at some of the cathedrals. When the queen's commissioners visited Exeter in 1559 they were moved by "the pittifull State of the said church beinge so great" and feared that reform would be difficult, since none of the residentiary canons was willing to appear before the visitors.[44] The unwise actions of Edmund Scambler, bishop of Peterborough and then of Norwich, are said to have ruined both sees and damaged their cathedrals.[45]

At Worcester articles of complaint were framed and sent to Archbishop Whitgift in 1587. The writer—unfortunately we do not know his identity—began with the general charge that "the estate of the Cathedrall Church of Worcester ys greatly wasted and myserably shaken, by the bad husbandry of the late Deane and the now Prebendaries there." More detailed complaints allege that members of the chapter have diverted the common treasure to their private use "and have not lefte one penny in the Treasury to helpe the Churche." They have cast the church into debt by failing to collect rents from some tenants and by allowing buildings to fall into disrepair. They took advantage of the late Dean Wilson's "Infirmitie, when he knew not what he did" and was "almoste senselesse," to convert cathedral property to their own uses. "It is Constantly reported," the complaint concludes, "that he toke yt heavely, and [his] sorrowe hastened his ende."[46]

Whitgift sent the bishops of Worcester and Hereford (Freake and Westfaling) to investigate these charges. The depositions they collected make it appear that the complaints were ill founded or, at best, exaggerated. The chapter clerk, aged sixty-eight, and a sexton, now

---

[43] It is interesting to note that bishops and large lay landowners behaved in much the same way as the cathedrals. Lawrence Stone has shown that noblemen were loath to increase rents, perhaps because of the prevailing doctrine of social responsibility, and faced legal difficulties in extracting the potential value of lands from copyholders; see *The Crisis of the Aristocracy, 1558–1641* (Oxford: Clarendon Press, 1965), pp. 303–322. Similarly, bishops followed a policy of cautious conservatism; they were more concerned about the honesty of officials than about increasing the revenues from their estates (Heal, *Of Prelates and Princes*, pp. 48–49). There is no reason to think that the cathedrals were especially sensitive to charges of rapacity.

[44] MS. 3552, fol. 142, Exeter Cathedral Library.

[45] Cf. *VCH, Norfolk*, 2: 275.

[46] Accounts, A25, Worcester Cathedral Library.

eighty-two, did indeed remember "great treasures"—crosses, chalices, candlesticks, paxes, copes, and other vestments—that had disappeared from the church. Some had been divided among the prebendaries, but this had taken place at the beginning of Elizabeth's reign, when John Pedder was dean. The sexton agreed that "the late deane was greatly decayed in his sences at his later tyme, yet this deponent neuer knew him in that case that he knew not whatt he did."[47] One concludes that there had been problems and irregularities, but that these were not so great as the dissident grumbler had alleged.

The troubles at Chichester, on the other hand, were perfectly genuine; they arose out of the urgent need to repair the steeple in 1562 and the realization that ordinary revenues would never be adequate for the task. Faced with this crisis, the Dean and Chapter decided to sell plate and vestments that were not needed for Protestant worship. Application was made to the Queen's Council for permission to proceed, which was granted on condition that an inventory be made. This survives and is of considerable interest. The plate designated for sale amounted to 349 ounces of silver gilt and 158 ounces of ordinary silver; this included two great crosses, six chalices and patens, a monstrance, two pax boards, six cruets, two candlesticks, two censers, and an image of Christ taken from one of the crosses.

The list of vestments and other furnishings is more detailed and of even greater value, since relatively few descriptions of ecclesiastical needlework from the Tudor period survive. Among the articles in this inventory are seven altar frontals (each is referred to as "a fronte and subfronte"): one of red velvet wrought with gold; another of red velvet adorned with flowers and a crucifix; one "of russels" (a strong twilled woolen cloth), blue and red; one of white "branched" damask with images and fleurs-de-lis; one of white silk "called bawdkyn" (brocade); one of blue damask with an embroidered crucifix and flowers; and one of white, red, and green satin from Bruges. In addition there were silk curtains, one set yellow and blue, another red and blue, and three "very old" frontals of bawdkyn.

The numerous copes were of several colors, to fit the changing seasons of the church year. Among the nine "good" red copes were three of velvet wrought with gold, "whereof one hath the Image of Saint Pawle in the Cape;" another with the image of Saint Michael; one plain, without images; one embroidered with stars and roses; one with blue orphreys; and one "with the Salvation in the Cape." There were also four "old, bad" red silk copes. The white copes included one bear-

47 Ibid.

ing the arms of a Cardinal, another with the image of Christ and Our Lady, and an intriguing one "with the Trinity in the cape" (this was the sort of thing that particularly infuriated the reformers!); among the blue copes were one decorated with wreaths of gold and another ornamented with gold flowers. Red, white, blue, green, and black "vestments"—this probably means chasubles—are listed, sixteen in all. The inventory concludes with a sepulcher cloth (it is not clear whether this was a funeral pall or a covering for the Easter sepulcher) of "branched" velvet embroidered with images, several cushions, and an old chair covered in red velvet.[48]

It is not in fact certain that the frontals and vestments were sold, for we hear no more of them. It would probably have been difficult to find a market for such popish needlework, unless it was exported. But William Bradbridge, the cathedral chancellor, did sell 507 ounces of plate in 1563, receiving £128 19s. 9½d., of which his expenses, including the cost of obtaining a license from the council, consumed £34 18s. ½d. The remaining sum was not large enough to cover the actual cost of repairing the steeple, which amounted to £126 19s. 8½d., so some of the cathedral's ordinary income had to be applied.[49]

The Chichester accounts contain detailed information about the repairs to the steeple, again valuable because there are no other such records. The Dean and Chapter consulted a master mason from Salisbury (his name was William Phillips) who was presumably experienced in the problems of maintaining great spires. On his first visit Phillips merely inspected the steeple. Later he returned to instruct the local carpenters, who appear to have installed new timber framing. Phillips also supervised the pointing of the stonework; he was paid £22 for all of his services.[50]

The most severe financial distress occurred at Chester, as a result of what R.V.H. Burne aptly called the "rape" of cathedral lands. This had taken place in 1553, when the dean (William Cliffe) and two prebendaries were imprisoned in the Fleet on the order of Sir Richard Cotton, comptroller of the king's household, on trumped-up charges alleging that they had "tak[en] down the lead of their church and

---

[48] Chichester Accounts, cap. 1/4/6/2, West Sussex Record Office.

[49] Chichester Accounts, cap. 1/23/3 (1563), West Sussex Record Office. It is hard to imagine the tower of Durham carrying a spire, but the accounts for 1571–1572 record expenditures for repair of the steeple. It must have been a small lead spike, since a plumber repaired it and the cost was not great (Treasurer's Book 9, Prior's Kitchen, Durham).

[50] Chichester Accounts, cap. 1/23/3, West Sussex Record Office. The accounts refer to a separate book listing all the individual charges for this project, but the book does not appear to have survived.

[done] other disordered things." The dean was kept in prison for twenty days without trial; finally, while sick with gout, he agreed to appease Cotton by granting him the fee farm of most of the cathedral lands in exchange for an annual payment of £603 17s. Since the rents on the property amounted to more than £700, this was immediately damaging to the cathedral, and the future implications were still worse since the Dean and Chapter would have no power to increase rents or levy fines.[51]

Partly because of this alienation of revenues the cathedral grew more and more impoverished. The records of a visitation held by the archbishop of York in 1578 say that the church is dilapidated and the school building scarcely usable: stones have dropped from the vault on the scholars' heads and winter storms are unbearable. Nonresidence was also a serious problem. The subdean, John Nutter, told the visitors that the dean had not been in Chester more than twice since 1573; as for the canons, Hawford had come but once in ten years, Herle once in three years, Bulkeley and Hyde but once a year. (The dean, Richard Longworth, was in London attending the queen, Hawford at Cambridge, Hyde at Oxford.)[52]

At about this time, perhaps stung by these complaints, the chapter inaugurated a campaign to recover the lands. The fact that Cotton had made favorable leases to the leading gentlemen of Cheshire made it all the harder to do so, and the cost of litigation was enormous. Finally the earl of Leicester, having been bribed with the promise of six-years' rent of the lands, took an interest in the matter, and in 1579 Leicester, Burghley, Hatton, Mildmay, and Wray decreed a compromise settlement, generally referred to as the "Leicester award." Under its terms, Cotton's heir retained his rights, but the cathedral's annual rent was increased to £802 1s. 2d. This sum remained fixed for the next two centuries, and the unfortunate arrangement continued to contribute to the cathedral's poverty.

The total income of Chester cathedral in the years after the Leicester award was £986 13s. 4d. a year. The terms of the award specified how the £150 that it added to the revenues was to be spent: £4 for a divinity lecturer, £5 6s. 8d. in increased salary for the schoolmaster, £2 6s. 8d. additional for his assistant, and another £2 6s. 8d. to the organ-

[51] Burne, *Chester Cathedral*, pp. 24–25. The grant to Cotton, which was to run for an indefinite term of years, is in the Chapter Lease Book, fols. 16–17, Chester Cathedral Library.

[52] Burne, *Chester Cathedral*, pp. 12, 55–56, 60–61. Longworth, who was master of St. John's College, Cambridge, from 1564 to 1569, had been deprived of a canonry at Durham in 1570 because he had been in residence only one week in three years (Marcombe, "Dean and Chapter of Durham," p. 35).

ist and master of the choristers. Until the buildings had been refurbished, £24 a year was to be spent on the cathedral itself and £6 on repair of the frater so that it could serve as a common dining hall. The master of the works was to receive £10 a year, and £4 was to be spent annually on books for the cathedral library. Once these purposes had been accomplished the new revenues were to be divided among the dean (who was to have £20 a year), the six prebendaries (£4 each), and the petty canons (a total of £6 13s. 4d.). Nearly £100 was actually spent in repairs to the cathedral in a six-month period following the award, so the chapter may have spoken honestly when they told visitors in 1585 that they had allocated £200 for the first year and £100 annually thereafter. But the Dean and Chapter certainly did not follow the provisions of the Leicester award in detail. They were mainly interested in augmenting their own salaries, and after 1590 they simply gave everyone an annual bonus.[53]

STATISTICS quantifying the inflation of the later Tudor period may help us appreciate the financial distress facing the cathedrals and those who worked in them. The best table, which takes the price of a composite unit of consumables with the years 1451–1475 as its base, shows relatively stable prices until about 1520. By the end of Henry VIII's reign, they had doubled (the index for 1547 is 231). After having reached the amazing figure of 409 in the last year of Mary's life, the index declined to 230 in 1558, but it hit 300 again in 1570 and was 448 at the time of Elizabeth's death.[54]

The cost of consumable products, then, had doubled in Elizabeth's reign and quadrupled since the compilation of the *Valor Ecclesiasticus*, while cathedral incomes remained virtually unchanged. It is true that the price index does not perfectly represent the cost of all the goods and services needed by the cathedrals, for wages did not rise so rapidly as the price of consumables and most of the cathedral revenues went into salaries. But fixed stipends must have created distress for the clergy and singing men who had to pay higher prices for food, clothing, and other necessities. It must be remembered, too, that most of

[53] Burne, *Chester Cathedral*, pp. 72–75, 84–85. The Leicester award is copied in the Chapter Lease Book, fol. 41, Chester Cathedral Library. A visitation of 1583 revealed that there was still only one canon permanently in residence, although two others met the technical requirements so that they could receive the emoluments.

[54] Figures from E. H. Phelps Brown and Sheila V. Hopkins, "Seven Centuries of the Price of Consumables, Compared with Builders' Wage-Rates," in *Essays in Economic History*, ed. E. M. Carus-Wilson, 2 vols. (New York: St. Martin's Press, 1962), 2: 194–195.

these men were now attempting to care for families on incomes that in many cases had been barely adequate for single persons a generation or two earlier.

When every possible allowance is made, it is still clear that the cathedrals were much less well off at the end of the Tudor period than they had been at its beginning. A handful of deans and canons still enjoyed comfortable, privileged positions, but even they could never hope to live like such predecessors as Prior More. Most of those who served in the cathedral churches found life increasingly Spartan. If there were great rewards, they were not of this world.

8

CATHEDRAL MUSIC AND
MUSICIANS

BECAUSE sung services formed such a prominent part of the work of the cathedrals, musicians were important members of the cathedral establishments. Those who loved church music might have been prepared, as many of their twentieth-century counterparts would be, to argue that the cathedrals existed mainly for the purpose of singing the praises of God and nurturing the finest music that can be made by man. The Puritans, as has been shown, disagreed vehemently with this sense of priorities and would have been glad if they could have shifted the emphasis from singing to preaching, even to the point of disbanding the musical establishments entirely. In this matter, however, their views did not prevail; throughout the Tudor period musicians made up a majority of the persons serving in all of the English cathedrals, and musical standards remained high. This chapter will consider the duties, living conditions, and general status of the vicars choral, singing men or lay clerks, petty canons, choristers, and organists, and it will draw together some information about such matters as organs and choral repertoire, especially during the Elizabethan age.[1]

LONG before the sixteenth century, the men who sang in the choirs of the old secular cathedrals—the cathedrals of the old foundation— were organized into colleges of vicars choral. These establishments were altered relatively little by the Reformation; the vicars choral re-

---

[1] For general studies of these and related topics see Peter Le Huray, *Music and the Reformation in England, 1549–1660* (London: Herbert Jenkins, 1967); Denis Stevens, *Tudor Church Music* (New York: Norton, 1966); Hugh Benham, *Latin Church Music in England, c. 1460–1575* (London: Barrie and Jenkins, 1977); Walter L. Woodfill, *Musicians in English Society from Elizabeth to Charles I* (Princeton: Princeton University Press, 1953), esp. chap. 6; David Wulstan, *Tudor Music* (London: J. M. Dent, 1985). A preliminary account of the cathedral musical establishments can be found in Stanford E. Lehmberg, "The Reformation of Choirs: Cathedral Musical Establishments in Tudor England," in *Tudor Rule and Revolution*, ed. D. J. Guth and J. W. McKenna (Cambridge: Cambridge University Press, 1982), pp. 45–68. There is some interesting related material in Nicholas Temperley, *The Music of the English Parish Church*, 2 vols. (Cambridge: Cambridge University Press, 1979), although Temperley does not deal directly with the cathedrals.

TABLE 8.1
Vicars Choral

Cathedral and date	Number	Cathedral and date	Number
York		Exeter	
1557	14	1550	20
1565	15	1563	16
1572	13	Chichester	
Lincoln		1550	12
1547, 1591	12	1570, 1585	9
Wells		1597	8
1564, 1587	15	Lichfield	
1594	17	1576, 1603	12
Salisbury		Hereford	
1574	14	1583	12
1562	9	St. Paul's [a]	
1575	7	1554	6

[a] St. Paul's also had 12 minor canons who sang in the choir; it was the only one of the old secular cathedrals to employ minor canons.

mained in existence at York, Lincoln, Wells, Salisbury, Exeter, Chichester, Lichfield, Hereford, and St. Paul's. Indeed, most of these corporations of singers lasted almost unchanged into the nineteenth century, and their influence extends into the twentieth.

After some fluctuation at midcentury the numbers of vicars choral stabilized under Elizabeth. Everywhere these colleges were smaller than they had been before the Reformation, as can be seen in table 8.1.[2]

[2] Sources, mainly financial records, include *York*: Accounts, E1/80, E1/88, E1/91, York Minster Library; *Lincoln*: MS. ciij/45/10, Lincolnshire Record Office; *Wells*: Fabric Accounts, 1390–1600, Wells Cathedral, ed. L. S. Colchester (typescript), app. C, Wells Cathedral Library (Wells in theory had fifty-three vicars' places after 1549, but most of these were kept vacant and the revenues transferred to the fabric; figures are for the actual number of vicars present); *Salisbury*: Act Books, MS. 80, fol. 22; MS. 81, fols. 29–30; Communars' Accounts, Box 104, nos. 126, 159, Salisbury Cathedral Library; *Exeter*: MS. 3686, fol. 30; *Chichester*: Chichester Accounts, cap. 1/23/2, fols. 69, 121–126, 202; Ep. 1/20/4, West Sussex Record Office; *Lichfield*: Thomas Harwood, *The History and Antiquities of the Church and City of Lichfield* (Gloucester: J. Harris, 1806), p. 257; *Hereford*: statutes (1583) and charter (1587), HCA 4254, Hereford Cathedral Library; *St. Paul's*: MS. W.D. 32, fol. 75 (Michael Shaller's Note-Book), St. Paul's Cathedral Archives, City of London Record Office. At Chichester the Dean and Chapter admitted that they had only six singing men in 1589 but said they were willing to appoint more whenever "eny man meete for the servyce of the church shall seeke vnto vs" (Chichester Accounts, cap. 1/4/8/2, West Sussex Record Office). For pre-Reformation figures, see above, Chapter 1.

After the Reformation the requirement that vicars choral take holy orders was generally dropped. Some of the vicars were still priests, but their number declined during the later sixteenth century. So far as we know, there were virtually no deacons or subdeacons; the vicars who were not priests remained laymen. The surviving records do not always state exactly what the proportion of clerics to lay singers was, but we know enough to chart the trend.[3] At Exeter, where all twenty-four vicars were required to be priests before the Reformation, there were six clerics and ten laymen in 1563, only four priests and ten laymen in 1586. The appointment of a layman at Salisbury in 1547 was clearly novel and its specific conditions were noted in the chapter act book,[4] but the twelve vicars present in 1568 were evenly divided between priests and laymen. At Lincoln a layman was admitted as a vicar of the second form as early as 1556, though this was a temporary arrangement, not supposed to last longer than two years.[5] Lichfield had five priests and seven laymen during the period from 1576 to 1603. At Chichester, only the priests were referred to as vicars choral, the laymen being called lay clerks; here there were four vicars and five lay clerks in the 1570s, five vicars and four lay clerks in 1585. With the chantries gone, and with infrequent celebrations of Communion, there was less need for priests than had earlier been the case, and the colleges of vicars choral came more and more to be made up of laymen who sought careers in music and probably turned to the Church mainly because there was little employment outside it.[6]

Vicars choral were generally appointed by the Dean and Chapter, often on the nomination of the precentor. At Wells the arrangements were laid out quite precisely in the charter granted by Elizabeth in 1592: when vacancies occur, the Dean and Chapter shall name a candidate within three months. He must be found acceptable by a majority of the existing vicars. Should the Dean and Chapter not nominate a vicar within three months, the vicars themselves may do so.[7]

[3] The sources are those cited in n. 2 above.

[4] Act Book, MS. 80, fol. 19, Salisbury Cathedral Library.

[5] R.E.G. Cole, ed., *Chapter Acts of the Cathedral Church of St. Mary of Lincoln, A.D. 1547–1559*, Lincoln Record Society, no. 15 (Horncastle, 1920), p. xxiv.

[6] Some of the priest vicars were pluralists drawing income from parishes they seldom visited. One of the vicars choral at Chichester, for instance, was vicar of Eastbourne and Burwash; it is said that he had not seen his parishioners more than once in two years, and that he employed an uneducated man as his curate. See Roger B. Manning, *Religion and Society in Elizabethan Sussex* (Leicester: Leicester University Press, 1969), p. 176. At Lincoln a vicar choral was parish priest of St. Mary Magdalene, but since this church stood opposite the west front of the cathedral there should have been little difficulty in his serving it (Lincoln Chapter Acts, A/3/7, fol. 48, Lincolnshire Record Office).

[7] MSS of the Vicars Choral, D. 5, Wells Cathedral Library.

It was common for newly appointed vicars to serve a probationary year, after which their qualifications would be reviewed by the other vicars prior to the granting of permanent tenure. At Wells the vicars choral were particularly careful about the probationary term for young men; they appointed a senior vicar to supervise each of the probationers and did not always recommend perpetuation.[8] Sometimes the evaluations are quite detailed; at Salisbury the vicars stated that one Richard Smith "hath no fitt voyce to singe the tenor for that it is to small, neither the countertenor for that it is not tunable thervnto, neither the bass for that itt is vtterly vnfitt for that parte," though "as concerning his knowledge they think him therin sufficient."[9] There was some complaint about the abilities of vicars choral who had been installed at Exeter in the 1590s under the patronage of the organist, Arthur Cocke, and it was reasserted that no one was to be perpetuated unless he had been judged fit by a majority of the vicars.[10] At Lichfield a vicar choral who survived his probationary year was expected to give his colleagues a banquet, called his "Senie Feast," at a cost of £8 or £10.[11] Having gained permanent status a vicar could generally stay on until he died or found a better position, but dismissals are not unknown; in 1596 John Hodson, a vicar choral at Chichester, was told to look for different employment since his voice was decayed and he had neglected his duties.[12]

Occasionally we find reference to the need for a specific voice. Salisbury was able to add two countertenors in 1551, one of the appointments being possible only after another claimant renounced his right to the first vacancy, and a man identified as a tenor was employed in 1590.[13] In 1593 Hereford promised the next vacant position for a tenor or countertenor to Thomas Boyce, "now or late of the Cathedral Church of Wells." Perhaps Boyce did not find the singers at Hereford as competent as those at Wells; in 1596 "he did abuse the company by depraving them behind their backs," and was ordered to reform his behavior.[14]

---

[8] Act Book H, fol. 32, Wells Cathedral Library, records the appointment of supervisors; for dismissal of a probationary vicar who did not have a competent voice and was of evil conversation, see HMC, *Calendar of the Manuscripts of the Dean and Chapter of Wells*, 2 vols. (London, 1907, 1914), 2: 206.

[9] MS. 81, fol. 136, Salisbury Cathedral Library.

[10] J. F. Chanter, *The Custos and College of the Vicars Choral of the Choir of the Cathedral Church of St. Peter, Exeter* (Exeter: W. Pollard, 1933), p. 21.

[11] Harwood, *Lichfield*, p. 264.

[12] W. D. Peckham, "The Vicars Choral of Chichester Cathedral," *Sussex Archaeological Collections* 78 (1938): 151.

[13] MS. 80, fol. 29 and MS. 82, fol. 20, Salisbury Cathedral Library.

[14] Vicars Choral Act Book 1, fols. 88, 98–99, Hereford Cathedral Library. Boyce had

At Wells we are presented with the interesting case of William Taws-well, who was praised by the other vicars for his "scientia[m] et vocem" and in 1586 was granted the next vacancy for a tenor, unless the Dean and Chapter insisted on the appointment of a priest. Tawswell was given permanent status in July 1587. It is not clear just what happened next. Tawswell seems to have had a fine voice but an irascible temper-ament, and it looks as if he was ejected or agreed to resign. But in October 1588 he was readmitted, again for a probationary year under the supervision of William Jeffries. At the end of the year, the vicars said that they approved of his demeanor and voice, but the Dean and Chapter rejected him because of "certain [unspecified] causes." In 1592 he sought restoration and was accepted by the chapter, once again for a probationary year. After he swore to abide by the statutes and customs of the church he was perpetuated in 1593, but in 1600 he was in trouble again, accused of illicit relations with the wife of another vicar. We last hear of him in 1601, when he admitted that he had spent the night outside the cathedral close, playing "tables" with friends in the town. He was suspended for a month but not, so far as we know, removed from his position.[15]

The colleges of vicars choral were substantial institutions, with sev-eral officials and numerous employees. A presiding officer was cho-sen, sometimes annually and sometimes for a longer period, from the senior, more experienced vicars. At Exeter he was called the custos; the position was held from 1586 to 1593 and again from 1598 to 1605 by Thomas Irish, an interesting figure because of his longevity. He was a priest vicar for forty-five years (1582–1627) and may have been a lay vicar before that; he was married and had a daughter, Grace, who in turn married a vicar choral. Her husband, named Robert Par-sons, served most of the seventeenth century, from 1619 until his death in 1676.[16]

Hereford also had a custos, as well as a steward of the garner, two collectors of rents, two auditors, two clavigers, and a clerk. All were bound in sureties for the true performance of their office: the custos had to put up a bond of 100 marks (about £67), the clavigers £20, and the others £10 each.[17] Servants included a laundress, a brewer and his

---

been admitted as a vicar choral of Wells in 1585 (Act Book H, fol. 32, Wells Cathedral Library).

[15] Act Book H, fols. 35, 42, 92; Act Book, 1591–1607, fols. 153, 161, Wells Cathedral Library.

[16] Chanter, *Vicars Choral of Exeter*, p. 19. This is not the composer Robert Parsons and was probably not related to him; see the entries in *The New Grove Dictionary of Music and Musicians* (London, 1980).

[17] Vicars Choral Act Book 1, fols. 4–5, Hereford Cathedral Library.

helper, a porter, and a cook. In 1581 the brewer was directed to make no ale, only beer, but ale was being brewed again ten years later, when the brewer was ordered not to serve it until it was at least four days old. The amount of malt used for brewing was limited by the queen's visitors in 1582 and by the college itself in 1590, while another order of 1582 stated that no one should be given ale or beer earlier than eight o'clock in the morning or three o'clock in the afternoon.[18]

The vicars probably spent more time drinking the college's beer than reading the college's books. One of the vicars was designated overseer of their library. In 1585 he was told to call in the volumes that had been lent,[19] but testimony at a visitation in 1588 suggests that there were not many of these. One of the vicars said that there was indeed "a library and a number of ould bookes therein safely kept, but to little proffitt of anye; for that the most parte doe not vnderstand the lattine tonge; but if anie of your worships do want any of the said bokes, we would verie gladly exchaunge for some newe writers, whereby we might be occupied in godly studye."[20]

Some of the vicars had taken wives as early as the 1540s, when marriage was first permitted for men in holy orders. We know that four vicars at Lincoln were married during the reign of Edward VI.[21] The married men, or at least their wives, were expelled under Mary. Marriage became increasingly common under Elizabeth; despite the queen's lack of enthusiasm, both priest and lay vicars brought wives and families to live with them in the close. Since surviving records seldom refer to the marital status of the vicars, it is impossible to produce statistics documenting the decline of celibacy. Such references as we have tend to be tangential. There is a note of allowances for the widows of two vicars choral at Hereford in 1595 and 1596, and the act book for 1600 provides that fines shall be levied against vicars whose sharp-tongued wives abuse or slander other members of the college.[22]

A decline in the frequency with which the vicars dined together in their common hall is clearly related to the fact that most of the choir men had married and preferred to eat their meals with their families. A problem had arisen at Chichester as early as 1568, when the vicars were enjoined to dine communally, as directed by their statutes. The

[18] Ibid., fols. 29, 38, 39, 77, 82.
[19] Ibid., fol. 52.
[20] HCA 3395, statement by Bartholomew Mason, Hereford Cathedral Library. Most vicars choral were not highly educated; at York none of them had attended a university. See Claire Cross, *York Clergy Wills, 1520–1600: I. Minster Clergy* (York: Borthwick Institute, 1984), p. viii.
[21] Cole, *Lincoln Chapter Acts, 1547–1559*, p. xxiii.
[22] Vicars Choral Act Book 1, fols. 93, 98, 116, Hereford Cathedral Library.

order must have had little effect, and in 1583 the existing situation was accepted by a new injunction that required them to dine in hall only once a month. Even this limited reminder of the old common life did not continue, however; in 1634 the vicars leased out their hall and kitchen and abandoned their dinners altogether.[23] At Hereford the vicars attempted to give up the common table for a year beginning in September 1587, arguing that the cost of obtaining a new charter from the queen had made them unable to maintain their accustomed hospitality, but the Dean and Chapter refused to permit them to do so. They were still having dinners in 1588, and they agreed to have supper as well four nights a week during Lent, "provided it be very sparing and not to exceed one dish of fish and another of butter and ye same to be deducted from their accustomed dinners on ye same day." In 1599 six vicars requested permission "to depart out of commons," and no objections were recorded.[24]

Some remarkable surviving documents for the Bedern at York vividly chronicle these changes. Here the individual houses were unsuitable for wives and certainly too small for families; the records refer to them as "cubicles," probably similar to the rooms occupied by students at Oxford and Cambridge. There does not seem to have been any attempt to knock out walls and unite two or more houses into a single larger dwelling, as was probably done in the Vicars' Close at Wells. Instead, the vicars moved out as they married and outsiders came to rent the chambers, so that most of the houses were not actually occupied by vicars at the end of Elizabeth's reign. Still, the vicars choral continued to take one meal together each day. Their Kitchen Book, beginning in 1563, lists the main courses served. During the second and third weeks in November 1567, for instance, they were:

Sunday	Goose	Roast beef
Monday	Beef	Mutton
Tuesday	Mutton	Veal
Wednesday	Haddock	Lampreys
Thursday	Rabbit	Rabbit
Friday	Whiting	Whiting
Saturday	Milk & eggs	Milk & eggs

Other entries give expenses. A roast goose cost 5s. 3½d., a pig 4s., "capons roste" 4s. 5d. Salmon was less, only 2s. 11d. In all, the charges

<hr/>

[23] Peckham, "Vicars Choral of Chichester," p. 136.
[24] Vicars Choral Act Book 1, fols. 61, 66, 112; Dean and Chapter Act Book 2, fol. 130, Hereford Cathedral Library.

for a typical week's food amounted to 54*s*. 1*d*.[25] Considerable "Howshoulde stoof" was needed to prepare and serve these dinners. An inventory compiled in 1564 lists, among other things:

> In primis xix sylver spones. Item one masure, lased about with silver with a cover and a knope of silver.
> Item one drinking cuppe of silver and a cover of silver.
> Item one pece of silver with a cover parcell guilt.
> Item four iugges and xv drinkinge pottes.
> Item two dosen of trenchers.
> Item iiij basens, four vres, and four candlesticks, four saltes peuter and one skeele.
> Item one stampe with xxx counters. And a paire of waightes, with Calvens institutions [*sic!*].
> Item one Duble table cloth of lynninge.
> Item two new table clothes for the table and one owlder.
> Item xlviij napkins.
> Item two table clothes for the servauntes table.
> Item one great Christ [crucifix?] in the inner howse.[26]

According to a statute accepted by eleven vicars choral late in Edward's reign, those who were "absent and furthe of commons" were to be fined 2*d*. a week. Even if they were sick they were to pay a penny.[27] These payments are recorded in the Kitchen Book, which shows that only four or five of the older vicars (presumably the unmarried ones) dined regularly in the early 1570s.[28] The end came in 1574, when a melancholy entry states:

> M[d] that the subchaunter Burlande, S[r] Kay, Swaine, Iverson, Richardson, Hunter, Lee and Burges bretheren and felowes of the Colledge called the Bederne, did geve vpp howse kepinge or kepinge of commons together in the hall this weeke vppon Satturday the xxvij[th] day of June Anno Dni 1574 by all ther consentes for so long tyme as they shoulde thinke goode therof.

A further note in another hand explains that

> this commons was broken vp by the sute of the maryed men being vicars chorall to the Deane called Mathew Hutton who gave license so to do, for that the maryed men shuld not be duble

[25] Vicars Choral Kitchen Book, 1563–1644, fols. 1–22, York Minster Library.
[26] Ibid., fol. 23.
[27] Vicars Choral Statute Book, fol. 130, York Minster Library.
[28] Kitchen Book, fols. 144–181.

charged. Wherfore all the hoole company of the sayd vicars chor-
all dyd so agree vnto the same as is afore sayd.[29]

The property of the college was divided among the vicars beginning
in 1577, although some silver spoons remained as late as 1591, when
it was decided to give each vicar two and the subchanter three.[30] Similar events, less well documented, occurred elsewhere; at Salisbury and
Exeter the common table seems to have been out of use before the
end of the century.[31]

Dinners in hall, while they lasted, must have been pleasant social
occasions. There was a tradition that visiting musicians might be invited; sometimes they were not to be fed unless they had helped sing
a service.[32] All of the vicars from Hereford may have journeyed to
Lichfield in 1593, when 8s. 1d. was paid for a special meal, not in the
vicars' hall but at the Angel.[33] In 1590 it was agreed that the individual
vicars of Hereford should pay for drinks that they gave to strangers
at the buttery, if these were above the three "cues" a day allowed the
vicar himself.[34] The poor were sometimes fed as well; it was customary
for "two poore folkes . . . to have relief with meat and drink in the
Colledge hall" at Hereford, and the vicars there gave up their "bevers"
or evening drinks and snacks on Wednesdays, Fridays, and Saturdays
during the "time of dearth" in 1597 so that they could contribute to
"ye relief of ye poore."[35] Similarly, the vicars of Lichfield gave 27s. 6d.
to those suffering from the plague in 1594, but all was not bleak; they
had wine "when Mr. Strethay invited the company to the Swan," and
Lord Paget sent them a buck from Beaudesert Park.[36]

Everywhere the vicars choral shared in the financial distress common to all who were associated with the cathedrals, as their resources
failed to keep pace with inflation and had to be stretched to cover the
needs of wives and children. At Chichester, uniquely, they had no independent income but merely received fixed stipends from the Dean

[29] Ibid., fol. 193.
[30] Ibid., fol. 202. For a fuller account of the Bedern, see Frederick Harrison, *Life in a Medieval College: The Story of the Vicars-Choral of York Minster* (London: John Murray, 1952), esp. pp. 214–280.
[31] Cf. Woodfill, *Musicians*, p. 138.
[32] In 1582 the vicars of Hereford ordered that no one should bring guests who were not either visiting singing men or the vicars' tenants, and that the kitchen should be no-tified in advance (Vicars Choral Act Book 1, fol. 39, Hereford Cathedral Library).
[33] Harwood, *Lichfield*, p. 271. In the following year 8d. was paid to a visiting singing man of Wells (p. 268).
[34] Vicars Choral Act Book 1, fol. 77, Hereford Cathedral Library.
[35] Ibid., fols. 62, 103.
[36] Harwood, *Lichfield*, pp. 268, 270.

and Chapter.[37] The Bedern at York had endowments of its own, but the college received a set amount from the cathedral treasury as well: £24 2s. 8d. a year, plus £7 0s. 6d. for the common table and a small sum for each individual vicar.[38] The situation at Lichfield seems to have been more common. Here the college of vicars choral was entirely responsible for handling its own finances. Income was received as rent from several hundred properties, mainly houses within Lichfield itself, the annual total approximating £150. For many years the treasurer carried forward the complaining notation that more than £5 had been "lost by the fall of money," that is, by the recoinage of 1560, when debased coins were called in and exchanged for new ones at rates lower than their face value. Rents for the Cardinal's Hat (probably a tavern) and for two pastures (called Bullmoors and Hobmoors) were also uncollectible items carried forward from year to year. The annual accounting, called the restore, was made before the subchanter and vicars in their common hall on the Feast of the Assumption of the Virgin (August 15); money remaining on hand at this time was divided among the vicars choral. This sum stayed constant, very close to £30 annually, throughout the 1570s and 1580s, but it declined during the last decade of Elizabeth's reign and was only £24 11s. 1d. at the time of her death. Occasionally charitable contributions are recorded: in 1590, for example, the 20s. paid as a fine for the renewal of Isabel Shenton's lease on her house was given to her "towardes her maryage."[39]

References to supplementary funding for the vicars choral—a recognition that existing revenues were inadequate—are found at a number of the cathedrals. In 1562 the canons of Salisbury agreed to pay a shilling apiece (presumably once each year) to the communar of the vicars choral, since the vicars were no longer attached to individual canons who were responsible for giving them hospitality.[40] A similar arrangement was entered into at Wells, where after 1583 the vicars choral received £3 6s. 8d. a year from the Dean and Chapter in lieu of the "meate and drinke" to which they had been entitled. Perhaps the

[37] Peckham, "Vicars Choral of Chichester," pp. 129, 142.

[38] Accounts, e.g., E1/81/1 (for 1562), York Minster Library.

[39] Vicars' Muniments, C.1, C.2, C.3, Lichfield Joint Record Office. The entries for the Cardinal's Hat were misinterpreted by J. Charles Cox, ed., *Catalogue of the Muniments and Manuscript Books Pertaining to the Dean and Chapter of Lichfield*, William Salt Archaeological Society, pt. II, vol. 6 (London, 1886), p. 195n, as a fee paid at the time of a visitation by Wolsey. The vicars received rents for several other inns, including the Swan and the Unicorn.

[40] Act Book, MS. 80, fols. 152–153, Salisbury Cathedral Library. During this period there were eight canons, four of them resident, and fourteen vicars choral.

singers were granted additional vacation in place of additional stipends: in 1584 their annual holiday was doubled, from three weeks to
six.[41] By the 1590s the vicars choral of Salisbury were receiving the
money that had formerly gone to altarists as a supplement to their
salaries, but it was acknowledged that this was improper.[42]

It appears that the Dean and Chapter of Lincoln were so eager to
secure the services of John Cheseman, evidently an exceptional musician, that they agreed to pay him £10 a year in 1594 even though the
other vicars were receiving only £4. The inequity must have caused
friction; the situation was regularized in 1598 when the vicars' salaries
were raised to £8 and Cheseman voluntarily agreed to accept the same
amount.[43] An individual vicar at Hereford had been granted an augmentation of £2 a year from vacant vicarages in 1557, and one of the
singing men of Chichester demanded £7 0s. 10d. even though his colleagues were paid only £5 10s. 6d. (this was about 1589).[44] In 1591 the
vicars choral of Hereford wrote the archbishop of Canterbury for permission to increase their stipends, evidently out of existing revenues,
but we do not know whether this was agreed to.[45] A number of individual vicars added to their livelihood by holding offices within the
vicars' college, or other posts in the cathedral; one of the singers at
Exeter was excused from the choir one day a week, and presumably
paid an additional fee, for mending copes and vestments, work in
which he was said to be expert.[46]

The wills of several vicars choral were copied into the vicars' act
book at Hereford, no doubt because these vicars had made bequests
to the college. Roger Carwardyn, who died in 1567, left an estate of
£29 12s. 8d. He was not married, though he had been accused two
years earlier of having an improper relationship with one Elenora
Whyte. She is not mentioned in the will; the bequests include £5 for
the poor, 40s. each for brothers and sisters, and a trifling 6d. to the
cathedral. Another vicar was to have Carwardyn's best gown and
surplice. Thomas Salte, who died in 1569, was also unmarried. He
presented a gold cup to the college of vicars and gave 10s. toward the
repair of its kitchen. The poor were to be given five dozen loaves of

[41] Act Book H, fols. 22–23, Wells Cathedral Library.

[42] Dora H. Robertson, *Sarum Close* (London: Jonathan Cape, 1938), p. 144.

[43] Lincoln Chapter Acts, MS. A/3/7, fol. 120, and MS. A/3/9, fols. 1–2, Lincolnshire Record Office.

[44] Dean and Chapter Act Book 1, fol. 150, Hereford Cathedral Library; Chichester
Accounts, cap. 1/4/82, West Sussex Record Office.

[45] Vicars Choral Act Book 1, fol. 80, Hereford Cathedral Library.

[46] MS. 3552, fol. 15, Exeter Cathedral Library, calendared in Herbert Reynolds, ed.,
The Use of Exeter Cathedral (London: Church Printing Co., 1891), p. 27.

bread and the residue of the estate after other bequests to relatives and college servants were made; 4s. 8d. was to be used for the repair of highways. William Davys, identified as "my boy," was given 40s. and Salte's blue cloak. Davys was very likely a chorister who lodged with the vicar; the will of Henry Mynde, proved in 1580, made similar bequests of 6s. 8d. each to Thomas Ferrett, "a lytle boye whiche ys in my Chambor" and Richard Hosyar, "the Ladd that vseth to come to my Chambor." We know from other entries that Ferrett was admitted as a chorister in 1581 and that Thomas Hosyar, probably the father of the "Ladd," was a vicar choral, later to be a prebendary of the cathedral. Like Robert George, who died in 1581, these men wished to be buried "in the accostomed place for ye buryall of Vicars," in the cloister. Mynde's testament bequeathed his soul "to the handes of Allmyghtie god my only redemer and maker, into whose mercye I committe my self nowe and at all tymes, that when he shall please hym to call me out of this miserable worlde I truste I shalbe in the nombre of them whiche he hathe redemed with his most precious blood." Such phrases are common in pre-Reformation wills, but it is unusual to find them as late as 1580.[47]

Some wills of vicars choral have survived at York as well. In cases where a valuation of their goods is given, figures range from £23 to £66; the richer vicars also served as parish priests. It was common for these men to make bequests to their fellow vicars (William Bait, who died in 1558, left such things as surplices, jackets, and spectacles to eleven vicars and an archdeacon) and to request burial at the customary place within the minster. The possessions mentioned are generally meager and include only one book, a Latin dictionary (*Hortus vocabulorum*) published in 1500.[48]

In cathedrals of the new foundation—the former monastic cathedrals and Henry VIII's new establishments of the 1540s—the size of the choir and the stipends of its members were regulated by statute. Instead of vicars choral, these cathedrals were served by men who fell into two groups—the minor canons and the lay clerks or singing men.

Minor, or petty, canons were expected to be in holy orders and were thus comparable to the priest vicars in the colleges of vicars choral; their position is in some ways reminiscent of that of the former chantry priests. In the first instance, many of them were former monks

47 Vicars Choral Act Book 2, fols. 18, 52, 66, 86, 89, Hereford Cathedral Library.
48 Cross, *York Clergy Wills*, pp. vii–viii, 6–7, 92–95.

who remained when their houses were refounded. Although they had been ordained, they were not highly educated; in contrast to the higher-ranking major canons, or prebendaries, few of them had university degrees. They have been aptly referred to as "efficient liturgical machines," for the pay was too poor, and the work too routine, to attract men of outstanding ability.[49] Lay clerks, as the name implies, had not taken orders. One often thinks of the lay clerks alone as providing the countertenor, tenor, and bass parts in the choirs, but the statutes given to these cathedrals in the 1540s make it quite clear that the minor canons were expected to join with them in "chant[ing] the praises of God and the canonical hours continually in the temple of the Church."[50]

If one adds the numbers of minor canons and lay clerks specified in the statutes, one finds that the musical establishments of these cathedrals were supposed to be somewhat larger than those where the vicars choral continued to serve. The numbers are given in table 8.2.[51]

The statutes ordain that "those who praise God together in the choir" should also "praise God together at table." So the minor canons and the unmarried lay clerks ("quotquot uxores non habent") are to dine together in a common hall, presided over by the precentor, with a steward appointed to provide all things necessary.[52] We know that the former monastic misericord was converted for use as the petty canons' hall at Chester, and that it was still in use in 1585.[53] At Worcester the monks' refectory became the hall. It ceased to function about 1560, for the same reasons that dining in the Bedern came to an end. But the Peticanons Hall at Canterbury (the former monastic dormitory) lasted until 1609.[54] Communal life seems to have broken down at Durham by 1580, when three minor canons—probably the last three who remained unmarried—were ordered "to keep house to-

[49] David Marcombe, "The Dean and Chapter of Durham, 1558–1603" (Ph.D. thesis, Durham University, 1973), p. 44. Only two of the dozens of men who were minor canons at Durham studied at a university (in this case, Cambridge), and only one of them completed his degree. The usual pattern was service as a chorister and secondary education at the grammar school in Durham before appointment to a minor canonry. Those who attended the university continued to draw their stipends (£10 a year) as minor canons.

[50] A. Hamilton Thompson, ed., *Statutes of the Cathedral Church of Durham*, Surtees Society, no. 143 (Durham, 1929), pp. 133–135. The statutes of the other cathedrals are similar.

[51] Figures from the various statutes; generally the same figures can be found in E 315/24, fols. 1–80, PRO, the two sets of financial proposals for the refoundation of cathedrals.

[52] Thompson, *Statutes of Durham*, pp. 150–153.

[53] Account Book 2, fols. 5–10, Chester Cathedral Library; R.V.H. Burne, *Chester Cathedral* (London: SPCK, 1958), p. 42. The cost of the common table was £10 5s. 8d. a month.

[54] Michael Craze, *College Hall, Worcester*, pamphlet (Worcester: King's School, 1982), pp. 4, 11.

TABLE 8.2
Number of Minor Canons and Lay Clerks

Cathedral	Minor canons	Lay clerks
Canterbury	14	12
Winchester	12	12
Durham	8	10
Worcester	10	8
Ely	8	8
Norwich	8	8
Rochester	6	6
Carlisle	8	4
Westminster	12	12
Peterborough	8	8
Chester	6	6
Oxford (Osney)[a]	6	6
Gloucester	6	6
Bristol	6	6

[a] These numbers were altered somewhat after the cathedral moved to Christ Church. In 1549 there were nine "ministri in ecclesia," or minor canons (including the chanter or precentor), and eight lay clerks ("clerici"), but during most of Elizabeth's reign there were ten lay clerks and only three or four "ministers" (Register, 1547–1619, fols. 2–42, Christ Church Archives, Oxford).

gether as the petty canons are bound to do."[55] At Westminster, while the Abbey was a cathedral, there was "contencyon rysen emonge the peticanons abowght their beyng in commyns," and in 1551 it was decreed that "it shalbe free for euery peticanon to be owte of commyns at his plesure, whether he be maryd or vnmaryd."[56]

Married lay clerks and minor canons seem to have found houses for their families close to the cathedrals they served. The *Rites of Durham* tells us that a countertenor named Nicholas Suffield (he was also a joiner by trade) had a house and little garden at the east end of the churchyard, and that it was occupied by Thomas Tyler, a bass, after Suffield's death.[57] The lease of a house in the close to a petty canon of

[55] Marcombe, "Dean and Chapter of Durham," p. 49; Act Book, 1578–1583, fol. 34, Prior's Kitchen, Durham.

[56] Act Book, 1542–1609, fol. 51, Westminster Abbey Library.

[57] *A Description or Briefe Declaration of all the Ancient Monuments, Rites, and Customes belonginge or beinge within the Monastical Church of Durham before the Suppression*, ed. James Raine, Surtees Society, no. 15 (Durham, 1842), reprinted with additional editorial material by J. T. Fowler, Surtees Society, no. 107 (Durham, 1903), pp. 163–164.

Norwich was recorded in 1573.[58] A survey of the minster precincts at Peterborough conducted during the Interregnum refers to seven or eight sets of chambers for the petty canons in the former monastic almonry and five houses for singing men (here known as "conducts") adjoining the former infirmary hall; in 1567 the petty canons had been ordered to live in these houses themselves, not rent them out.[59] The petty canons of Norwich were likewise told not to let their houses to outsiders.[60] Those who sang at Westminster Abbey are said to have found houses or lodgings in the immediate vicinity of the church.[61]

The cathedral statutes generally provided that minor canons and lay clerks were to be named by the dean with the advice of the chapter.[62] Sometimes more elaborate arrangements were made. At Westminster Abbey an exceedingly complex scheme was adopted in 1546, when the chapter agreed to divide these and other appointments (of choristers, scholars, bell ringers, and sextons) into fourteen portions, the dean holding two and each other canon one. Originally all nominees were to be examined by the whole chapter before admission. But in 1547 it was decided to allocate the places to the patronage of individual canons under a system of "lots and balls," with no further consideration by the chapter. At Ely a similar system was put into effect in 1551: the dean was allowed to nominate two singing men and all eight choristers, and each of the eight canons was to name one singing man. The precentor was chosen from among the minor canons according to an established rota.[63] At Carlisle the dean, who was not resident, wrote the chapter requesting the next vacant singing man's room for his nominee.[64] Reversionary rights were sometimes granted at Norwich, and singing men were sometimes employed as probationers—"yf he prove not sufficient to sing his part, then he must geve place," the chapter acts say of Erasmus Tuddenham in 1602. Here there is also an unusual instance of a singing man (Henry Smith) who was promoted to a petty canon's position in 1567, presumably upon ordina-

[58] Norwich Chapter Book 1, fol. 36, Norfolk Record Office.

[59] W. T. Mellows, ed., *The Foundation of Peterborough Cathedral*, Northamptonshire Record Society, no. 13 (Northampton, 1941), pp. xlviii–xlix; MS. 30, fol. 42, Peterborough Cathedral Archives, Cambridge University Library.

[60] Act Book 1, fol. 1, Norfolk Record Office.

[61] C. S. Knighton, "Collegiate Foundations, 1540 to 1570, with Special Reference to St. Peter in Westminster" (Ph.D. thesis, Cambridge University, 1975), p. 349.

[62] See Thompson, *Statutes of Durham*, pp. 132–133.

[63] Knighton, "Collegiate Foundations," pp. 80–83. Information about the Abbey comes from the Act Book, fols. 30, 39, Westminster Abbey Library; the regulations at Ely are found in one of Archbishop Parker's papers, MS. 120, pp. 288–289, Corpus Christi College, Cambridge.

[64] Chapter Registers, vol. 3, fol. 179, Carlisle Record Office.

tion.[65] In 1595 the chapter of Gloucester doubted whether they should appoint John Jenyns, probably the son of a former dean, as a lay clerk, but agreed to do so despite his lack of experience since he "daily takes pains" to learn.[66]

The salaries of these singers were fixed by the cathedral statutes, petty canons generally receiving £10 a year and lay clerks most often £6 13s. 4d. (At Canterbury and Norwich their stipend was £8, and there is an instance of a bass, perhaps a particularly fine musician, who was granted £10 a year for life in 1567.[67]) Occasionally there were opportunities for additional employment within the cathedral itself: a petty canon of Norwich was keeper of the treasury, for instance, and a singing man also served as gospeler.[68] One of the minor canons of Durham, William Smith, was an organ builder, and another was a bookbinder.[69] The case of a singer who was also a joiner has already been noted. At Peterborough a butcher, or at least a former butcher, was to be appointed in the early seventeenth century "if he could be made fit for the quire."[70] But it was not acceptable to keep a tavern, and one of the singing men of Norwich was dismissed in 1604 for refusal to "suppresse" an alehouse he had erected within the cathedral precinct.[71] Occasionally the petty canons served as vicars of parishes; at Durham this was permitted if their cures lay within twenty-four miles of the cathedral. The income from such positions was generally between £10 and £30 a year.[72]

Since the established wages were not sufficient to attract able men, unfilled vacancies existed frequently, especially among the petty canons. At Carlisle two of their positions had been converted into posts for lay clerks by 1594.[73] The stipends of lay clerks at Durham were augmented by funds from vacant petty canonries.[74] But such supplements were often inadequate; in 1581 the Dean and Chapter gave £9 10s. 8d. to one of the singing men, William Cooke, "towardes the relieve of him self, his wiffe and children, and payinge of his debtes"— £6 was an outright gift, the rest to be repaid in quarterly installments.

[65] Act Book 1, fols. 5, 40, Norfolk Record Office. Two petty canons appointed in 1571 were unusual in having held the M.A. (fol. 27).
[66] F. S. Hockaday, ed., "Episcopal Visitations of the Dean and Chapter of Gloucester, 1542–1751" (typescript, Gloucester Cathedral Library, safe 34), p. 65.
[67] Act Book 1, fol. 6, Norfolk Record Office.
[68] Ibid., fols. 20, 26.
[69] Marcombe, "Dean and Chapter of Durham," p. 46.
[70] Mellows, Foundation of Peterborough, p. xlviii.
[71] Act Book 1, fol. 41, Norfolk Record Office.
[72] Marcombe, "Dean and Chapter of Durham," pp. 47–48.
[73] Chapter Registers, vol. 3, fol. 181, Carlisle Record Office.
[74] Marcombe, "Dean and Chapter of Durham," p. 44.

Two more loans were recorded in 1582, the singers "being sore charged and haveing nothing but their stipends." Sometimes alms totaling £6 13s. 4d. a quarter were given to the singing men of Durham, but this was at the dean's discretion and could not be counted on: the distribution was made in 1565 and 1566 and again in 1579, but not between 1567 and 1570.[75] At Bristol the stipends of four of the singing men, here called cantors, were augmented by £1 6s. 8d. each after 1562, and one of the minor canons was given an additional 13s. 4d. The alms distributed in 1581 included one shilling to a poor singing man, but it is not clear whether he was one of those in the cathedral's employ. By the 1580s the composition of the choir had changed; there were eight cantors and only four minor canons rather than the six laymen and six clergy originally planned. In 1602 its size was reduced, evidently because of financial difficulties, so that there were only three minor canons and six cantors.[76]

In contrast to modern cathedral choirs, sixteenth-century musical establishments always included fewer boys than men. The numbers are shown in table 8.3.[77]

In several cases we know that these numbers were reduced during the later sixteenth century. This was easier to do in cathedrals of the old foundation, where the size of the establishment was under the control of the Dean and Chapter, than in cathedrals of the new foundation, where it was fixed by statute. At Salisbury, for instance, the number of choristers had dropped from fourteen to eight as early as 1550; during Elizabeth's reign it varied from eight to ten.[78] At Lincoln the arrangements had been altered in 1549, when the number of choristers in the old foundation was reduced from twelve to four but it was agreed to turn the Burghersh chantry into an endowment for the support of additional boys as "Burghersh chanters." The total number remained at twelve until about 1560, when it fell to nine.[79] Despite its statutes Bristol reduced the number of boys from six to only four in

---

[75] Act Book, 1578–1583 (not paginated), Prior's Kitchen, Durham.

[76] Bristol Cathedral Accounts, DC/A/9/1/4, Bristol Record Office.

[77] Sources as in notes 2 and 51 above.

[78] Robertson, *Sarum Close*, pp. 126–127. At cathedrals of the old foundation the choristers often enjoyed their own separate revenues; this was certainly true at Hereford and Lincoln as well as Salisbury.

[79] Cole, *Lincoln Chapter Acts, 1547–1559*, p. xxiv; A. R. Maddison, *A Short Account of the Vicars Choral, Poor Clerks, Organists, and Choristers of Lincoln Cathedral* (London, 1878), p. 23.

TABLE 8.3
Number of Choristers

Cathedrals of the old foundation			
Salisbury	14	St. Paul's	10
Exeter	14	Chichester	8
York	12	Hereford	7
Lincoln	12	Wells	6
Lichfield	12		

Cathedrals of the new foundation			
Canterbury	10	Rochester	8
Winchester	10	Peterborough	8
Durham	10	Chester	8
Westminster	10	Oxford	8
Worcester	8	Gloucester	8
Ely	8	Carlisle	6
Norwich	8	Bristol	6

1602.[80] We know that the full number of choristers was not always present in some of the other cathedrals, and it is likely that there were undocumented vacancies almost everywhere.[81]

At Lincoln the chapter acts sometimes record the ages of boys entering the choir. These range from six (surprisingly young) to fourteen (surprisingly old, and possibly a sign that voices changed later in the sixteenth century than today), with most boys coming at eight or nine. Here the admission of a new singer was a formal ceremony held in the chapter house following vespers. The boys were always designated as choristers or "Burghersh boys"; there was an exceptionally large turnover in 1584, when six new boys were admitted at the same time.[82]

In cases where we know the boys' background, it turns out (as we would expect) that most came from the cathedral city itself or from the surrounding countryside. Nicholas Orme, who has studied the

[80] Bristol Cathedral Accounts, DC/A/9/1/14, Bristol Record Office.

[81] Thurston Dart suggested that only half of the boys (that is, only four) were on duty at Chichester in any given week, and that this "half choir" may explain the phrase "in medio chori" found in the works of Weelkes, but I do not find his arguments convincing ("Music and Musicians at Chichester Cathedral, 1545–1642," *Music and Letters* 42 [1961]: 221).

[82] Lincoln Chapter Acts, A/3/7, fols. 33, 80, 86, 91, 97; A/3/9, fol. 11, Lincolnshire Record Office.

choristers of Exeter between 1535 and 1558, found that their parents included two gentlemen (in one case the boy was illegitimate), a merchant, two yeomen, five husbandmen, a brewer, a miller, a weaver, and a widow. Some may have been sons of the tenants of cathedral lands.[83] In many cases there is reason to think that the boys were related to vicars choral, lay clerks, prebendaries, or the organist. Thus we find Stephen Bull, possibly the son of the organist Thomas Bull, as a chorister at Canterbury in 1558; James and John Lant, probably sons of Bartholomew Lant, the organist at Christ Church, Oxford, in 1564; William Warrocke, perhaps the son of Thomas Warrocke, organist at Hereford, in 1586; and two sons of Ellway Bevan, organist and master of the choristers at Bristol, in 1602. Two sons of Edmund Inglott, the organist at Norwich, were choristers, and one of them (William) went on to serve as a lay clerk and finally to succeed his father as organist (1608–1621). At Winchester, Robert and Philip Belfelde, choristers from 1561 to 1567 and 1573 to 1580, were very likely the sons of Henry Belfelde, lay clerk (1553–1579), and four boys (Leonard, George, John, and William, choristers in the period between 1576 and 1595) may have been related to the subsacrist William Wodeson (1553–1581). The choristers at Oxford also included boys named Calfhill and Bernard, very likely sons of prominent prebendaries. During Mary's reign, when priests were not supposed to have wives or children, there was a dispute about the admission of a boy who was the son of a priest at Hereford (not necessarily a member of the cathedral establishment), but in the end he was accepted.[84]

The boys generally lived together in a choristers' house. At Salisbury, the same building in Bishop's Walk had been used for this purpose since 1340.[85] The choristers' house at Lincoln had been purchased by the Dean and Chapter as early as 1283. In 1475 it was damaged by fire, and the choristers are said to have lost all their clothes. The house was rebuilt—indeed in a more modern form it still stands, adjoining the Chancery, although now used for a different purpose.[86] In most places the choristers ate together, in the choristers'

[83] Nicholas Orme, *The Minor Clergy of Exeter Cathedral, 1300–1548* (Exeter: University of Exeter, 1980), pp. xvi–xvii.
[84] MS. M.A. 40, Canterbury Cathedral Library; Register, 1547–1619, fol. 24, and Disbursement Book, 1578–1579, p. 41, Christ Church Archives, Oxford; Act Book 1, fol. 148, and Act Book 2, fol. 123, Hereford Cathedral Library; Bristol Cathedral Accounts, DC/A/9/1/5, Bristol Record Office; Chapter Book, 1553–1600, Winchester Cathedral Library; Noel Boston, *The Musical History of Norwich Cathedral* (Norwich: Friends of Norwich Cathedral, 1963), p. 67.
[85] Robertson, *Sarum Close*, p. 64.
[86] Maddison, *Vicars Choral*, p. 35; Stanley Jones, Kathleen Major, and Joan Varley, *The*

house or in a common hall shared with the lay clerks and minor canons. At Exeter, for instance, the injunctions of 1559 direct that the boys shall sit together at table and complain that there had been no specific provision for their meals earlier.[87] The choristers of Winchester ate in the choristers' house in the close; in 1541 the organist was paid £8 6s. 8d. "pro the dyette, rayment and other necessarys pro the same choristars" plus a further 20s. "for the co[o]kes wages servying the same choristars."[88] At Lichfield the choristers' house was leased to a layman in 1593; it appears that the choristers were lodged and fed in various places.[89] At Hereford the boys boarded with the canons, at Norwich and Chester with the organist.[90] During the 1570s York Minster paid the organist, Henry Thorne, about £18 a year for the board of twelve choristers, plus about £9 for their gowns.[91] In 1559 one of the singing men at Rochester contracted with the Dean and Chapter to care for the eight choristers for an annual payment of £26 13s. 4d.; he was to "provide, ffynde and geve vnto the said Eight Choristers meate, drynke, wollyne, lynen, hose, shoes, lodging and washing, holsome good sufficient and necessarie, with all other thinges for suche childeryn beyng nedefull."[92] At Wells it was agreed in 1587 that "the choristers shall from henceforth remayne att home"—evidently all of them were from the city itself—and they were allowed 20s. a quarter for their expenses.[93]

In most cathedrals a master of the choristers was responsible for the boys' training. Although he might serve as organist as well, this was not always the case. Specific responsibilities were often laid down when a new master (sometimes called an informator) was appointed. At Salisbury, for instance, the singing instructor agreed to teach the choristers "playnsonge, prycksonge, faburdon [and] distento."[94] Frequently the master was expected to teach the choristers, at least the older and more apt ones, to play the organ. At Exeter he taught them

---

Survey of Ancient Houses in Lincoln: I. Priorygate to Pottergate (Lincoln: Lincoln Civic Trust, 1984), pp. 47–50.

[87] MS. 3674, fol. 55, Exeter Cathedral Library. Earlier the choristers and secondaries were supposed to have been fed by the residentiary canons, who were granted 12d. a week from the common fund for this purpose in 1544 (MS. 3552, calendared in Reynolds, *Use*, p. 30).

[88] John Crook, *A History of the Pilgrims' School and Earlier Winchester Choir Schools* (Chichester: Phillimore, 1981), p. 7.

[89] Act Book 5, fol. 35, Lichfield Joint Record Office.

[90] Act Book 1, fol. 37, Hereford Cathedral Library; Account Book 1, Chester Cathedral; Boston, *Musical History of Norwich*, pp. 47, 66.

[91] Accounts, e.g. E1/93b for 1578, York Minster Library.

[92] DRC/A001/1, Rochester Cathedral Archives, Kent Record Office.

[93] Act Book H, fol. 42, Wells Cathedral Library.

[94] Robertson, *Sarum Close*, p. 122.

how to perform on "vyalls" (viols) as well, and at Lincoln "docile and suitable boys" were "to be taught to play on the instruments called clavichords."[95] At Westminster Abbey, while it was a cathedral under Henry VIII, it was ordered "yt [Robert] Fox, the M[aster] of our Choristars, shall have the whole gouerning of the Choristers to teache them, to provide for meate & drink & to se them clenly and honestly apparailed in all things, & he to have the whole Stipend."[96]

During Elizabeth's reign, there were often problems with these arrangements. At Salisbury, Thomas Smythe, the music master in the 1560s, was a drunkard and dicer who quarreled with the organist; it is said that the boys "utterly mock[ed] him" until he was removed by Bishop Jewel.[97] In 1561 the seneschal, or steward, of the choristers at Lincoln complained that he did not have enough money for their food, and in 1584 the Dean and Chapter withheld the salary of their teacher, Thomas Butler, because of his negligence.[98] The choristers of Hereford attended the King's School, receiving only their musical instruction directly at the cathedral. This was not an uncommon arrangement—the choristers of Westminster Abbey, for instance, attended Westminster School, while at Lincoln the boys were sent to the grammar school from 6 to 9 A.M. and 1 to 3 P.M.—but it does not seem to have worked well at Hereford. During a visitation in 1588, one vicar choral reported that the boys were "not so sufficientlye instructed in their musick and gramer as they should be," while another said that he did not know "howe they are trayned vp in Grammer, but in Singinge, nothinge at all to any purpose."[99] Things were still bad at Salisbury in 1602, when the Dean and Chapter complained that the choristers "are not at this present able (by reason of their want of knowledge and practise in the Church songes & musicke) to sing suerly and perfectly but doe often misse and faile & are out in their

<hr />

[95] MS. 3552, fol. 50, Exeter Cathedral Library, calendared in Reynolds, *Use*, p. 36; Margaret Bowker, *The Henrician Reformation: The Diocese of Lincoln under John Longland, 1521–1547* (Cambridge: Cambridge University Press, 1981), p. 93. The organist of Lincoln, Thomas Butler, was warned several times in 1594 and 1595 about his "insignem negligentiam" in not instructing the boys in playing the organ; he promised to teach the more able ones ("aptiores") (Lincoln Chapter Acts, A/3/7, fol. 121, Lincolnshire Record Office). Boys who learned how to perform on instruments may have had opportunities to play them during services, for instrumental music was not limited to the organ. Instruments were sometimes played from minstrels' galleries; in addition to the famous example in the nave at Exeter, there were others in the transepts there, one at Wells, and perhaps more elsewhere.

[96] Edward Pine, *The Westminster Abbey Singers* (London: Dennis Dobson, 1953), p. 46.

[97] Robertson, *Sarum Close*, p. 139. Smythe later promised to reform, was pardoned, and eventually became the organist.

[98] Lincoln Chapter Acts, A/3/7, fols. 11, 97, Lincolnshire Record Office.

[99] HCA 3395, Hereford Cathedral Library; Lincoln Chapter Acts, 1559–1597, A/3/7, fol. 58, Lincolnshire Record Office.

singing to the greate shame of the teacher & disgrace of so eminent a Church to which so many strangers doe repaire." John Bartlett, the boys' master, claimed that it was not his duty to teach the children, but only to find them food and apparel. He seems to have failed in this, too, for the choristers' house was said not to be clean and decent, so that the boys had been taken home by their parents and friends and no one had lived in the house for a month.[100]

It was frequently difficult to find talented boys for the choirs, and financial records occasionally include payments to the organist or master of the choristers for trips to search for them. Thus, during Mary's reign, Canterbury paid 13s. "to take vpp children to serve our church," while under Elizabeth, Bristol allowed expenses of 5s. for a journey "to provide some mete choristers for our choir."[101] In 1541 Winchester paid 3s. 4d. for the expenses of a chorister who came from Guildford.[102] Fuller and more interesting documentation comes from Westminster Abbey, unfortunately dating from the period before it became a cathedral. One of the special privileges of the Abbey, shared by the Chapel Royal and ratified by royal warrants such as that issued by Henry VII in 1497, was the power of impressing outstanding men and boys from other choirs.[103] A fascinating instance of this perquisite in operation is provided in the account book of William Fyttz, subalmoner in the early sixteenth century. In November 1512 Fyttz traveled from Westminster to the City of London "to take too chyldren with the commyssyon, the tone callyd Richard Bemond, the other callyd Wyllyam ffynnes." Parents had to be mollified, as several entries show:

Item gevyn to Wyllyam ffynes Master lying seke by cause he had no body to help hym in his syckenes, iijs. iijd.
Item to the same W. ffynes moder to haue hyr good wylle, xijd.
Item to Richard Bemondes master by cause of hys good wylle, xijd.

. . . .

Item spent of Ric. Bemonde ffader & moder W. ffynes moder when the[y] came to Westminster to se the children, xijd.

Later another boy, Peter Best, was recruited from St. Olave's Church; his father, the parish clerk, obtained 2s. 6d. for his good will, and subsequently (together with Fynes' mother and sister) he received another

[100] Choristers' Accounts, 2/4, Salisbury Cathedral Library.
[101] MS. M.A. 39, fol. 18, Canterbury Cathedral Library; Bristol Cathedral Accounts, 1581, DC/A/9/1/4, Bristol Record Office.
[102] Treasurer's Book, 1541–1542, fol. 11, Winchester Cathedral Library.
[103] Pine, *Westminster Abbey Singers*, pp. 27–28.

payment, probably for expenses in visiting at Westminster. When one of the boys fell ill, 10s. was paid to his father "for his surgery & phisyk in ye tyme of his seknes," and Robert Medellan's wife received 8s. "for kepyng of W. Whyght, one of the syngyng chyldern, viij weks." A bill from the "potycary" amounted to 5s. 2d.[104]

Naturally the cathedrals were unhappy when their best choristers were spirited away to Westminster, and sometimes they fought to prevent such raiding of their choirs. In 1493 the Dean and Chapter of Wells gave 6s. 8d. to the king's servants to persuade them not to take away three choristers, and they paid another 10s. in 1505.[105] Nearly fifty years later Canterbury allowed 8s. to the organist, Thomas Bull, "for his charges to London to saue our queresters."[106] We know that one of the choristers of Wells was indeed taken to the Chapel Royal in the 1580s, for the queen herself wrote the cathedral about him. The boy, named John Pitcher, had been "brought hither to serve us in the rome of a childe of our chapel, in which place he remayned nighe this six yeares, diligent in service and to our good likings, till nowe, that his voice begynneth to chaunge, hee is become not soe fitt for our service." Elizabeth asked the Dean and Chapter to give him "a singinge mans rome" that she understood was "voide in the saide church," but despite her "expresse commaundement," they do not appear to have done so. They were later told that she was miffed at their refusal.[107]

When their voices broke, the boys were usually sent to the local grammar school with stipends from the cathedral. Peterborough allowed them five years of schooling at £3 6s. 8d. a year, as did Exeter, provided that the choristers had served that cathedral for at least five years.[108] Similar provisions, generally not so well documented, were in place at Durham, Lincoln, Winchester, Canterbury, and doubtless elsewhere. Alan Marden, son of the master of the choristers at Canterbury, may serve as an example of a chorister who proceeded to the grammar school there in 1576.[109] Choristers were supposed to have preference in being named scholars at the King's School in Worcester but were not always appointed; only one of the choir boys named in the accounts for 1543–1544, for instance, became a King's Scholar.[110]

[104] WAM 33301, fols. 2–20, Westminster Abbey Library. Some extracts are printed in Pine, *Westminster Abbey Singers*, pp. 30–36.

[105] HMC, *Wells*, 2: 132, 182. Wells seems to have had an unusually close relationship with the Chapel Royal and the Abbey.

[106] MS. M.A. 39, fol. 18, Canterbury Cathedral Library.

[107] HMC, *Wells*, 2: 314, from Act Book H, fol. 52, and Ledger F, fol. 113, Wells Cathedral Library.

[108] MS. 30, injunctions of 1559, Peterborough Cathedral Archives, Cambridge University Library; MS. 3674, injunctions of 1547, Exeter Cathedral Library.

[109] MS. M.A. 41, Canterbury Cathedral Library.

[110] Craze, *College Hall, Worcester*, p. 24.

Some of the former choristers attending the grammar school at Lincoln became poor clerks and received a total stipend of 5 marks a year; similarly they might serve as altarists at Salisbury or secondaries at Exeter.[111] An occasional clever boy might proceed from the grammar school to Oxford or Cambridge, still supported by the Dean and Chapter, and finally be appointed vicar of one of the parishes for which the cathedral was patron.[112] Those who were less academically inclined might receive assistance in establishing other careers: in 1622 (admittedly after the period under discussion) the organist of Winchester "put out ... the boy Jenings" when his voice changed but promised "to healpe him to somewhat to put him to a trade; 20s. they usually have when they goe off."[113] The Dean and Chapter of Salisbury out of "special grace" gave 26s. 8d. to John Wright, a departing chorister, in 1565.[114] Those who continued to be interested in music might eventually become vicars choral, like Robert White of Wells, a former chorister who was named a vicar in 1488 and served until his death twenty years later.[115] Other choristers who became vicars choral included Thomas King, William Smith, and John Raison, admitted as singing men at Lincoln in 1479, 1544, and 1561, respectively.[116]

Special events and recreations provided moments of diversion in the choristers' lives, which may otherwise have been fairly monotonous and drab. Before the Reformation, the chief of these was the Festival of the Boy Bishop, which began on St. Nicholas' Day (December 6) and continued with events on Holy Innocents' Day, sometimes called Childermas (December 28) and for several weeks thereafter. Throughout this holiday period one of the choristers, chosen by the boys themselves, was dressed as a bishop; he was conducted to the bishop's throne with due ceremony and was allowed to bless the people, to participate in processions and banquets, and occasionally to preach, though since he was not a priest he could not of course cele-

[111] Cole, *Lincoln Chapter Acts, 1547–1559*, p. 14; Act Book, MS. 81, fol. 11, Salisbury Cathedral Library; MS. 3552, fol. 139, Exeter Cathedral Library, calendared in Reynolds, *Use*, p. 51. Every chorister of Exeter was entitled to a secondary's place for two years, with the usual stipend plus 20s. a year for books so long as he remained at the grammar school. These young men were expected to attend services on holy days.

[112] For this happening at Durham, see Marcombe, "Dean and Chapter of Durham," p. 320. At Lincoln one of the poor clerks (John Huddleston, probably related to the singing man George Huddleston) was allowed to attend Oxford or Cambridge beginning in 1578, drawing his stipend as if resident (Lincoln Chapter Acts, 1559–1597, A/3/7, fol. 86, Lincolnshire Record Office).

[113] *The Diary of John Young S.T.P., Dean of Winchester, 1616 to the Commonwealth*, ed. F. R. Goodman (London: SPCK, 1928), p. 73.

[114] Act Book, MS. 81, fol. 11, Salisbury Cathedral Library.

[115] Liber Ruber, fols. 21, 26, 152, Wells Cathedral Library.

[116] Lehmberg, "Reformation of Choirs," pp. 49–50; Lincoln Chapter Acts, 1559–1597, A/3/7, fol. 11, Lincolnshire Record Office.

brate the mass. Dean Colet, approving of these ceremonies, ordered that the boys of St. Paul's school hear the boy bishop's sermon in the cathedral, and several surviving examples suggest that the choristers preached quite seriously, admonishing both their elders and their contemporaries to devotion and virtue. Henry VIII condemned such "chyldysh observances" in a proclamation of 1541 and ordered them to be abandoned, and many of the reformers joined the king in inveighing against them, but we know that they were revived under Mary and may have continued, in modified form, even longer.[117]

The boys of Salisbury were treated to "kockfyghtyngs and potations" in 1526, while the choristers of Bristol joined other members of the cathedral establishment in commemorating Elizabeth's accession with an annual banquet throughout her reign.[118] When John Redford, the composer and dramatist, came from St. Paul's to visit Chichester in 1543 he was given 5s. in appreciation of "his kindness to the choristers of our church."[119] He may have done no more than praise their singing, but it is possible that he helped them present a play. Certainly Redford was involved with the "children of Paul's" who formed a dramatic company under Elizabeth; they performed regularly in a building adjacent to the cathedral, and occasionally before the queen, who issued a license to the master of the choristers to take up children in any part of the realm to be trained for such entertainments. The Puritans, of course, disapproved.[120] Unauthorized frivolities, for which the boys were reprimanded, included playing "le tenez" (tennis) in Lincoln (in 1530) and football games in the close at York (earlier than this period, in 1409).[121]

IT is of some interest to see how long the cathedral musicians remained in office. Fortunately for the historian, payments to them are entered regularly in the accounts of some cathedrals, making it possible to calculate longevity and to note specific cases of special concern.

[117] See J. G. Nichols, ed., *Two Sermons Preached by the Boy Bishop*, Camden Society, n.s., 14 (London, 1875); Robertson, *Sarum Close*, pp. 78–94; and Richard L. DeMolen, *"Pueri Christi Imitatio*: The Festival of the Boy-Bishop in Tudor England," *Moreana*, no. 45 (1975): 17–28. A sermon preached by the bishop of Ely, John Alcock, for the boy bishop was printed in London by Wynkyn de Worde under the title *In die Innocencium sermo pro episcopo puerorum* (undated; probably temp. Henry VII).

[118] J. G. Nichols, *Two Sermons*, p. 10; Bristol Cathedral Accounts, DC/A/9/1/4, Bristol Record Office.

[119] Accounts, Cap. I/23/2, fol. 63, West Sussex Record Office.

[120] H. H. Milman, *Annals of St. Paul's Cathedral* (London: John Murray, 1868), pp. 312–314.

[121] Lehmberg, "Reformation of Choirs," p. 49.

A study of the singing men employed at Durham during Elizabeth's reign, excluding those whose careers began before 1558 and those whose terms extended beyond 1603, reveals that fourteen such men served an average of twenty years each.[122] Two men are recorded as being present for a single year, possibly a sign that they proved unsuitable or found that they disliked the work. (One, employed only during 1558, may have found the Elizabethan Settlement unpalatable.) At the other extreme, one finds instances like that of Miles White, who had been a chorister and then scholar in the grammar school under Mary. He took his place as a singing man in 1562 and was still in office forty-one years later, when Elizabeth died. Robert Masham, also a former chorister and scholar, sang for thirty-eight years (1565–1603). With the exception of the two men who sang for a year or less, all of these musicians were employed for at least a decade, and many of them must have had no other occupation during their mature lives.

Similar calculations for the minor canons produce a list of thirty-seven men whose average period of service was almost twelve years. Here one finds a much larger number who were employed for a single year; these twelve men, being priests, may have been able to move on to more lucrative positions in parishes. If they are disregarded, the term of employment averages fifteen years. The most interesting case—and one that is difficult to sort out—is that of William Smith. Evidently there were two men with this name, possibly father and son although the records do not differentiate them or indicate their relationship. The elder was in office by 1547 and is probably last mentioned in 1570; the younger was a chorister from 1565 to 1570, a scholar in the grammar school in 1571–1572, and a minor canon from 1577 to 1600. During the last decade of his life he was also master of the choristers.[123] Another singer, Michael Patteson, had an even longer career, running from 1571 into the reign of James I.

Choristers, naturally, could not remain so long. The seventy-one boys listed by the treasurers for this period served an average of about four and a half years. Imperfect records probably account for what appears to be a large turnover in 1581 and again in 1588, with a num-

[122] These statistics, and those about minor canons and choristers which follow, have been calculated from Treasurers' Books 1–19, Prior's Kitchen, Durham. There are gaps between 1572 and 1576 and between 1581 and 1587 that may affect the figures: some of the musicians may in fact have served longer terms than those revealed by the accounts.

[123] Neither of these men was the composer of the preces and responses still frequently used in the cathedrals, although they may have been related since the composer was also a Durham man. (According to the *New Grove Dictionary*, his dates are 1603–1645.) Our William Smith the Younger was probably born a bit later than 1550, the date suggested in *Grove*, since it is not likely that he would have been so old as fifteen when first appointed a chorister.

ber of boys mentioned only once; if these are discounted, the true term of service was about five years. Two cases of longevity are surprising: George Dobson appears to have sung for twelve years and Robert Watson for eleven. If the records are correct, they must have been very young when they entered the choir. Nineteen of the choristers went on to become scholars in the grammar school; three of them (including the younger William Smith) later served as minor canons, and two as singing men. Several may have been the sons of singing men and one (Robert Wright) was possibly a second-generation chorister.

In each cathedral where we can trace the careers of the musicians there are instances of men who sang for two decades or more, but some of the choirs do not seem to have had the high degree of stability recorded at Durham. At Chester, for instance, only two of the six "conducts" listed in 1585 were still there in 1591, while at Hereford half of the twelve vicars choral enrolled in 1602 had come in 1593 or later.[124] The longest careers seem to have occurred at Exeter, where William Woke was a vicar choral for seventy-two years and John Hicks for seventy.[125] (Were they even able to attend the services by the end of their lives, one wonders, much less add to the musical quality of the choir?) At Westminster Abbey the tenure of Christopher Brickett was nearly as long; a chorister in the old monastic Lady Chapel, he attended the grammar school, then served as a choirman from 1549 until his death on Ascension Day, 1596.[126] A petty canon of Norwich, Thomas Sadlington, served for fifty-nine years (1579–1638).[127] The life of Jerome Loveday, who sang at Lincoln, is particularly well documented. He was admitted as a chorister in 1547, became a poor clerk in 1555 and a subdeacon in 1558, was married at St. Margaret's Church within the cathedral close in 1567, saw several of his children baptized there, and died in February 1578.[128] A whole dynasty of men, appropriately named Base, served at Chichester; they included Richard (1548–1570), Owen (1559–1585), John (1559–1601), and Henry (1570–1588).[129]

---

[124] Account Book 3, fol. 115, Chester Cathedral Library; Vicars Choral Act Book 1, fol. 124, Hereford Cathedral Library.

[125] Chanter, *Vicars Choral of Exeter*, p. 21.

[126] Knighton, "Collegiate Foundations," p. 349.

[127] Norwich Chapter Book 1, Norfolk Record Office; also J. F. Williams and B. Cozens-Hardy, eds., *Extracts from the Two Earliest Minute Books of the Dean and Chapter of Norwich Cathedral, 1566–1649*, Norfolk Record Society, no. 24 (Norwich, 1953), pp. 20–21.

[128] Cole, *Lincoln Chapter Acts, 1547–1559*, p. 156.

[129] Peckham, "Vicars Choral of Chichester," pp. 156–159; caps. I/23/2 and I/23/3, West Sussex Record Office.

31. Monument to Osbert Parsley, Norwich Cathedral.

The best known of the Tudor singing men, Osbert Parsley, sang at Norwich for half a century. His monument in the cathedral nave (fig. 31) is the only such memorial to a lay clerk. Framed by simple classical columns, a black marble panel carries this poetic inscription:

OSBERTO PARSLEY

Musicae Scientissimo
Ei quondam Consociati
Musici posuerunt Anno 1585

Here lies the Man whose Name in Spight of Death
Renowned lives by Blast of Golden Fame
Whose Harmony survives his vital Breath,
Whose Skill no Pride did spot whose Life no Blame

Whose low Estate was blest with quiet Mind:
As our sweet Cords with Discords mixed be:
Whose Life in *Seventy* and *Four* Years entwined
As falleth mellowed Apples from the Tree.
Whose Deeds were Rules whose Words were Verity:
Who here a Singing-man did spende his Days.
Full *Fifty* Years in our Church Melody
His Memory shines bright whose theme we praise.

If the dates on the monument are correct, Parsley became a singing man in 1535 at the age of twenty-four; he may have been a novice in the cathedral priory before the Dissolution, or he may have been a lay musician employed to assist the monks with their services. By 1558 Parsley had married and bought a house in St. Saviour's parish; shortly before his death, with his family grown, he sold it again. His will, dated December 9, 1584, leaves all his property to his wife, Rose, and mentions seven children—three sons and four daughters. Parsley was a composer as well as a singer. His service, which includes both morning and evening canticles, is still sung occasionally. He also left a setting of the Lamentations and a Latin anthem, "Conserva Me Domine," possibly written before the introduction of the Prayer Book.[130]

Another particularly interesting musician is Richard Bramston. Probably born in the 1480s, he became a vicar choral of Wells in 1507. Two years later the chapter insisted that he receive holy orders, but he was evidently unwilling to take the vow of celibacy and left the cathedral for the Augustinian Abbey in Bristol. In 1510 he appeared back at Wells "in privy and disguised apparel," as the chapter complained, "to have had away one of our best choristers, that is to say Farre." This attempt at kidnapping was soon forgotten, however; sometime between 1512 and 1515 Bramston returned to his position at Wells, without any requirement that he be ordained. A versatile man, he became both master of the choristers and clerk of the works, and he was a composer as well—two of his Latin antiphons survive, and Morley is known to have studied with him. After 1531 he gave up his post with the choristers but remained as a vicar choral and master of the works for the rest of his life. He appears to have been a shrewd businessman, involved in, among other things, the sale of sheep from the Cistercian abbey of Old Cleeve. His will, dated May 26, 1554, shows that he had become prosperous. Married but without children, he left much of his wealth for charitable purposes, including £100 to

---

[130] Boston, *Musical History of Norwich*, pp. 30–34.

the city of Wells for interest-free loans to young men eager to set up in trade or at a craft.[131]

ALTHOUGH the Chapel Royal functioned as the true center of musical creativity through Elizabeth's reign, most of the great composers also held positions as organist or master of the choristers in the cathedrals.[132]

A few had begun their careers before the Reformation. Thomas Tallis, the best known of these, had been organist at Dover Priory and then at Waltham Abbey prior to the Dissolution. When Waltham was suppressed he served briefly as a lay clerk at Canterbury (1541–1542), but about 1543 he was appointed to the Chapel Royal and in later years had no cathedral connections.[133] Although Christopher Tye had been born about the same time as Tallis (ca. 1505), he was never involved with the monasteries; he was educated at Cambridge and became a lay clerk of King's College Chapel in 1537. In 1543 he was appointed master of the choristers at Ely. A protégé of Richard Cox, he may have taught music to Edward VI while Cox was the boy's tutor, but he did not follow Cox into exile under Mary. After Cox became bishop of Ely, Tye was ordained to the priesthood, and he held several rich livings in the diocese during his later life. Occasionally irascible, Tye is said to have exchanged barbs with the queen: when she sent a verger to tell him that he was playing out of tune, "he sent word yt her eares were out of Tune." In 1562 Tye's son-in-law Robert White followed him as master of the choristers at Ely, later serving in similar positions at Chester and Westminster Abbey (1569–1574).[134]

William Byrd, the greatest and most prolific composer of the Tudor period, was very likely born in Lincoln and began his career as organist there in 1563, while he was still a young man. His qualifications must already have been impressive, for he was given a larger salary than usual and was granted the lease of a valuable rectory in addition. While at Lincoln he was married, and two of his children were baptized at the parish church within the close. He joined the Chapel Royal

[131] Nicholas Orme, "Two Tudor Schoolmaster-Musicians," *Somerset and Dorset Notes and Queries* 31 (1980): 19–26.

[132] Information about their lives and works is conveniently available in Le Huray, *Music and the Reformation*. On the Chapel Royal, see Woodfill, *Musicians*, pp. 161–176.

[133] *New Grove Dictionary*, s.v. "Tallis, Thomas"; Paul Doe, *Tallis* (London: Oxford University Press, 1968).

[134] *New Grove Dictionary*, s.v. "Tye, Christopher." The ancedote about Elizabeth comes from Anthony Wood.

in 1570 but for several years divided his time between the chapel and the cathedral; when appointed joint organist of the Chapel Royal (with Tallis) in 1572 he left Lincoln, but for nearly a decade he continued to receive a quarter of his former stipend on condition that he send his new "songs and services" to the cathedral from time to time.[135] John Bull similarly served both a cathedral and the queen's chapel. As a boy he had been taken from the choir at Hereford to serve as a chorister in the Chapel Royal. Appointed organist and master of the choristers at Hereford in 1582, he was soon in trouble because of his frequent absences, and after three years he was suspended. But he continued to have rooms in the college of vicars choral; indeed he was granted better ones in 1587 and again in 1591, on this occasion because of the personal intervention of Archbishop Whitgift.[136]

All of these men left superlative church music. So did Thomas Morley, although he is better known as a madrigalist than as a religious composer. Morley was probably a chorister at Norwich, where his father was a brewer and perhaps also a verger. For several years in the 1580s Morley was organist at Norwich. By 1591 he had moved on to St. Paul's, and he was also active in the Chapel Royal. Like Byrd he had Roman Catholic leanings, and his writings include Latin motets as well as English anthems and services.

Of the several cantankerous composers, the worst was John Farrant. Farrant was admitted as a lay clerk at Salisbury in 1571, having probably held brief appointments in the choirs at Ely and Bristol. In 1572, after finishing his probationary year, he was married to Margaret Andras, a niece of John Bridges who became dean of the cathedral six years later. From the beginning Farrant had charge of the choristers, and in 1587, on the retirement of Thomas Smythe, he became organist as well. By this time his son, also named John, was a chorister.

The elder Farrant had a violent temper and had been involved in brawls with another vicar choral, Christopher Cranborne, but it was a feud with Dean Bridges that ruined his career. The whole story is recounted in the chapter act book. Farrant's wife, it seems, had complained to her uncle that she was being mistreated. In February 1592 Bridges sent for Farrant, who appeared during a meeting of the chapter and insisted that the dean had no right to interfere in his domestic

[135] *New Grove Dictionary*, s.v. "Byrd, William"; Edmund H. Fellowes, *William Byrd* (London: Oxford University Press, 1936).

[136] *New Grove Dictionary*, s.v. "Bull, John"; Watkins Shaw, *The Organists and Organs of Hereford Cathedral* (Hereford: Friends of Hereford Cathedral, 1976), pp. 7–8; Act Book 2, fols. 108, 117, and Vicars Choral Act Book 1, fols. 59, 78, Hereford Cathedral Library. In later life, Bull was accused of adultery and fled to the Netherlands, where he lived from 1613 until his death in 1628.

quarrels. Indeed, he threatened Bridges, saying that he would deal with him later when he was alone. The occasion arose on Saturday, February 5. Farrant left the cathedral after the first lesson at evensong and forced his way into the dean's study, swearing by God that he would talk with Bridges whether it was convenient or not. Throwing off his surplice, Farrant unsheathed a knife and told the dean, "Thou goest to take away my living but Gods Wounds Ile cutt thy throat." "What, Vilane wilt thou kill mee?" replied Bridges. In the end Farrant did no more than tear Bridges' gown. The dean barricaded himself in his bedroom, "and when the said Farrant saw that all hope of entering [the] bedchamber was taken away from him, he went off and sang the Anthem without attaining his purpose." A choirboy had accompanied him on the whole escapade. When summoned before the chapter to account for his behavior, Farrant fled to Hereford, where he was briefly employed as a vicar choral but was dismissed after uttering "filthy rayleing & contumelious speeches against ye Custos of ye said Colledge at supper time." His later life, probably spent in London, is obscure; his son, who possessed a calmer temperament, served as organist of Salisbury from 1598 to 1618.[137]

John Fido also caused trouble at Hereford. It appears that his original appointment as organist in 1591 was the result of a recommendation by Archbishop Whitgift. He lasted only a year, being succeeded by Farrant; when Farrant was dismissed Fido returned, although the vicars choral resolved not to admit him to their company because he had spoken "most slanderous words" against them. He left Hereford in 1595 and spent a year as organist of Worcester but was back in Hereford by January 1597. Within a few months he was gone again; early in the seventeenth century he was briefly a vicar choral of Wells and later a minor canon of Worcester.[138]

The most pathetic case is that of the brilliant composer Thomas Weelkes, who was named organist, master of the choristers, and a Sherburne clerk at Chichester in 1601 or 1602. His career started well, for he held a degree in music from Oxford and was married to the daughter of a wealthy merchant. After 1608 he was probably associated with the Chapel Royal, and his colleagues at Chichester complained of his unauthorized absence. By this time he had taken to

[137] Act Book, MS. 82, pp. 39–44, Salisbury Cathedral Library; Vicars Choral Act Book 1, fol. 84, Hereford Cathedral Library; Robertson, *Sarum Close*, pp. 146–158; *New Grove Dictionary*, s.v. "Farrant, John." Shaw, *Organists of Hereford*, pp. 10–11, is probably wrong in thinking that the same Farrant was a vicar choral of Wells from 1594 to 1599.
[138] Shaw, *Organists of Hereford*, pp. 10–12; Act Book 2, fols. 143, 163; Act Book 3, fols. 172; Vicars Choral Act Book 1, fols. 93, 101, Hereford Cathedral Library.

drink; his drunkenness was reproved as early as 1613 and was said to be a public scandal by 1616. The next year he was dismissed as organist. He died in London, at a friend's house, in 1623.[139]

Minor composers with cathedral connections, in addition to Fido, included John Thorne, organist at York from 1542 to 1573; John Mudd, organist at Peterborough in the 1580s; Nathaniel Giles, organist at Worcester in the same decade; Thomas Bateson, organist at Chester in the early years of the seventeenth century; Nathaniel Patrick, organist of Worcester; William Lawes, a vicar choral of Salisbury; Elway Bevin, a vicar choral of Wells and organist at Bristol; and William Mundy, a vicar choral of St. Paul's as well as a gentleman of the Chapel Royal for much of Elizabeth's reign.[140]

ALTHOUGH no Tudor organs, or even their specifications, survive, it is possible to learn a good deal about them from financial records, act books, and other miscellaneous sources.

Organs were used in cathedrals even before the Norman Conquest. One such instrument at Winchester was described by Wulfstan (d. 963). It had four hundred pipes and twenty-six bellows worked by seventy men. "Like thunder the iron tones batter the ear, so that it may receive no sound but that alone. To such an amount does it reverberate, echoing in every direction, that everyone stops with his hand to his gaping ears, being in no wise able to draw near and bear the sound, which so many combinations produce. The music is heard throughout the town, and the flying fame thereof is gone out over the whole country." Two monks were needed to play it.[141]

Sixteenth-century organs were much smaller instruments—one or two manuals without pedals. Most cathedrals possessed several organs located in different parts of the building, suitable for accompanying singing in the choir, the nave, the Lady Chapel, or wherever else sung services might be held. Before the Reformation, Durham had four

[139] David Brown, *Thomas Weelkes: A Biographical and Critical Study* (London: Faber and Faber, 1969); *New Grove Dictionary*, s.v. "Weelkes, Thomas"; Dart, "Music at Chichester," p. 225.

[140] There are modern editions of works by all of these men. See Le Huray, *Music and the Reformation*, pp. 408–426. The vicars of Salisbury had been concerned about Lawes' appointment in 1595 because he was suspected of bigamy but finally agreed to admit him on account of the excellence of his voice. He later cleared himself of the bigamy charge (Act Book, MS. 82, fols. 74–75, Salisbury Cathedral Library).

[141] Betty Matthews, *The Organs and Organists of Winchester Cathedral*, 2d ed. (Winchester: Friends of Winchester Cathedral, 1975), p. 1; Frank L. Harrison, *Music in Medieval Britain* (London: Routledge and Kegan Paul, 1958), p. 205.

pairs of organs, described by the author of the *Rites of Durham*. The largest, over the choir door, was played only at principal feasts; its pipes were "all of the most fine wood and workmanshipp, very faire, partly gilded uppon the inside and the outside of the leaves and covers up to the topp, with branches and flowers finely gilted, with the name of Jesus gilted in gold." Only two organs in England, one in York and one at St. Paul's, could compare with it. A second organ in the choir, called "the Cryers," was played only when the four doctors of the church (Augustine, Ambrose, Gregory, and Jerome) were read, while a third was used for ordinary services. Still a fourth organ stood in the Galilee, which was used as the Lady Chapel; here "Our Lady's mass was daily sung by the master of the song school, with certain deacons and choristers, the master playing vpon a paire of faire orgaines."[142] New organs had been installed in many of the cathedrals during the fifteenth century. At Lincoln, where an organ is first recorded in 1311, a new organ was placed in the Chapel of St. John Baptist, where the Lady mass was sung, and repairs to the great organs in the choir were made in 1428, while in 1442 a new and better instrument for the choir was made by one "Arnald Organer" of Norwich.[143]

The sixteenth century saw the introduction of more new instruments. In 1513 the large sum of £165 15s. 7½d. was spent on organs at Exeter, placed on the choir screen, or "pulpitum."[144] At Hereford a new organ for the choir appears to have cost only £14, which was taken from the bequest of a former prebendary, Hugh Greene, in 1524.[145] There is a reference to mending the bellows of new organs at Chichester in 1533.[146] In 1540 Norwich acquired an organ from the dissolved house of the Black Friars.[147] The cathedral had previously (in 1510) spent £13 6s. 8d. from the estate of Lady Anne Heydon for an organ in the choir, replacing one that had burned in a fire the year before. This instrument appears to have been destroyed at the order of two Puritan-minded canons in 1576, but it was replaced in time for the queen's visit in 1578 by an organ costing £16 12s., its wind pressure stabilized hydraulically. This organ in turn was demolished when the cathedral spire fell in 1601.[148]

---

[142] *Rites*, 1903 ed., pp. 3–5.

[143] Maddison, *Vicars Choral*, pp. 27, 31, 35.

[144] Betty Matthews, *The Organs and Organists of Exeter Cathedral* (Exeter: Dean and Chapter of Exeter Cathedral, n.d.), p. 1. One often finds the plural form "organs" or "a pair of organs" in contemporary records.

[145] Act Book 1, fol. 36, Hereford Cathedral Library; Shaw, *Organists of Hereford*, p. 27.

[146] Cap. I/23/1, fol. 71, West Sussex Record Office.

[147] Liber Miscellaneorum 3, DNC, R226A (not paginated), Norfolk Record Office.

[148] Boston, *Musical History of Norwich*, p. 7.

At Exeter the organs in the Lady Chapel were sold to a parish church for £5 6s. 3d., but new ones must have been installed since there is a further reference to the sale of the Lady Chapel organs in 1545.[149] This may have been part of the reformers' campaign against elaborate music, as well as against the veneration of the Virgin Mary. At Worcester organs in the chapels dedicated to Saints Edmund and George were pulled down by Dean Barlow in 1550, and even the great choir organ was taken down on August 30, 1551, but a new organ was installed on the north side of the choir in 1556.[150] Dean May ordered that organ playing at St. Paul's be discontinued in 1550, and he may have gone so far as to command the removal of the instrument. If so his wishes were not obeyed, for the organ was in use again to celebrate the accession of Queen Mary.[151] New organs at Worcester had been set up by 1556, while at Westminster Abbey eight stops were added to the instrument at the beginning of the Catholic queen's reign.[152] A pair of organs erected at Canterbury at about the same time cost £6 18s. 4d.[153] The "chaire" organ at Gloucester with its fine case (fig. 32) survives as part of the present instrument; it dates from 1579.[154] Rochester installed a new organ in 1590, and Wells was planning to do so in 1600.[155]

The best known organ builders of this period were John Howe I and II. Between them the father (d. 1519) and son (d. 1571) developed a virtual monopoly, especially of the work in and near London, and they seem to have driven other men out of business: the guild of organ builders became extinct in 1531, and the younger Howe subsequently joined the Skinners Company. The Howes' workshop was located in Walbrook, "at the sign of the Organe Pype." For ordinary repairs and maintenance John Howe was paid a retainer of 12s. a year at Westminster, 13s. 4d. at St. Paul's, and 5s. 8d. at Rochester.[156]

Less well known men worked elsewhere. Arnold the organ maker

---

[149] MS. 3552, Exeter Cathedral Library, calendared in Reynolds, *Use*, p. 30.

[150] Vernon Butcher, *The Organs and Music of Worcester Cathedral* (Worcester: The Cathedral, 1981), p. 7; Cecil Clutton and Austin Niland, *The British Organ* (London: Batsford, 1963), p. 54.

[151] Milman, *Annals of St. Paul's*, p. 227.

[152] Butcher, *Organs of Worcester*, p. 7; Knighton, "Collegiate Foundations," p. 150.

[153] MS. M.A. 40, accounts for 1556 (not paginated), Canterbury Cathedral Library.

[154] Clutton and Niland, *British Organ*, p. 178 and pl. 3.

[155] Paul Hale, *The Organs of Rochester Cathedral* (Rochester: The Cathedral, n.d.), p. 1; L. S. Colchester, Roger Bowers, and Anthony Crossland, *The Organs and Organists of Wells Cathedral*, rev. ed. (Wells: Friends of Wells Cathedral, 1974), p. 3; Act Book, 1591–1607, fol. 156, Wells Cathedral Library.

[156] WAM 33618–33619, Westminster Abbey Library; W.D. 32, fol. 77, Archives of St. Paul's, London Record Office; DRC/FTb3, Kent Archives Office; *New Grove Dictionary*, s.v. "Howe, John"; Clutton and Niland, *British Organ*, pp. 49–50.

32. Chair organ case, Gloucester Cathedral.

received payments at Norwich in the 1540s; he may have been de-
scended from the "Arnald Organer" of Norwich mentioned a century
earlier at Lincoln.[157] One Richard Frencham was paid for mending,
tuning, and gluing the organs at Canterbury in the 1550s. A man
named Blackarde was working there in 1580, and George Pendleton
in 1600.[158] Peter Joyner (the surname must represent his trade) and a
helper received 14*d.* a day for mending the bellows of the great organs
at Chichester in 1533.[159] At Hereford a troublesome vicar choral

[157] DCN, R226A, accounts for 1540, Norfolk Record Office.
[158] MSS. M.A. 40, 41, Canterbury Cathedral Library.
[159] Cap. I/23/1, fols. 69, 71, West Sussex Record Office.

named John Hichons worked on the organs in the 1520s and 1530s; he was suspended for incontinence in 1532 but was allowed to complete an organ that he had begun to build, and in 1533 he was readmitted provided that he repaired two other instruments.[160] Howell and Raynold cared for the organs at Exeter in 1545, and a Hugh Chappington was "granted the office of Organ Mender" there in 1554, at 13s. 4d. a year.[161] The organists of Wells usually served as keepers of the organs there; payments for maintenance were made to Nicholas Prynne in the 1550s and to William Lyde in the following decade.[162] William Smith, the petty canon of Durham whose interest in organs has already been noted, undertook repairs there in the 1580s and 1590s, while one John Odams was employed at Ely in 1598.[163] Thomas Dallam, founder of a dynasty of organ builders that lasted throughout the seventeenth century, was just becoming established at the time of Queen Elizabeth's death and does not seem to have undertaken work of any consequence for the Tudor cathedrals. He was sent to Constantinople in 1599 with a mechanical organ and clock as a gift to the sultan. On his return he built fine instruments for King's College, Cambridge; Worcester Cathedral; and Eton College.[164]

THE cathedral archives reveal a very large number of disciplinary actions taken against vicars choral and singing men. They were often charged with incontinence and adultery, negligence and absence, or quarreling and violent behavior.

During the period before the Reformation, when these singers were expected to remain celibate, most of the complaints dealt with sexual offenses. One of the vicars choral of Salisbury, charged with maintaining a concubine in the fourteenth century, alleged that every vicar kept a mistress, either in the close or out of it. Charges of keeping

---

[160] Act Book 1, fols. 44, 66, 70, 71, Hereford Cathedral Library; Shaw, *Organists of Hereford*, p. 27.

[161] MS. 3552, Exeter Cathedral Library, calendared in Reynolds, *Use*, p. 30; Matthews, *Organs of Exeter*, p. 1. A few years later it was said that Chappington had not done the work and that another "cunning" man had offered to mend the organs without charge (MS. 3686, fol. 80, in Reynolds, *Use*, p. 63).

[162] Communar's Accounts, 1552–1553 and 1559–1560, Wells Cathedral Library.

[163] Conrad Eden, *Organs Past and Present in Durham Cathedral* (Durham: Dean and Chapter, 1970), pp. 4–5; EDC 3/1/3b, Receiver's informal accounts, 1597–1635, fol. 12, Ely Cathedral Archives, Cambridge University Library. Similar payments for repairing bells and clocks are found in most of the cathedral archives.

[164] *New Grove Dictionary*, s.v. "Dallam, Thomas"; Clutton and Niland, *British Organ*, pp. 48, 53–54.

women occur frequently in the fifteenth century as well. It was sometimes hoped—at Chichester, for instance—that the erection of collegiate buildings for the vicars choral would be sufficient to correct such
abuses, but in fact they continued.[165]

The situation at Wells was probably fairly typical of that faced in
cathedrals of the old foundation. In 1493 Simon Lane, a vicar choral
and chantry priest, admitted that he had committed adultery with the
daughter of William Welmote, a local burgess; as a penance he was
required to go before the procession in the cathedral on the following
Sunday, with a wax taper that he was to offer at the image of St. Andrew, and he was suspended from wearing his habit or receiving his
pay for six months. In 1501 John Braddon was suspended because he
persisted in maintaining a relationship with Joan Millward, a married
woman, despite earlier warnings. He confessed his guilt and was pardoned but was made to sit on the second form and go in the lowest
place during processions. When charged in 1504 with continuing this
liaison and with neglecting to say mass he became abusive; he refused
to do penance, appeared in church carrying a long knife under his
garments, and was finally deprived, eventually renouncing his right of
appeal to the archbishop of Canterbury or the pope. (He was back in
office by 1507 but had to undergo another probationary year.) Early
in 1502 Gilbert Jacob confessed committing adultery and submitted to
correction, and John Salter admitted beating a woman named Kath-
erine. In 1507 two vicars were accused of fighting in the house of a
suspect woman and were told not to see her again, but one of them
(John Harryes) disregarded the warning, was involved in another
fight, and was suspended briefly.

In 1509 John Skynner was deprived because he had left Wells without permission and was wont to sleep at the house of Maud Preston,
outside the close. Later in the same year Thomas Prowse admitted that
he had fathered the child born to Ellen Dyke and was warned to ab-
stain from the company of women (within six months he was again
accused of incontinence), while John Harman was charged with an
adulterous relationship with Joan Plummer and was given a penance
(saying part of the Psalter while kneeling before the image of St. Andrew). This made little impact, and in 1510 he was excommunicated
for a few days when he admitted having a child by a woman named
Maud. All of these offenses occurred within the first quarter century
of the Tudor period.[166]

[165] Peckham, "Vicars Choral of Chichester," p. 132.
[166] HMC, *Wells*, 2: 117, 119; Liber Ruber, fols. 41, 85, 89, 103, 110, 146–147, 157, 160,
174–175, 183, 197, Wells Cathedral Library.

The situation at Salisbury was similar. Two vicars choral were accused of keeping company with suspect women in 1502. Another was charged with adultery in 1503, three more with "indecorous life" and fornication in 1523.[167] At York many of the vicars, at least in the fifteenth century, openly kept mistresses in their rooms within the Bedern.[168] A vicar choral of Lichfield was "corrected" for incontinence in 1491 and forced to make compurgation on the oaths of five other vicars and ten chantry priests.[169] At Hereford, Roger Palmer was charged with incontinence in 1517 and finally resigned; David Mey confessed his fault in 1519 and was given penance (saying the seven penitential psalms); Richard Baker was accused of relations with at least five women at about the same time. (He did not mend his ways and was finally forced to leave in 1528.) William Chall was similarly in trouble in 1521. Two vicars were charged with incontinence in 1522; John Here confessed and was given a penance, but David Mey now denied the accusation, failed to appear before the chapter, was declared contumacious, and was eventually made to resign.[170]

Charges of negligence are also common. At Wells the Dean and Chapter regularly warned the vicars choral to be present for services, although some of the older men were excused from night matins. In 1504 Oliver Grendon, one of the vicars, was suspended for a month because he had failed to read the Gospel when scheduled to do so, and John Braddon, already in trouble because of his liaison with a woman, was accused of neglecting to celebrate mass, to the grave scandal of the church and detriment of his soul. He confessed that he had often done so. In 1510 Richard Paty was sentenced to stand on the second step in the choir wearing a surplice but no habit throughout vespers, matins, and high mass on the Feast of Corpus Christi because of frequent absence from services. When he presumptuously entered the choir in his habit the dean called him and said, "Why are you not doing your penance?" "I will not do public penance," he replied. "I would rather go away." Then the dean said, "Go away." Paty later repeated his statement in a formal meeting of the chapter, which declared him no longer a vicar.[171] The vicars of Hereford were also warned, fined, and sometimes deprived for negligence and absence.[172]

[167] Act Book, MS. 80, pp. 13, 15, 43, 44, Salisbury Cathedral Library.
[168] G. E. Aylmer and Reginald Cant, eds., A History of York Minster (Oxford: Clarendon Press, 1977), p. 91.
[169] Chapter Act Book 3, fol. 8, Lichfield Joint Record Office.
[170] Act Book 1, fols. 12, 18, 30, 32, 41, Hereford Cathedral Library.
[171] HMC, Wells, 2: 166, 169, 176, 179; Liber Ruber, fols. 89, 94, 100, 103, 177, Wells Cathedral Library.
[172] Act Book 1, fols. 35, 61, Hereford Cathedral Library.

Later in the century, after vicars were permitted to marry, complaints about their relations with women naturally declined. There was still the occasional problem, like that at Lincoln in 1595, when Augustine Trauson was deprived because of infamous living and "impregnacione cuiusdam mulieris infra ci[vita]tem Lincoln."[173] Neglect of duty remained a problem, and charges of violence and drunkenness increased.

The vicars choral of Lincoln seem to have been a particularly quarrelsome lot—or perhaps their disputes merely happen to be better documented than most. In 1576 a junior vicar was accused of quarreling with one of his senior colleagues; he was admonished and placed under supervision for a quarter. In 1583 two more junior vicars charged with contempts and violent wrongs were threatened with expulsion. The vicars were involved in a long controversy over the dean's right to claim payment for residence—if this were disallowed the vicars would share in the distribution of revenues. One of the vicars, George Huddleston, appears to have been especially lazy, argumentative, rash, and nosy. He was examined by the archdeacon in 1594 to ascertain "How he came to ye knowledge of the contents of a certayne lettre sente by hym [the archdeacon] to Mr Deane elected, and how much therof he knew." Huddleston claimed that he had merely found a scrap of paper in the body of the church and had read it. In 1599 the Dean and Chapter had a full discussion of the "intollerabil negligens" of the vicars choral, poor clerks, and choristers and sent the head vicars a stern warning.[174]

Differing religious views may have been responsible for some of the discord. This seems to have been the case at Salisbury in 1567, when a feud erupted between the supervisor of the vicars choral, John Meakins, and John Sheppard, a prebendary. Sheppard said that

on Sonday last . . . in the tyme of eveninge prayer the said Sʳ John Meakins in the quire made his prayer, viz. "O my god delyver vs from false preachers & from all thes hypocrites & dissemblers, &

---

[173] Lincoln Chapter Acts, A/3/7, fol. 121, Lincolnshire Record Office. He later married the woman. In 1567 a petty canon of Norwich, John Colles, was warned to "avoyd from ye Compeny of Margaret Porter now the wyfe of Christofer Cristelowe in all suspect places within the precynct . . . and especially that the said John shall not suffer the sam Margaret to resort to his chambr . . . vpon peyn of expulcyon" (Norwich Chapter Book 1, fol. 3, Norfolk Record Office). At Hereford a vicar choral was accused of having a woman in his room in 1578; when her husband came looking for her, she was found hiding "in a cole howse vnder a stayer." The vicar was merely admonished (Act Book 2, fol. 79, Hereford Cathedral Library).

[174] Act Book 2, fols. 81, 95, 97, 120, Hereford Cathedral Library; Lincoln Chapter Acts, A/3/9, fols. 3, 6–20; Bj 3.3, Lincolnshire Record Office.

sende vs trewe preachers that their workes & preachinges may agree," and after evenyng prayer was don in the quire he spake thes wordes openly, viz. "What hath light to do with darkenes? . . . Almightie God I beseche the sende vs trew faithfull catholique & sounde preachers & geve them grace to follow that in deede they professe in worde." And being asked to what ende he did so pray and whether he knoweth any suche preachers of his churche, he awnswereth that he will not brande any man ther with, butt leave that to his conscience.

Meakins escaped with a warning.[175] Earlier, in 1556, there had been dissension at Westminster Abbey, while it was a cathedral, and one of the priests was disciplined because he "dyd breake John Wodes heade (being one of the clarkes) with a pote."[176] It is not certain just what had caused the violence, but it may have been diversity of opinion in religion.

A quarrel arose at Hereford just before Christmas 1579. The dean publicly chastised a vicar choral, Richard Madox, for departing "before the tyme of sayinge the Letanye, leavinge the Chore vnserved . . . and also with often goinge without licence to Gloucester." Madox retorted that "the seid Dean sayed not trewe" and added that "he was as good as the seide Dean in everie respecte, further sayinge that he wold sewe hym for that & other thinges in the Storre Chambor." The dean threatened to deprive him, he continued to talk of a Star Chamber suit, and there, so far as we know, the matter ended. Certainly Madox remained in office. Indeed, he was admitted to a prebend two years later.[177]

We do not know just what constituted the "flagrant disobedience" for which Robert Bostoke was warned at Exeter in 1540.[178] At Norwich the Dean and Chapter had to prescribe seating arrangements for the singers in 1592 after "a greate disorder [was] comitted in the church by the sayd quire for places in tyme of devine seruice."[179] A lay vicar named Thomas Nodell was packed off to the cathedral prison (called Paradise) at Salisbury in 1567 for "writing certain infamous books."[180]

[175] In 1583 Sheppard had to make a written apology for a sermon in which he had criticized the earl of Pembroke and indiscreetly mentioned the story of Jehoram, king of Judah (Act Book, MS. 81, fols. 26–27, 98, Salisbury Cathedral Library).

[176] Act Book, 1542–1609, fol. 98, Westminster Abbey Library.

[177] Act Book 2, fols. 82–88, Hereford Cathedral Library.

[178] MS. 3552, fol. 40, Exeter Cathedral Library, calendared in Reynolds, *Use*, p. 34.

[179] Norwich Chapter Book 1, Norfolk Record Office; Williams and Cozens-Hardy, *Extracts*, p. 39.

[180] Act Book, MS. 81, fol. 28, Salisbury Cathedral Library.

The younger vicars of Lincoln had been charged with frequenting taverns as early as 1540.[181] Similar charges, in addition to those described above, were laid against Meakins at Salisbury in 1568.[182] In 1595 Robert Kirby was expelled from his position at Salisbury for frequent drunkenness, especially at a tavern called the Bell, just outside the east gate to the close.[183] Two years later William Davis was fined a month's wages at Hereford "for yt he did offend in ye sin of drunkenness most filthily" and was threatened with deprivation.[184] Dicing, quarreling, and fighting sometimes accompanied these bouts with drink.

In general it appears that there are fewer complaints against singing men at the end of Elizabeth's reign than there had been earlier. Perhaps the musicians had adjusted to the changes in religion and living conditions that had proved unsettling during the middle years of the century. But there are some charges right up to the end: a vicar choral of Wells was still being accused of adultery in 1599, and the vicars of Lincoln still had to be admonished to attend services faithfully in 1602.[185] Because of the character of the surviving documentation, it is impossible to produce statistics; one must be content with anecdotal evidence. It seems likely, however, that most cathedrals at most times had one or two singers who were habitually troublesome and a larger number who were occasionally negligent.

THE worst aspects of the cathedral musical establishments are revealed in these attempts to maintain discipline and punish offenders. The best they had to offer must have been expressed in the music itself rather than in the all-too-human lives of the singers.

It is unfortunate that we have very little precise information about the choral repertoire which was actually performed during the sixteenth century. Nowhere is there documentation listing the anthems, services, or voluntaries which were sung or played day by day. One can only presume that the great works of Tudor church music circulated among the cathedrals, in manuscript or in early published edi-

[181] Maddison, *Vicars Choral*, p. 46.
[182] Act Book, MS. 81, fol. 38, Salisbury Cathedral Library.
[183] Act Book, MS. 82, fols. 72–73, Salisbury Cathedral Library. The Bell is still there.
[184] Vicars Choral Act Book 1, fol. 104, Hereford Cathedral Library.
[185] Act Book H, fol. 120, Wells Cathedral Library; Lincoln Chapter Acts, A/3/9, fol. 26, Lincolnshire Record Office.

tions, and that these formed the basis of the sung services.[186] This view is corroborated by the statement that Dean Whittingham of Durham, despite his Puritan leanings, "was very carefull to provide the best songs and anthems that could be got out of the queen's chapell, to furnish the quire with all, himselfe being skillfull in musick."[187]

Catalogs listing the musical holdings of the cathedral libraries are also lacking for the Tudor period. There are, however, two such lists from the seventeenth century; many of the items mentioned in them were probably already available by 1603. At Chichester a short catalog of song books compiled in 1622 includes eight or ten copies each of "a new book for men only"; a book "of Mr Weekes pricking"; services by Tallis, Farrant, and Byrd; a "longe anthem booke" called "B"; and the anthem "A poore desire I haue to amend mine ill," by an unidentified composer.[188]

A substantially longer inventory survives at Norwich. This was made later in the century, perhaps just before 1681, when it was recorded as being in the custody of the chapter clerk; it is actually not a list of music originally purchased by the cathedral but rather of books bequeathed to the Dean and Chapter by an anonymous donor. A number of printed volumes are included, some of them containing madrigals rather than church music:

Mr Birds Psalmes and Sonnets 5 partes printed
Mr Birds songs of 5 and 6 partes printed
Mr Bird and Mr Tallis Latten Songs printed
Mr Birds Gradualia Liber Secunda of 5 and 6 parts printed
Mr Birds Gradualia of 4 and 5 [parts] printed
Mr Yonge of 5 and 6 partes printed
Mr Morleyes Oriana of 5 and 6 partes printed
Mr Morleyes Fa las of 5 partes printed
Mr Wilbies first sett of 5 and 6 partes printed
Mr Phillips of 8 partes printed

A number of "pricked," or manuscript, books are listed as well.[189] It is tempting to suppose that this music was collected by the organist or one of the singing men and that much of it had been performed in the cathedral. In only a few places can actual Tudor music be traced

[186] On Elizabethan music publishing, especially William Byrd's three volumes, see Le Huray, *Music and the Reformation*, pp. 370–405.
[187] *Life of Mr. William Whittingham, Dean of Durham*, Camden Society, no. 104 (London, 1870), p. 23.
[188] Cap. I/4/6/3, West Sussex Record Office, printed in Le Huray, *Music and the Reformation*, p. 94.
[189] Liber Miscellaneorum, 2, DCN, R226A, fols. 308–390, Norfolk Record Office.

in the cathedral libraries. One of the earliest of these rare survivals is a set of part books at Wells containing compositions by Adrian Batten.

The mere fact that cathedral choirs could sing the difficult works of Tallis, Byrd, and Weelkes is one argument for musical quality. Another derives from listeners' comments. It is true that virtually none of these have survived from the Tudor period itself. But things were probably much the same in the 1630s as they had been in the late sixteenth century, and we are fortunate in having a number of descriptions from that decade. Lieutenant Hammond's travel diary for 1635, for instance, records favorable experiences at several cathedrals. At Rochester, "her Organs though small, yet are they rich and neat; her Quiristers though but few, yet orderly and decent." At Canterbury he "saw and heard a fayre Organ sweet and tunable, and a deep and rauishing consert of Quirsters." At Winchester "they sing sweet and heauenly Anthems," and the organist is one of the rarest in the land. Exeter possessed "a delicate, rich, and lofty Organ which has more additions [stops?] than any other, as fayre Pipes of an extraordinary length, and of the bigenesse of a man's Thigh"; the "melodious and heauenly Harmony [was] able to rauish the Hearers Eares." Only at Chichester and Peterborough was the singing indifferent.[190]

The reactions of worshipers, then as now, must have varied. When interrogated about the matter during a visitation in 1596 one of the vicars choral of Hereford very sensibly said, "Our singinge & songes is as it is in all other Cathedral Churches, but what devocion or pyetie it stirres vp in the myndes of the hearers I knowe not."[191] At least for some, services could be moving experiences. Perhaps the best testimony comes from the great poet George Herbert. While vicar of Bemerton in the early seventeenth century, he made his way twice a week to Salisbury Cathedral, "and at his return he would say, that his time spent in prayers and cathedral music elevated his soul, and was heaven on earth."[192]

[190] L. Wickham Legg, ed., "A Relation of a Short Survey of the Western Counties," *Camden Miscellany 16*, Camden Society, 3d ser., no. 52 (London, 1936), pp. 9, 11, 34, 46, 74, 87.
[191] Archive 4588, Hereford Cathedral Library.
[192] Izaak Walton, "The Life of Mr George Herbert," in *The Works of George Herbert* (London: Frederick Warne, n.d.), p. 35.

9

CANONS, PREBENDARIES,
AND DEANS

THE higher-ranking cathedral clergy—canons, prebendaries, and deans—are an exceptionally interesting group for historical study. They form a clearly defined elite professional class; their lives are exceptionally well documented, and analysis of the surviving records can tell us a good deal about social and geographical mobility, educational qualifications, marriage and family, and life expectancy. Such issues as pluralism, nonresidency, and appointment of laymen to ecclesiastical positions can also be addressed by the techniques of prosopography, or collective biography.

In order to examine these matters, I have created a computerized data bank based upon Le Neve's *Fasti Ecclesiae Anglicanae*, a listing of principal officeholders in the Church of England. The *Fasti* was originally published in 1716 and a three-volume edition edited by Duffus Hardy appeared in 1854, but the more accurate revised edition now in progress at the Institute of Historical Research has been utilized wherever possible. To fill gaps in these sources, listings published by individual cathedrals themselves have been used, supplemented by information from the cathedral archives, primarily the financial records, where necessary.[1]

---

[1] These sources are:

John Le Neve, *Fasti Ecclesiae Anglicanae, 1300–1541*, 12 vols. (London: Athlone Press for Institute of Historical Research, 1962–1967), compiled by Joyce M. Horn except where otherwise stated: vol. 1, *Lincoln Diocese*, comp. H.P.F. King; vol. 2, *Hereford Diocese*; vol. 3, *Salisbury Diocese*; vol. 4, *Monastic Cathedrals (Southern Province)*, comp. B. Jones; vol. 5, *St. Paul's, London*; vol. 6, *Northern Province*, comp. Jones; vol. 7, *Chichester Diocese*; vol. 8, *Bath and Wells Diocese*, comp. Jones; vol. 9, *Exeter Diocese*; vol. 10, *Coventry and Lichfield Diocese*, comp. Jones; vol. 11, *The Welsh Dioceses*, comp. Jones; vol. 12, *Introduction, Errata, and Index*.

Idem, *Fasti Ecclesiae Anglicanae, 1541–1857*, 5 vols. (London: Athlone Press for Institute of Historical Research, 1969–1979), compiled by Joyce M. Horn except where otherwise stated: vol. 1, *St. Paul's, London*; vol. 2, *Chichester Diocese*; vol. 3, *Canterbury, Rochester, and Winchester Dioceses*; vol. 4, *York Diocese*, comp. Horn and David M. Smith; vol. 5, *Bath and Wells Diocese*, comp. Horn and D. S. Bailey.

Also, Bertram H. Green, comp., *Bishops of Worcester and Deans of the Cathedral* (Worcester: Russell, 1979); Patrick Mussett, comp., *Lists of Deans and Major Canons of Durham, 1541–1900* (Durham: Prior's Kitchen, 1974); J. F. Williams and B. Cozens-Hardy, *Extracts from the Two Earliest Minute Books of the Dean and Chapter of Norwich Cathedral, 1566–1649*,

Officeholders whose names were obtained in this way have been searched for in standard biographical dictionaries: the *Dictionary of National Biography*,[2] of course, and—since so many of the higher clergy attended one of the universities—listings and dictionaries of graduates of Oxford and Cambridge.[3] Biographical information in Christina H. Garrett's study of Marian exiles has also been used.[4]

These files include all identifiable persons who held a major position in a cathedral between 1485 and 1603. Some of them entered office before the accession of Henry VII, and some continued to serve long after the death of Queen Elizabeth. Bishops have not been included as such, although most of the Tudor bishops began their careers with cathedral appointments and so are counted in those capacities. Similarly, archdeacons have been included only if they were also prebendaries or canons, since as archdeacons they served the bishop and diocese rather than the Dean and Chapter. Most of the Tudor archdeacons did in fact have positions in cathedrals and so are part of the data base. Men who were priors of monastic cathedrals before the Reformation have been included in the files, since their role was in part comparable to that of a dean. But ordinary monks in the cathedral priories have not been studied in this way, nor have minor canons, vicars choral, or singing men. Generally the sources are not adequate for this sort of analysis of the monastic population or those holding lower offices. In all, we have some information for 2,849 individuals—probably not quite a complete group of all those who held higher office in the cathedrals but closely approaching it.[5]

Norfolk Record Society, no. 24 (Norwich, 1953); typescript version of the new Le Neve for Salisbury and manuscript material for Oxford, Bristol, Peterborough, Coventry and Lichfield, Lincoln, Exeter, Hereford, and Gloucester, 1541–1603, kindly provided by Joyce M. Horn; archival materials for Ely, Carlisle, Chester, and Worcester; John Le Neve, *Fasti Ecclesiae Anglicanae, England and Wales*, ed. T. Duffus Hardy, 2 vols. (Oxford: Oxford University Press, 1854).

[2] 22 vols. (London: Oxford University Press, 1908–1909).

[3] For Oxford: A. B. Emden, *A Biographical Register of the University of Oxford to A.D. 1500*, 3 vols. and supp., 1501–1540 (Oxford: Clarendon Press, 1957, 1974); Joseph Foster, *Alumni Oxonienses*, 4 vols. (Oxford: Parker, 1891); Anthony à Wood, *Athenae Oxonienses*, 2 vols. (London: Rivington, 1813–1820). For Cambridge: C. H. Cooper and T. Cooper, *Athenae Cantabrigienses*, 3 vols. (vols. 1, 2, Cambridge: Deighton, Bell, 1858, 1861; vol. 3, Cambridge: Bowes and Bowes, 1913); John Venn and J. A. Venn, *Alumni Cantabrigienses*, pt. 1, 4 vols. (Cambridge: Cambridge University Press, 1922–1927).

[4] *The Marian Exiles* (Cambridge: Cambridge University Press, 1938).

[5] This number includes a few men identified in Le Neve only as chancellors, treasurers, or precentors; they have been included because most men who held such positions were canons as well, and the lack of a reference to their appointment probably reflects a deficiency in the sources. Only in cathedrals of the old foundation were precentors likely to be prebendaries, and only there have they been counted. In cathedrals of the new foun-

The amount of information available varies enormously from individual to individual. In a large number of cases we have nothing more than a man's name and the position, or several positions, that he held. Information about university education is frequently forthcoming and can generally be matched easily enough with the names of the cathedral clergy. In some cases, of course, problems arise because there are several individuals with identical or similar names. It is less common to find data about social status, place of birth, marriage, and children, but such evidence occurs often enough to justify discussion of these topics. We must be careful not to assume that the documented cases are typical or that they represent a random sample of the entire population, for it is the most prominent clergy, not the common or modestly successful men, whose careers are detailed in the biographical sources.

CAVEATS about the nonrepresentative nature of the existing evidence are particularly appropriate in any consideration of the social status or class background of the cathedral clergy, for we have information in only 208 cases (about 7 percent of the total). It is likely that analysis of this data produces results that are skewed in favor of the higher classes, since men with aristocratic or gentle backgrounds were probably more likely to attain prominent, well-documented positions than those born in more humble circumstances. But the available material is of considerable interest so long as we do not try to make unwarranted generalizations from it.

For what they are worth, the results of analysis are found in table 9.1.

In most instances, nothing further is known about those listed in the sources as commoners or of humble parentage. A few are described as sons of yeomen, peasants, or cowherds. Thirteen of the fathers are referred to as tenants of a college at one of the universities or Winchester College. Three illegitimate sons of obscure ancestry are included in this group. The situation of Thomas Godwyn was unusual: he was the son of poor parents but was adopted and educated by Richard Layton, the prominent visitor of monasteries and dean of York.

A variety of urban trades and crafts, together with considerable disparities in wealth, are reflected in the next category. Here the fathers' occupations include baker, tailor, draper, clothworker, weaver, butcher, grocer, tanner, blacksmith, tallow chandler, apothecary, gold-

---

dation, precentors were chosen by the Dean and Chapter from the group of minor canons.

TABLE 9.1
Social Background of Cathedral Clergy

Father's Status or Occupation	Known cases	% (rounded)
Commoner, tenant farmer	65	31.5
Merchant, artisan, tradesman	38	18
Gentry, "good family"	77	36
Noble	7	4
Clergy	16	8
Foreigners	5	2.5
TOTAL	208	100

smith, painter and stainer, schoolmaster, notary public, bailiff, scrivener, and town clerk. Four of the cathedral clergy were sons of mayors. John Colet's father, Sir Henry, was a wealthy mercer who rose to become lord mayor of London. John Lee was the bastard son of another mayor of London, while both Thomas Aldrich and Edmund Suckling were sons of mayors of Norwich.

As might be expected, a substantial number of the higher clergy were recruited from the ranks of the gentry, for a career in the Church was one of the principal options open to younger sons who would not inherit landed estates. At least twelve of the seventy-seven clergymen who fall into this category were sons of knights and had thus grown up amid considerable wealth and prestige. These men were George Carew, John Constable, Oliver Dynham, Thomas Fitzherbert, Roger Leyburn, Francis and Theodore Newton, Leonard Pilkington, John Stapulton, Richard Swale, William Tresham, and Humphrey Tyndall. Some further prominent gentry families include Arundel (of Cornwall), Blaikston (of Durham), Whittingham (of Cheshire), Isham (of Northamptonshire), Deryng, Fitzhugh, Fitzwilliam, Heywood, and Twynhoo.

Although a relatively small number of churchmen could claim noble ancestry, the individual instances represented here are of special interest because these men were likely to gain the greatest preferments. Three became bishops: Reginald Pole, Mary's archbishop of Canterbury; James Stanley, son of the first earl of Derby, who was bishop of Ely early in the sixteenth century; and Gilbert Berkeley, bishop of Bath and Wells under Elizabeth. The deans include Elizabeth's kinsman George Boleyn, dean of Lichfield.[6] Another relative of the queen,

[6] Elizabeth once offered to make George Boleyn bishop of Worcester, but he declined the appointment; see Thomas Harwood, *The History and Antiquities of the Church and City of Lichfield* (Gloucester: J. Harris, 1806), p. 183.

William Boleyn, was archdeacon of Winchester. Humphrey de la Pole, a nephew of Edward IV, was a prebendary of St. Paul's, and Alan Percy, third son of the fourth earl of Northumberland, became a prebendary of York.

The offspring of prominent clerics also had a head start in ecclesiastical careers. John Aylmer, bishop of London, appointed his son Theophilus a prebendary and archdeacon there; William Barlow, bishop of St. David's and then of Chichester, may have helped his son William gain preferment at Wells, although the younger man's posts at Winchester, Lichfield, Salisbury, and York were obtained after the bishop's death; Emmanuel Barnes, canon of Durham, was named by his father, Richard, the bishop; George Downham, son of William, bishop of Chester, collected prebends at Chester, Gloucester, Wells, and St. Paul's; John Freake was archdeacon of Norwich, where his father, Edmund, held the bishopric. Francis Godwyn, prebendary of Wells and later bishop of Hereford, was the son of Thomas, bishop of Bath and Wells. (Two more Elizabethan prebendaries of Wells, Paul and Robert Godwin, may have been his relatives as well but because of uncertainty have not been included in the calculation.) Thomas Rands, prebendary of Lincoln, was a son of the bishop, Henry Holbeach or Rands. Edwin Sandys, archbishop of York, gave his son Miles a prebend there despite the fact that the son was a layman, and another layman, Sylvanus Scory, was a prebendary of Hereford, where his father, John, was the bishop. The most curious case of nepotism involves Edmund Bonner, the Marian bishop of London: he named John Wymmesley alias Savage, the bastard son of his half-brother, the Reverend George Savage, to a prebendal stall at St. Paul's. Three more of the cathedral clergy were the children of priests.

The five churchmen born abroad were from widely divergent backgrounds. Anthony Rodolph Chevallier was of noble Norman ancestry. John Garbrand was the son of a Dutch bookseller who settled in Oxford. The papal collector Giovanni Gigli was the child of a merchant of Lucca, while another Italian, Bernardino Ochino (famous because he renounced the Church of Rome) was the son of a barber. Finally there is the curious career of John Emmanuel Tremellius, son of a Jew of Ferrara: converted to Christianity by Cardinal Pole, he later embraced Protestantism and was forced into exile under Mary.

It is unfortunate that our knowledge of social background is so sketchy. If we had more complete information we would probably find a great many more common folk from the countryside and tradesmen from the cities, a goodly number of gentry, and a small handful from aristocratic or clerical families. It is clear that the cathedral clergy were drawn from all classes, and that such careers offered a path of upward mobility to young men who were poor but clever (and fortunate enough to obtain the necessary education). It was possible, as the case of George Abbot proved, for the son of a rural clothworker to become archbishop of Canterbury. The rise of Cardinal Wolsey, son of a butcher of Ipswich, was notorious in his own time. But entry into the Church and attainment of its highest offices were easier if one was well connected.[7]

PLACE of birth is better documented than social status. In all, we know the geographical origin of 628 of the cathedral clergy—nearly a quarter of the entire group.

The basic figures are of limited interest. They show, as we would expect, that young men from all parts of the country were drawn into the Church and rose to the higher offices that the cathedrals offered. Not surprisingly, the largest number (48) came from Yorkshire, the largest county. This was followed, less obviously, by Lancashire (37), Lincolnshire (35), Somerset (31), Kent (29), and Hampshire (26, including three from the Isle of Wight). Fewer men than we might have guessed are recorded as being born in London—only 47, with another 6 from Middlesex. The number known to have come from other cities and towns is far smaller. Most had been born in cathedral or university cities: there were 6 from Norwich, 5 from Canterbury, Oxford, and Worcester, 4 from Lincoln, Salisbury, Carlisle, Gloucester, and Lichfield, 3 from York, Bristol, and Wells, and 2 from Winchester, Durham, Chichester, Ely, and Cambridge.

The statistics regarding birthplace assume greater interest when they are correlated with the university attended and with the place of first cathedral appointment, for the question of geographical mobility within a Tudor professional class can be addressed in this way. The figures for the universities are set out in table 9.2.

These figures demonstrate quite dramatically that virtually all of the higher clergy possessed a university education. In only eight instances

[7] The social origins of English bishops in the first half of the sixteenth century were not very different from those of the cathedral clergy; see Felicity Heal, *Of Prelates and Princes: A Study of the Economic and Social Position of the Tudor Episcopate* (Cambridge: Cambridge University Press, 1980), p. 173. David Marcombe, "The Durham Dean and Chapter: Old Abbey Writ Large?" in *Continuity and Change*, ed. Rosemary O'Day and Felicity Heal (Leicester: Leicester University Press, 1976), pp. 125–144, contains valuable comments about the social status of prebendaries of Durham. On the social background of Oxford students in the Tudor period, see Lawrence Stone, "The Size and Composition of the Oxford Student Body, 1580–1909," in *The University in Society*, by Stone et al., 2 vols. (Princeton: Princeton University Press, 1974), 1: 3–110; and James McConica, "Scholars and Commoners in Renaissance Oxford," in ibid., 1: 151–182.

TABLE 9.2
Place of Birth and University Attended

Place of Birth	Total	Oxford		Cambridge	
		(a)	(b)	(a)	(b)
London	47	33	24	27	23
Southeast	(49)	(30)	(29)	(27)	(19)
Middlesex	6	4	4	3	2
Kent	29	17	16	19	12
Surrey	9	5	5	4	4
Sussex	5	4	4	1	1
East Anglia	(61)	(25)	(9)	(57)	(51)
Essex	8	3	0	8	8
Cambridgeshire	7	2	0	8	7
Hertfordshire	13	7	3	10	9
Huntingdon	2	0	0	2	2
Rutland	1	0	0	1	1
Norfolk	15	5	1	15	14
Suffolk	15	8	5	13	10
Northeast	(83)	(41)	(25)	(63)	(58)
Lincolnshire	35	18	11	26	24
Yorkshire	48	23	14	37	34
North	(40)	(24)	(14)	(30)	(26)
Co. Durham	8	5	2	6	6
Northumberland	12	7	4	9	8
Cumberland	10	5	4	8	6
Westmorland	10	7	4	7	6
Northwest	(49)	(31)	(20)	(38)	(29)
Lancashire	37	24	15	30	22
Cheshire	12	7	5	8	7
West	(45)	(37)	(33)	(15)	(10)
Gloucestershire	15	13	13	5	2
Herefordshire	5	4	4	1	0
Shropshire	8	5	4	3	3
Worcestershire	17	15	12	6	5
Southwest	(20)	(19)	(19)	(2)	(1)
Devon	18	17	17	1	1
Cornwall	2	2	2	1	0
South	(83)	(80)	(78)	(13)	(5)
Dorset	11	10	9	2	2
Hampshire	26	26	26	3	0

TABLE 9.2 (*cont.*)

Place of Birth	Total	Oxford		Cambridge	
		(a)	(b)	(a)	(b)
Somerset	31	29	28	8	3
Wiltshire	15	15	15	0	0
Midlands	(42)	(18)	(16)	(31)	(26)
Derbyshire	7	2	2	6	5
Leicestershire	7	3	3	7	4
Northamptonshire	10	6	5	5	5
Nottinghamshire	5	0	0	5	5
Staffordshire	13	7	6	8	7
Home Counties	(54)	(44)	(38)	(25)	(16)
Bedfordshire	4	2	1	3	3
Berkshire	17	13	12	6	5
Buckinghamshire	13	10	7	8	6
Oxfordshire	13	12	12	5	1
Warwickshire	7	7	6	3	1
Wales	40	33	31	13	9
Foreign	(15)	(9)	(8)	(7)	(7)
Scotland	1	1	0	1	1
Calais	1	0	0	1	1
Italy	5	3	3	2	2
France	3	1	1	2	2
Germany	3	2	2	1	1
Netherlands	1	1	1	0	0
Spain	1	1	1	0	0
TOTAL	628	424	344	348	280

NOTE: Numbers in parentheses are subtotals for the regional areas. For an explanation of columns (a) and (b), see p. 234.

where the place of birth is known do we lack information regarding study at Oxford or Cambridge. Four of these are cases of men born abroad, all of them Italians like Polydore Vergil and Bernardino Ochino who had completed their education before coming to England. The four Englishmen with known birthplaces who cannot be identified in university lists (one each from the counties of Kent, Hertford, Hereford, and Shropshire) may well have attended nevertheless; as will be seen later, the records of Oxford and Cambridge are incomplete, especially for the earlier part of this period.

Since many men attended both universities, it has proved useful, especially for purposes of studying geographical mobility, to compile two sets of figures. Column (a) in the table lists all men known to have attended the university in question at some time in their lives, while column (b) is limited to those who attended only that university or attended it first, later studying at the other or incorporating their status there. This second listing is especially interesting in revealing the close ties that existed between certain parts of the country and one of the universities; it shows a prevailing sense of regional loyalty and a likelihood that one would be drawn to the closer of the two institutions. Thus most young men from East Anglia, Lincolnshire, Yorkshire, and the north went to Cambridge, while most of those born in the home counties, the south, the west country, and Wales matriculated at Oxford. No students (or at most a single isolated individual) went to Cambridge from Wiltshire, Hampshire, Hereford, Oxfordshire, Warwickshire, Devon, or Cornwall, and relatively few men from Gloucestershire, Worcestershire, Somerset, Dorset, and Sussex were attracted there. Conversely, Oxford numbered no natives of Cambridgeshire, Essex, Huntingdon, Nottinghamshire, or Rutland, and a mere handful of those born in Derbyshire, Norfolk or County Durham. Londoners, born roughly equidistant from the two universities, divided into roughly equal numbers. The figures in column (a) show that quite a large number of the higher clergy had ties with both universities, not just a single institution. In all, 81 Cambridge men were later affiliated with Oxford, while 69 students from Oxford subsequently migrated to Cambridge. The larger size of Oxford during the sixteenth century is reflected in the totals for both columns.[8]

The limited geographical mobility characteristic of the sixteenth century is revealed also by a correlation of the clergy's birthplaces with the dioceses within which they held their first cathedral appointment. This analysis shows that 121 of the cathedral clergy (between one-fifth and one-sixth of those with known places of birth) obtained their initial cathedral position within their native diocese. Since there were never fewer than nineteen cathedrals, and for the later part of the period either twenty-two or twenty-three, the likelihood of appointment close to home was far greater than that which would have been produced by chance. Thus geographical mobility was restricted, and to a considerable extent there was a regional rather than national market for the talents of young clerics.[9] The number of instances is too

[8] These figures correspond well with those for regional distribution of matriculants at Oxford given in Stone, *University in Society*, 1: 102, table 10. No comparable calculation has been made for Cambridge.

[9] In a review of the new Le Neve volume for Bath and Wells, Claire Cross pointed out

TABLE 9.3
Places of Birth and First Appointments

Name	County of Birth	Earliest Appointment	Date
Andrewes, Lancelot	London	St. Paul's	1589
Angel, John	Gloucester	Gloucester	1571
Arscott, Alnetheus	Devon	Exeter	1519
Ascham, Roger	York	York	1559
Babthorpe, Robert	York	York	1544
Banks, Thomas	Denbigh	St. Asaph	1585
Battye, Edmund	Lincoln	Lincoln	1591
Beacon, John	Suffolk	Norwich	1574
Belassis, Anthony	Durham	Durham	1540
Bell, John	Worcester	Worcester	1518
Beresford, James	Derby	Lichfield	1507
Bilson, Thomas	Hants	Winchester	1577
Bisse, James	Somerset	Wells	1583
Bisse, Philip	Somerset	Wells	1571
Blaikston, Marmaduke	Durham	Durham	1599
Blake, Anthony	York	York	1562
Boket, William	Somerset	Wells	1480
Bourne, Gilbert	Worcester	Worcester	1542
Branche, William	Wiltshire	Salisbury	1482
Buckley, William	Stafford	Lichfield	1548

great to permit a complete table here; the point is perhaps most easily driven home by listing the cases of men whose surnames began with the letters *A* and *B* (see table 9.3).

Some cases demonstrate even greater geographical stability than the table suggests. Thus, for instance, Thomas Bilson was an alumnus of Winchester College, and after serving as a canon of Winchester Cathedral he became bishop of Winchester (1597–1616). John Bell of Worcester was named bishop of that diocese in 1539. Robert King of Oxfordshire was the first bishop of Oxford; John Ponet of Kent became bishop of Rochester after a stint as canon of Canterbury; Thomas Thirlby, born in Cambridge, was Queen Mary's bishop of Ely; Thomas Watson, a native of the county of Durham, was dean and then bishop there, again under Mary.

In addition to the instances in which we can equate place of birth

that most of the prebends at Wells were worth £10 a year or less and that these did not attract ambitious churchmen from outside the diocese; the list of prebendaries "reads as a roll call of West Country clergy most of whom did not go on to higher office in the national church" (*English Historical Review* 96 [1981]: 643).

and place of initial appointment, there are a number of further cases that manifest regional considerations. Two men born in London (Thomas Browne and William Wickham) became canons of Westminster. Several men from Oxford held office at Lincoln during Elizabeth's reign: Oxfordshire had been a part of the diocese of Lincoln prior to the 1540s, and a special relationship doubtless remained. Thomas Brent of Charing, Kent, was a prebendary of St. Paul's at the opening of the Tudor era, and Richard Rogers, also of Kent, held a prebend there through most of Elizabeth's reign. Robert Crowley of Gloucestershire was a prebendary of neighboring Hereford, and William Fleshmonger of Hampshire served in the adjacent diocese of Chichester. The list could easily be extended.

A large number of the cathedral clergy, as will be seen shortly, held office in several places during their careers, as they accumulated positions or moved to more influential and lucrative posts. In these later appointments, regional considerations can frequently be detected, but once established the higher clergy were more likely to move to other parts of the country where greater opportunities awaited them. The higher the position, the less important were local ties. Especially within the episcopate, ability, experience, and political patronage counted for more than regional connections. It is probably also true that there was greater geographical mobility in the second half of the sixteenth century, following the Reformation. David Marcombe has shown that the monks of Durham, for instance, were generally born in the locality, to parents who were yeoman or artisans, while the prebendaries of the refounded secular cathedral were drawn from a much wider area. Many were still northerners, often from substantial landowning families, but a number came from the south and a few were Scotsmen.[10]

In only 164 cases do we know which grammar schools the cathedral clergy attended. Not surprisingly, the evidence is weighted in favor of the great schools, with relatively few documented instances of graduation from a local institution.

Eton and Winchester dominate the list. Curiously enough the number known to have attended these foundations was precisely equal: fifty-eight men could claim to have been educated in each. The ties that linked Eton with King's College, Cambridge, and Winchester with New College, Oxford, show up with amazing clarity. All fifty-eight of

[10] Marcombe, "Durham Dean and Chapter," p. 136.

the Winchester students matriculated at Oxford, with five of them later studying at Cambridge and four at one of the Italian universities. Fifty-four Etonians migrated to Cambridge, only four to Oxford. Fourteen of these Cambridge men were later associated with Oxford, three of the Oxonians with Cambridge. Again, four eventually studied abroad—three in Italy and one in Spain (at Valencia).

Figures for other schools are much smaller: scattered, unrepresentative, and of little significance. Twelve boys attended Westminster (most of them then went to Oxford). St. Paul's and the Merchant Tailors' School could claim six students each. All but one of the St. Paul's boys matriculated at Oxford; all but one of the Merchant Tailors' at Cambridge. Four men, including Thomas Linacre and Thomas Stapleton, are known to have attended the cathedral school at Canterbury. Three were educated at Manchester. No other school could claim more than one or two.

HIGHER education is much better documented. We have information about the universities attended by 1,493 men, just over half of the complete group. An additional 592 (21 percent) are listed as holding degrees, although the granting institution is not known. This means that nearly three-quarters (actually 74 percent) of the cathedral clergy can be identified as graduates.[11] Deficiencies in the records of the universities exist throughout the sixteenth century and are particularly severe for the period before 1580, so the number possessing a university education must be substantially higher than this. Overall, one may hazard a guess that about 90 percent of canons and prebendaries were graduates.[12]

---

[11] There are thirty cases in which we know that a man attended one of the universities but have no record of his receiving a degree. Some, like Thomas Cromwell, no doubt went down before graduating, but most instances probably reflect defects in the sources. The very small handful of men who achieved appointment as prebendaries without degrees included a few who had begun their careers as vicars choral. We know of three such instances at York, where none of the sixteenth-century vicars attended a university, as well as one at Rochester (Walter Hayte). But these cases are most exceptional; generally there was a great gulf between the uneducated vicars and the learned canons. See Claire Cross, *York Clergy Wills 1520–1600: I. Minster Clergy* (York: Borthwick Institute, 1984), pp. vii–viii, 7–8, 69–70, 99; DRC/AO12, Rochester Cathedral Archives, Kent Record Office. At Durham, only two of the canons appointed under Elizabeth lacked degrees, and one of these subsequently obtained his M.A. and B.D. from Cambridge; see David Marcombe, "The Dean and Chapter of Durham, 1558–1603" (Ph.D. thesis, Durham University, 1973), p. 23.

[12] For discussion of the lacunae in the sources for Oxford, see Stone, "Oxford Student Body," esp. pp. 12, 82–88, 91, 109. Guy Fitch Lytle, "Patronage Patterns and Oxford

This high level of educational qualification was in marked contrast to the situation among the parish priests. It is impossible to ascertain exactly what proportion of the lower clergy were university graduates, but such evidence as we do have agrees that it was low. In the diocese of Chester, only one of the 282 men ordained during the 1560s was noted as a graduate.[13] This was admittedly one of the distant corners of the realm. But even at York only 2 or 3 of the priests who served the city churches during the sixteenth century had attended a university.[14] In the diocese of Lincoln, only 9 of 76 men ordained between 1520 and 1544, surveyed to determine their knowledge of Latin, were listed as graduates. And many of the parish priests who had attended a university were nonresident pluralists. During the episcopate of Bishop Longland at Lincoln (1521–1547) only about 25 percent of the resident parish priests were graduates.[15] The situation was worse during the earlier years of Elizabeth's reign: a visitation of 1576 revealed that only 36 of the 215 parish clergy (about 17 percent) in the diocese of Lincoln were graduates. Only in the last decades of the sixteenth century did the situation improve, as shown by the visitation of 1585, which revealed 80 graduates among the 195 priests ordained in Lincolnshire during the previous nine years. By 1603 a third of the priests within the diocese of Lincoln had attended a university; of 1,184 clergymen, 544 held degrees in the arts and 101 in theology.[16] The proportion of graduates in the diocese of Canterbury rose from 18 percent in 1571 to 60 percent in 1603. In the diocese of Worcester, 19 percent of the priests were graduates in 1560, 23 percent in 1580, and 52 percent in 1620; in Lichfield, only 24 percent of the clergy in 1603 held degrees.[17]

Throughout the Tudor period, then, the cathedral clergy formed

Colleges, c. 1300–c. 1530," in Stone, *University in Society*, 1: 124, has shown that the number of canonries and prebends presented to university graduates rose significantly between 1300 and 1500: at Salisbury from 57.6 percent to 80.6 percent, at Lichfield from 50 percent to 91.1 percent, and at St. Paul's from 66.7 percent to 93.5 percent.

[13] Rosemary O'Day, "The Reformation of the Ministry, 1558–1642," in *Continuity and Change*, ed. O'Day and Felicity Heal (Leicester: Leicester University Press, 1976), p. 61.

[14] Henry Moore, a pluralist prebendary, was the sole graduate incumbent of a parish during Elizabeth's reign (Cross, *York Clergy Wills*, p. 141).

[15] Margaret Bowker, *The Henrician Reformation: The Diocese of Lincoln under John Longland, 1521–1547* (Cambridge: Cambridge University Press, 1981), pp. 127–129.

[16] Philip Hughes, *The Reformation in England*, 3 vols. (London: Hollis and Carter, 1950–1954), 3: 137–140.

[17] A. G. Dickens, *The English Reformation* (London: Batsford, 1964), p. 308; D. M. Palliser, *The Age of Elizabeth* (London: Longman, 1983), pp. 331–332; cf. Patrick Collinson, *The Religion of Protestants* (Oxford: Oxford University Press, 1982), p. 94; and Jo Ann Hoeppner Moran, *The Growth of English Schooling, 1340–1548* (Princeton: Princeton University Press, 1985), pp. 138–149.

TABLE 9.4
University Degrees Held

Degree	Number
B.A., B. Grammar	895
M.A., "Magister"	1,266
B.D.	604
D.D.	476
B. Civil Law	306
D. Civil Law	249
B. Canon Law	207
D. Canon Law	138
B. Medicine	16
M.D.	33
B. Music	3

an intellectual elite, far better educated than their brethren in the parishes. Of the 1,493 known graduates associated with the cathedrals, 783 or 52.4 percent were educated at Oxford, 438 or 29.3 percent at Cambridge. An additional 272 (18.2 percent) attended both; if this figure is added, we have 1,055 Oxonians (70.7 percent) and 710 Cantabrigians (47.6 percent). There were 54 (3.6 percent) who studied abroad, generally after completing a degree in England. Italian universities attracted most of these men: 15 studied at Bologna, 8 at Padua, 6 at Ferrara, and 4 at Turin—a total of 33, or 34 if one includes a vague reference to study "in Italy." We know that 7 went to Paris, 2 to Orléans, one each to Lyons and Tours; 3, all Marian exiles, studied at Basel. There are records of 2 at Louvain, one each at Heidelberg, Valencia, and Douay. (This last, as one would surmise, is an Elizabethan recusant, the famous controversialist Thomas Stapleton, who was deprived of his prebend at Chichester in 1563 and subsequently became a professor of divinity at Douay and canon of Louvain.)

It is possible to tabulate the specific degrees that the cathedral clergy are known to have held (see table 9.4).

The number of advanced degrees is extraordinary. Aside from the university faculties themselves, there could not have been a more highly educated group in the realm. In all, we know of 896 doctorates held by cathedral clerics. Some men held more than one such degree; in most instances these men were lawyers, both canonists and civilians. (Before the Reformation it was common to be a *doctor utriusque juris*.) At least one man (Cardinal Bainbridge) held three doctorates, in divinity as well as civil and canon law, and there are two cases (John Argentyne and John Talbot) of clergy with degrees in both divinity and medicine.[18] The total number of men holding one or more doctorates is 841.

Closer examination reveals that the degrees in divinity or theology are almost evenly divided between Oxford and Cambridge, while something like two-thirds of the degrees in civil and canon law were granted by Oxford. Men with foreign degrees were most likely to have studied canon or civil law at Bologna, Ferrara, or Padua, all of which had distinguished legal faculties. Virtually all of the medical degrees came from Oxford.[19]

The chronological distribution of the higher degrees is of some interest as well. The academic study of canon law was abolished in 1535, in the wake of the Submission of the Clergy, and no further degrees in canon law were awarded after that date. This was a change of considerable significance, for the practice of canon law had been an important clerical profession, and many ecclesiastical lawyers held cathedral appointments.[20] The study of civil law continued, but the number of doctorates awarded in the field declined, or at best remained constant, in the years following the break with Rome; the largest number—seventeen—were granted in the 1520s. The study of divinity, on the other hand, increased in popularity following the Reformation. If, as Lacey Baldwin Smith has suggested, most of the lawyers were conservative and most of the theologians were reformers, the growing ascendancy of Protestant theology within the cathedral chapters is borne out by the statistics (see table 9.5).[21]

A number of these learned prebendaries continued to hold university offices and were nonresidents in their cathedrals. The ties between Cambridge and Ely were particularly close, and one finds among the

[18] On Bainbridge, see William E. Wilkie, *The Cardinal Protectors of England* (Cambridge: Cambridge University Press, 1974), pp. 40–52.

[19] These figures correspond reasonably well with those developed by Mark Curtis, *Oxford and Cambridge in Transition, 1558–1642* (Oxford: Clarendon Press, 1959), p. 150. Curtis's table is broken down by decades and indicates the increasing number of graduates during Elizabeth's reign.

[20] The dominance of canon law within the universities during the early Tudor period is emphasized in Hugh Kearney, *Scholars and Gentlemen: Universities and Society in Pre-Industrial Britain, 1500–1700* (London: Faber and Faber, 1970), pp. 15–16. There was a brief attempt to reestablish canon law studies at Oxford under Mary Tudor; see Elizabeth Russell, "Marian Oxford and the Counter-Reformation," in *The Church in Pre-Reformation Society*, ed. Caroline M. Barron and Christopher Harper-Bill (Woodbridge, Suffolk: Boydell Press, 1985), p. 218.

[21] Cf. Lacey Baldwin Smith, *Tudor Prelates and Politics* (Princeton: Princeton University Press, 1953).

TABLE 9.5
Number of D.D., D.Civil L., and D.Cn.L. Degrees, by Decades

Date	D.D.	D.Civil L.	D.Cn.L.
Before 1480	11	15	17
1480–1489	9	12	7
1490–1499	10	6	15
1500–1509	30	15	15
1510–1519	26	8	18
1520–1529	20	17	16
1530–1539	37	13	2
1540–1549	23	13	—
1550–1559	22	10	—
1560–1569	38	14	—
1570–1579	30	12	—
1580–1589	48	12	—
1590–1599	35	1	—
1600–1609	33	0	—

NOTE: These figures reflect only degrees for which dates are known. There are a number of additional instances where the degree is listed without date.

prebendaries of Ely such men as Richard Wilkes and Edward Barwell, masters of Christ's College; Henry Hervey, master of Trinity Hall and vice-chancellor in 1560; Giles Eyre, fellow and vice-provost of King's; John Fuller, Edward Gascoyne, and John Duport, masters of Jesus; Thomas Bacon, master of Gonville Hall; Thomas Peacock, master of Queens'; and Edward Leeds, master of Clare. No attempt has been made to collate all known cases of overlapping college and cathedral appointments, but we may note one further instance, that of John Piers, dean of Chester, who was successively master of Balliol and dean of Christ Church, Oxford, in the 1570s.[22]

A SUBSTANTIAL number of the cathedral clergy have left published writings. In all, there are 197 men whose works are listed in the *Short-Title Catalogue*, which includes books printed in England, Scotland, and Ireland between 1475 and 1640, as well as books written in the

[22] He ended his career as archbishop of York, 1577–1594. Piers had been born to humble parents at South Hinksey.

TABLE 9.6
Subject of Published Writings

Theology	222
Sermons	184
Popular religious tracts, catechisms, etc.	130
Anti-Catholic tracts	101
Pro-Catholic tracts	18
Travel, cosmography, science	34
Education	29
History	20
Poetry	37
Published letters, "remains"	23
Injunctions, directives	9
Miscellaneous or unclear	40

English language and printed abroad.[23] According to other sources a further 116 of these churchmen produced writings other than letters or administrative documents. A few of these were works written in Latin and printed abroad, hence not included in the *Short-Title Catalogue*; others may have been published but have not survived; still others remained in manuscript.[24] Just over 300 of the cathedral clergy, then, can be identified as authors, either scholars or popular writers.[25]

Tabulation of the entries in the *Short-Title Catalogue* produces a list of 830 separate titles, with an additional 512 reprints or new editions of these works (1,342 entries in all). Classification of the separate titles by subject is interesting (see table 9.6).

A number of famous books are found alongside many lesser, ephemeral works. The theological writings include the monumental

[23] A. W. Pollard and G. R. Redgrave, eds., *A Short-Title Catalogue of Books Printed in England, Scotland, and Ireland, 1475–1640* (London: Bibliographical Society, 1946). The complete revised edition was not available when this study was begun; it would provide somewhat greater accuracy but would not alter the general situation significantly except in showing a larger number of reprints and new editions.

[24] Some men known to have contributed to the *Bishops' Book* or the translation of the Bible under King James are included in this group. Three of the prebendaries from Wales are said to have contributed to the translation of the Bible into Welsh.

[25] Much interesting material about early English publishing is included in the two volumes by H. S. Bennett, *English Books and Readers, 1475 to 1557*, 2d ed. (Cambridge: Cambridge University Press, 1969); and *English Books and Readers, 1558 to 1603* (Cambridge: Cambridge University Press, 1965).

Laws of Ecclesiastical Polity by Richard Hooker, who was a prebendary at Salisbury, together with such things as obscure Biblical commentaries by Andrew Willet, a scholarly prebendary of Ely, or the *Propugnaculum* against Martin Luther published in 1523 by the leading Oxford theologian Edward Powell, who held prebends at Lincoln and Salisbury.[26] There are also such intriguing technicalities as Hugh Broughton's discussion of whether the high priests' ephod was silk or wool.

None of the popular tracts has achieved the status of a classic. One can easily enough imagine the contents of John Alcock's *Mons perfeccionis, or the hyll of perfeccion* (1496), John Gibson's *Easie entrance into the principall points of christian religion* (1579), Edward Hutchins' book called *Dauids sling against great Goliah* (1581), Edward Vaughan's *Nine obseruations howe to reade the Bible* (1591), or Francis Bunny's *Exposition of the Lordes praier* (1602). The most prolific writers of devotional literature were Thomas Becon, whose most popular work, *The sicke mans salue*, ran through seventeen editions between 1561 and 1632; Edward Dering, author of such things as *Godly priuate praiers for housholders to meditate vpon, and to say in their families*; and John Norden, now remembered as a geographer but best known in his own time for *A pensive mans practice*, *A poore mans rest*, and *A sinfull mans solace*. Both Dering and Becon had some of their writings gathered into editions of collected works. Becon's ran to three volumes (1560).[27] The most widely used catechisms were those composed by Alexander Nowell, dean of St. Paul's; there are nearly fifty editions of four such works, some of them translations into Latin and Greek.

The sermons of Lancelot Andrewes were printed more frequently than those of any other preacher. Most of his published ones were delivered during the reign of James I, often before the king himself, even though Andrewes was a prebendary of St. Paul's as early as 1589. Several of John Longland's sermons for Henry VIII at Greenwich were printed in the 1530s, as were Thomas Lever's for Edward VI two decades later. *A sermon of Cuthbert* [Tunstall] *Bysshop of Duresme vpon Palme Sondaye before Kynge Henry the viii* was published in 1536. At least one of Whitgift's sermons before Elizabeth was printed.

Funeral orations form a considerable subgenre of sermon literature. One of the most famous was Matthew Parker's sermon *Howe we ought*

---

[26] I am grateful to Guy Fitch Lytle for calling my attention to Powell's work, which is representative of that done by the conservative theology faculty at Oxford during the earliest stages of the Reformation. Sir Thomas Elyot contributed the preface to the *Propugnaculum*, a fact that I did not know when I wrote my biography of Elyot and that may be important in linking him with Oxford and with religious conservatives.

[27] On Becon, see John N. King, *English Reformation Literature: The Tudor Origins of the Protestant Tradition* (Princeton: Princeton University Press, 1982), pp. 113–121.

to take the death of the godly, preached at Cambridge for the burial of Martin Bucer in 1551.[28] The only work of Archbishop Grindal to be printed was his sermon on the death of Emperor Ferdinand; this was published in both English and Latin editions in 1564. The actual number of published funeral sermons is somewhat larger than the figures would indicate, since some of them were not printed as separate items and are not listed by author in the *Short-Title Catalogue*.[29]

Occasionally a volume of collected sermons was published at the time of the preacher's own death. An example of this is the *Six learned and godly sermons* by Richard Eedes, prebendary of Salisbury, Hereford, and Oxford as well as dean of Worcester, printed in 1604. Several of John Foxe's sermons saw publication; *A sermon of Christ crucified* received five editions in English and one in a Latin translation, and there was also his *Sermon preached at the christening of a certaine Jew* (1578), again printed in both languages. A number of sermons delivered at Paul's Cross in London were printed. Not all of these were by famous men, as *A sermon preached at paules crosse on the xxv. day of June* (1587) by William Gravet, a prebendary of St. Paul's, will show.[30] Among the clearly Protestant homilies are *Fouretene sermons concernyng the predestinacion and eleccion of god* given by Bernardino Ochino and published in 1550.

The quantity of literature attacking the Catholic church and its doctrines is extraordinary. Perhaps the best-known works are those by William Turner: *The huntyng and fynding out of the Romishe fox*, published under a pseudonym in 1543; *The second course of the hunter at the Romishe fox* (1545), again issued under a pseudonym; and *The huntyng of the Romyshe vuolfe* (1554). John Bale, later to be a canon of Canterbury, joined the fray with his diatribe *Yet a course at the Romyshe foxe* (published in 1543 under the pen name J. Harryson). The pursuit continued throughout the century, with a canon of Rochester, Thomas Bell, issuing his own *Hunting of the Romish foxe* in 1598. Bell's other titles include *The anatomie of popish tyrannie, The downefall of poperie, The Popes funerall*, and *The woefull crie of Rome*. Bale's most influential writing was *The Image of Both Churches*, a commentary on Revelation that compares the true reformed Church with the false establishment of the pope and Antichrist. He also published such

[28] This received a second edition about 1570.

[29] This was the case, for instance, with a sermon by Thomas Montford, a prebendary of St. Paul's, preached at the funeral of Lady Blount in 1619 (Pollard and Redgrave, *Short-Title Catalogue*, no. 3135). I am indebted to Retha Warnicke for this information.

[30] See Millar MacLure, *The Paul's Cross Sermons, 1534–1642* (Toronto: University of Toronto Press, 1958).

items as *An expostulation or complaynte against the blasphemyes of a franticke papiste of Hamshyre* (ca. 1551) and *The pageant of Popes* (1574).[31]

The largest number of pieces attacking the papists was published by Matthew Sutcliffe, a prebendary of Wells and dean of Exeter. His pen produced *An abridgement or survey of Poperie, A challenge concerning the Romish Church, A brief examination of a certaine disleal petition presented by certaine laye papistes*, and *The unmasking of a Masse-monger*, as well as two books denouncing Cardinal Bellarmine and two more attacking the English Jesuit Robert Parsons. Specific issues were dealt with by Jean Veron, a Protestant immigrant from France who held a prebend at St. Paul's; he wrote *A stronge battery against the inuocation of saintes* and *A stronge defence of the maryage of pryestes*, both published in 1562. Another prebendary of St. Paul's, Robert Crowley, issued *A briefe discourse against the outwarde apparell of the popishe church*. Further general items include *Truth and falshood, or a comparison between the truth now taught in England and the Romish church* by Francis Bunny, canon of Durham and Carlisle; *The hatefull hypocrisie, and rebellion of the Romishe prelacie* by Lewis Evans, prebendary of Salisbury and Wells; and the ballad *A free admonition without any fees To warn the papists to beware of three trees* by William Birch, canon of Durham.

Catholics also wrote, but in much smaller numbers. During the last year of Henry's reign Richard Smith published *A defence of the sacramente of the aulter* and *A defence of the blessed masse*. Silent under Edward, he reemerged under Mary to issue *A bouclier of the catholike fayth* in two parts, 1553 and 1554. John Seton, who held positions at York and Winchester, published a Latin panegyric on the accession of Queen Mary. From Antwerp, Thomas Stapleton conducted a campaign against the "vntruthes" in John Jewel's *Apology*. Christopher Bagshaw, a Jesuit who had been imprisoned in 1587, issued *A true relation of the faction begun at Wisbich* under an assumed name in 1601.

Some of Bale's anti-Catholic writings took the form of plays. Some contained comic elements (*A Comedy Concernynge Thre Laws*, written during Edward's reign, is an example); some were adaptations of mystery plays, like the *Chefe Promyses of God*, probably intended to be performed by choir boys. Thomas Becon wrote a Protestant nativity play called *Dialog betwene thangell & the Shepherdes*. The "ryght pithy, pleasaunt and merie comedie" called *Gammer Gurtons Nedle* was probably the work of William Stevenson, a canon of Durham; it shares with

---

[31] On Turner and Bale, see William A. Clebsch, *England's Earliest Protestants* (New Haven: Yale University Press, 1964); on Bale, see also King, *English Reformation Literature*, pp. 56–75, 418–428, e.g.

Udall's *Ralph Roister Doister* the distinction of being the earliest actual English comedy.[32]

Robert Crowley deserves to be remembered as more than an anti-Catholic pamphleteer. His place in the history of English literature rests primarily on his work as editor and publisher of the first printed edition of *The Vision of Piers Plowman* (1550). He was also a poet of some merit, perhaps the finest writer of verse during the mid-Tudor period. Much of his work was prophetic, like *The Voyce of the Laste Trumpet*. His masterpiece, now insufficiently appreciated, is a satire about counsel and misrule at court called *Philargyrie of Greate Britayne* (1551). He was also responsible for compiling the first complete metrical Psalter in English, published (with music) in 1549.[33]

Some of the scholarly writings published by the cathedral clergy are of greater continuing value than the popular or controversial religious literature. Polydore Vergil, William Camden, and John Foxe are better known as historians than as ecclesiastics, yet all held prebends: Vergil was a pluralist with stalls at Wells, St. Paul's, Lincoln, and Hereford, and Foxe's work was supported by appointments at Salisbury and Durham, while Camden was content with a single post at Salisbury. Vergil's history of the reigns of Henry VII and Henry VIII was published by Grafton in 1546 and ran through four more editions in the sixteenth century.[34] Camden's *Annales* of the reign of Elizabeth was issued in both English and Latin versions soon after her death. Foxe's *Acts and Monuments*, or *Book of Martyrs*, remains the greatest achievement of Protestant historical scholarship in the English Reformation; it was one of the most popular works of the sixteenth and seventeenth centuries, second only to the Bible. Another important work of historical and literary scholarship was John Bale's bibliography, *Illustrium maioris Britanniae scriptorum summarium*, published abroad during Bale's years of exile.

Matthew Parker, who was a prebend of Ely and dean of Lincoln under Edward VI, might well have remained at Cambridge studying the history of the Anglo-Saxon church had not Elizabeth insisted upon naming him archbishop of Canterbury in 1559. His treatise *De antiquitate Britannicae ecclesiae Cantuariensis* first appeared in 1572. Laurence Humphrey wrote a life of John Jewel, published in Latin in

[32] On Reformation drama, see King, *English Reformation Literature*, pp. 271–318. The title page of *Gammer Gurtons Nedle* merely attributes it to "Mr. S., Master of Arts."
[33] Crowley has been studied at some length by King, *English Reformation Literature*, pp. 319–357, 469–477.
[34] Since the name is so unusual, one may guess that Polydore Heliar, a prebendary of Wells from 1548 to 1573, was named for Vergil, who may have been his patron.

1573. Less well known but of some lasting use was the *Catalogue of the bishops of England* compiled by Francis Godwyn (son of the bishop of Bath and Wells, himself later bishop of Llandaff, then Hereford). Godwyn also wrote annals of the reigns of Henry VIII, Edward VI, and Mary, as well as a curious piece called *The man in the moon or a discourse of a voyage thither.*

Real voyages were the subject of *The principall navigations* by Richard Hakluyt, a canon of Bristol, the city from which many of the expeditions had departed. Robert Johnson, who held preferments at Rochester, Peterborough, Norwich, and Lincoln, wrote specifically of the "fruits of planting in Virginia" in his *Nova Britannia* of 1609. Robert Langton left an account of his pilgrimage to the shrine of St. James the Greater at Santiago de Compostela (1522) and Giles Fletcher a description *Of the Russe common wealth*, written after an embassy to Russia in 1588.

The geography of Britain itself was studied by Norden, briefly in his book *England: an intended guyde for English travailers* (1625) and with greater detail in the volumes of *Speculum Britanniae* covering Middlesex and Hertfordshire (1593, 1598). He also wrote *The surveyors dialogue* (1607). John Rudd, a canon of Durham, does not seem to have published himself, but he was a mapmaker and taught the great cartographer Christopher Saxton.[35] London was described in several volumes by Richard Johnson, a prebendary of Salisbury under Elizabeth and James; these included *The nine worthies of London, The pleasant conceites of Old Hobson, the merry Londoner*, and *The pleasant walkes of Moorefields*.[36] One of Camden's lesser works was a descriptive catalog of the tombs and monuments in Westminster Abbey, published in 1600.

The science of navigation was a special interest of William Barlow, archdeacon of Salisbury and prebendary of Wells, Lichfield, Winchester, and York; his works included *Magneticall aduertisements* and *The nauigators supply*. The greatest scientist among the canons was William Turner, the Protestant controversialist. Botany was his field. He published an herbal, a listing of *The names of herbes in Greke, Latin, Englishe, Duche and Frenche*, a book about "the properties of the bathes in Englande," and *A new boke of the natures of all wines*.[37] The genre of popular

---

[35] Marcombe, "Dean and Chapter of Durham," p. 22.

[36] Johnson's writings also include such songs as "A Crowne Garland of Goulden Roses," and *The history of Tom Thumb*, which sold so well that nine reprintings were necessary.

[37] On Turner as a naturalist, see C. E. Raven, *English Naturalists from Neckam to Ray* (Cambridge: Cambridge University Press, 1947), pp. 48–137, and A. G. Dickens, *Lollards and Protestants in the Diocese of York, 1509–1558* (London: Oxford University Press, 1959), pp. 192–194.

medicine also included *The garden of health* by a prebendary of Lich-field, William Langham.

Arithmetic, dialectic, and logic were expounded by John Seton, the Catholic whose panegyric for Mary has already been noted. John Case, a prebendary of Salisbury, published several studies of Aristotle's physics as well as *The praise of music* or, in its Latin version, *Apologia musices*. Ralph Lever wrote on logic. John Chamber, who had studied medicine and held a stall at Salisbury, published *A treatise against judicial astrologie* (1601), and Francis Coxe, prebendary of Chichester and Lichfield, set forth *A short treatise declaringe the detestable wickednesse of magicall sciences* (1561).

The best-known Tudor treatise on education was *The scholemaster* by Roger Ascham, a prebendary of York, who also wrote an account of the history of archery, called *Toxophilus*. Latin grammar was a concern of several prominent churchmen; those who published on this subject included John Colet, Thomas Linacre, Cuthbert Tunstall, and (per-haps surprisingly) Thomas Wolsey.[38] Other grammarians with cathe-dral connections were Thomas Lupset, Richard Mulcaster, John Stan-bridge, and John Holt. Thomas Cooper, the bishop of Winchester, published a famous Latin dictionary, *Thesaurus linguae Romanae & Bri-tannicae*, only to be lampooned in one of the Martin Marprelate tracts on the grounds that he had plagiarized Sir Thomas Elyot's earlier dic-tionary. (Cooper freely admitted that his work was based on Elyot's, and such borrowings were in any case common in the sixteenth cen-tury.) Jean Veron also issued a Latin-English dictionary (1575), and Anthony Corano, a native of Spain who gained prebends at Chiches-ter, Lichfield, and St. Paul's, published a book on "Spanish grammer" for Englishmen (1590).

There is less writing on political theory than one might have ex-pected. Hooker's work of course belongs in this category as well as in theology. There is also John Ponet's *Shorte treatise of politike power* (1556). The only other publications of any significance are those by Richard Morison, one of Cromwell's humanist protégés, who argued the case for royal supremacy in two treatises of 1539, *An exhortation to styr all Englyshe men to the defence of theyr countreye* and *An inuective ayenste treason*.

I T is harder to study marital status than educational qualifications, for most of the sources do not indicate whether the clergy took wives or

---

[38] Wolsey's only published work was *Rudimenta grammatices et docendi methodus* (1529).

had children. In cases where we have full biographical information, marital status is generally known, and some study of it is rewarding. Because of the small number of cases yielding data, statistics are not very useful. Still, some numbers can be obtained and some interesting cases identified.[39]

In all, we know of at least 190 cathedral clergy holding positions between 1485 and 1603 who were married.[40] Clerical marriage was illegal until 1549—a bill to sanction it had passed Convocation and the Commons in 1547 but failed to clear the Lords, and the prohibitions were not removed until the second parliament of Edward VI.[41] Those who married earlier had to resign their positions, as did Anthony Denys, an obscure prebendary of Salisbury, in 1538. Even a prominent reformer like Thomas Cranmer, convinced that clerical marriage was desirable, was compelled to keep his German wife, Margaret, a secret for sixteen years.[42] A substantial number of priests married openly and lawfully during Edward's reign, only to be forced to abandon either their wives or their jobs under Mary. Despite Elizabeth's dislike of clerical marriage, it was again permitted after 1558. At Durham practically all the Elizabethan canons were married, even a few who were former monks, and the same situation probably existed elsewhere.[43]

Since wedding dates are seldom available, it is not possible to construct a table showing the increasing frequency of marriage directly. Some idea, however, can be gained by placing the clergy into groups based on the date of their death. This produces the results found in table 9.7. Several of these figures call for comment. The number of married men who died in the 1550s includes five who were executed by Mary: Cranmer; Bishop Robert Ferrar of St. David's; John Rogers,

[39] For discussion of marriage among bishops, see Joel Berlatsky, "Marriage and Family in a Tudor Elite: Familial Patterns of Elizabethan Bishops," *Journal of Family History* 3 (1978): 6–22; and Heal, *Of Prelates and Princes*, pp. 176–178.

[40] In addition to sources cited earlier, see the list of married clergy within the diocese of York in A. G. Dickens, *The Marian Reaction in the Diocese of York* (York: Borthwick Institute, 1957), pt. 1, pp. 22–31. It includes seven canons and three vicars choral who were priests.

[41] The enabling statute is 2 & 3 Edw. 6, cap. 21.

[42] Margaret Cranmer, who was related to the Lutheran pastor Osiander, came to England with Cranmer in 1532, returned to Germany when the Act of Six Articles was passed in 1539, came again to England in 1543, and left at the time of Mary's accession. After Cranmer's execution she married the exiled English printer Thomas Whitchurch; they returned to England on Elizabeth's accession. After Whitchurch died in 1561 Margaret married Bartholomew Scott, a Surrey J.P. She herself died soon after 1571. She bore Cranmer two children—a daughter who married the lawyer and M.P. Thomas Norton, and a son, Thomas, evidently a quarrelsome and disreputable character. See Jasper Ridley, *Thomas Cranmer* (Oxford: Clarendon Press, 1962), pp. 46–47, 151–152.

[43] Marcombe, "Dean and Chapter of Durham," p. 26.

TABLE 9.7
Married Clergy: Decades of Death

Date	Number of Clergy	Date	Number of Clergy
1540–1549	3	1580–1589	25
1550–1559	15	1590–1599	22
1560–1569	12	1600–1609	25
1570–1579	18	1610–1619	29

a prebendary of St. Paul's; Laurence Saunders, prebendary of York; and Rowland Taylor, prebendary of Hereford and Rochester. Only ten of the married men died natural deaths during this decade. The number of married clergy reaching the end of their lives rose during the first half of Elizabeth's reign, as more and more clergy took wives and those who did so finally met death, and finally stabilized in the 1580s.

Several cathedral clergy are known to have married twice. These include Leonard Pilkington, a canon of Durham, whose second wife was the widow of Bishop Richard Barnes; John Ponet, bishop of Winchester;[44] William Overton, bishop of Coventry and Lichfield; Edwin Sandys and Thomas Young, archbishops of York; Alexander Nowell, dean of St. Paul's; Owen Owens, prebendary and archdeacon of Bangor; and Thomas Staller, a prebendary of Hereford and archdeacon of Rochester. Richard Fletcher, prebendary of St. Paul's and Lincoln, dean of Peterborough, and bishop of Bristol, Worcester, and London successively, was suspended from his position as chaplain to Queen Elizabeth because she disapproved of his second marriage. Edmund Suckling, a prebendary of Norwich under Elizabeth and dean of the cathedral in the time of James I, married three times.[45]

[44] His first marriage, which was dissolved, was a bigamous association with the wife of a butcher; his second wife, Maria Haymond, was of respectable parentage. See Heal, *Of Prelates and Princes*, p. 177n.

[45] Little is known about the social background of the wives. Even Heal, working with a smaller number of better-documented cases in her study of Tudor bishops, could ascertain only that Barlow's wife was a former nun, Mrs. Hooper and Mrs. Cranmer were foreigners, Mrs. Holgate was a lady of "good family," and Mrs. Coverdale was of uncertain origin but was the sister-in-law of the reformer Dr. Joannes McAlpine (ibid., p. 177n). The wife of Toby Matthew (dean of Oxford and Durham, then bishop of Durham and archbishop of York) was the daughter of Bishop Barlow; her first husband had been a son of Matthew Parker, so she could claim "a bishop to her father, an archbishop to her father-in-law, four bishops to her brethren and an archbishop to her husband" (G. E. Aylmer and Reginald Cant, eds., *A History of York Minster* [Oxford: Clarendon Press, 1977], pp. 210–211). According to Marcombe ("Dean and Chapter of Durham," pp. 26–

At least seventy-six of the men under consideration are known to have had children. The actual number was doubtless far greater. In two cases these offspring were illegitimate, born before clerical marriage was lawful: there is the famous instance of Thomas Wolsey's son, Thomas Wynter, who was sent to study on the Continent while collecting the revenues from the deanery at Wells and prebends at York, Salisbury, and Lincoln, in all amounting to something like £2,700 a year,[46] and the little-known case of James Stanley, a son of the first earl of Derby, who held positions at Ely, Salisbury, and York and left two sons and a daughter when he died in 1515.

Some of the early clerical families were large. Both the martyr John Rogers and Richard Parry, dean and later bishop of St. Asaph, left eleven children. Ralph Lever had ten, John Pilkington and Rowland Taylor nine, Owen Owens eight, Richard Cox and William Whittingham seven.[47] One of the five children of Henry Parry, who held prebends at Bath and Wells, Salisbury, York, and Lincoln, grew up to become bishop of Worcester. Arthur Wake, a prebendary of Oxford, had only two sons, but they attract attention because he christened them Abraham and Isaac. Some men died leaving behind small children. Laurence Saunders was survived by an infant son when he was burned in 1555, and William May, dean of St. Paul's, left a seven-year-old daughter when he died naturally in 1560.

Several men lived to see sons or other close relatives follow them into the Church and provided patronage that brought about lucrative appointments. Besides Parry, noted above, there were the instances of John Aylmer, Edmund Bonner, William Downham, Edmund Freake, Henry Holbeach (or Rands), and Edwin Sandys, all mentioned earlier. Bishop Cox's son-in-law John Duport became a prebendary of Ely, and Dean Nowell's nephew William Whitaker served as chancellor of St. Paul's. One of the sons of Owen Owens, archdeacon of Bangor, became bishop of St. Asaph.

A few more married men, interesting for one reason or another, may be mentioned in passing. John Hodgkin, originally a Dominican friar, was deprived of his prebend at St. Paul's because he was married, but he repudiated his wife and was restored to office at Elizabeth's accession. He was also suffragan bishop of Bedford, in which capacity he served as one of the consecrators of Matthew Parker as

---

27), most of the wives of the canons at Durham were of the same social status as their husbands, and some were very remarkable women.

[46] See A. F. Pollard, *Wolsey* (London: Longmans, Green, 1929), pp. 308–312.

[47] Of Dean Whittingham's sons, one became a knight, one a tailor, and one a bandit; see Marcombe, "Dean and Chapter of Durham," p. 43.

archbishop of Canterbury. The reformer Nicholas Shaxton, bishop of Salisbury from 1535 to 1539 (until forced to resign because he could not swallow the Six Articles), was convicted of heresy in 1543 but escaped in 1546 by renouncing both his Protestant views and his wife. Mary was willing to tolerate him as a suffragan bishop of Ely; he died halfway through her reign. Finally, John Foxe commands attention because of his *Book of Martyrs*; a prebendary of Salisbury and canon of Durham, he was a family man with a wife, two sons, and a daughter, and may be taken as a type of the married Protestant minister and scholar.

SINCE the charge of pluralism and nonresidency has been leveled against the cathedral clergy, both by their own contemporaries and by modern scholars, it is useful to know just how common it was to hold several ecclesiastical appointments concurrently. Strictly speaking, the cathedral clergy did not come within the meaning of pluralism as defined by canon law, which held (in Maitland's words) that it was "the simultaneous tenure by one clerk of more than one benefice involving cure of souls," for cathedrals were not parishes and members of the chapter did not have the cure of souls.[48] Nevertheless it is important to know how prevalent pluralism (understood generally rather than technically) actually was.

Collation of information about canons, prebendaries, and deans reveals that the great majority held office in a single cathedral.[49] As table 9.8 shows, only 731 men held posts in two or more cathedrals; this is about one-quarter of the total group. Pluralism was especially rare among the clergy in the Welsh cathedrals.

Most of these pluralists held their positions concurrently, although there are a few cases of men resigning some appointments when ac-

[48] F. W. Maitland, *Roman Canon Law in the Church of England* (London: Methuen, 1898), p. 149. Occasionally in the sixteenth century itself one finds the view that deans held the cure of souls for other members of the cathedral community—for instance, vicars choral—although there are references to vicars marrying and having their children baptized in a parish church.

[49] This calculation excludes appointments as bishop. A number of cathedral clergy were nominated to bishoprics, but it was customary for them to resign their cathedral preferments upon consecration. Exceptions were occasionally made for the poor Welsh bishoprics; thus Francis Godwyn continued to hold a prebend at Wells while bishop of Llandaff but resigned it when translated to Hereford in 1617. Unfortunately the sources do not permit separate calculations for residentiary canons.

TABLE 9.8
Number of Cathedrals in Which
Clergy Held Appointments

Two	440	Six	14
Three	159	Seven	6
Four	70	Eight	7
Five	33	Nine	2

cepting others.[50] It was quite common for men to hold a prebend in conjunction with another office in the same cathedral; many served as precentor, treasurer, subdean, or chancellor while holding a stall.

In cathedrals of the old foundation, where there were large numbers of prebends that varied significantly in value, it was quite usual for members of the chapter to move from prebend to prebend as more desirable appointments became available. This practice was especially common at Chichester, Salisbury, Lincoln, Wells, Lichfield, and Hereford. An extreme example is provided by Edward Finch, who held nine prebends at Salisbury in succession during the years between 1514 and 1539, serving also as archdeacon of Salisbury and prebendary of Chichester. Henry Rawlyns moved through eight prebends at Salisbury in a shorter time (1513–1526); he, too, was archdeacon there and prebendary of both Wells and Lincoln. Christopher Massingberd held offices only at Lincoln, but between 1509 and 1553 he was treasurer, precentor, chancellor, and archdeacon as well as holder of seven successive prebends there; Henry Martyn had five appointments as prebendary of Hereford (1504–1524) and again was an archdeacon of the diocese. It was not customary for one man to hold several prebends in the same cathedral concurrently, but, if one can trust the sources, such pluralism did occasionally occur: Edward Hanson, for instance, is recorded as enjoying two of the prebends at Lincoln during the period between 1504 and 1507.

Multiple appointments at the same cathedral did not of course imply nonresidence. Indeed, it was most likely that they would be given to men whose chief energies were in fact devoted to the work of the cathedral. Overlapping positions in two or more cathedrals, however, certainly necessitated nonresidence, especially since a number of these

[50] For example, William Harford, listed as a canon of Peterborough, 1541–1549, and then a prebendary of Chichester, 1559–1571. It is possible that Harford actually remained in office at Peterborough until Mary's reign, then was deprived and had to wait until Elizabeth's accession before he could obtain another position.

lucrative preferments went to prominent government officials who never lived within a cathedral close.

The most egregious pluralists were William Knight and Richard Sampson, both of whom accumulated appointments in nine cathedrals while serving Henry VIII as ambassadors and administrators. Knight (d. 1547) held prebends at Lincoln, St. Paul's, Salisbury, Bangor, Westminster, and Wells, was archdeacon of Chester, Coventry and Lichfield, Lincoln, and York, and eventually became bishop of Bath and Wells. Secretary to both Henry VII and Henry VIII, he was sent as ambassador to the pope during the discussion of Henry VIII's divorce. Sampson (d. 1554) was a prebendary of St. Paul's, York, Lincoln, Wells, and Lichfield; archdeacon of Norwich, Bath and Wells, and Exeter; dean of Westminster, Lichfield, and St. Paul's. He became bishop of Chichester, then of Coventry and Lichfield, and was active as president of the Council of Wales.

Among those who held office in eight cathedrals were Christopher Urswick, the scholarly ambassador, friend of Erasmus, and dean of York (d. 1522); Hugh Oldham, a chaplain to Henry VII and bishop of Exeter from 1504 to 1519; Giovanni Gigli, the papal collector in England and English ambassador in Rome (d. 1498); Peter Carnelian, court poet and Latin secretary to Henry VII and Henry VIII; Edmund Chaderton, treasurer of the chamber for Henry VII; and John Boxall, principal secretary to Queen Mary.

Some other prominent pluralists include John Bourchier (d. 1495), nephew of the archbishop of Canterbury; John Dogett (d. 1501), another nephew of Cardinal Bourchier; Robert Morton (d. 1497), nephew of Cardinal Morton, the next archbishop; Thomas Barrow (d. 1499), master of the rolls; Thomas Bedyll (d. 1537), an ecclesiastical lawyer who was active in the royal divorce proceedings; John Chamber, physician to both Henrys; John Gunthorpe (d. 1496), humanist and diplomat; Cardinal Bainbridge; bishops Gardiner and Tunstall; Richard Gwent (d. 1544), a canon lawyer and sometime prolocutor of Convocation; William Horsey (d. 1543), who had been involved in the celebrated case of Richard Hunne; Oliver King (d. 1503), secretary of state and ambassador; Rowland Lee (d. 1543), who dominated the Council of Wales while bishop of Coventry and Lichfield; John London (d. 1544), Warden of New College, Oxford, and active in the dissolution of the monasteries before his conviction for perjury and his death in the Fleet; William Smith (d. 1514), a royal councilor and co-founder of Brasenose College, Oxford; Richard Pace (d. 1536), diplomat and scholar; Thomas Ruthall (d. 1523), another royal councilor, secretary, and ambassador; Peter Vannes (d. 1563), the Italian who was Latin secretary to Henry VIII and Edward VI and ambassador to Venice; and—not surprisingly—Cardinal Wolsey, who held five prebends and two deaneries in addition to his higher honors. All of these men held positions in four or more cathedrals.

Sometimes pluralists held their various offices within circumscribed geographical areas. Thus the five prebends enjoyed by John Williams (d. 1558) were in the adjoining dioceses of Salisbury, Wells, Bristol, Gloucester, and Hereford, while the three held by William Lawson (d. 1583) were at Exeter, St. David's, and Hereford. Such men may well have visited each cathedral yearly, possibly preaching when they came.

It is worth noting that most of the pluralists accumulated their offices under Henry VII or Henry VIII. Such appointments under Elizabeth were rare, the only significant instances being those of Matthew Hutton and Toby Matthew, both of whom became bishop of Durham and subsequently archbishop of York after holding prebends and deaneries. It should be pointed out that the revenues drawn out of the cathedrals to fatten the purses of courtiers came mainly from the old secular cathedrals, which before the Reformation had substantial endowments and were accustomed to supporting large numbers of nonresidents.

These instances of pluralism and nonresidency do not of course tell the whole story, for they are limited to positions within the cathedrals themselves. Much larger numbers of the cathedral clergy held appointments in parishes, and some were also fellows or masters of colleges at Oxford and Cambridge. It is not possible to compile figures that account for all cases of pluralism.[51] The evidence suggests that it was indeed common at the beginning of the Tudor period but declined in the second half of the sixteenth century. Perhaps agitation in the Reformation Parliament and a statute against pluralism passed in 1529 marked the beginning of a new attitude.[52] Puritan criticism, which reached a head in Elizabeth's reign, may also have had something to do with the change. But it seems more likely that a fundamentally altered situation resulted from the growing secularization of

[51] In a recent study of pluralism at Norwich between 1370 and 1406, T. E. Carson found 38 cases of priests holding both a prebend and a parish out of a total of 241 active pluralists; see "The Problem of Clerical Irregularities in the Late Medieval Church: An Example from Norwich," *Catholic Historical Review* 72 (1986): 191.

[52] Cf. Stanford E. Lehmberg, *The Reformation Parliament, 1529–1536* (Cambridge: Cambridge University Press, 1970), pp. 82, 92–93. The actual statute (21 Hen. 8, cap. 13) is filled with exceptions to the general premise that clergy should not have more than one benefice with cure of souls, for it allowed four positions if these were acquired before 1530 and had other exemptions for those employed by the king or as chaplains to noblemen, judges, and bishops, as well as for those with university degrees in divinity and law.

the government, with fewer churchmen named to high civil office after the Reformation and thus fewer government officials whose financial support came from multiple appointments in the cathedrals. The end of careers in canon law must be involved as well, since so many of those who combined service to the State with appointments in the Church had been trained as canon lawyers.

Especially in the case of the pluralists, it is important to know who was responsible for their appointments. In theory the situation was relatively simple. At cathedrals of the old foundation prebendaries were named by the bishop and the dean was elected by the chapter. There were of course no prebendaries in the monastic cathedrals before the Reformation, and the monks elected their prior. The original charters of cathedrals of the new foundation appoint the Dean and Chapter by name, a sign of royal patronage. As these cathedrals gained statutes, all appointments were left in the hands of the monarch; both deans and canons were to be nominated by the Crown.[53] But these constitutional arrangements do not tell the whole story. Even in cathedrals of the old foundation, deans were generally nominated by the Crown.[54] At both Durham and Chester the right of naming the canons was granted to the bishop by Queen Mary.[55] Elsewhere the monarch seems to have retained the nomination. Royal patronage itself bears further investigation, however, since the leading councilors and churchmen were responsible for making recommendations to the monarch. At Durham, for instance, Dean Whittingham probably owed his appointment to Ambrose Dudley, earl of Warwick, while both Toby Matthew and William James, deans later in Elizabeth's reign, were supported by Leicester and the Cecils.[56] Bishops probably kept more personal control of their rights of presentation, but they, too, were subject to various pressures. A bill passed by Parliament in 1576 but vetoed by the queen complained that prebends and deaneries, as well as fellowships at the universities, were sometimes sold.[57] This may have been so, although we have no evidence for it. Each case was unique and would have to be investigated separately, were surviving documentation adequate. What can be said is that the sovereign and

[53] See A. Hamilton Thompson, ed., *The Statutes of the Cathedral Church of Durham*, Surtees Society, no. 143 (Durham, 1929), pp. xxxiii, xlii, 87, 103.

[54] An exception appears to be St. Asaph, where the deanery was in the gift of the bishop; see Le Neve, *Fasti*, ed. Duffus Hardy, 1: 81n.

[55] Marcombe, "Durham Dean and Chapter," p. 133; R.V.H. Burne, *Chester Cathedral* (London: SPCK, 1958), p. 34.

[56] Marcombe, "Dean and Chapter of Durham," pp. 53–71.

[57] G. R. Elton, *The Parliament of England, 1559–1581* (Cambridge: Cambridge University Press, 1986), p. 226, based on evidence in the Lords and Commons Journals.

the bishops (who were of course themselves named by the king or queen) were ultimately responsible for the appointments, including those of the pluralists. Nowhere was royal supremacy more evident than in the Tudor cathedrals.[58]

SINCE the prebendaries, canons, and deans did not hold the cure of souls, there was no canonical requirement that they be priests, and a few laymen were certainly appointed to these positions. Most of the sources do not indicate whether officeholders were ordained, so it is impossible to produce a complete list of laymen. At least twenty-nine can be identified, and it seems likely that there were in all something like twice this number. Even that, of course, would be a very small proportion, less than 2 percent of the entire group.

Some of the laymen who profited from cathedral preferments have already been mentioned. The most notable case is that of Thomas Cromwell, dean of Wells from 1527 until his fall in 1540. Elizabeth was more active than her father in naming members of her court and council to positions in cathedrals. She made Leicester a prebendary of York and Roger Marbeck, her chief physician, a prebendary of Salisbury, Hereford, and Oxford. Sir Thomas Smith, one of her principal secretaries, was restored to the deanery of Carlisle that he had held under Edward VI, and after he relinquished this in 1577, he was named a prebendary of Chichester. Sir John Wolley, the queen's Latin secretary, followed Smith as dean of Carlisle; Thomas Wilson, a principal secretary, was named dean of Durham in 1580 but died the next year; and Valentine Dale, a diplomat, held Cromwell's old deanery at Wells from 1574 to 1589.

Sixteen men with cathedral appointments can be identified as members of Parliament. Since it was unconstitutional for priests to sit in Parliament, on the grounds that they were represented in Convocation instead, these must have been laymen.[59] They include Sir John Mason, dean of Winchester from 1549 to 1554 (Mary gave him an annuity of £240 for resigning this office, which she did not think him qualified to hold); John Rogers, son of the martyr; Miles Sandys, son of the archbishop of York; Silvanus Scory, son of the bishop of Here-

---

[58] On the issue of patronage, see Lytle, "Patronage Patterns," pp. 111–149.

[59] The case of Alexander Nowell made it clear that clergy could not sit in the Commons. Returned in September 1553 for the Cornish borough of West Looe, Nowell was not allowed to take his place on the grounds that he was a prebendary of Westminster, "therby having a seat in the convocation house"; see S. T. Bindoff, ed., *The House of Commons, 1509–1558*, 3 vols. (London: Secker and Warburg, 1982), 3: 28–29.

TABLE 9.9
Social Background of Deans and Archdeacons

Father's Status or Occupation	No. of Deans	No. of Archdeacons
Commoner, tenant farmer	12	7
Merchant, artisan, tradesman	14	12
Gentry, "good family"	15	24
Noble	4	2
Clergy	2	8
TOTAL KNOWN CASES	47	53

ford; Sir Richard Morison, the political theorist, a prebendary of Salisbury; Ralph Skinner, dean of Durham; and Robert Weston, dean of Wells in the 1570s. The Protestant botanist William Turner was also an M.P.—he sat in 1547 through the influence of Protector Somerset. A deacon at the time, he finally took priest's orders in 1552, just after his first appointment as dean of Wells.[60] Three Welsh prebendaries sat in the Commons. It is conceivable that these parliamentarians, drawing income from the cathedrals, were disposed to defend them against attacks by Puritans and other reformers, but it would be rash to argue the matter strongly in the absence of fuller evidence.

TURNING from prebendaries to deans and archdeacons, one finds a number of interesting points, especially regarding mobility to higher office within the Church. The files contain information about 256 deans (including 43 men who were priors of monastic cathedrals before the Reformation) and 352 archdeacons who held cathedral positions (this includes 65 men who were both deans and archdeacons, and are counted here in both categories).

In terms of social background, these men who rose to higher offices were not much different from the entire group of cathedral clergy. The number of known cases remains small (see table 9.9).

An examination of educational qualifications reveals a very high proportion of men with doctorates (see table 9.10). About half of the deans and archdeacons held doctoral degrees, as opposed to something like one-quarter of the entire group including prebendaries and

---

[60] As has been shown, he was deprived by Mary but reinstalled by Elizabeth.

TABLE 9.10
Doctorates Held by Deans and Archdeacons

Degree	No. of Deans	No. of Archdeacons
D.D.	100	95
D.Civil L.	32	87
D.Canon L.	13	45
M.D.	4	7
TOTAL	149	234

TABLE 9.11
Previous Cathedral Appointments Held by Deans and Archdeacons

Office	No. of Deans	No. of Archdeacons
No previous appointment	63	102
Prebend or canonry, same cathedral	38	143
Prebend or canonry, different cathedral	70	105

canons. Clearly higher degrees eased the way to higher offices. The number of doctorates in canon and civil law held by archdeacons is especially notable. Such training was of course appropriate, since archdeacons were involved in diocesan administration and, frequently, in legal proceedings. Before the Reformation many of the archdeacons held doctorates in both civil and canon law. Since some deans, as well as some archdeacons, held advanced degrees in both divinity and law, the number of men with doctorates is smaller than the number of such degrees awarded.

Although a few men gained appointment as deans or archdeacons without having held previous cathedral offices, this was relatively unusual; a larger number had experience as prebendaries or canons, often in the same diocese but sometimes in another. The figures are set out in table 9.11. Archdeacons, more than deans, were frequently drawn from the cathedral chapter itself rather than from outside; this was the case in nearly a third of the appointments to archdeaconries. It was almost universal for archdeacons to hold prebends or canonries concurrently, while many deans resigned prebends upon assuming office. The post of archdeacon was less prestigious than that of dean and was often a steppingstone to a deanery: 47 men moved from the office of archdeacon to that of dean, as against only 10 who changed positions in the other direction. It was not usual to hold the two preferments concurrently, only 4 men violating the custom of resigning one when accepting the other.

Almost all deans and archdeacons were pluralists with offices in several cathedrals and very likely in several parishes as well: 11 deans held 2 deaneries, either simultaneously or in succession, and 5 held 3. Archdeacons were even more likely to accumulate positions; 43 held 2 archdeaconries concurrently or successively, while 9 held 3 each and 4 men held 4 archdeaconries apiece.

Perhaps the most significant aspect of these positions is the frequency with which they led to bishoprics. We know that 55 deans became bishops, 10 of them receiving their first episcopal appointment in the diocese where they had served as dean, and 62 archdeacons were promoted to the bench of bishops, 8 of them in the same diocese.[61] And 10 deans and 6 archdeacons became archbishops.[62] At least 129 of the 195 men consecrated as bishops between 1485 and 1603 had previously been prebendaries, canons, archdeacons, or deans; if one excludes the 45 men who served the 4 Welsh dioceses, 109 of the 150 English bishops had cathedral backgrounds. Through the Tudor period the high road to episcopal office was paved with cathedral preferments.

Study of a handful of exceptionally well documented cases can help explain the life patterns common among the cathedral clergy. We can examine the ages at which men received their university degrees and their initial appointments at the cathedrals, the ages at which they were advanced (if indeed they were) to higher office, the length of their tenures, and their ages at death (see table 9.12).

We know from these and a number of other cases that it was most common for young men to matriculate at Oxford or Cambridge at the

---

[61] This does not count John Young, who was a suffragan bishop with the title "Bishop of Gallipoli *in partibus*."

[62] These figures include a few men, such as George Abbot, who held cathedral appointments prior to 1603 but were not raised to the episcopate until the reign of James I.

TABLE 9.12
Life Patterns of Cathedral Clergy

Name	Birth	B.A.	Apt.	Dean	Bishop	Abp.	Death
George Abbot	1563	1582	1600	1600	1609	1611	1633
Lancelot Andrewes	1555	1575	1589	1601	1605	—	1626
Roger Ascham	ca. 1515	1534	1559	—	—	—	1568
Thomas Cranmer	1489	1512	bef. 1533	—	—	1533	ex. 1556
Richard Croke	1489	1510	1548	—	—	—	1558
John de Feckenham	ca. 1518	B.D. 1539	1554	1554	—	—	1585
Alexander Nowell	ca. 1516	1536	1551	1560	—	—	1602
Matthew Parker	1504	1525	1541	1552	—	1559	1575
Nicholas Ridley	ca. 1500	1523	1541	—	1547	—	ex. 1555
Nicholas West	1461	1487	1496	—	1515	—	1533
John Whitgift	1530	1554	1568	1571	1577	1583	1604
Thomas Wolsey	ca. 1475	1485	1508	1509	1514	1514	1530

age of sixteen or seventeen.[63] The bachelor's degree was normally awarded four years later, when the student was twenty-one, the master's after another three years, when he was twenty-four.[64] The earliest age at which men could canonically be ordained to the priesthood was twenty-three. The cathedral clergy who possessed doctorates were generally in their thirties when the degree was granted; often they held an appointment already, but if not they usually gained it shortly thereafter. A few more examples, this time set out according to ages (table 9.13), will show the usual pattern.

It is interesting to note the advanced ages to which these men lived. Investigation of the 288 cases where we have information about the date of birth (not often available, especially before the 1540s) as well as death reveals that the average age at death was 63, which was also the median age. The greatest longevity was achieved by Lawrence Chaderton, a prebendary of Lincoln from 1598 to 1640, who was probably 102 when he died. John Ebden, who held positions at York,

[63] Some were younger. Wolsey, famous as the "boy bachelor," was said to have gained the degree at fifteen, although the registers do not verify this (Pollard, *Wolsey*, p. 12); and Alexander Nowell in old age reminisced about entering Oxford at thirteen (Bindoff, *House of Commons*, 3: 28).

[64] Cf. Stone, *University in Society*, 1: 30; Curtis, *Oxford and Cambridge*, p. 86; J. B. Mullinger, *The University of Cambridge from the Royal Injunctions of 1535 to the Accession of Charles the First* (Cambridge: Cambridge University Press, 1884), p. 398.

TABLE 9.13
Life Patterns, by Ages

Name	B.A.	M.A.	D.D.	Initial Apt.	Dean	Bp.	Abp.	Death
Robert Hovenden	21	25	36	26	—	—	—	69
Edward Hutchins	20	23	—	31	—	—	—	71
Matthew Hutton	?	?	36	31	38	60	66	77
William James	20	24	32	35	42	64	—	75
John May	22	25	36	36	—	49	—	70
Thomas Neville	21	24	40	38	43	—	—	67
Richard Nix	?	?	36	42	—	54	—	89

St. Paul's, Winchester, and Salisbury, lived to the age of 98, and both Miles Spencer (prebendary of York and Norwich) and John Thornborough (dean of York, then bishop of Worcester) reached 90. Since men usually obtained their first positions in the cathedrals when they were in their 20s or 30s, the files tell nothing about infant or adolescent mortality. Once associated with a cathedral, relatively few died young. Nicholas Mercer, a prebend of Exeter, was the only man to be carried off before his thirtieth birthday; he died in 1597, aged 29. Eight more died in their thirties. This group includes Thomas Lupset and Edward Dering, both of whom had already made their mark as writers.

If we assume that most of the clergy received their B.A.s at the age of 21, it is possible to supply approximate birth dates for an additional 474 men, the date of whose death is known. This produces a large sample of 762 men for whom reasonably accurate birth and death dates are available—just over one-quarter of the entire group, and probably representative of the whole. Calculations made from this larger base show a median age at death of 61. Arranged by decades, the ages at which men died are shown in table 9.14.

These figures accord well with those which have been calculated for other groups in Tudor society. Mark Curtis has shown that the median age at death of all persons born between 1558 and 1640 for whom the *Dictionary of National Biography* gives birth and death dates was 63 and that the average life span of an Elizabethan or Jacobean student, based on the sample of matriculants at Gonville and Caius Colleges, Cambridge, was 60 years.[65] Percival Boyd's "Index of London Citizens,"

[65] Mark Curtis, "The Alienated Intellectuals of Early Stuart England," *Past and Present* 23 (1962): 31.

TABLE 9.14
Age at Death, Cathedral Clergy

Age	Number	% (Rounded)
20–29	2	0
30–39	39	5
40–49	125	18
50–59	192	25
60–69	213	28
70–79	139	18
80–89	45	6
90–99	6	1
Over 100	1	0
TOTAL	762	101

TABLE 9.15
Age at Death

	Cathedral Clergy (%)	London Citizens Born 1550–1569 (%)
Under 30	0	4
Under 40	5	17
Under 50	23	33
Under 60	48	52
Under 70	76	71
Under 80	94	93
Under 90	99	—

held by the library of the Society of Genealogists, also provides valuable comparative data.[66] Significantly fewer cathedral clergy than citizens of London died young, at ages up to 50, but from that age on, the figures are quite similar (see table 9.15). The longevity of cathedral clergy is thus not unique among those groups in Tudor society which are well documented (and hence, by definition, privileged), but it may surprise some who are not familiar with recently calculated morbidity statistics.

[66] Information taken from Peter Earle, "Age and Accumulation in the London Business Community, 1665–1690," in *Business Life and Public Policy: Essays in Honour of D. C. Coleman*, ed. Neil McKendrick and R. B. Outhwaite (Cambridge: Cambridge University Press, 1986), p. 59.

Long tenures of ecclesiastical offices also attract attention as one looks at the records. Few could compete with Samuel Proctor, who was a prebendary of Salisbury for half a century (1589–1639); Michael Reniger, a canon of Winchester for 49 years (1560–1609); or Leonard Parry, who served at Salisbury for 48 years (1566–1614). But it was common enough to hold a cathedral position for thirty years, as did Paul Methwyn, a prebendary of Wells from 1577 to 1607, or even 41, like Robert Swift (d. 1603), who obtained a canonry at Durham when he was 28 and held it until his death at 69. Bishops, being older when appointed, were not so likely to have lengthy tenures, but there are the cases of Richard Nix, bishop of Norwich for 35 years, John May, bishop of Carlisle for 21, John Whitgift, a bishop for 27 years and archbishop of Canterbury for 19, and Toby Matthew, archbishop of York for two decades in the early seventeenth century. There was no tradition of retirement from ecclesiastical positions, and those who served the cathedrals normally remained in office until they died.

THERE are very few charges of immorality against canons and prebendaries, in contrast to the large number brought against vicars choral and singing men. Most of the remaining complaints are found in the act books at Salisbury. Here Robert Ryve, a prebend, was accused of sodomy in 1562, when a woman testified that he had enticed her son into his house, kissed him, and forced him to reveal his "secreta membra." But Ryve was able to clear his name with the help of compurgators who swore to his reputation, one of them a medical doctor from Winchester, where Ryve also held a canonry. Ryve was later accused of failure to attend services and was declared contumaceous by the Dean and Chapter.[67]

It was also in 1562 that Leonard Bilson was found guilty of witchcraft and was placed in the pillory at the Cheap in London. He was still in prison in 1568 but retained his prebend at Salisbury until 1572, presumably the year of his death, although he lost a canonry at Winchester in 1562. In 1570 Thomas Mynthorn, or Myntryn, another prebendary of Salisbury, was charged with keeping "mulieres peregrinas anglice voc. vagabond women" in his house, including one "vulgariter vocat a roge," but he denied any wrongdoing.[68]

At Durham, Dean Whittingham was charged with drunkenness and adultery, the latter unproved, and William Todd, a canon who was

---

[67] Act Book, MS. 80, fols. 160–165, Salisbury Cathedral Library.
[68] Act Book, MS. 81, fol. 21, and MS. 82, fol. 49, Salisbury Cathedral Library.

deprived because of his Catholic views in 1567, was said to be a drunkard and unkempt. Toby Matthew was suspected of having an affair with the wife of his chaplain Henry Ewbank, and Ralph Lever was regarded as being unbalanced and neurotic.[69] All in all, the surviving complaints are few and insignificant, and serious moral turpitude was virtually unknown.

WILLS and probate inventories made by a number of cathedral clergy survive. Perhaps better than any other source, they convey an idea of the wealth, status, and intellectual liveliness of these men.

There is room here for only three examples, all drawn from the *York Clergy Wills* published by Claire Cross. William Melton, prebendary and chancellor of York Minster from 1496 until his death in 1533, held a D.D. from Cambridge, where he had been master of Michaelhouse and a teacher of Bishop John Fisher. His estate was valued at £124 19s. 7d.; the inventory of his goods includes a list of ninety books, chiefly patristic theological works but also volumes by Erasmus and Pico della Mirandola. Melton maintained a household at Acklam as well as the Chancery in York, and the inventory provides detailed information about such things as furniture, kitchen implements, chapel fittings, and plate in both places.

Edward Kellett had been a member of the chapter since 1524 and served as precentor during the last year before his death in 1539. His fine library, running to nearly fifty titles, was more oriented toward law than Melton's; it contained such things as Gratian's *Decretals*, together with Plato's works, the writings of Plutarch and Boccaccio, and an anti-Lutheran tract by William Barlow. Kellett's executors valued his estate at £360 18s. 7d.[70]

Thomas Atkinson belonged to a younger generation; he died in 1571. He had attended Eton and King's and was a convinced Protestant, married with children. His inventory reveals the possession of luxurious clothing, furniture, and plate, as well as a library of twenty-eight volumes, most notably the paraphrases and commentaries of Erasmus and the works of Calvin and Melanchthon. The books were appraised at only £2 4s. 4d. in a total estate of £233 7s. 2d.

[69] Marcombe, "Dean and Chapter of Durham," pp. 24–25.

[70] Cross, *York Clergy Wills*, pp. 9–25, 38–45. It is interesting to compare these estates to those of vicars choral at York, which ranged from about £24 to £60, and of chantry priests, whose stipends were only £6 a year but who were occasionally able to accumulate property worth as much as £30.

These inventories, together with an anecdotal account of Brian Higden (dean of York from 1516 to 1539) riding to church on Christmas Day preceded by fifty gentlemen in tawny coats and followed by thirty yeoman "in like coats guarded with saffron,"[71] help one visualize the lives of the higher clergy. Although their wealth and prestige declined somewhat as the Reformation affected their cathedrals, they retained the high social status that their learning, patronage, good fortune, and professional acumen gained for them.

[71] Ibid., pp. 112–119, 36.

10

CATHEDRALS IN ENGLISH
SOCIETY

WHAT WAS the actual role of cathedrals in Tudor England? Were they important parts of society in England and Wales, interacting in significant ways with the lives of lay people, or were they isolated pockets of privilege, havens for lazy rich clerics who had little concern for outsiders? If they did have a valuable contribution to make, where did it lie and what were its dimensions? What difference would it have made if the cathedrals, like the monasteries, had been dissolved during the Henrician Reformation?

Fundamental questions of this sort are the ultimate ones that any study of sixteenth-century cathedrals ought to answer, yet paradoxically they are the most difficult ones to attack. None of the sources created during the period itself relates to them directly, for such queries were never clearly posed. They can be tackled only by using inadequate materials that were originally intended to serve other purposes. Only through a combination of tangential approaches can one hope to penetrate to the heart of the matter. In this concluding chapter I will seek to do so.

CRITICISMS of the cathedrals and their clergy were common in the sixteenth century, and many of them were voiced by bishops or other knowledgeable observers sympathetic to the Church. Their comments deserve to be taken seriously.

Late in life Bishop Sherburne wrote of the "ancient squalor" that he had found early in the sixteenth century at Chichester Cathedral, so great that eminent men would be deterred from residing there.[1] Shortly after the break with Rome, Bishop Latimer visited the cathedral at Worcester (still monastic) and wrote, "I evydentlye perceve the ignorance and neglygance of dyverse relygiouse persons in this monasterye to be intollerable and not to be sufferyde, for that therby dothe

---

[1] Quoted in F. G. Bennett, R. H. Codrington, and C. Deedes, eds., *Statutes and Constitutions of the Cathedral Church of Chichester* (Chichester: Charles Knight, 1904), pp. 77–78.

reign Idolatre and many kindes of supersticions and other Enormyties."[2] When he was considering constitutional arrangements for cathedrals of the new foundation, Archbishop Cranmer concluded that the "sect of prebendaries" was not "a convenient state or degree to be maintained and established," for "commonly a prebendary is neither a learner, nor teacher, but a good viander. . . . I would wish that not only the name of prebendary were exiled [from] his Grace's foundations but also the superfluous conditions of such persons." It would be no great loss if they perished altogether, along with the monks, for in the days of the Apostle Paul there had been no prebendaries in the Church of Christ.[3] A third Marian martyr, Bishop Hooper, voiced similar sentiments in 1552. "Ah, Mr. Secretary," he wrote Cecil, "that there were good men in the cathedral churches. God then should have much more honour than he hath, the king's majesty more obedience, and the poor people more knowledge. But the realm wanteth light in such churches where as of right it ought most to be."[4]

Some of the Elizabethan bishops penned similar laments. In a letter to Peter Martyr, written in 1559, John Jewel described a visitation in which he had found that "the cathedral churches were nothing else but dens of thieves, or worse, if anything worse or more foul can be mentioned."[5] Three years later, prescribing reforms for Salisbury, he began with a mixed metaphor, saying that the cathedral should shine brightly among other churches like a city set on a hill, while instead "we found in our late ordinary visitation that there were not only elsewhere on every side but even in the close itself many things amiss, a fact which . . . we took much and grievously to heart."[6] At about the same time John Scory found the cathedral at Hereford "a very nursery of blasphemy, whoredom, pride, superstition, and ignorance."[7]

Writing to Grindal regarding the prophesyings in 1576, Richard

[2] Muniments, A.6 (iii), fols. 17–18, Worcester Cathedral Library.

[3] Quoted in Joan Simon, *Education and Society in Tudor England* (Cambridge: Cambridge University Press, 1966), pp. 184–185, from Cranmer's *Miscellaneous Writings*, Parker Society, no. 16 (Cambridge, 1846), pp. 396–397.

[4] Quoted in F. Douglas Price, "Gloucester Diocese under Bishop Hooper, 1551–3," *Transactions of the Bristol and Gloucestershire Archaeological Society* 60 (1938): 127–128, from Hooper, *Later Writings*, Parker Society, no. 21 (Cambridge, 1852), pp. xix–xx.

[5] *Zurich Letters*, Parker Society, no. 51 (Cambridge, 1842), p. 45.

[6] Act Book, MS. 80, fol. 148, Salisbury Cathedral Library, printed in Christopher Wordsworth and Douglas Macleane, *Statutes and Customs of the Cathedral Church of the Blessed Virgin Mary of Salisbury* (London: W. Clowes and Sons, 1915), p. 397. The "city on a hill" analogy is especially inappropriate for Salisbury, considering its location in a valley after the hilltop site at Old Sarum was abandoned.

[7] Quoted in Henry Gee, *The Elizabethan Clergy and the Settlement of Religion* (Oxford: Clarendon Press, 1898), p. 161.

Cox thought that if "the byshopps earnestly see to the ministers" there was little need of new orders, "savinge that the cathedrall churches would be brought to some better frame touchinge exercise of learninge, whose exercyse now is onely in singinge and very little in aedifyinge."[8] At Durham, Bishop Barnes found "an Augean stable . . . whose stink is grievous in the nose of God and of men and which to purge far passeth Hercules' labours." This was in 1578.[9] When examined the prebendaries admitted the partial truth of the charges: "It hath been cast in our teeth," they said, "that we teach others but amend not ourselves, that we speak of charity but live in hatred, talk of concord but sow discord. We are ashamed to hear it, but the accusation is true in some part, we cannot deny it."[10]

One of the fullest critiques comes from John Field's tract, *A View of Popish Abuses*. It is worth quoting at some length.

We should be too long to tell your honours of cathedral churches: the dens aforesaid of all loitering lubbers, where master Dean, master Vicedean, master Canons or Prebendaries the greater, master petty Canons or Canons the lesser, master Chancellor of the church, master Treasurer (otherwise called Judas the pursebearer), the chief chanter, singing men (special favours of religion), squeaking choristers, organ players, gospellers, pistlers, pensioners, readers, vergers, etc., live in great idleness, and have their abiding. If you would know whence all these came, we can easily answer you: that they came from the pope, as out of the Trojan horse's belly, to the destruction of God's kingdom. The church of God never knew them; neither doth any reformed church in the world know them.[11]

[8] Laud-Selden-Fairhurst MS. 2003, fol. 7, Lambeth Palace Library, printed in Stanford E. Lehmberg, "Archbishop Grindal and the Prophesyings," *Historical Magazine of the Protestant Episcopal Church* 34 (1965): 125.

[9] Lansdowne MS. 25, fols. 161–162, BL, quoted in David Marcombe, "The Dean and Chapter of Durham, 1558–1603" (Ph.D. thesis, Durham University, 1973), p. 251.

[10] York Book, fol. 84, Prior's Kitchen, Durham, quoted in Marcombe, "Dean and Chapter of Durham," p. 262. Half a century later a complaint lodged against Marmaduke Blaikston, a canon of Durham from 1599 to 1633, said, "you thinke you doe service ynough to God and the Church, yf you sit now and then in your stall, like an idle drone (as allwaies you have ben), to hear piping and chaunting, and oberve devoutly your son Cosin his new ceremonies" (*The Correspondence of John Cosin*, pt. 1, Surtees Society, no. 52 [Durham, 1869], p. 185).

[11] John Field, *A View of Popish Abuses*, sec. 17, printed in W. H. Frere and C. E. Douglas, *Puritan Manifestoes* (London: SPCK, 1907), p. 32; and in H. C. Porter, *Puritanism in Tudor England* (Columbia: University of South Carolina Press, 1971), p. 133. The tract, which was originally published as part of *An Admonition to Parliament* (1572), was issued anony-

This was echoed with even greater bitterness in a "Petition to Parliament for the succession and restoring of Christ to his full regiment," probably dating from 1587.

> These are indeed very dens of thieves, where the time and place of God's service, preaching and prayer, is most filthily abused in piping of organs, in singing, ringing, and trouling of the psalms from one side of the choir to another, with squeaking of chanting choristers, disguised (as are all the rest) in white surplices, others in cornered caps and filthy copes, in pistelling and gospelling with such vain mockeries, contrary to the commandment of God and true worshipping of God, imitating the manners and fashions of antichrist, the pope, that man of sin and child of perdition, with his other rabble of miscreants and shavelings. . . . These unprofitable members, for the most part dumb dogs, unskilful sacrificing priests, destroying drones, or rather caterpillers of the Word, they consume yearly, some £2500, some £3000, some more, some less, whereof no profit, but rather great hurt cometh to the church of God and this commonwealth. They are dens of lazy, loitering lubbards, the very harbours of all deceitful and timeserving hypocrites.[12]

Each of these complaints needs to be understood in its context. Bishop Sherburne was explaining why he had founded the four "Wiccamical" prebends and instituted other reforms at Chichester; he believed that the situation there improved greatly under his leadership. Latimer, Hooper, and Cranmer were in the vanguard of reformers and often felt that their work was hampered by conservative cathedral clergy. Jewel, Cox, and Scory, writing early in Elizabeth's reign, were troubled by men who had held office under Mary and still adhered to popish views. Barnes, on the other hand, found himself in opposition to the extreme Protestantism that developed in the chapter at Durham under Dean Whittingham. Field was one of the most radical of the Elizabethan Puritans; he could see little that was good in the Established Church. The petitioners were also advanced Protestants, leaders of the movement that introduced abortive Puritan bills into vir-

mously, but Porter has ascribed it to Field, partly on the basis of his signature, which appears on the flyleaf of a copy of the *Admonition* in the Cambridge University Library.

[12] Quoted by Claire Cross, " 'Dens of Loitering Lubbers': Protestant Protest against Cathedral Foundations, 1540–1640," in *Schism, Heresy and Religious Protest*, ed. Derek Baker, Studies in Church History, vol. 9 (Cambridge: Cambridge University Press, 1972), pp. 231–232, from A. Peel, ed., *The Second Parte of a Register*, 2 vols. (Cambridge: Cambridge University Press, 1915), 2: 211.

tually every session of Parliament during the 1570s and 1580s.[13] One can explain the reasons for their positions and discount their views accordingly. Sometimes one can refute their comments directly: the preceding chapter has shown that the prebendaries were not "dumb dogs," and their income did not reach the sums alleged. Still, such views were too common and too sincerely held to be ignored.[14]

THERE is some evidence that cathedral chapters regarded services as their own corporate offering to God, which laymen were not encouraged to attend and at which they were not entirely welcome. At Chichester, Bishop Story had ordered in 1481 that the great doors to the choir should be kept shut on festival days so that strangers could not come in and disturb the celebrations, as they had been doing.[15] In 1486 the Dean and Chapter of Lichfield emphasized that the cathedral was not a parish church, and that they did not hold the cure of souls, by ordering that such sacraments as marriage, extreme unction, and burial not be given to any lay persons save members of the choir and relatives of the canons.[16]

At Exeter, as noted, the clergy tried to drive some townspeople out early in Elizabeth's reign, for they had disturbed the ministers by singing "certain vernacular ryming songs," probably metrical Psalms. After some controversy Archbishop Parker ruled that lay persons should be admitted, provided that they were willing to worship according to the lawfully established services of the church.[17] At both Worcester and Carlisle there were orders that the doors to the cathedral should be kept locked except during services, a two-edged regu-

[13] Cf. J. E. Neale, *Elizabeth I and Her Parliaments, 1559–1581* (London: Jonathan Cape, 1953), pp. 191–217, 291–304; idem, *Elizabeth I and Her Parliaments, 1584–1601* (London: Jonathan Cape, 1957), pp. 58–83, 145–165, 216–232; Patrick Collinson, *The Elizabethan Puritan Movement* (London: Jonathan Cape, 1967), pp. 291–332.

[14] Two more recent comments may be noted. Early in the nineteenth century a prebendary of Lincoln wrote that "the cathedral . . . is in no true sense the mother church of the diocese. Rather it resembles an extraneous ornament or decorative addition to the diocesan edifice" (quoted in Owen Chadwick, *The Victorian Church*, 2 vols. [London: A. and C. Black, 1970], 2: 383). And as recently as 1979 Nicholas Temperley published the judgment that "cathedrals have been essentially aristocratic institutions. . . . Forming rather less than one per cent of the total number of Anglican places of worship, they have been insulated from the public, and indeed have had no clear social function since the Reformation severed them from foundations of learning and education" (*The Music of the English Parish Church*, 2 vols. [Cambridge: Cambridge University Press, 1979], 1: 1–2).

[15] Bennett, Codrington, and Deedes, *Statutes of Chichester*, p. 18.

[16] Act Book 2, fol. 14, Lichfield Joint Record Office.

[17] MS. 3552, fol. 145, Exeter Cathedral Library.

lation suggesting that visitors were to be discouraged but worshipers allowed.[18] In 1595 the chancellor of Norwich commanded "that in tyme of devine service the officers attendant, viz. the twoe Sextens and verger, shold see that the noyse made and used in the church in the tyme of devine service maye be herafter appeased, wherby the service may be the more quietly performed."[19] This again implies that laymen frequented the building, but without much devotion or piety.

Although the English cathedrals themselves did not serve as parishes, parts of their buildings were often set aside for parochial use. At Chichester the nave was used in this way; since the subdean of the cathedral served as vicar, this was referred to as the subdeanery parish.[20] A portion of the abbey at Chester was designated as St. Oswald's parish church. Probably one of the chapels served until the 1530s, when the monks, sensing that the end was near, gave the parishioners the large south transept.[21] At Carlisle the parish used the nave, the Dean and Chapter the choir.[22] St. Luke's chapel at Norwich functioned as a parish church. At Ely the beautiful Lady Chapel was given to the parishioners of St. Cross in 1562, when their own building was so decrepit that it could no longer be occupied. This arrangement continued until 1938.[23] Three of the Welsh cathedrals were also parishes. Christ Church cathedral at Oxford never housed a parish but served instead as a college chapel, this function perhaps making its outreach to the nonacademic community more difficult. In many other places, small parish churches were located within cathedral closes, sometimes nestled against the cathedral building itself. These were usually staffed by priests from the cathedral, and it was here that vicars choral and other persons employed by the cathedrals were baptized, married, and buried. The situation in the city of Exeter was unique, for here

[18] MS. A. 74, fol. 9, Worcester Cathedral Library; Chapter Registers, vol. 3, fol. 187 (1583), Carlisle Record Office.
[19] J. F. Williams and B. Cozens-Hardy, eds., *Extracts from the Two Earliest Minute Books of the Dean and Chapter of Norwich Cathedral, 1566–1649*, Norfolk Record Society, no. 24 (Norwich, 1953), p. 38.
[20] Gerald Cobb, *English Cathedrals: The Forgotten Centuries* (London: Thames and Hudson, 1980), p. 20, refers to the north transept and its chapel serving as a parish church until 1853. This was called St. Peter's the Great.
[21] R.V.H. Burne, *The Monks of Chester* (London: SPCK, 1962), pp. 138–139.
[22] C.M.L. Bouch, *Prelates and People of the Lake Counties: A History of the Diocese of Carlisle, 1133–1933* (Kendal: Titus Wilson, 1948), p. 188. The parish retained its dedication to St. Mary, although the cathedral was called the Cathedral Church of the Holy and Undivided Trinity after 1541.
[23] Cobb, *English Cathedrals*, pp. 81–82. The parish evidently did not appreciate the elegance of the building, for in later centuries the walls were encrusted with whitewash and the windows hidden behind long, dingy draperies. Substantial restoration had to be undertaken when the cathedral reclaimed the space.

the parish churches did not possess cemeteries. Funerals for all lay men and women were conducted in the cathedral, with burial in the cathedral close. When space limitations made it necessary to reuse graves, older bones were taken to a charnel house that remained in existence until the 1550s or 1560s.[24]

References in fifteenth- and sixteenth-century documents often make it clear that members of the civic oligarchy attended services in their local cathedrals. About 1495 depositions were collected at Hereford regarding the traditional right of the Dean and Chapter to precede the mayor and aldermen in civic processions, presumably processions to cathedral services. Someone had suggested that the mayor should be given a place at the head of the procession, immediately after the dean, but the chapter did not find this acceptable and it was determined that all the clergy would continue to precede the laymen.[25] An agreement made in 1516 to settle various matters that had been in dispute between the convent and citizens at Worcester provided that city officials might have their maces borne before them when they entered the cathedral, even though they had no jurisdiction within its liberties.[26] Prior More, always eager to remain on good terms with his lay neighbors, had given wine to the bailiffs and citizens on Christmas Day, and it is likely that his successors continued the tradition.[27] During Mary's reign, the Privy Council wrote to the mayor and aldermen of Bristol, requiring them "not to absent themselfes" from sermons and processions at the cathedral church as they had been doing (possibly as a sign of their dislike of the restored Catholic services) and not to expect the Dean and Chapter to "fetche them out of the cittie with their crosses and procession, being the same very unsemely and farre out of order."[28] Relations had probably improved by 1581, when the cathedral accounts record the payment of 10s. to the mayor's servants and the waits at Christmas.[29]

We know that members of the corporation attended Sunday services at Worcester regularly during Elizabeth's reign; they even paid for their own tiered seating.[30] All of the freemen of Winchester were obliged to meet the mayor at the High Cross of the city and accom-

---

[24] Nicholas Orme, *Exeter Cathedral as It Was* (Exeter: Devon Books, 1986), pp. 1–5.

[25] HCA 2958, Hereford Cathedral Library.

[26] Muniments, A.6 (ii), fol. 101, Worcester Cathedral Library.

[27] Ethel S. Fegan, ed., *Journal of Prior William More* (Worcester: Worcestershire Historical Society, 1914), p. 202.

[28] *Acts of the Privy Council*, 32 vols. (London: HMSO, 1890–1907), 6: 158.

[29] Bristol Cathedral Accounts, DC/A/9/1/4, for 1581, Bristol Record Office.

[30] Alan D. Dyer, *The City of Worcester in the Sixteenth Century* (Leicester: Leicester University Press, 1973), p. 232.

pany him to the cathedral on Sundays and feast days; those failing to
do so were fined 4*d*., or twice that sum if they were members of the
Council of Twenty-Four.[31] Attendance is also well documented at Lincoln, where it is clear that the emphasis was on attending sermons
rather than services. Few of the city's parish priests were educated
men, and "preaching of the Word" was centered almost exclusively in
the minster.[32]

Civic processions to St. Paul's were particularly splendid. It had long
been the custom for the lord mayor and aldermen of London, the
sheriffs, and members of the great guilds or companies to go in solemn procession to the cathedral on such festival days as All Saints,
Christmas, St. Stephen's, St. John's, Epiphany, the Feast of the Cir-
cumcision, and the Purification of the Virgin.

> On Whitsunday, the Mayor and City Dignitaries met at St. Peter's,
> Cornhill. This seems to have been the most splendid procession.
> The Mayor, Recorder, Aldermen, every one with his *Livery* (each
> of whom, according to his rank, received on that day gifts of robes
> and vestments of honour), the Sheriffs, and the great City Com-
> panies, preceded by the Rectors of the London parishes, marched
> along Cheapside to the north-east corner of the churchyard.
> There they were met by the procession of the Cathedral Clergy,
> along the south side of the churchyard, through the close of Wat-
> ling Street round to the great West door. There they stopped,
> while the hymn "Veni Creator" was sung antiphonally by the Vic-
> ars-choral with the organ, and with the incense-bearers incensing
> as they went on. The Mayor and Aldermen then advanced to the
> high altar and made their offering. That ceremony was repeated
> on Whit Tuesday, only that they met and set forth from St. Bar-
> tholomew's.[33]

Another source tells us that on All Saints, 1561, "the Mayor and Al-
dermen went in the afternoon to St. Paul's, with all the crafts in their
Liveries, attended with fourscore men, all in blue, carrying torches.
The Bishop of London preached the Sermon. They tarried in the
Church till night; and so the lord mayor and his company went home

[31] Tom Atkinson, *Elizabethan Winchester* (London: Faber and Faber, 1963), p. 65. On
one occasion a search for recusants was interrupted so that the officials could attend
matins at the cathedral (p. 106).

[32] J.W.F. Hill, *Tudor and Stuart Lincoln* (Cambridge: Cambridge University Press, 1956),
pp. 100–101.

[33] H. H. Milman, *Annals of St. Paul's Cathedral* (London: John Murray, 1868), pp. 165–
168.

all with torch-light."[34] A similar procession was held to honor the solemn inauguration of each new lord mayor. St. Paul's was also the site for special services at which the Te Deum was sung to celebrate such events as Henry VIII's safe return from Calais in 1532 or the birth of Princess Elizabeth in 1533.[35]

In 1602 the Dean and Chapter of Salisbury referred to the cathedral as an "eminent Church" to which "many strangers doe repaire."[36] At Chester it was said that "the whole city came" to services until the 1630s, when trouble arose because the chapter refused to allow the mayor to have his sword borne before him within the cathedral. The mayor, a former chorister, had been accustomed to attending daily and sitting opposite the dean. After the altercation, services were boycotted and "scarce five lay people" were present.[37] At Wells the sextons customarily provided cushions for persons attending services; in 1585 they were ordered not to charge for them.[38] At Hereford the chapter paid "for making a backe for a new seate for the gentlemen of the citie, on promise that [the carpenter] would make it lower, that the people may see the pulpit and heare the better." This was in 1588.[39] In the seventeenth century Laud issued orders for the removal of pews from cathedral churches (this was done at Lichfield and Worcester); he also commanded that the mayor and aldermen, together with the wives of prebendaries and other women of quality, no longer be given seats in the choir at Durham, York, and Salisbury.[40] His directive, and the fact that it aroused opposition, suggests that these persons had been in the habit of attending earlier.

MOST of the people who came to the cathedrals heard sermons. Preaching was regarded as important long before the Reformation, and it came to be thought of as even more essential as Protestant views prevailed. In London crowds resorted to Paul's Cross, the outdoor pulpit adjoining the cathedral. Worcester also had a tall stone cross where sermons were delivered in the open air, with seats for the prin-

[34] John Nichols, *The Progresses and Public Processions of Queen Elizabeth*, 3 vols. (London: John Nichols and Son, 1823), 1: 105.

[35] E. W. Ives, *Anne Boleyn* (Oxford: Blackwell, 1986), pp. 201, 230.

[36] Choristers' Accounts, 2/4, Salisbury Cathedral Library.

[37] R.V.H. Burne, *Chester Cathedral* (London: SPCK, 1958), pp. 114–115. Another chorister who became a prominent civic leader was Robert Chafe of Exeter.

[38] Act Book H, fol. 31, Wells Cathedral Library.

[39] R. 588 (Fabric Roll, 1587–1591), Hereford Cathedral Library.

[40] Christopher Hill, *Economic Problems of the Church from Archbishop Whitgift to the Long Parliament* (Oxford: Clarendon Press, 1956), p. 179.

cipal citizens near the church wall.[41] In other places preaching normally took place indoors, often in the cathedral nave.

When establishing his new prebends at Chichester, Bishop Sherburne laid down statutes that mandated preaching. The prebendaries were ordered to preach regularly and were given guidance about the subjects to be covered: their sermons were to deal mainly with the vices of detraction, perjury, neglect of the duty of educating children, and murmuring against God whenever things did not turn out prosperously.[42] At Lincoln special arrangements were made for sermons during Lent and Advent, 1505. Those in Lent were to be delivered in the nave, the Advent sermons being preached in the chapter house.[43] It is said that Ralph Collingwood, dean of Lichfield from 1512 to 1521, preached for half an hour every Sunday, and that he was the first to do so.[44] The act book for Westminster Abbey records that when the church became a cathedral it was "decreyd yt sermondes shuld be mayd euery sonday."[45]

The statutes given to cathedrals of the new foundation generally require that each canon deliver at least four sermons a year and that the dean preach himself, or by sufficient deputy, on the principal feast days. The importance attached to preaching is underscored in statements like that for Durham: "Because the Word of God is a lamp unto our feet, we therefore appoint and will, nay by the mercy of God we implore, that the Dean and all the Canons be diligent in season and out of season in sowing the Word of God both in the country and especially in this Cathedral Church."[46] Elizabethan injunctions often contain similar passages.[47]

Members of the chapter at Durham can hardly be accused of shirking this responsibility. During Elizabeth's reign there were at least 170 sermons and lectures a year, generally of high quality. In 1585 the

[41] Cobb, *English Cathedrals*, p. 164.

[42] Bennett, Codrington, and Deedes, *Statutes of Chichester*, pp. 58–59.

[43] Margaret Bowker, *The Secular Clergy in the Diocese of Lincoln, 1495–1520* (Cambridge: Cambridge University Press, 1968), p. 177. Bowker emphasizes the role of the cathedral as a center for instruction and refers also to the sermons preached before the visitation of the bishop.

[44] Thomas Harwood, *The History and Antiquities of the Church and City of Lichfield* (Gloucester: J. Harris, 1806), p. 181.

[45] Act Book, 1542–1609, fol. 10, Westminster Abbey Library.

[46] A. Hamilton Thompson, ed., *The Statutes of the Cathedral Church of Durham*, Surtees Society, no. 143 (Durham, 1929), p. 109. Cf. the Statute Book, sec. 13, Chester Cathedral Library; J. E. Prescott, *The Statutes of the Cathedral Church of Carlisle* (London: Elliot Stock, 1903), sec. 14.

[47] See, for instance, those for Peterborough, MS. 30, fol. 1, Peterborough Cathedral Archives, Cambridge University Library, and injunctions for Wells issued in 1559 and 1592, *VCH, Somerset*, 2: 41.

dean, Toby Matthew, preached 28 sermons in the cathedral. He delivered 19 in 1586 and 27 in 1587. During his eleven years in office, Matthew is said to have preached 721 sermons, most of them in the cathedral but 15 or 20 a year in parish churches. Initially Dean Whittingham was disappointed that relatively few of the "stiff" townspeople came to hear the preaching, but in 1563 he thought that "now of late they begin to resort more diligently to the sermons and service."[48] The situation was quite different at Chester, where for some years the subdean, John Nutter, was the only member of the chapter actually in residence. Yet even here he was said to preach often, "godly and sincerely."[49]

Theology lectures, often given by Puritans, frequently supplemented the sermons. Divinity lectures at Durham began in 1559; they were delivered in the chapter house two or three mornings a week. Attendance by both major and minor canons was supposed to be compulsory. Hugh Broughton, the lecturer in the 1580s, was especially popular and attracted large crowds.[50] Among the various lecturers referred to in the records of other cathedrals is Thomas Thackham, a former prebendary of York, who was appointed at Hereford in 1581.[51]

The cathedral clergy frequently preached in parish churches, especially those in which the Dean and Chapter held the tithes. In 1578 the canons of Durham delivered more than 300 sermons in parishes, 215 within County Durham and 88 in Northumberland.[52] Worcester paid members of the chapter 3s. 4d. for each sermon delivered in a parish church, or twice that sum if it was more than twenty miles distant. At Chester the fee was always 6s. 8d.[53]

A NUMBER of the cathedrals received visits by the king, queen, or other members of the royal family. Coronations of course took place in Westminster Abbey; Edward VI and Mary were crowned during its brief incarnation as a cathedral. Coronation processions often stopped

[48] Marcombe, "Dean and Chapter of Durham," pp. 10–11, 306, (Landsdowne MS. 7, fol. 24, BL).

[49] Nutter later amassed such wealth, mainly during his years as dean (1589–1603), that Elizabeth referred to him as the "Golden Ass" (Burne, *Chester Cathedral*, pp. 56, 64).

[50] Marcombe, "Dean and Chapter of Durham," p. 11.

[51] Act Book 2, fol. 90, Hereford Cathedral Library.

[52] Marcombe, "Dean and Chapter of Durham," p. 306.

[53] MS. A. 74, fol. 1, Worcester Cathedral Library; Account Book 3, for 1590, Chester Cathedral Library.

near St. Paul's. During the pageantry held in 1533 to honor Anne Boleyn, for instance, two hundred children, including those from St. Paul's School, declaimed translations from the Latin poets from a platform erected at the east end of the churchyard.[54] Marriages, baptisms, and funerals might occur in cathedrals outside of London. We do not know just where the union between Henry VII and Elizabeth of York was celebrated.[55] The couple's older son, Prince Arthur, was born in Winchester and baptized in the cathedral there. As a boy, Arthur visited the cathedral at Worcester, accompanied by his parents and his grandmother, Lady Margaret Beaufort. A few years later he was buried there, and the chantry chapel described earlier was built in his honor. His marriage to Catherine of Aragon had been solemnized at St. Paul's. Henry VII and Elizabeth were interred at the Abbey, in the lofty fan-vaulted chapel added east of the shrine of Edward the Confessor.

Catherine of Aragon had visited Exeter Cathedral in 1501, spending several days at the deanery shortly after her initial landing at Plymouth.[56] She married Henry VIII in the Franciscan church at Greenwich, not in the Abbey or a cathedral, and Henry was buried at Windsor rather than Westminster. The marriage of Philip II and Mary, as noted above, took place at Winchester. In 1554 Philip attended a great service at St. Paul's honoring the arrival in England of Cardinal Pole.[57] Mary and Pole visited Canterbury in 1557, when the chapter had to make special payments for cleaning the chapter house, carrying away rubbish, and preparing the library and tombs for royal inspection.[58] During her father's reign Mary had paid several visits to Worcester, where she was entertained by Prior More, both in Worcester itself and at his manor of Battenhall. Perhaps she was especially attracted by Prince Arthur's chantry, with its armorial references to her mother, Catherine of Aragon. In 1526 she stayed from January 7 through Easter, leaving only on April 15. She returned again in August for the Feast of the Assumption of the Virgin.[59] Mary's funeral took place in Westminster Abbey, and she is buried there.

Elizabeth's progresses took her to several of the cathedrals. Her visit to Canterbury in 1573 is described in a letter sent by Archbishop Parker to Grindal, then archbishop of York.

---

[54] Ives, *Anne Boleyn*, p. 281.
[55] S. B. Chrimes, *Henry VII* (London: Eyre Methuen, 1972), p. 66.
[56] Orme, *Exeter Cathedral*, p. 53.
[57] Milman, *Annals of St. Paul's*, p. 239.
[58] MS. M.A. 40, for 4 & 5 Phil. & M., Canterbury Cathedral Library.
[59] Fegan, *Journal of Prior More*, pp. 37, 224, 234.

I met her Highness, as she was coming to Dover, upon Folkston Down. The which I rather did, with all my men, to shew my duty to her, and mine affection to the Shire, who likewise there met her. And I left her at Dover, and came home to Bekesborne that night: and after that, went to Canterbury to receive her Majesty there. Which I did, with the Bishops of Lincoln and Rochester, and my Suffragan, at the West door: where, after the Grammarian had made his Oration to her upon her horseback, she alighted. We then kneeled down, and said the Psalm *Deus misereatur* in English, with certain other Collects briefly; and that in our chimers and rochets. The Quire, with the Dean and Prebendaries, stood on either side of the Church, and brought her Majesty up with a Square-song, she going under a canopy, born by four of her Temporal Knights, to the traverse placed by the Communion board; where she heard Evensong, and after departed to her lodging at St. Austin's, whither I waited on her. . . . And so her Majesty came every Sunday to Church, to hear the Sermon; and upon one Monday it pleased her Highness to dine in my great Hall, thoroughly furnished, with the Council, Frenchmen, Ladies, Gentlemen, and Mayor of the Town, with his Brethren, &c. her Highness sitting in the midst, having two French Ambassadors at one end of the table, and four Ladies of Honour at the other end.[60]

After staying fourteen days at Canterbury the queen returned to her palace at Greenwich, stopping on the way to attend a Sunday service at Rochester Cathedral and hear a sermon there.[61]

In 1575 Elizabeth visited Lichfield, where she stayed from July 20 to August 3,[62] and then journeyed to Worcester, arriving on Saturday, August 13. The next day she attended a service in the cathedral.

Her Majestie proceeded into the Churchyard and the Church with a cheerful countenance; and at three several places in the Church, being upon the greftes, or steppes, she turned herself back, shewing herself unto the people; who crying "God save your Majestie!" she also with a loud voice gave them hartie thanks as before; and into the Chancell; and being settled in her traves, or seate, rychly decked and adorned in the upper end of the Chancell, next to Prynce Arthur's Chapell, and hering a great and solem noyse of syngyng of service in the Quier, both by note and

---

[60] John Nichols, *Progresses of Queen Elizabeth*, 1: 345.
[61] Ibid., 1: 353.
[62] Harwood, *Lichfield*, p. 304.

279

also plaing with cornetts and sackbutts; which being finished, Mr.
Doctor Langworth, a Prebendary ther, did reade the Epistle, and
Mr. Dr. Wilson, Dean, did reed the Gospel; and which ended,
Doctor Bullyngham, Byshop of Worcester, did preach before her
Majestie and the Nobles, and others being present, and a gret au-
dience.

She lodged in the Bishop's Palace.[63] Three years later, in 1578, her
progress into East Anglia took her to the cathedral at Norwich.[64]

The queen attended services at St. Paul's on numerous occasions.
An amusing episode occurred on New Year's Day, 1562. Dean Nowell
had obtained from a foreigner some fine engravings or woodcuts de-
picting saints and martyrs, and he had these bound into a copy of the
Prayer Book that he laid at the queen's place, intending to give it to
her for a New Year's gift. When she saw it she was displeased. "She
opened the book, and perused it, and saw the pictures; but frowned
and blushed, and then shut it (of which several took notice); and, calling for the verger, bad him bring her the old book, wherein she was
formerly wont to read." After the service she interrogated the dean,
who admitted that he was responsible for the volume. "Have you for-
got our Proclamation against images, pictures, and Romish reliques?"
Elizabeth asked. Nowell insisted that he meant no harm and had
hoped to please her. After some further interchange the queen left
with the parting command, "Let no more of these mistakes ... be
committed within the Churches of our Realm."[65]

In her later years Elizabeth seems to have been more attracted to
country houses than to cathedrals. Occasionally her courtiers took her
place. In preparation for a visit by Leicester in 1583 the Dean and
Chapter of Chester had to have eight loads of filth carted away and a
hole in the courtyard filled.[66]

Even when the queen was not present, the cathedrals honored her.
At Chester there is a record of bells ringing to celebrate her "happy
accession"—doubtless this was true everywhere, even if documents do
not prove it—and many of the cathedrals, including Rochester, rang
peals annually on the anniversary of her succession. Bristol celebrated

[63] John Nichols, *Progresses of Queen Elizabeth*, 1: 539. During this visit the citizens hoped
to arouse the queen's interest in the financial problems caused by the decline of the clothing industry. Cf. Michael Craze, *King's School, Worcester, 1541–1971* (Worcester: Baylis,
1972), p. 40.
[64] Noel Boston, *The Musical History of Norwich Cathedral* (Norwich: Friends of Norwich
Cathedral, 1963), p. 7; Ian Dunlop, *Palaces and Progresses of Elizabeth I* (London: Jonathan
Cape, 1962), pp. 128–138.
[65] John Nichols, *Progresses of Queen Elizabeth*, 1: 105–106.
[66] Burne, *Chester Cathedral*, p. 61.

"Her Majesty's Day" with both ringing and a bonfire.[67] At Hereford there was a bonfire in October 1587 to celebrate the queen's deliverance, presumably from the treachery of Mary, Queen of Scots.[68] After her execution, Mary had been buried in Peterborough Cathedral, where there was an elaborate funeral, with heralds and noblemen as chief mourners. The bishop of Lincoln preached, taking his text from the Thirty-ninth Psalm ("Lorde, let me knowe myne ende") and quoting Martin Luther ("Many an one that liueth a papiste, dieth a protestante").[69] Despite the circumstances Elizabeth was intent on honoring Mary's royal status.

THE relationship that existed between the cathedrals and ordinary members of the laity is much less well documented than that which involved the royalty and nobility.[70] One way of approaching it is to examine artifacts rather than documents, in this case the tombs and monuments of lay people erected within the Tudor cathedrals. These can surely be read as proof of interaction between the cathedrals and the laity, a sign that prestige was associated with burial in a cathedral or lasting commemoration there.[71] It seems certain, too, that the funerals of the civic leaders and aristocrats commemorated in the cathedrals were attended by throngs of laymen.[72]

During the centuries before the Reformation, chantry chapels were memorials as well as locations for requiems and obits. All the cathedrals had chantries, and most of them had elaborate chantry chapels. Some of these, like Sir John Speke's chantry at Exeter, described in

---

[67] Bristol Cathedral Accounts, DC/A/9/1/4, under 1581, Bristol Record Office.

[68] R. 591 (Claviger's Roll, 1586–1587), Hereford Cathedral Library.

[69] MS. 11 (Dean Fletcher's Ledger Book, 1587–1642), Peterborough Cathedral Archives, Cambridge University Library.

[70] Among the small number of studies to approach this topic may be mentioned Ann M. Kettle, "City and Close: Lichfield in the Century before the Reformation," in *The Church in Pre-Reformation Society*, ed. Caroline M. Barron and Christopher Harper-Bill (Woodbridge, Suffolk: Boydell Press, 1985), pp. 158–169.

[71] Cf. Clare Gittings, *Death, Burial and the Individual in Early Modern England* (Dover, N.H.: Croom Helm, 1984).

[72] See Mervyn James, *Society, Politics and Culture* (Cambridge: Cambridge University Press, 1986), pp. 176–187, for a description of the funeral of William, Lord Dacre, held at Carlisle Cathedral in 1563 (it is interesting to note that the Salkelds were dependents of the Dacres); and Lawrence Stone, *The Crisis of the Aristocracy: 1558–1641* (Oxford: Clarendon Press, 1965), p. 572, for more general comments on aristocratic burial ceremonies. It was not unusual for several hundred mourners to participate in processions, and sometimes cathedral deans preached even if interment was in a parish church rather than the cathedral. The dean of Chester, for instance, conducted the funeral of Edward, earl of Derby, in 1572 although it was held in Ormskirk church.

Chapter 1, were erected during the sixteenth century (Speke died in 1518), and some of them include iconography suggesting friendship and mutual respect between laymen and clerics.[73]

After the Reformation and the dissolution of the chantries, monuments took over the role of memorializing lay men and women, though they were not of course centers for the prayers and masses that had existed earlier.[74] Two of the monuments at Worcester are especially interesting; both depict local Elizabethan merchants who died early in the seventeenth century. Robert Wilde, a wealthy clothier who died in 1608, is commemorated by an altar-tomb that includes full-size recumbent effigies of Wilde and his wife (fig. 33).[75] The Moores, memorialized with even greater grandeur, were drapers who made a fortune by financing and managing the cottage industry of spinning and weaving, dyeing and selling the finished goods themselves. Their monument (fig. 34) contains six kneeling figures carved in the round out of white stone, including John and Anne Moore, their son Thomas Moore (who is shown in his alderman's robes), and his wife Mary. "Here born, here bred, here buried, December Anno 1615," the memorial to Thomas concludes.

Hereford has the tomb of Alexander Denton (d. 1576) and his wife (fig. 35), depicted in recumbent effigies much like those of the Wildes. A child is shown with them. At Gloucester one finds a large monument to Thomas Machen, an alderman who died in 1615; he and his wife are shown kneeling at a prayer desk, while below them are smaller figures of four sons and a grandson, four daughters and two granddaughters. Edward Cole, a wealthy lawyer who died in 1617 after several terms as mayor of Winchester, is commemorated by a memorial in the north aisle of the cathedral there.[76]

Ely Cathedral contains grandiose monuments to Sir Robert and Sir Mark Steward (d. 1570 and 1603, respectively). Despite a bogus claim of relationship to the Stuart royal family, these men—father and son—were descendants of Robert Steward, the last prior and first dean of Ely. They had grown rich out of their connections with the

[73] See above, Chapter 1. The Speke chantry included coats of arms of bishops Courtenay, Oldham, and Fox, as well as Dean Veysey. See Nicholas Orme, "Sir John Speke and His Chapel in Exeter Cathedral," *Reports and Transactions of the Devonshire Association* 118 (1986): 25–41.

[74] Cf. Brian Kemp, *English Church Monuments* (London: Batsford, 1980).

[75] In 1544 Wilde's father had bought one of the finest houses in Worcester, called the Commandery. This was Charles II's headquarters during the battle of Worcester and is now a museum illustrating the role of Worcester in the Civil War. Wilde was a graduate of the King's School; see Craze, *King's School, Worcester*, p. 23.

[76] Atkinson, *Elizabethan Winchester*, p. 71.

33. Tomb of Robert Wilde and his wife, Worcester Cathedral.

cathedral, for the Dean and Chapter had been persuaded to grant them a number of profitable leases and tithes. Sir Robert is shown reclining but propped up on his elbow, wearing a tabard emblazoned with his arms (fig. 36); Sir Mark's tomb (fig. 37), pompous and blustering, has many coats of arms beneath his figure and, above, a great crest containing his own escutcheon, supported by *putti* and flanked by two obelisks, a common symbol of eternity. A neighboring tablet, with some Renaissance touches, commemorates Sir Robert's son-in-law William Lynne (d. 1589).[77]

One of the most haunting monuments at Canterbury (fig. 38) depicts the tragic death of two generations of the Hales family: a painted panel shows the suicide by drowning of Sir James Hales in 1554, after his mind had been unsettled by the rapid religious changes, while a relief pictures the burial at sea of his son, the younger Sir James, who

[77] See Edmund Esdaile, *The Monuments in Ely Cathedral* (Ely: Dean and Chapter, 1973), pp. 8–9.

34. Monument to John Moore and his wife, Worcester Cathedral.

35. Tomb of Alexander Denton and his wife, Hereford Cathedral.

36. Monument to Sir Robert Steward, Ely Cathedral.

died aboard a disease-stricken warship in 1589.[78] Chester has a monument to Thomas Greene (d. 1602), shown flanked by his two wives (fig. 39), and a memorial tablet, without effigy, for Sir William Gerrarde (d. 1581), a former lord chancellor of Ireland and vice-president of the Council for Wales (fig. 40). Here the inscription is framed by Ionic columns and topped by an entablature with strapwork. The similar monument to the singing man Osbert Parsley at Norwich has already been noted. The cathedral at Oxford has an affecting memorial (originally a carved brass) to Henry Dow, son of a merchant tailor of London, who died in 1578 at the age of twenty-one after having studied at Christ Church for two years and six months.

[78] The elder Hales, a serjeant-at-law and judge, had handled legal business for the cathedral under Henry VIII. See MS. M.A. 40, miscellaneous accounts for 1542–1575, fol. 7, Canterbury Cathedral Library; cf. Kemp, *Church Monuments*, p. 71.

37. Monument to Sir Mark Steward, Ely Cathedral.

Less useful in establishing connections between the cathedrals and lay people, but often of higher artistic quality, are the monuments to members of the clergy and cathedral dignitaries. A number of these depict bishops. Perhaps the finest of the late medieval style is Bishop Sherburne's tomb at Chichester (1536); his reclining body is shown full length, clad in episcopal vestments, while beautiful alabaster angels surround his coat of arms and bear his miter up to heaven (fig. 41). The tomb of Bishop Booth of Hereford is of about the same date, similar in composition but less elegantly wrought. The first bishop of Oxford, Robert King (d. 1557), is buried in the south transept of his cathedral, in a tomb boasting an elaborately carved canopy but without any effigy. The curious monument to Nicholas Bullingham of Worcester (d. 1576) includes a life-size representation of the bishop,

38. Monument to Sir James Hales and his family,
Canterbury Cathedral.

but the inscription occupies the center of the space so that only the
prelate's torso and legs are visible (fig. 42).

The artistic quality of the later Tudor monuments, considered as
pieces of sculpture, is markedly less high than that of the early sixteenth-century work, which had been vigorous, progressive, and
adaptable.[79] The post-Reformation pieces often seem unsophisticated
in conception and parochial in execution. But, since more of the monuments were erected by laymen, their social significance is probably
higher than that of the earlier tombs and chantries. Some lay people

[79] The adjectives are from Lawrence Stone, *Sculpture in Britain: The Middle Ages* (Harmondsworth: Penguin Books, 1955), p. 232.

287

39. Monument to Thomas Greene and his wives, Chester Cathedral.

clearly cared about the cathedrals or they would not have chosen to be memorialized in them.

CHURCH buildings, including cathedrals, were often used for secular purposes. This subject has been considered so carefully by J. G. Davies that it is necessary here only to summarize his conclusions.[80]

The secular use of church buildings can be traced back to the patristic period and became even more widespread in the Middle Ages. In the case of English parish churches, it was the responsibility of the laymen to maintain the nave, the rector being charged only with upkeep of the chancel; it was hard, therefore, to deny parishioners the use of the nave, which came to function as a village hall, employed for a variety of purposes. That financial arrangement did not apply to cathedrals, but there, too, the naves were put to nonreligious uses, as gathering places or locations where business could be transacted and goods sold. Indeed, William Harrison, in his *Description of England* (1587), complained that cathedral naves were "rather markets and

[80] J. G. Davies, *The Secular Use of Church Buildings* (London: SCM Press, 1968). I am grateful to Professor Davies for several interesting discussions of this topic while he was a visiting professor at the University of Minnesota.

40. Monument to William Gerrarde, Chester Cathedral.

shops for merchandize, than solemn places of praier."[81] Contracts often specified that rents were to be paid at the cathedral font, or even on the altar. There were actually thoroughfares running through several cathedrals, including those at Winchester, Salisbury, Exeter, Norwich, and Worcester as well as St. Paul's.

The extent to which St. Paul's was used for secular purposes was notorious. The nave was little better than a marketplace; animals were driven through the building; promenading, gossiping, hiring, transacting business, obtaining legal counsel—all of these activities took place in Paul's Walk. Early in Henry VIII's reign Dean Colet objected, with little effect, and in 1554 the lord mayor issued a proclamation "for the preventing of Profanation and Abuses offered to St. Paul's."

[81] Quoted in D. M. Palliser, *The Age of Elizabeth* (London: Longman, 1983), p. 334.

41. Tomb of Bishop Sherburne, Chichester Cathedral.

This lamented that many people "commonly use and accustom themselves very unseemly and unreverently (the more the pity) to make their common Carriage of great Vessels full of Ale and Beer, great Baskets full of Bread, fish, Flesh and Fruit, and such other things; Fardels of Stuff, and other gross Wares and Things" through the church, "some leading Mules, Horses and other Beasts through the same." These activities were forbidden and penalties were prescribed, ranging from a fine of 3s. 4d. for the first offense to two-days' imprisonment for persistent violators. The actual sale of merchandise may have been stopped, but walking and talking continued for centuries, a writer in 1628 likening the noise to the buzzing of bees. In the eighteenth century, and doubtless earlier, the naves of York and Durham also served as fashionable promenades. When there were no other

42. Tomb of Bishop Bullingham, Worcester Cathedral.

large public buildings it was probably inevitable that cathedrals would be used for secular purposes. Indeed it is still common for their naves to be used as concert halls, not necessarily for the performance of religious music.

In their role as sanctuaries, churches were also fulfilling an essentially secular function. Once again this custom goes back to the earliest years of Christianity and, indeed, has pagan origins. Although all churches might provide refuge for those fleeing criminal prosecution, Westminster Abbey and Durham Cathedral were most important in this regard; it is said that more than three hundred persons sought sanctuary in the cathedral priory at Durham between 1464 and 1524.[82] According to his memoranda Thomas Cromwell would have liked to abolish sanctuaries altogether, but this was not done until the reign of James I. Instead, the rights of sanctuary were limited by statutes passed in 1529, 1536, and 1540.[83] We know that there were sanc-

[82] Davies, *Secular Use*, pp. 145–146, 183, 202–203, 142–154, 203; 19–21, 42. The famous Norman knocker on the door to the nave at Durham was intended primarily for use by those seeking sanctuary at times when the building was locked. The archival records of the cathedrals themselves contain virtually no information about sanctuary.

[83] Stanford E. Lehmberg, *The Reformation Parliament, 1529–1536* (Cambridge: Cambridge University Press, 1970), pp. 98, 126, 204, 230; idem, *The Later Parliaments of Henry VIII, 1536–1547* (Cambridge: Cambridge University Press, 1977), p. 100. See also Isobel D. Thornley, "The Destruction of Sanctuary," in *Tudor Studies Presented to A. F. Pollard,*

tuary men at Westminster during Mary's reign because they took part in a procession when Feckenham was installed as abbot. Feckenham was later involved in a controversy with Parliament when he refused to relinquish special rights guaranteed by an old charter (now known to have been forged).[84] In 1566 the dean of Westminster appeared in the House of Commons to assert the historical claims of sanctuary there: Parliament was considering a bill that would have deprived defaulting debtors of sanctuary rights.[85] After his disquisition the bill was voted down, but sanctuaries continued to be unpopular. There was a general belief that their existence encouraged lawlessness.

THE impact of cathedrals on the economy of the cities in which they were located should be pointed out, even if it is not possible to provide hard, quantitative evidence. Many of the cathedral cities were dominated by their great churches, economically as well as physically. This was of course especially true of such small towns as Ely, Wells, and Canterbury, but the economic influence of the cathedral was significant everywhere, except perhaps in London.

Because the cathedrals drew their principal revenues from scattered landholdings, the economic effect was to redistribute income from rural areas where it was generated to the cities where it was spent. In addition, the Dean and Chapter often owned large numbers of urban houses and tenements, renting them to lay people ranging from prominent merchants to poor widows and thus interacting with the lives of many townspeople, at least so far as their dwellings were concerned. At Worcester, for instance, the cathedral owned almost two hundred houses, somewhere between 10 and 20 percent of all the dwellings in the city, while at Winchester many of the shops and stalls in the High Street belonged to the Dean and Chapter.[86] In many places the bishop and the dean were the richest residents, employing a number of servants. Everywhere the prebendaries formed an elite group, able to spend significant sums of money on food, furniture,

---

ed. R. W. Seton-Watson (London: Longmans, 1924), pp. 182–207; and E. W. Ives, "Crime, Sanctuary, and Royal Authority under Henry VIII," in *On the Laws and Customs of England*, ed. M. S. Arnold et al. (Chapel Hill: University of North Carolina Press, 1981), pp. 296–320.

[84] Thornley, "Destruction of Sanctuary," pp. 204–205; D. M. Loades, *The Reign of Mary Tudor* (London: Macmillan, 1979), pp. 448–450.

[85] G. R. Elton, *The Parliament of England, 1559–1581* (Cambridge: Cambridge University Press, 1986), p. 301.

[86] Dyer, *City of Worcester*, p. 230; Atkinson, *Elizabethan Winchester*, p. 20.

books, and household staff. Vicars choral were less well off, but they, too, enriched the civic economy and were frequently noted as visitors to taverns and alehouses. Before the Reformation, pilgrims attracted to shrines provided custom for inns and shopkeepers; when the famous statue of the Virgin, said to be ten feet tall, was removed from the cathedral in Worcester, a townsman created a disturbance by protesting that the city would be impoverished.[87] The tradition of visiting cathedrals was continued to some extent by tourists in later years. Skilled artisans and more ordinary practitioners of the building trades were needed to keep the cathedrals in repair. In short, virtually every aspect of the local economy was linked with the life of the cathedral.

It is impossible to quantify all of this, but reference to the known income of the individual cathedrals helps to gauge the scale of this impact.[88] Even the poorest cathedrals (Bristol and Carlisle) had revenues exceeding £600, while their richer cousins (Canterbury, Lincoln, Winchester, and Durham) could expect to receive several times that amount. If even half of this found its way into the local economy— and it is hard to see how that could fail to be the case—the effect must have been marked. No doubt trade was more important than the church in places like Norwich and Bristol, as well as London, and the university certainly outstripped the cathedral in bringing money into Oxford. In most other cities a large proportion of the townspeople must have been able to trace a good part of their livelihood back to the cathedral close.

A PORTION of the income received by the cathedrals was set aside for charitable purposes. In cathedrals of the new foundation this was usually mandated by their statutes.

Documents drawn up when the new foundations were under consideration include references to poor men who were to be maintained by the cathedrals and to the allocation of funds for their support.[89] Generally they were allowed £6 13s. 4d. a year, the same sum ordinarily provided as a pension for former monks and as a stipend for singing men. Simple living accommodations and sometimes food were also supplied. The number of almsmen was specified in the statutes; it var-

---

[87] This was in 1538, when Latimer had been so pleased that the people turned "from ladyness to godliness"; see above, Chapter 3, and Dyer, *City of Worcester*, p. 231.

[88] Since the clergy were exempt from parliamentary taxation, we cannot compare their wealth directly with that of merchants and townsmen listed on local assessment rolls.

[89] E 315/24, PRO.

ied according to the size and wealth of the cathedral, Canterbury and Winchester being made responsible for twelve; Worcester for ten; Durham for eight; Carlisle, Chester, Ely, Peterborough, and Rochester for six; Bristol and Gloucester for only four.[90] We know from other sources that Westminster Abbey, while a cathedral, had twelve and Oxford the surprisingly high number of twenty-four.[91]

The statutes describe the sort of persons who were to be appointed: "men oppressed with poverty and distressed by want, or crippled and mutilated in warfare, or worn out with old age, or in some other way reduced to weakness and want." They also provide that the almsmen shall attend services daily and, if physically able, assist in ringing bells and lighting candles and lamps.[92] If they are negligent or slothful they are to be corrected by the dean. We know that this was occasionally necessary: at Hereford a poor man named David Griffith had to be admonished in 1586, and at Oxford the queen herself expressed distress that the almsmen seldom attended the services and ordered them to reform. This was in 1562.[93] At Carlisle the register for 1594 includes the entry, "It is decreed that John Carlill a beademan shall amend his lief and conuersacion &c., this is the second admonicion."[94]

The Crown retained the right to name almsmen, and royal letters of nomination exist in several of the cathedral archives. These often describe the men named. Elizabeth had granted Carlill his position on account of his blindness and poverty.[95] At Peterborough she appointed John Watson, who had served her and her father "in the warres bothe in Fraunce and Scotland, and wherein he was maymed of his lefte hande, and now by reason therof not hable to serve any longer," and Thomas Delariewes, "being a man blynde and not hable to gett his living."[96] Sometimes other persons tried to obtain places for their dependents: the mayor and aldermen sought a position at Carlisle for "a poor blynde man borne in this Cittie," and Lord Scrope was

---

[90] Thompson, *Statutes of Durham*, pp. 146–149. Possibly the poor men at Durham were thought of as successors to the fourteen poor men whose feet had been washed on Maundy Thursday in the years of the monastic establishment, and who had been given food and money; see *A Description or Briefe Declaration of all the Ancient Monuments, Rites, and Customes belonginge or beinge within the Monastical Church of Durham before the Suppression*, ed. J. T. Fowler, Surtees Society, no. 107 (Durham, 1903), p. 77.

[91] Westminster: E 315/24, fols. 5, 38, 82, PRO; Oxford: Act Book, 1549–1619, fol. 291, and Disbursement Book, 1577–1578, Christ Church Archives.

[92] Thompson, *Statutes of Durham*, p. 147.

[93] Act Book 2, fol. 122, Hereford Cathedral Library; Act Book, 1549–1619, fol. 291, Christ Church Archives, Oxford.

[94] Chapter Registers, vol. 3, fol. 177, Carlisle Record Office.

[95] Ibid., fol. 168. Other royal appointments are recorded on fols. 170–171.

[96] W. T. Mellows, ed., *The Foundation of Peterborough Cathedral*, Northamptonshire Record Society, no. 13 (Northampton, 1941), p. lvii.

able to name an almsman there in 1587.[97] Inevitably there was occasional confusion, for Elizabeth was sometimes tempted to grant positions when there were no vacancies, and the chapter was likely to yield to other requests when they did not receive word from the court. Such a situation occurred at Peterborough in 1576, when the queen complained that "by [the] subtill practises and dealing of some evill disposed parsons there" her nominee had not been admitted. She "straightly charge[d] and commaunde[d]" the Dean and Chapter to give him his place, even if this necessitated ejecting another almsman.[98]

Specific gifts for the relief of distressed lay men and women are perhaps of greater interest than the continuing support of the almsmen. Many such items are recorded in act books and accounts. Payments made at Chester in 1585 included 40s. given to the mayor "to the use of the poore therein," 4s. "geven by speciall appoyntment of Mr. Subdean vnto one Sr. Cuthbart a Bachelor of Arte of Cambridge being in great povertye for want of lyvinge & now in way of preferment," 12d. to a poor minister "beinge in great povertye," and like amounts to a poor woman with a child and to the prisoners in the castle. The payment to the mayor recurs annually.[99] Oxford provided clothing and shoes for Margery the poor woman of the kitchen and made grants "to the healing of a poor boy's arms," "to olde mother Saye bedreden," "to a pore widow that hathe many children," "to a pore maried cople," and "to an Irish soldier."[100] Lichfield gave 27s. 6d. to plague victims in 1594.[101] When the singing men of Norwich were fined for tardiness or absence from services one-third of the money was given to the poor.[102]

At Durham gifts ranging from 3s. 4d. to 16s. 8d. were made regularly during Elizabeth's reign; recipients included a poor man whose house was burned, a cripple, a man who had been robbed, prisoners, a destitute widow who was a minister's wife, poor scholars at Oxford and Cambridge, a singing man from Southwell, the curate of St. Margaret's "because his stipend was so small," and the poor of the French church in London.[103]

[97] Chapter Registers, vol. 3, fols. 168, 180, Carlisle Record Office.

[98] Mellows, *Foundation of Peterborough*, p. lvii.

[99] Account Book 3, for the 1580s and 1590s (not paginated), Chester Cathedral Library.

[100] Disbursement Books, 1548, 1577–1578, 1578–1579, Christ Church Archives, Oxford.

[101] Harwood, *Lichfield*, p. 268.

[102] Liber Miscellaneorum, 2, DCN, R226A, fol. 107, Norfolk Record Office.

[103] Treasurers' Books 2–19, Prior's Kitchen, Durham.

The amount that cathedrals of the new foundation were supposed to spend on alms was specified in their statutes. The total at Canterbury was £140, at Winchester £100, and at Durham £86 13s. 4d. Most cathedrals were allocated £40 for this purpose, poorer ones like Carlisle only £30.[104] Some of the money was to be used for the maintenance of roads and bridges, despite the seeming irrelevance of this work to charity or the religious mission of the church: £40 at Canterbury was to be given to these public works, £20 at Durham, and £15 at Carlisle. The remaining sum was to be distributed to the poor and needy, and detailed accounts were to be kept, ready for inspection when required.

Expenditures at Durham were close to the prescribed figure, £76 3s. 3d. being given to the poor in 1564–65, £56 8s. 4d. in 1566–1567, and £66 13s. 4d. (exactly the statutory figure, and therefore perhaps suspect) in 1576–1577. Comparable figures are hard to obtain. It appears that the Dean and Chapter of Chester gave only £9 8s. 6d. to the poor in 1591–1592.[105] In addition to this there were the stipends of the almsmen. When interrogated during the royal visitation of 1559 the Dean and Chapter of Canterbury had to admit that they had not given the poor the full £100 a year mandated by their statutes, because of "our great charges of reparations and other extraordinary business." In fact their alms during Mary's reign had ranged from £53 6s. 8d. to £100 13s. 4d. Expenditures on highways had been as small as £22 13s. 4d. rather than the required £40. Trying to excuse themselves, the Dean and Chapter insisted that "we did ever purpose, as yet we may, to satisfy the same in such due time as we conveniently may."[106]

Even when they distributed as alms the full amounts required by their constitutions, the cathedrals were not devoting significant portions of their revenue to this purpose. Since the annual income of Durham was about £1,800, the annual allocation for charity was less than 4 percent.[107] Charitable contributions at Chester were only one percent in 1591–1592, when the income was £964 15s. 5d.[108] Chester was of course one of the poorest cathedrals, struggling to maintain its buildings with inadequate revenues. But even Canterbury, refounded with an endowment of £2,542, spent less than 4 percent on alms. As

[104] Thompson, *Statutes of Durham*, pp. 170–173; J. E. Prescott, *Statutes of Carlisle*, p. 82.

[105] Account Book 3, Chester Cathedral Library.

[106] W. H. Frere and W. M. Kennedy, eds., *Visitation Articles and Injunctions*, 3 vols., Alcuin Club, nos. 14–16 (London, 1910), 3: 51–52.

[107] The figure is derived from Treasurers' Book 13* (Prior's Kitchen), where a note reads, "yf ther were a diligent and good receivor, ther might be yerelie receyved abowte £1835."

[108] Account Book 3, Chester Cathedral Library.

charitable institutions, the cathedrals did help relieve distress in a number of individual cases, and comments or descriptions written into their records suggest that members of the chapter did feel compassion for the unfortunate. But the proportion of their revenue devoted to such purposes was not large.

THE educational institutions associated with the cathedrals made a much greater impact on Tudor society than their charitable activities. The situation was altered dramatically by the Reformation, but the role of the cathedrals remained undiminished and was if anything greater than at the beginning of the sixteenth century.

In all of the medieval cathedral cities except perhaps Rochester, ancient schools still flourished in the fifteenth century. Song schools were of course needed for the choristers. The monastic cathedrals had almonry schools that provided education for poor boys, often relatives of the monks. Grammar schools were affiliated with the secular cathedrals. St. Peter's School at York Minster was the largest and most distinguished of these; it probably had more than one hundred students, both poor boys and fee-paying sons of local merchants or wealthy country families.[109] Lincoln, Exeter, Salisbury, and Wells also possessed grammar schools that were quite separate from the choristers' school.[110] In some places new endowments were provided during the reign of Henry VII: at Lichfield, Bishop William Smith turned a decayed hospital into a grammar school in 1495; at Chichester, Bishop Edward Story converted one of the prebends into an endowment for the cathedral school.[111]

The impact of the New Learning was first evident in London, where John Colet established the new St. Paul's School in 1509 to provide education in classical Latin and Greek. Dean Colet gave most of his own estate to the school as an endowment, so that free education could be provided to all the students. (He was a rich man, since his father had been a lord mayor of London, and he was the sole surviving heir out of a family of twenty-two children.) His stated desire was to provide education for young men who sought careers in the world, not in

[109] Jo Ann Hoeppner Moran, *Education and Learning in the City of York, 1300–1560* (York: Borthwick Institute, 1979), pp. 5–8. See also idem, *The Growth of English Schooling, 1340–1548* (Princeton: Princeton University Press, 1985), pp. 106–112.

[110] Nicholas Orme, *Education in the West of England, 1066–1548* (Exeter: University of Exeter, 1976), p. 2.

[111] Nicholas Orme, *English Schools in the Middle Ages* (London: Methuen, 1973), pp. 214–215.

the Church; for this reason, and probably also because he distrusted the conservative canons of the cathedral, he left the government of the school in the hands of the Mercers' Company rather than the Dean and Chapter. This arrangement was not emulated elsewhere, but the classical curriculum and to some extent the secular emphasis became increasingly common.

Schools were provided for in virtually all the cathedrals of the new foundation. Expansive original proposals that would have established centers of higher learning at Canterbury, Westminster, and Durham as well as grammar schools in all the cathedrals were scaled down, but the provisions written into charters and statutes were still substantial. The new institutions regarded Henry VIII as their founder and are generally still called the King's Schools. Their size varied according to the wealth and prestige of the cathedral in question: Canterbury was to provide free instruction for fifty boys, Worcester for forty, Chester and Ely for twenty-four, Peterborough and Rochester for twenty. Durham, probably because its statutes were not issued until Mary's reign, was ordered to maintain only eighteen scholars.[112] No new foundation was thought necessary at Winchester, where Wykeham's college remained intact and began to admit more local boys as commoners. The school at Oxford did not survive the transfer of the cathedral to Christ Church and its amalgamation with the college. Henry VIII's original letters patent for Norwich ordered that twenty poor children be educated, but statutes were never provided during the Tudor period and, probably for that reason, the cathedral does not actually seem to have had a school at all.[113]

Edward VI's royal injunctions for cathedrals, issued in 1547, required the old secular cathedrals as well as the new foundations to maintain free grammar schools. No details are set out, and no new endowments were given the cathedrals, which were told to pay the headmaster 20 marks a year and the usher or junior master half that sum out of normal cathedral revenues.[114] Under Mary an attempt was made to turn some of the schools into seminaries for Catholic priests, but, except perhaps at Lincoln and York, it had little effect.[115]

[112] Thompson, *Statutes of Durham*, pp. 142–144.

[113] When a free school was founded at Norwich under Edward VI, it was placed under the control of the city, and it does not appear to have had any real connection with the cathedral (Orme, *English Schools*, pp. 263–266; letters patent, in DCN, R226A, fols. 23–53, sec. 26, Norfolk Record Office).

[114] Frere and Kennedy, *Visitation Articles*, 2: 138–139.

[115] Orme, *English Schools*, pp. 286–287. A statute of 1554 had granted the queen authority to issue new statutes for the grammar schools established under Henry VIII and Edward VI; this was the constitutional basis for the Catholic initiative.

Students accepted into the cathedral schools were to know how to read and write and to possess an elementary knowledge of grammar. Ordinarily they were to be fifteen or younger when admitted and were to remain for four years, or five if the dean judged that appropriate; former choristers might be allowed to enter even if older than fifteen, and were to have preference over other boys. Those who proved to be slow or dull were to be expelled by the dean, "lest," say the statutes, "like mildew, [they] consume the honey of the bees."[116] The masters were to be named by the Dean and Chapter; an undermaster was to instruct the younger boys, with the headmaster handling the upper forms.

It was originally planned that cathedrals would provide exhibitions (i.e., scholarships) for the brightest young men graduating from the grammar schools, so that they could attend Oxford or Cambridge. The number of such awards was to vary from twenty-six at Canterbury to four at Rochester. Financial records at Worcester, Chester, Winchester, and Hereford as well as Canterbury show that university students were indeed supported for a few years in the 1540s, but the system did not survive the financial crisis of Henry VIII's last years; the cathedrals were forced to restore the endowments devoted to higher education to the Crown, and the exhibitions vanished.[117] In a few places, private philanthropy helped fill the gap. Archbishop Parker endowed four exhibitions at Corpus Christi College, Cambridge, where he had been master, for boys from the King's School, Canterbury; these were to run for three years, or six if the scholars were candidates for ordination.[118] While dean of Exeter, Simon Heynes had proposed the establishment of scholarships for twelve students at Oxford and twelve at Cambridge, but his scheme was never put into effect.[119]

The largest and finest of the new establishments, both still flourishing, were the King's Schools established at Canterbury and Worcester. We are fortunate in having good histories of both, sympathetically written by former students.[120] The first headmaster at Canterbury, John Twyne, was an active, picturesque character, a Member of Parliament, alderman, and sheriff as well as a scholar. Suspected of conjur-

---

[116] Thompson, *Statutes of Durham*, p. 145.

[117] Orme, *English Schools*, p. 265, and cathedral financial records.

[118] D. L. Edwards, *A History of the King's School, Canterbury* (London: Faber and Faber, 1957), pp. 76–77.

[119] Orme, *Education in the West of England*, p. 54.

[120] See D. L. Edwards, *King's School, Canterbury*; and Michael Craze, *King's School, Worcester*. There is also valuable information in Craze, *College Hall, Worcester*, pamphlet (Worcester: King's School, 1982).

ing and popery, and dismissed for drunkenness in 1560, he lived on until 1581, spending his last years studying early British history.[121] Less is known about John Pether, the first headmaster at Worcester, but he was described as a "fit" man for the position and held a M.A. from Oxford. His successor, Thomas Bradshaw, was able to take over the former monastic refectory in the cathedral cloister as College Hall; in the early seventeenth century as many as two hundred boys were educated there.

Alexander Nowell was headmaster of Westminster School. When he became dean of St. Paul's, Nicholas Udall followed him at Westminster. Famous as the author of "Ralph Roister Doister" and as a grammarian, Udall was thought guilty of sexual relations with his students and would probably have been removed had he not conveniently died. When Westminster Abbey ceased to be a cathedral the school was refounded a second time (it thus regards Elizabeth as *fundatrix*), and provision was made for as many as one hundred twenty students. Scholarships were also created so that five or six graduates a year could go on to Christ Church, Oxford, or Trinity College, Cambridge.[122] The first two headmasters at Durham were not university graduates, and Dean Whittingham wrote Cecil that he had to teach the boys himself three or four hours a day. But Robert Cooke, Francis Key, James Calfhill, and Peter Smart, successive masters between 1570 and 1600, all held M.A.s from Oxford or Cambridge. The founding headmaster of College School, Gloucester, was Robert Alfield, who had studied at Eton and King's College, Cambridge, and had taught at Eton before moving to Gloucester. Described as "eminent for his learning and piety" and notable for the ease with which he shifted his religious views under Edward and Mary, he remained at the school until 1575, when he left to become rector of Bourton-on-the-Water.[123]

Generally, grammar schools in the cathedral cities had closer links with the cathedrals themselves after the Reformation than before. The Dean and Chapter appointed the masters and paid their salaries, and the schools were usually housed within the cathedral precincts, often in former monastic quarters.[124] Education was free; in earlier centu-

---

[121] His chief historical work, *De Rebus Albionicis, Britannicis atque Anglicis*, was published posthumously by one of his sons in 1590; it suggests a connection between British and Phoenician civilization (see Edwards, *King's School, Canterbury*, pp. 68–74).

[122] C. S. Knighton, "Collegiate Foundations, 1540 to 1570, with Special Reference to St. Peter in Westminster" (Ph.D. thesis, Cambridge University, 1975), pp. 245–320.

[123] See J. N. Langston, "Robert Alfield, Schoolmaster, of Gloucester; and His Sons," *Transactions of the Bristol and Gloucestershire Archaeological Society* 56 (1934): 141–163.

[124] At Lincoln there had been two grammar schools, one controlled by the city and one by the cathedral, but they were united in 1584 under an agreement whereby the Dean

ries this was not always the case. The quality of the teaching improved during Elizabeth's reign, as more of the masters possessed higher education themselves. The interaction of the schools with lay society seems to have become greater as well. Cathedral grammar schools functioned less and less as breeding grounds for priests, and increasingly as institutions to prepare promising young men for study at the universities or for professional careers.

TUDOR cathedrals were occasionally centers of entertainment as well as education. The famous mystery plays had of course been performed in the cathedrals during the Middle Ages, and the theatrical tradition continued, secularized, throughout the sixteenth century. Bishop Bonner, it is true, tried to prohibit plays and interludes in the churches of London during Mary's reign. But Elizabeth delighted in performances by the "Children of Powles," ordering them to appear at Nonesuch Palace and at court as well as within the cathedral itself. These players were choristers, but the boys of St. Paul's School also produced dramas and were encouraged to do so by Dean Colet's statutes.[125]

Almost the only evidence regarding plays put on by choristers and students from other cathedrals comes from Wells. Here the headmaster of the grammar school was reprimanded by the Dean and Chapter in 1583 because "he did carrye with him the children of the Grammerskoole and the Choristers of the saide Cathedral Churche vnto Axelbridge to playe in the parishe churche theare." As a punishment he was ordered to pay 2s. to each of the twenty-four poor persons in the almshouse.[126] It is not clear just what the objection was: the Dean and Chapter may have disapproved of plays generally, as frivolous entertainments unworthy of the cathedral, or (more likely) they may simply have disliked having the children carted around to outlying parishes. Possibly they thought that the headmaster had profited personally from the performance.

In many places, cathedral accounts record payments to traveling players and musicians. At Worcester, Prior More paid 4s. to Wolsey's minstrels in 1529, and 6s. 8d. to the king's players when they visited

---

and Chapter would name the headmaster, the mayor and aldermen the usher, with the cost of the school to be shared by the city and the chapter (see J.W.F. Hill, *Lincoln*, pp. 103–104).

[125] Milman, *Annals of St. Paul's*, pp. 311–314.

[126] Act Book H, fol. 20, Wells Cathedral Library.

his country house at Grimley. A few years later he gave the queen's minstrels another 6s. 8d.[127] In 1543 Chichester paid the earl of Arundel's mimes for performing in Christmas week "as usual."[128] The treasurer of Rochester gave 3s. 4d. to "my lorde protectors players," presumably a troupe maintained by Somerset under Edward VI.[129]

Payments become more common under Elizabeth. In 1563 Canterbury gave the large sum of £3 6s. 8d. to a "Mr. Russhe" for "settynge out of his plays yn Christmas."[130] The chamberlain's Accounts at York record payments to the earl of Essex's players, Lord Stafford's men, a group of players from Lancashire, and "the Scollars of the Horsfaire players," who were students at one of the local schools.[131] Durham presented 26s. 8d. to the earl of Leicester's players in 1580.[132] The cathedral at Chester paid 6s. "for a barell of bere to geve to the pleares to make them to drinke" in 1567. The queen's players and the earl of Essex's musicians visited Chester several times between 1588 and 1591. Their performances may have been an especially welcome diversion in this relatively poor, remote area.[133]

APPROACHING the question of the cathedrals' role in society from a very different point of view, one can consider the career opportunities that cathedrals provided for two specific groups of men.

Cathedral music has already been discussed fully; here it is necessary only to point out how few other opportunities were open to professional singers and composers. The court and Chapel Royal employed a small group of fine performers, some of them men born and trained abroad. A few noblemen kept one or two musicians in residence, some cities employed a few men as waits, some large collegiate churches like Southwell and Beverley had paid singing men, and a handful of the Oxford and Cambridge colleges had professional organists. Some minstrels wandered the country, perhaps loosely under the patronage of a nobleman or member of the royal family. But the cathedral choirs provided the main source of employment for trained

[127] Fegan, *Journal of Prior More*, pp. 296, 298, 393. The queen in question would have been Anne Boleyn.

[128] Cap. 1/23/2, Communar's Accounts, fol. 63, West Sussex Record Office.

[129] DRC/FTb3, Rochester Cathedral Archives, Kent Records Office.

[130] MS. M.A. 40 (not paginated), Canterbury Cathedral Library.

[131] Accounts, E2/21, St. Peter's Part, 1572–1600, York Minster Library.

[132] *Extracts from the Account Rolls of the Abbey of Durham*, Surtees Society, no. 103 (Durham, 1901), p. 717.

[133] Account Book 2, fol. 52; Account Book 3, for 1588–1591, Chester Cathedral Library.

musicians in the sixteenth century, and positions as organists in the cathedrals were held by the greatest composers of the period. If laymen wished to hear music performed by professionals, there were few places they could go other than the cathedrals, for public concerts had not yet begun and common folk would not normally have been admitted to musical entertainments at court or in the homes of aristocrats.

A second and more important group includes the canons, prebendaries, and deans, the highly educated clergy who served the cathedrals and enjoyed good livings from their endowments. Again, there were not many other professional opportunities to tempt the educated elite of the sixteenth century—the university graduates and especially those with higher degrees from Oxford and Cambridge. Bright young men who were not in line to inherit titles or landed estates had few options. Some might make names for themselves and possibly acquire fortunes in the government or at court. The law, perhaps coupled with service in the House of Commons, was already appealing. But the Church offered the best hope for many aspiring young men, especially for those from humble backgrounds whose chief assets were their brains. Within the Church, only a select few could expect to attain the status of bishops. Parish churches were numerous—there were nearly ten thousand in England and Wales—but the wages of parish priests were so low and the likelihood of intellectual stimulation in many villages so small that most educated men would have been dissatisfied with parochial appointments. It was far more appealing to be a member of a cathedral chapter.

Fortunately for those who wished to make their careers in the cathedrals, an unusual number of positions were available in the mid-sixteenth century as a result of successive religious changes that drove groups of men from office. In addition, matriculations at the universities declined around the middle of the century, so that there were fewer graduates to compete for choice appointments. By the last years of Elizabeth's reign, the situation had changed dramatically: there were more graduates and fewer openings. Inevitably, some who sought careers in the Church were disappointed, receiving less desirable appointments than they thought they deserved or perhaps no office at all. Mark Curtis has suggested that this frustration was one of the reasons for alienation among early Stuart intellectuals; although his view of career prospects for the clergy was too pessimistic, it probably remains true that opportunities were not so great in the seventeenth century as they had been earlier.[134]

[134] Mark Curtis, "The Alienated Intellectuals of Early Stuart England," *Past and Present*

In his study of social mobility, Lawrence Stone concluded that English landed society in the years between 1540 and 1880 was not really an open elite, ready to receive ambitious young men who wished to move up into its ranks.[135] During the Tudor period the Church was more open than the country-house aristocracy; within the Church, it was the cathedral chapters that formed the elite.

Looked at in this light, the use of prebends as rewards for learned men who were not actually resident at the cathedrals can be better understood.[136] The sixteenth century, unlike the twentieth, had no other scheme of grants for scholars. Tudor cathedrals were, among other things, forerunners of modern foundations or national endowments. In the era before free public education, the opportunity for poor boys to have places in the free cathedral schools was also socially significant. These functions were not necessarily religious ones, any more than the maintenance of highways was, and it might have been just as well if all of them had been handled in other ways. But, in the absence of other systems, the cathedrals were of considerable social importance because of the professional opportunities they offered.

THE place of cathedrals in English society was altered significantly during the sixteenth century, largely as a result of the Reformation. To begin with an obvious and indisputable point, there were simply more cathedrals at the end of the Tudor period than there had been at the beginning. They served smaller dioceses, so that a larger proportion of the populace lived within a reasonable distance of one of them. Thus more lay men and women, if they wished, could resort to cathedrals in order to attend services, hear sermons, admire architecture, or listen to music.

To what extent did they do so? The question is hard to answer, for the evidence is unsatisfactory and mixed. Certainly lay people did attend masses and other services before the Reformation, and some

---

23 (1962): 25–42. His arguments are challenged by Ian Green, "Career Prospects and Clerical Conformity in the Early Stuart Church," ibid., 90 (1981): 71–115. See also Lawrence Stone, "The Educational Revolution in England, 1560–1640," ibid., 28 (1964): 41–80; and idem, "Social Mobility in England, 1500–1700," ibid., 33 (1966): 16–55.

[135] Lawrence Stone and Jeanne C. Fawtier Stone, *An Open Elite? England 1540–1880* (Oxford: Clarendon Press, 1984).

[136] It is interesting to note that Thomas Starkey shared this view. He wrote, in a marginal note to the manuscript of his dialogue between Lupset and Pole, "Prebendys schold be premia to yong gentylmen maryd and lernyd in scripture, by thys mean scripture schuld be more communyd then hyt ys" (sp 1/90, fol. 112, PRO). I am grateful to Thomas F. Mayer for this reference.

were deeply attached to the old forms of worship. But this was not essential so far as the cathedral clergy were concerned; their chief goal was the glory of God rather than the edification of man. Especially in the case of the monastic cathedrals, participation by the laity was unimportant and perhaps unwelcome prior to the 1530s. Later in the century, as preaching gained in importance, a serious attempt was made to provide frequent sermons of high quality and to attract hearers to them. It can thus be argued that cathedrals were more outward looking in the years following the Reformation, and in that sense more intimately related to lay society.

Cathedrals were more closely involved in education as well. The new cathedral schools trained hundreds of young men, not merely for positions in the Church but now for life in a larger community. In many cases those who had been associated with the cathedrals as boys must have retained an affection or attachment in later life. Some of them, if they prospered in trade or at law, perpetuated their ties by erecting monuments in the cathedrals. Involvement in charity and in entertainment was less significant but was no doubt appreciated by those who benefited from it.

Finally, the possibility of holding attractive positions in the cathedrals brought men of outstanding and varied abilities into the Church. This was of course true long before the coming of the Reformation, but it may be that the possibility of marrying and having a family while still serving the Church widened the appeal of the ecclesiastical establishment, making it in some ways a stronger body than it had been in the late Middle Ages.

Many things did not change. The great buildings remained, modified to suit new needs and a new theology but not demolished or allowed to fall into ruin. The influence of cathedrals in civic economies and the importance of clergy in local communities shifted in subtle ways but remained strong. Where there was change, not all was gain. Much that was beautiful was destroyed. A great legacy of medieval art was lost when statues were torn down, shrines demolished, windows smashed, chalices melted, altars removed, manuscripts thrown away, embroidered frontals and vestments rejected. Beautiful, mystical liturgies, too, were given up in favor of a simpler, more rational Book of Common Prayer. Sometimes loss and gain were intertwined: the abandonment of Latin services fostered and even forced creativity, especially among musicians, who composed some of England's greatest music to fit new English words.

The role of cathedrals—indeed the whole rationale for their existence—was transformed. In the medieval church cathedrals were cherished primarily because they maintained an unceasing round of prayer and praise. They served man, generally, because they helped him glorify God, and more specifically because their masses for the dead might shorten the time spent by souls in purgatory. After the Reformation, prayers for the dead, veneration of relics and images, and pilgrimages to shrines were eliminated, since they were thought to be superstitious practices that had no place in a purified church. Cathedrals then functioned mainly as centers of teaching and preaching, of instruction and admonition. They served God by showing men and women how to live soberly and worship reverently. The emphasis moved from sacraments to sermons as the Eucharist came to be celebrated infrequently (certainly not several times a day, as at the beginning of the century) while preaching rose in importance.

Unlike the monasteries, the cathedrals survived the crisis of the sixteenth century. Restructured, renewed, secularized, modernized, they accepted an altered role in society, different from the position they had enjoyed in the Middle Ages but no less vital because of the impact of the Reformation.

INDEX

Abbot, George, 231, 261
Alcock, John, 22, 56, 59, 78, 243
Aldrich, Thomas, 229
Alfield, Robert, 300
almsmen, 293–95
altarists, 22–25
altars, destruction of, 116–17, 121; Eliza-
   bethan orders concerning, 144
Andrewes, Lancelot, 235, 243, 261
Angel, John, 235
annuellars, 22
archdeacons, 258–60
Argentyne, John, 240
Arnold, organmaker, 216–17
Arscott, Alnetheus, 235
Arthur, Prince, 62, 68, 109–11, 278
Arthur of Evesham, 48
Ascham, Roger, 235, 248, 261
Atkinson, Thomas, 265
Audley, Edmund, 22
Augmentations, Court of, 81, 106, 108
Augustine, Saint, 3, 38
Aylmer, John, 132, 230, 251
Aylmer, Theophilus, 230

Babthorpe, Robert, 235
Bacon, Thomas, 241
Bagshaw, Christopher, 245
Bainbridge, Christopher, 239, 254
Bait, William, 193
Baker, Richard, 220
Baker, Walter, 162
Bale, John, 244–46
Bangor Cathedral, 34–35, 125, 161; use
   of, 113
Banks, Thomas, 235
Barlow, John, 216
Barlow, William, 98, 124, 133, 147, 230
Barlow, William, the younger, 230, 247,
   265
Barnes, Emmanuel, 230
Barnes, Richard, 161, 250, 269
Barnes, Robert, 72
Barrow, Thomas, 254
Bartlett, John, 203
Barwell, Edward, 241
Base, Henry, 208
Base, John, 208
Base, Owen, 208
Base, Richard, 208

Bateson, Thomas, 214
Bath Abbey: architecture, 59–61; early
   history, 38–39; finance, 46; suppressed,
   82
Batten, Adrian, 225
Battye, Edmund, 235
Beacon, John, 235
Bearpark (Beaurepaire), 40, 136, 168
Beckington, Thomas, 15
Beckwith, Sir Leonard, 129
Becon, Thomas, 243, 245
Bedern, 14, 24, 188–90
Bede, 73
Bedyll, Thomas, 254
Beeley, Richard, 132
Belfelde, Henry, 200
Belfelde, Philip, 200
Belfelde, Robert, 200
"Bell Harry" tower, Canterbury, 53–55
Bell, John, 55, 235
Bell, Thomas, 244
Bellasis, Anthony, 235
Bemond, Richard, 203
Benedict, Saint, 38
Beresford, James, 235
Berkeley, Gilbert, 229
Best, Peter, 203
Bevin, Elway, 200, 214
Bilson, Leonard, 264
Bilson, Thomas, 235
Birch, William, 245
Bisse, James, 235
Bisse, Philip, 235
Black Rubric, 121
Blackard, organ mender, 217
Blaikston, Marmaduke, 235
Blake, Anthony, 235
Blythman, William, 73
Bocket, William, 235
Boleyn, Anne, 67–68, 98, 278
Boleyn, George, 229
Boleyn, William, 230
Bonner, Edmund, 103, 104, 124, 136,
   230, 251, 301
Book of Common Prayer (1549), 112–16;
   (1552), 119–21; (1559), 141, 145; re-
   jected under Mary, 124
Booth, Charles, 36, 286
Bostoke, Robert, 222
Bourchier, John, 254

307

INDEX

37; secular uses, 288–91; sermons, 275–77

Catherine of Aragon, 51, 67–68, 109–10, 278

Chad, Saint, 31, 72–73

Chaderton, Edmund, 254

Chaderton, Lawrence, 261

Chaderton, William, 151

Chall, William, 220

Chamber, John, 249, 254

Champion, Richard, 97

chancellor, office of, 6

chantries, 20–25, 105–9

Chappington, Hugh, 218

charity, 293–97

Charles V, Emperor, 51–52, 126, 137

Cheseman, John, 192

Chester Cathedral: almsmen, 284; and Book of Common Prayer, 115; charity, 295–96; choristers, 199, 201; confiscation of vestments, 119; Elizabethan Settlement, 150–52; exhibitions, 299; finance, 89, 166–67; foundation, 86; laity at services, 275; leases of land, 174–75; lectures, 162; minor canons and lay clerks, 195, 208; monuments, 285, 288–89; old customs at, 99; as parish church, 272; plays, 302; "rape" of lands, 178–80; refurbished under Mary Tudor, 129–30; removal of altar, 116; school, 298; sermons, 277; visited by Leicester, 280

Chevallier, Anthony Rodolph, 230

Chichester Cathedral: canons, 5; chantries, 23; choristers, 19, 199, 206; condition before Reformation, 36; criticism of, 267, 270; demolition of St. Richard's shrine, 71; dissolution of chantries, 107; Elizabethan Settlement, 148–50; finance, 26–29, 31, 33, 166, 170; high altar, 76; leases, 33; and Marian exiles, 132; and Marian martyrs, 134; monuments, 286, 290; music catalog, 224; organ, 215, 217; as parish church, 272; plays, 302; refurbished under Mary Tudor, 129; removal of altars, 116–17; renounces pope, 68; repair of steeple, 177–78; residence of canons, 170; school, 297; sermons, 276; and Thomas Weelkes, 213–14; vestments, 177–78; vicars choral, 13, 15, 183–85, 187–88, 190–91, 208, 219

choristers, 19–20, 198–208

Christopherson, John, 135

Chrodegang, Bishop of Metz, 5

Clement VII, Pope, 67

Cliffe, William, 178–79

Clyffe, George, 153

Cobham, Lord, 84

Cocke, Arthur, 185

Cole, Edward, 282

Cole, Henry, 135

Cole, Thomas, 132

Colet, John, 12–13, 51–52, 206, 229, 248, 289, 297, 301

Colet, Sir Henry, 229

Collingwood, Ralph, 276

Colman, Robert, 128

communion, frequency of, 160

communion cups, 150–51

Constable, John, 229

Cooke, Robert, 300

Cooke, William, 197

Cooper, Thomas, 248

cope silver, 169

Corano, Anthony, 248

Courtenay, Peter, 22

Coventry Cathedral: early history, 38–39; finance, 45–46; prior of, 41; suppressed, 82

Coverdale, Miles, 114, 133–34

Cox, Richard, 87, 91–92, 101, 124, 132, 140, 143, 147, 158, 211, 251, 268–70

Coxe, Francis, 248

Cranborne, Christopher, 212

Cranks, John, 47

Cranmer, Edmund, 132

Cranmer, Thomas: and Book of Common Prayer, 112–16, 119–21; device for the succession, 123; and Edward VI, 101–3; and English Litany, 99; executed, 133; imprisoned, 124; life pattern, 261; marriage, 249; and Prebendaries' Plot, 96–97; opposes prebendaries, 268, 270

Crauden, Prior of Ely, 63

Croke, Richard, 261

Cromwell, Thomas, 6, 67–69, 79–81, 257, 291

Cross, Claire, 265

Crowley, Robert, 159, 236, 245–46

Curtis, Mark, 262, 303

Cuthbert, Saint, 73

Dale, Valentine, 257

Dallam, Thomas, 218

Daniel, William, 148

Davies, J. G., 288

Davis, William, 193, 223

Day, George, 91, 116–17, 124

deans: education, 231–41, 258–60; geographical origin, 231–36; income, 166; laymen as, 257–58; lives of, 227–28,

309

ons, 8–9; St. Peter's Portion, 172; school, 136, 297–98; secular uses, 290; use of, 113; vicars choral, 12, 13–14,

183, 188–91, 193, 220
Young, Thomas, 132, 250